D1643705

MEMOIRS OF THE
DUKES OF URBINO—III

Anderson

FRANCESCO MARIA II DELLA ROVERE, DUKE OF URBINO
After the picture by Baroccio in the Uffizi Gallery, Florence

MEMOIRS OF THE DUKES OF URBINO

ILLUSTRATING THE ARMS, ARTS & LITERATURE OF ITALY, 1440–1630

BY JAMES DENNISTOUN OF DENNISTOUN

A NEW EDITION WITH NOTES BY EDWARD HUTTON & OVER A HUNDRED ILLUSTRATIONS

IN THREE VOLUMES. VOLUME THREE

LONDON JOHN LANE THE BODLEY HEAD
NEW YORK JOHN LANE COMPANY MCMIX

WM. BRENDON AND SON, LTD., PRINTERS, PLYMOUTH

CONTENTS

BOOK SIXTH

(*Continued*)

OF FRANCESCO MARIA DELLA ROVERE, FOURTH DUKE OF URBINO

CHAPTER XXXIX

CHAPTER XL

CHAPTER XLI

BOOK SEVENTH

OF GUIDOBALDO DELLA ROVERE, FIFTH DUKE OF URBINO

CHAPTER XLII

CHAPTER XLIII

BOOK EIGHTH

OF FRANCESCO MARIA II. DELLA ROVERE

SIXTH AND LAST DUKE OF URBINO

CHAPTER XLIV

CHAPTER XLV

CHAPTER XLVI

CHAPTER XLVII

CHAPTER XLVIII

BOOK NINTH

OF LITERATURE AND ART UNDER THE DUKES DELLA ROVERE AT URBINO

CHAPTER XLIX

CHAPTER L

CHAPTER LI

CHAPTER LII

CHAPTER LIII

CHAPTER LIV

CHAPTER LV

APPENDICES

ILLUSTRATIONS

FACING PAGE

CHRONOLOGICAL TABLE

CHAPTER XXXIX

CHAPTER XL

CHAPTER XLI

CHAPTER XLII

CHAPTER XLV

CHAPTER XLVI

CHAPTER XLVII

CHAPTER XLVIII

CHAPTER XLIX

CHAPTER L

CHAPTER LI

CHAPTER LII

CHAPTER LIII

CHAPTER LIV

CHAPTER LV

APPENDICES

MEMOIRS OF THE
DUKES OF URBINO—III

NOTE.—The Editor's notes are marked with an asterisk.

BOOK SIXTH

(*continued*)

OF FRANCESCO MARIA DELLA ROVERE FOURTH DUKE OF URBINO

MEMOIRS OF THE DUKES OF URBINO

CHAPTER XXXIX

Causes which led to the sack of Rome—The assault—Death of Bourbon—Atrocities of his soldiery—The Duke of Urbino's fatal delays—The Pontiff's capitulation and escape—Policy of the Emperor.

OUR narrative of little interesting campaigns has now brought us to an event unparalleled in the horrors of modern warfare, by which the laws of nature, the dictates of humanity, the principles of civilisation were alike outraged. The sack of Rome inflicted a dire retribution for the restless shuffling that had disgraced the temporal policy of recent pontiffs; it was the crowning mischief to a long agony of ultramontane aggression; and in it was spent one of the last mighty waves of barbarian aggression that broke upon the Italian Peninsula.

Such are the difficulties in the way of a just and satisfactory judgment as to the causes which led to this outrage, that it may be well to review these, even at the risk of some recapitulation. The total demoralisation of Bourbon's army, the want of good understanding between him and other imperial leaders in Italy, the absence of zeal or common interests among the confederate powers and their officials, with the prevailing bad faith of all parties, form a combination of elements baffling to the historian as it must have been to the actors themselves. The petty motives and feeble measures of the Pontiff have already been amply exposed. Francis and the Venetians had originally entered the strife only from selfish views upon Lombardy, which they pursued without attempting any comprehensive or efficient operations, and, as soon as the storm had passed by them, their languor became indifference. Charles cared little for Italy, or the ill-defined claims of the Empire upon it, except as a fair field for aggrandising or securing, by intrigue or by arms, his already exorbitant dominions, and he left his officers there pretty much to their own discretion in the maintenance of his interests. His successive viceroys at Naples, perceiving the policy of Clement to be inherently adverse to their master's interests, were ever ready to annoy his frontier, or to cajole him away from the Lombard league. The Constable, finding that the cautious tactics of the Duke of Urbino kept his own movements in check, and impeded his appeasing with pillage a reckless host whom he could not pay, was ready to adopt any enterprise that might ensure occupation and plunder to his dangerous bands, not doubting that, whoever might suffer, success would justify him with the Emperor, to whose glory it must ultimately redound.

As soon as the Pope had ratified the truce of the 15th March, he, with an infatuation which even an empty treasury can ill excuse, dismissed two thousand of the *bande nere* who garrisoned Rome. A Swiss corps withdrew at the same time, on his refusal of their monthly pay in advance. When the imperialists drew southward, his chief care was for Florence, and, on hearing of the insurrection there, he sent one of his chamberlains to acknowledge Francesco Maria's good service, adding a vague hope that, in the event of Bourbon threatening Rome, he would contribute counsel and aid for its safety.

In reply, the Duke recommended that Viterbo, and Montefiascone should be secured, and Rome suitably defended by Renzo da Ceri and Orazio Baglioni, suggesting that his Holiness might betake himself to the strongholds of Orvieto or Civita Castellana : with these precautions, he added that an early and innocuous conclusion of the inroad would ensue, as the enemy, when shut out from plunder of the towns, must quickly disperse. But these counsels came too late, and, with a foolhardiness and folly savouring of judicial blindness, the Pontiff remained in the comfortable conviction that Bourbon would take up his quarters at Siena, on the representations of Lannoy.*[1] It was only about the 25th that his impending danger first dawned upon him. Rome had then, of regular troops, but two hundred foot and a few light cavalry, besides the Swiss guard, and the only officer of rank was Renzo da Ceri, whose personal courage and military capacity were in equal disrepute, and of whom Clement had on various occasions spoken with contempt. Yet upon this broken reed did he place his sole reliance for the defence of his capital. He commanded the weak points of the walls to be repaired and strictly guarded, distributing the artillery where most required. He pressed above three thousand men into his service; but these hasty levies were of the most useless description, composed of artizans, servants, and the scum of the population, "more used to handle kitchen spits and stable forks than military weapons." Resorting to fanatical expedi-

*[1] The army would not hear of a truce. Bourbon, really at their mercy, as he knew before he crossed the Apennines, asked them what they wished to do. "To march on," replied the Spaniards, "even without pay." The Germans after a time, though hungry for their wage, made common cause with them. "To march on," became almost a war-cry, and Bourbon was compelled to consent. He sent word to the Pope before he got into Val d'Arno that his men "were determined to push on, not only to Florence but to Rome, and dragged him with them as a prisoner." He asked for 150,000 ducats by April 15th to pay them with, that he might lead them back. The Pope, however, who had no faith in his power or honesty, sent nothing, trusting in Lannoy and that broken reed the Duke of Urbino.

ents, he proclaimed a plenary remission of their sins to such as should fall in the sacred struggle. But the greatest difficulty was to raise money for these purposes: the wealthy classes were so absorbed in egotism and luxury, so deluded by false security, that they would contribute nothing. Domenico de' Massini, one of the richest of them, would lend but a hundred ducats, a refusal for which he and his family paid bitterly in the sack. On the 11th of April, Girolamo Negri, a shrewd observer, wrote that the papal court had become a barn-yard of chickens, and that, though each day gave more manifest signs of evil times, every one relied on the Viceroy's mediation, failing which all would be lost.

At this juncture there appeared in Rome one of those strange fanatics whose mysterious aspect and unearthly character, taking strong hold of the popular imagination at particular crises, impart a supernatural character to their wild and dismal vaticinations. He was an aged anchorite, who, fancying himself another Jonah, had long attracted street audiences by vague declamations of coming convulsions, and, as the peril became imminent, warned the anxious people that a total revolution in church and state, and the ruin of the priesthood, were at hand. Rushing along the thoroughfares, he preached, with piercing voice and excited gesticulation, a general penitence and humble reliance on the offended Deity, as the only shelter from the impending storm. He even forced his way to the presence of his Holiness, and, in the midst of the court, repeated gloomy warnings and stern denunciations in harsh words seldom heard in such high places. "But," in the words of an old writer, "repentance is an irksome sound to the ears of hardened sinners," and "more is required to make a saint than sackcloth raiment, a crucifix, and philippics against vice"; so the prophet was committed to prison, to continue his preaching to a more limited audience. Yet it needed no stretch of superstition to regard the sack of Rome, with its accumulated horrors, as a Divine judgment. The gross vices which disgraced the papacy towards the close of the preceding century had, indeed, been considerably modified; but, as the reformation was rather in decency than in morals, it had not greatly influenced the people of Rome: the poison, though counteracted at the core, continued to circulate through the branches. In truth, the hearts of all were so indurated, and their judgment so blinded by pleasures, debaucheries, avarice, and ambition, that the forebodings of enthusiasts, and the many portentous omens of evil that occurred about the same time, were equally disregarded. Among these were, of course, blood-red suns and fiery meteors; but it was afterwards remembered that two aged men with long beards had been observed to stride solemnly along the chief thoroughfares of the city, bearing a large empty bag, and exclaiming at intervals with dolorous solemnity, "Behold the sack!"[1]

The measures of the government, superficial as they were, generated false security; and a general muster of the citizens which returned thirty thousand as capable of bearing arms, tended to confirm the fatal delusion. The Pope gave currency to it by setting forth on all occasions the reduced state of the imperialist army, the proximity of that of the league, and above all insisted that the invaders, being for the most part Lutherans, were no doubt conducted by Providence, to undergo a signal punishment for their heresies under the very walls of the Christian metropolis. To such a height was this foolhardiness carried, that the messenger, who arrived on the 3rd of May to demand

[1] The play of words applies equally in Italian and English, and the incident savours much of a carnival jest. A scarce little book of prophecies, dated 1532, has for *Envoye* a sonnet, foreshadowing the woes of Italy in consequence of—

"L' infando error de Sogdoma e Gomora,
Le profanate sacre binde e tempi,
L' occider Dio mille volte al hora."

free passage to Naples, was dismissed by Renzo with the threat of a cannon-ball at his head; and on the following day the Datary wrote to Count Guido Rangone, that a reinforcement of six or eight hundred men would suffice for defence of the city. But ere the messenger was well clear of the gate, the enemy were before it.[1]

The inhabitants, at length aroused to their danger by the presence of an army whom they supposed at Siena, were thrown into general panic, though some were so blinded as to suppose it the advanced guard of the confederates. Even now, bold and judicious expedients might have defended the walls until the arrival of the allies, whose first division actually reached the Porta Salara the same day on which the city was taken; and had the bridges been previously cut, as was urged upon Renzo in consideration of the weak defences of the Borgo S. Spirito, the principal portion of the city might have held out, even after these had been carried, whilst the Duke of Urbino would have had leisure to execute signal vengeance upon the ruffian invaders, demoralised by their leader's fall and by the pillage of its Transteverin quarters.

It is by no means easy to form an idea of the actual force of the invading army from the varying estimates that have come down to us. Muratori, who bestowed much

[1] It is difficult to reconcile the varying accounts of the sack, for which, besides the many printed authorities, we have drawn largely upon a collection of unpublished and very minute details, Vat. Urb. MSS. No. 1677. It is doubtful whether Bourbon arrived on the evening of the 4th or of the 5th of May, but the assault was unquestionably made upon Monday the 6th. Many of the incidents given in that MS. are too horrible for admission into these pages. The narratives of Guicciardini and Giacomo Buonaparte, and those printed in the second volume of Eccardius, may be consulted for such; the two first, indeed, have done little beyond arranging some documents of that MS. collection. We have also consulted the Narrative of Leonardo Santori, Vat. Ottob. MSS. No. 2607, and Sanuto's MS. Diaries; checking the whole by minute examination of the localities. * On the 3rd May Bourbon had passed Viterbo, on the 4th he was at Isola Farnese. As to the number of men which Renzo da Ceri had at command, 3000 seems nearer the truth than 30,000. Bourbon had scaling ladders but no artillery. Cf. GUICCIARDINI, *Il Sacco di Roma*, Milanesi, p. 163, and CASANOVA, *Lettere di Carlo V. a Clement VII.* (per nozze Firenze, 1894).

attention upon such military statistics, reckons the troops whom Bourbon carried from Milan at about five thousand Spaniards, four thousand Germans, and half as many Italians, besides five hundred men-at-arms, two thousand German cavalry, and an indefinite number of light horse, to whom were soon united the lansquenets of Fründesberg, originally fourteen thousand, but already somewhat reduced. This would give a total of twenty-six or twenty-seven thousand men, which exceeds by a few thousand infantry the calculation adopted by Giacomo Buonaparte, his multiplication of the men-at-arms by ten being obviously an accidental error. The same author supposes that the Imperialists who had marched from Montevarchi were about twenty thousand Germans, eight thousand Spaniards, three thousand Italians, with but six hundred horse. The impression current at Rome, and in the confederate camp, that Bourbon brought from forty to fifty thousand men before that city was therefore grossly exaggerated; indeed, some authorities diminish his effective force to half that number, while Buonaparte esteems it under thirty thousand. The allied army, according to Baldi, was twenty thousand strong, of whom one fifth were cavalry: but it, too, had melted away when mustered at Isola, as we shall in due time see. On the whole, it appears that the inequality of numbers was not such as to justify the Fabian tactics, or it may be the petted policy, of Francesco Maria.

On Sunday, the 5th of May, the Constable bivouacked in the meadows north-west of the city, having approached it without crossing the Tiber. He repeated by trumpet his summons in name of the Emperor for free passage to Naples; an idle insult, considering that the way beneath the walls lay open for him. He then explained to a council of his officers the perilous state of affairs,—the troops fatigued, starving, mutinous, with a powerful enemy pressing upon their rear, and the richest metropolis of

Europe ill-defended before them, urging that there was no alternative but that night to conquer its effeminate citizens, or next day be cut to pieces by the allied host. But, finding these representations received with cold indifference, he at dusk repeated them to the whole army in an energetic harangue, which he concluded by assuring them he had received, through Cardinal Colonna, assurances of support from the Ghibelline party within the city.

Ere the morrow's dawn his army was in motion, and, under cover of a singularly dense fog, approached the city between the modern gates of Cavallegieri and S. Pancrazio. The wall was there pierced by a loop-hole, serving as the window of a small and slightly built house that formed part of the defences; below it was another aperture into the cellar. These vulnerable points, which had been unpardonably overlooked by the papal engineers, were quickly noticed by the enemy, who brought the few guns they possessed to bear upon them, and soon effected a small breach. The exact site is loosely and contradictorily described as between one of the gates and the tower of S. Spirito, near Cardinal Mellini's, or Ermellini's, garden. Meanwhile the besiegers, protected by the mist from the guns of S. Angelo, vigorously attacked various points; and on the heights above the Strada Giulia, two Spanish colours were wrested from them. The walls and substructions now visible on that side, and those which separate the Lungara from the Borgo S. Spirito, are all of later date; and in constructing them, sixteen years subsequently, the aspect of the localities has been so changed as to baffle accurate comparison with descriptions of the assault. If we can suppose the external wall to have run from near the Porta S. Spirito towards that of S. Pancrazio, instead of being carried, as at present, along the Janicular ridge from the Porta Cavallegieri, it might be comparatively easy to reconcile these statements. At all events, it is certain that considerable resistance was made by some citizens who occupied the *Campo Santo* or burying ground, which then lay just outside of the gate from S. Spirito into the Lungara, and which, according to a mural inscription there, was removed in 1749 to its present site farther up the hill. This, being the brunt of the battle, was occupied by Bourbon, whose exertions throughout the morning had been unremitting. Whilst steadying a ladder with his left hand, and cheering on his men with his right, he was struck to the ground by a bullet which passed through his thigh. The credit of that lucky shot, which cut short a career commenced in treason, closed in sacrilege, is claimed by Benvenuto Cellini. He tells us that on hieing to the Campo Santo with two comrades, he beheld from the walls the enemy assaulting the spot where they stood; whereupon they discharged their pieces in terror, he aiming at a figure singled out in the mist from its commanding height. Having mustered courage to peep over the wall, he saw a great confusion occasioned by the Constable's fall, and, fleeing with his friends through the cemetery, escaped by St. Peter's to the castle of S. Angelo.*[1] This assertion, which has generally passed for gasconade, receives support from the Vatican MS., wherein the shot is ascribed to some silversmith lads who, from the Mount of the Holy Crucifix, aimed at the general's white mantle and plume; and a monumental tablet outside the Church of S. Spirito commemorates Bernardino Passeri, goldsmith and jeweller to Clement and his two predecessors, who was killed on the 6th of May, on the adjoining part of the Janicular, after slaying many of the enemy, and capturing a standard. About five hundred paces to the west of that reach of the modern city wall which commands the Cavallegieri gate, there stands on the road to the Fornaci a small oratory, called the Capella di Barbone, and pointed out by tradition as the spot where Bourbon was wounded.

*[1] Cf. *The Life of Benvenuto Cellini*, trans. by J. A. Symonds (Nimmo, 1896), p. 65–6.

No account, however, which I have seen, countenances the idea of his having fallen so far away; nor is it possible, even when no mist intervenes, to see either that point, or the site of the present exterior city wall, from the old cemetery of S. Spirito, whence the fatal shot appears to have been aimed. But from whatever spot or hand it proceeded, the wound was mortal, and the Constable died in his thirty-ninth year, ere he could witness the desecration or share the booty to which he had stimulated his followers. Yet had God's just judgment on the traitor been withheld for a time, his influence might, perhaps, have stayed the fury of the soldiery, and Rome might have been spared some portion of the misery that ensued. His body was carried to Gaeta, and his armour is still shown at the Vatican, a plain coat of immense strength. It, however, bears an indentation on the inner side of the right thigh, where the fatal bullet entered after grazing its steel edge.[1]

For a moment his troops wavered, dismayed by their leader's fall; but revenge and a consciousness of their perilous position rendered them desperate. The assertion of Mambrino Roseo, that the Swiss guard disputed every inch of the breach until only a drummer was left alive, wants confirmation from those narratives of eye-witnesses which I have examined. Be this as it may, it was about half-past eight that the first detachment, who had made their way into the Borgo, were observed by Renzo da Ceri. Instead of cutting them down with the body of horse who followed him, he in a loud voice gave the *sauve qui peut*, and, galloping round by the Ponte Sisto, reached that of S. Angelo, where he recklessly crushed and trod down

[1] In a set of miniatures executed by Giulio Clovio for Charles V., and illustrative of his military achievement, which were bequeathed by the Right Hon. Thomas Granville to the British Museum in 1847, Bourbon is represented falling backwards from a ladder placed against a round tower on the walls of Rome; but being composed without accurate knowledge of the localities, it throws no light upon the manner of his death.

the citizens, already rushing across it in masses to the castle.*[1] Had this craven caitiff rallied his men to the breach, it might have been repaired; and had he but held the Porta Settimiana, or even now cut the lower bridges, the invaders would have been confined within a small district of the city, until Guido Rangone arrived with succours.

The panic thus originated by the city's defender spread rapidly in all quarters. The Pontiff, who, from his chair in S. Peter's, had been thundering spiritual menaces against the foe, was hurried along the covered passage to S. Angelo, whither also flocked the cardinals, clergy, and citizens of all ranks, in such crowds that it was found impossible to close the gates. At length the portcullis was dropped, with great difficulty from its rusty condition, and several cardinals, who had been excluded, were afterwards drawn up in baskets. The terrified crowd who were thus shut out, rushed to escape by the city gates, but, finding these closed, they dispersed themselves among the palaces of the Ghibelline cardinals, upon which they vainly relied as sure asylums.

About three thousand got into the castle, with fourteen cardinals. It was very ill supplied with provisions, and the neighbouring shops were hurriedly emptied of whatever stores they contained. The Pontiff, in his alarm, would have attempted flight, but Bourbon's death inspired him with some hope of making terms. In fact, the besiegers, who had at first rushed in with cries of "Hurrah for Spain! slay! slay!" soon paused, discouraged by the loss of their leader, and anticipating a desperate resistance. In this state of matters, the Portuguese ambassador was authorised by his Holiness to propose an accommodation to the imperialist chiefs, who, finding themselves in

*[1] Creighton justly remarks that this was not in keeping with Renzo da Ceri's character. The tale is from Guicciardini. Renzo da Ceri was certainly no "craven caitiff."

possession of but a fraction of the city, with walls and gates on either side excluding them from the S. Spirito and Trastevere quarters, temporised for some hours. But as the bulk of their army entered at S. Pancrazio, and they ascertained the panic in the town, their misgivings passed away, and about two hours before sunset they suddenly advanced through the Porta Settimiana, in Via Lungara. Encouraged by its defenceless state, they pushed across the Ponte Sisto, which they found equally unguarded, and spread like a deluge over the devoted city.

Now began the horrors of the sack. The brutal soldiery, absolved from discipline, scoured the city at will, penetrating unchallenged into the most secret and most sacred places.*[1] Churches and convents, palaces and houses, were invaded and rifled; resistance was punished with fire and sword; rape and murder were the fate of the inhabitants. Passing over details too revolting for the imagination to supply, but too repulsive for a place in these pages, we may cite the feeling exclamations of one who seems to have witnessed them :—"Alas! how many courtiers, gentlemen, and prelates, how many devout nuns, matrons, and maidens became a prey to these savages! What chalices, images, crucifixes, vessels of silver and gold, were torn from the altars by these sacrilegious hands! What holy relics were dashed to the ground with derisive blasphemy by these brutal

*[1] They were of many nationalities—Germans, Spaniards, Italians—"a horde of 40,000 ruffians free from all restraint." They gratified their elemental passions and lusts at the expense of the most cultivated population in the world. The Germans were the worst: "the Lutherans amongst them setting an example which was quickly followed of disregard of holy places." The Spaniards, however, excelled them in deliberate cruelty. For three days this barbarism went on unchecked. On the fourth the barbarians began to quarrel amongst themselves over the division of the booty. "The Germans . . . turned to drunkenness and buffoonery. Clad in magnificent vestments and decked with jewels, accompanied by concubines who were bedizened with like ornaments, they rode on mules through the streets and imitated with drunken gravity the processions of the Papal Court." Cf. CREIGHTON, *op cit.*, vol. VI., pp. 342–3.

Lutherans! The heads of Saints Peter, Paul, Andrew, and of many others, the wood of the sacred Cross, the blessed oil, and the sacramental wafers, were ruthlessly trodden upon. The streets exhibited heaps of rich furniture, vestments, and plate, all the wealth and splendour of the Roman court, pillaged by the basest ruffians.[1]

After these miserable scenes had endured for three days, rumours of the Duke of Urbino's approach recalled the imperialist leaders to the necessity of defence.*[2] The command having devolved upon the Prince of Orange, a yellow-haired barbarian, further plunder was prohibited, under severe penalties; and the army, reduced to comparative order, betook themselves to enjoy their booty. But now a new drama of atrocities opened. The Germans had especially distinguished themselves by a thirst for blood, but the wily Spaniards taught them a means more effectual than murder of enriching themselves and punishing their victims. The prisoners had, in most cases, concealed whatever of greatest value they possessed, and recourse was had to every variety of torment in order to extract from them supposed treasures, and a ransom for their lives; so that those who had been spared in seeming mercy found themselves but reserved for a worse fate. After stripes and blows had been exhausted, when hunger and thirst had failed to force compliance, tortures the most brutal succeeded. Some were suspended naked from their own windows by a sensitive limb, or swung head downwards, and momentarily threatened to be let drop into the street. Others had their teeth drawn slowly and singly, or were compelled to swallow their own mutilated and roasted

[1] Vat. Urb. MSS. No. 1677, f. 19.

*[2] The Duke was very slow as usual. There was plenty of time for him to receive imploring letters. A career, which was a failure brought about by dilatoriness and treason, here seems to have reached its lowest point. As always, Dennistoun is too favourable in his judgment of anyone belonging to the Rovere house.

members. Others were forced to perform the most odious and menial services; and the greatest extremities were always used towards those who were suspected of being the most wealthy and noble. Even after the desired amount of gold had been thus extorted from them, their sufferings were sometimes resumed at the instance of new tormentors. When such cruelties palled, their inflictors had recourse to a novel amusement, by forcing from the victims a confession of their sins; and we are assured by the narrator of these enormities, himself a Roman, that the iniquities thus brought to light, as habitual in that dissolute capital, were such as to confound even the licentious soldiery of Bourbon. Over the outrages committed upon the women we draw a veil: when lust was satiated, they were prolonged in diabolical punishment, the husbands and fathers being compulsory witnesses to such unspeakable atrocities.

But the delight of these sacrilegious villains, especially of the German Lutherans, was to outrage everything holy. The churches and chapels, including the now blood-stained St. Peter's, were desecrated into stables, taverns, or brothels; and the choirs, whence no sounds had breathed but the elevating chant of prayer and praise, rang with base ribaldry and blasphemous imprecations. The grand creations of religious art were wantonly insulted or damaged; the reliquaries and miraculous images were pillaged or defaced. Nay, a poor priest was inhumanly murdered for his firm refusal to administer the blessed sacrament to an ass. Nor was any respect paid to persons or party feelings. The subjects of the Emperor who happened to be in Rome, the adherents of the Colonna and other Ghibelline leaders, were all involved in the general fate. Four cardinals attached to that faction had declined entering S. Angelo, calculating that they would not only

"Guide the whirlwind and direct the storm,"

but peradventure, promote their own interests in the mêlée. They were, however, miserably mistaken, for they, too, were held to ransom; and one of them (Araceli), after being often led through the streets tied on a donkey, behind a common soldier, was carried to church with mock funereal rites, when the office of the dead was read over his living body, and an oration pronounced, wherein, for eulogy, were loathsomely related all the real or alleged immoralities of his past life. Another outrage in especial repute with the Germans, was a ribald procession, in which some low buffoon in sacred vestments was borne shoulder-high, scattering mock benedictions among the mob, amid shouts of "Long live Luther!"

A great portion of the circulating wealth of the city was centred in the Strada de' Banchi, which, from being in a line with the castle and just across the river, was considered comparatively secure. But this fallacious hope quickly vanished, and during five hours that quarter of bankers, merchants, and jewellers was savagely sacked in sight of the papal court. In one of these shops a large money bag being discovered, a general scramble ensued for its contents, and forty-two of the soldiery lost their lives at their comrades' hands, fighting for what proved to be counterfeit coin. The Jews, who were not then enclosed in the Ghetto, suffered a full share of such miseries, to make them disgorge their secret treasures. Vast multitudes of citizens took refuge in the palaces of the cardinals and principal nobility, especially of those supposed to be friendly to the imperial interests; but these asylums were seldom respected. That of the Cancelleria, originally built by Cardinal Pietro Riario, and still one of the most spacious in the capital, was long spared; but on the 20th of May its turn came; and as it was the last to be pillaged, the outrages perpetrated upon its miserable inmates, including numerous ecclesiastical and diplomatic dignitaries, with a crowd of the high-born beauties of Rome, were perhaps the most signal and sanguinary of all. In other palaces the fugitives, though spared from violence, were held to ransom. The Dowager Marchioness of Mantua purchased immunity for her residence with 10,000 ducats, which the merchants whom it sheltered joined in paying, and which her son Ferdinando, one of the imperial leaders, was said to have basely shared. In the Vatican MS. is a backbond, signed by about five hundred persons, who had sought refuge in the palace of Cardinal Andrea della Valle, obliging themselves to repay, in sums varying from 10 to 4000 scudi each, the ransom of 40,000 ducats which he had advanced. Among the names is the King of Cyprus, and, what may have more interest for us, that of Peter Hustan from Scotland. The English Cardinal of St. Cecilia, Thomas Usher, Archbishop of York, was one of those who escaped into the castle.

But where, meanwhile, was the army of the League?*[1] The Duke of Urbino, after quelling the insurrection at Florence, had lingered there for some days at the instance of the Cardinal Legate, who represented to him that Rome was amply provided with means of defence. Yet, upon learning Bourbon's advance, the confederates despatched Guido Rangone from Incisa, where their army lay, to anticipate by forced marches his arrival at that capital. Taking five thousand light infantry of the *bande nere*, with a large force of cavalry, he pushed on, and at Otricoli met the Datary's foolish missive of the 4th of May, which, declining further relief, asked for but a few hundred troops as enough for the wants of the city. The Count, however, paid no attention to this news, and, hurrying across the Campagna, heard near the Ponte Salara that the enemy had that morning penetrated the walls. Had he but

*[1] Where indeed! The Duke of Urbino had left Florence on May 3rd, but it was the 22nd of that month before he reached Isola. Strangely enough, he marched much slower than the barbarians.

known the real state of the army, or by a headlong dash risked his all in the noble enterprise, his name would have been honoured as the saviour of Rome. But his genius was unequal to the opportunity, and he retired to Otricoli to await the arrival of his chiefs.

The Duke at length aroused himself, and moved rapidly forwards. On the 3rd he quitted Florence, and at Cortona separated the army into two divisions for facilitating the commissariat. One he led by Perugia, the other, under Saluzzo, took the Val di Chiana, with a common rendezvous at Orvieto.*[1] He was at the lake of Thrasimene on the day Rome fell, and arrested his march at Perugia to effect once more a revolution there, by substituting his friend Orazio Baglioni for Gentile, a partisan of the Medici. Santori justly observes, that "in the Duke of Urbino the desire of avenging old injuries was suspected to have prevailed over zeal for the honour of Italy and the safety of Rome": indeed, this ill-timed gratification of an old grudge cost several precious days. On the 9th, his advanced guard were met at Casalino on the Tiber by a fugitive from Rome with news of the fall of that city, and again halted. Thus it was the 16th ere he joined the other division of the army at Orvieto, where it had preceded him by five days, and whence, after cruelly sacking Città della Pieve, which refused supplies, he sent on a strong party of two thousand foot and five hundred horse to carry off the Pope. It was commanded by Federigo da Bozzolo, whose gallantry well qualified him for such an

*[1] This amazing route is inexplicable. The way by the Val di Chiana was, of course, a highway to Rome. The way by Perugia, "with a rendezvous at Orvieto," is inexplicable. No more fatuous proceeding can be imagined. From Florence he would keep the Via Aretina so far as Arezzo, following it indeed thence to Rigutino to Camuscia to the Case del Piano in the Perugino close to Trasimeno. If he went thence to Perugia he was merely trying to delay his march. It was off the main route, and would lead him into the valley of Spoleto. From Perugia to Orvieto there was no good road. If he wished for a road to Rome via Perugia he should have joined the Via Flaminia at Foligno and followed it directly to the Eternal City.

attempt; but his horse having unfortunately fallen upon him near Viterbo, disabling him entirely, the command of the expedition devolved upon a subaltern, who, finding it daylight ere he came in sight of S. Angelo, and his orders being for a night attack, retraced his steps without communicating with the castle.

Three days were now passed in consultations among the leaders, of which we have varying accounts. Guicciardini of course represents them in the most unfavourable light for Francesco Maria.*[1] He tells us that neither the letters of the Pontiff, nor the entreaties of the Proveditori and the French general, could rouse the Duke's stubborn nature to active measures; and he describes him as full of zeal in words and proposals, but ever interposing obstacles to the execution of any definite plan. On the other hand, Baldi asserts that an onward movement, suggested by the Duke at Isola,*[2] was, to his great regret, overruled by these authorities, and by Guicciardini himself; whilst the Bishop of Cagli [3] pleads as his excuse for inaction, that the Venetians, finding their duty very different from field-days and muster-rolls, refused to follow him, and even retired home in great numbers. But, assuming the truth of the last averment, should not the blame of such lax discipline attach to the general who had led these troops through

*[1] It is impossible to represent the Duke in a worse light than he appears. He behaved throughout the campaign like a selfish fool; he seems never to have understood the gravity of the situation or the enormity of his crime. His biographer does not seem to understand it either.

*[2] As we know, he did not reach Isola till the 22nd. Rome was then sacked. If Guicciardini delayed, as Baldi says, we know that it was for some good reason, for his integrity and his patriotism cannot be questioned. We may well doubt Baldi's tittle-tattle.

[3] Vat. Urb. MSS. No. 818, f. 5. Sanuto has preserved a letter which he says gave the first authentic information of the sack to the combined leaders, and which urges them to exertion in most pressing terms. It will be found in II. of the Appendix, with two other letters detailing the principal incidents of that direful event in terms which, though in a great measure anticipated by our narrative, show the impression made by them at the time, and probably conveyed the fullest information of the catastrophe to the Duchess of Urbino and to the Emperor. See the Pontiff's brieves illustrating his feeble policy, No. I.

several campaigns? and may not the moral paralysis which impeded effective tactics in the army be fairly adduced in mitigation of their unauthorised furloughs?

At length an advance was agreed upon, and on the 20th the head-quarters were at Isola di Farnese, nine miles from Rome, the Duke having marched by Nepi, and Saluzzo by Bracciano. Here distracted counsels again prevailed, and, in answer to urgent representations of his confederates, that the Pope must at all hazards be relieved, Francesco Maria ordered a muster of the army, which showed twelve to fifteen thousand men. Letters to the same purpose arriving from the Signory, and a message declaring that Clement had broken off a negotiation with his oppressors on the strength of speedy assistance, he at length consented that Rangone should once more attempt to bring off his Holiness, by leading a division to Monte Mario, whilst he advanced to his support with the main body as far as Tre Capanne. But on pretext of making a previous examination of the ground, he wasted so much time, that night had fallen when they reached that place; and the expedition being thereby delayed until morning, a general feeling then prevailed that the force was inadequate, and the troops were thereupon withdrawn. An even less creditable version of this evolution is given by an eye-witness in the Duke's service, who attributes as its motive the seizure of a quantity of booty, which had been removed from Rome to Monte Rotondo; adding that, on seeing signal fires over the Campagna, and hearing a vague rumour that the enemy were approaching in force, the Duke suddenly faced about and regained his quarters, his men in sad plight, and the rear stripped to their shirts by some skirmishers.[1]

[1] Memoirs of Antenore Leonardi, dictated by him in 1581, Vat. Urb. MSS. No. 1023, f. 85. Among the works dedicated to Francesco Maria II. is a *Treatise on Tides* by Annibale Raimondo of Verona [1589], who had served under his grandfather in Lombardy, and at this time. In the pre-

In order to cut short such discreditable scenes, the Duke, at a council of war, announced his resolution to attempt no offensive operations until his army should be recruited by fifteen thousand Swiss, some ten thousand other troops, and forty pieces of cannon, with ample funds for their pay; adding that, as S. Angelo was provisioned for three months, there would be sufficient time for raising these reinforcements. This opinion he embodied in a memorial, which he sent on the 30th from Isola, by the Bishop of Asti, to Francis I. It is preserved by Baldi, and in Sermonetta's Letters, and offers a verbose, laboured, and inconclusive defence of his drivelling tactics. The burden of it is the inferiority of the allied force to the enemy, the probable failure of aggressive movements, and an urgent appeal that the King should come in person, as the only means of giving unanimity to a council in which each desired to lead. Indeed, the whole proceedings of the army attest the

face, a somewhat inflated testimony is borne to that Duke's military talents, arguing that his tactics were ever aggressive when unimpeded by other leaders, who in the present instance prevented him from marching upon Rome. But the author was eighty-four when he wrote a statement palpably intended for an adulatory purpose, and his feeble or partial reminiscences cannot be considered of material weight. We have thought it right, in a passage so nearly touching the Duke of Urbino's fair fame, to embrace the conflicting views of our best authorities: the narratives of Paruta and Morosini, Venetians, who had no interest in his reputation, go far to reconcile these and justify him. They tell us that the Signory, profoundly moved by the Pontiff's danger, sent pressing orders for their army to support him; and that, in compliance therewith, Francesco Maria and the Proveditore Pisani resolved to advance upon Rome and rescue Clement, even at the hazard of a general engagement, but that the other Proveditore, Vetturi, formally protested against exposing the army to so great a risk: that disgusted by the failures brought on by these misunderstandings, the Signory superseded Vetturi, and grumbled against their general: that the latter, annoyed by unmerited reflections, wished to throw up his command, and that it was only after cool consideration, and flattering advances from the senate, that he consented to remain in its service. See his formal defence, App. III. * Nothing can justify him, and it is impossible to defend him with honour. After all the only excuse for a soldier is his success, and Francesco Maria knew not what success meant. The testimony of courtiers should go for nothing. History has tried him, and the ruin of Rome bears witness to the treason of this ineffectual Signorotto. The Pope surrendered Castel S. Angelo on June 7th.

mutual jealousies and disunion of its leaders, which form the best justification of the Duke's dilatory measures, amid difficulties which he had not energy or decision to overcome.

The Pontiff, thus abandoned to his fate, learned by better experience,

> "With what a weight that robe of sovereignty
> Upon his shoulder rests, who from the mire
> Would guard it, that each other fardel seems
> But feathers in the balance."

On the 18th he wrote to the Duke of Urbino, "amid these calamities and perils," begging a safe-conduct for a messenger as far as Siena, to induce Lannoy to repair to Rome, the envoy selected for this mission being Bernardo, father of Torquato Tasso. The Viceroy willingly responded to this summons, hoping to succeed Bourbon in command of the imperialists. But finding the Prince of Orange already chosen by the army to that post, he in disgust kept aloof from the capitulation, which was signed on the 5th of June, by the intervention of Gattinara. Its principal stipulations were these: 1. A safe-conduct to Naples for his Holiness, and such of the cardinals as chose to go, upon payment of 150,000 golden scudi, two thirds whereof within six days, the remainder on the expiry of twenty. 2. Security for the personal property within the castle, upon payment of as much more, for which hostages were to be given until it could be raised by a general impost or otherwise. 3. The removal of all censures from the Colonna, and their restoration to their estates and dignities. 4. The immediate surrender of S. Angelo, Civita Vecchia, Ostia, and Civita Castellana, with the further cession of Parma, Piacenza, and Modena to the Emperor, as an inducement for the army to evacuate Rome. This treaty was signed by nine cardinals, four bishops, and eighteen imperialist officers, and the castle was forthwith consigned to a guard of the invaders, in whose hands the Pontiff and his court remained virtually prisoners.[1]

But many difficulties impeded completion of the remaining conditions. The amount of ransom seems under various pretexts to have been considerably advanced, and is set down by most writers at 400,000 scudi. In order to raise this sum, all the church-plate, which had been saved in the fortress, was hastily coined into specie, and three scarlet hats were set up to sale. Two of them were at once secured for 160,000 scudi by the Venetians, ambitious of influence in the conclave. The third was bought for a creature of Pompeo Colonna, whose personal hostility to Clement had become somewhat mitigated by grief for the sufferings he had brought upon the city, and who, in a pathetic audience with his master, obtained his forgiveness and benediction. Still, a large balance of the besiegers' demands remained undischarged, and the stipulation regarding the fortresses was nullified, Civita Castellana being in the hands of the allies, and Ostia occupied by Andrea Doria, neither of whom would acknowledge the capitulation. Parma and Piacenza were also held for the Church, in consequence, as was suspected, of instructions secretly transmitted by Clement. In the hope of obtaining better terms, his Holiness successively directed more than one member of the Sacred College to proceed as legate to Charles, among whom was Cardinal Farnese, his successor on the papal throne; but none of them would execute the commission.

Meanwhile the miseries of the city were fearfully aggravated. The terrified peasantry having ceased to carry supplies where they were sure of misusage, scarcity was succeeded by famine; and the sewers, choked with bodies and abandoned to neglect, engendered a deadly epidemic, called by Muratori, the murrain, which spared neither

[1] Vat. Urb. MSS. No. 1677, f. 38.

friend nor foe. In August, the pestilence increased to a terrific degree; and the invading army being reduced by long licence to an undisciplined horde, portions of it rushed in masses from the city of the plague. Some of these bands, after attempting to hang the Pope's hostages, fled towards Terni and Spoleto, sacking the towns on their way, until cut to pieces by the confederates. Nor was the Pontiff exempt from scenes of suffering. Asses' flesh was served at his table; and a greengrocer's wife was hanged before S. Angelo, for dropping into the trenches a few salad leaves for his use. The contagion spread so rapidly in the castle, that the invaders, fearing their prey might slip from their grasp by death, removed his Holiness for some weeks to the Vatican Belvidere, until the scourge had abated.

Lannoy, having fallen a victim to the disease, was succeeded as viceroy by Ugo da Moncada, from whose mercy Clement knew he had nothing to expect, and whom Santori characterises as "an experienced, clever, and sagacious man of the world, devoid of religion, full of fraud, and no observer of his word." He arrived on the 31st of October, in order to effect some new arrangement, when the Pope purchased by further large sums an exemption from several of the former stipulations, in particular from putting himself and his cardinals into his enemy's hands by going to Naples.[1] To raise this fresh imposition, four more hats were thrown upon the market, and were purchased by adherents of the Emperor. At length, after many delays, the 9th of December was fixed for his liberation from a seven months' virtual captivity; but, distrusting every one, he escaped in disguise the previous night. Concealing his face and beard under an old slouch hat and cloak, and laden with baskets and bags, he passed the sentinels of S. Angelo as a pedlar or menial servant.

[1] The new treaty of November 26 is printed by Molini in the *Documenti di Storia Italiana*, I., 273.

At a secret postern in the Vatican garden, he found a fleet horse, with a single attendant, supposed to have been provided by Cardinal Colonna, and, riding all night by Celano and Baccano, after a short repose at Capranica, he reached Orvieto, which he had some days before fixed upon as an interim residence.

The diplomatic relations of the Holy See at Madrid were at this juncture in the hands of Count Castiglione, with whom we have formerly become acquainted in the service of Dukes Guidobaldo and Francesco Maria, and whom we last noticed as agent for the Marquis of Mantua at the Roman court in 1522, where he was again sent in the same capacity on the election of Clement VII. The position of the new Pontiff soon became one of great delicacy, and already were those difficulties closing around him, which, during his reign, completed the first great breach in the Romish church, and consummated the mischiefs of foreign invasion in the Peninsula. The struggle for universal dominion of those youthful rivals who occupied the thrones of France and the Empire, was convulsing civilised Europe, and Italy was obviously fated to become the permanent prey of the victor. In these circumstances, a character so deficient in energy and decision was singularly inadequate to cope with the necessities of the times; and Clement's influence at Florence, far from affording a prop to the tottering papacy, tended yet more to distract his irresolute purpose. Falling back upon the usual expedient of small minds, he adopted a neutral attitude between the two contending potentates: but the days were past when Pontiffs could grasp the balance of power, or curb a dangerous ascendancy; and Clement's views aimed not beyond siding with a momentary victor. To carry out such policy fine diplomacy was requisite, and Castiglione was selected to watch the interests of Rome at the Spanish court. In the autumn of 1524, he accepted this Nunziatura, to which was joined the lucrative collectorship of Spain; and after visiting the shrine of Loreto, he reached Madrid in the following March.

His negotiations for the next four years embraced the politics of Europe, to which those of Italy were but an episode. We cannot interrupt the thread of our narrative to notice them: a sketch of their progress, in No. IV. of the Appendix, may afford some idea of the difficulties of Castiglione's position, as the medium of communication between a master who, leaving him habitually without information, recalled his most momentous instructions after they had been acted upon, and a monarch whose public measures were in uniform contradiction to his private assurances. That diplomacy so conducted should have issued in disgrace to Clement, ruin to Rome, and a broken heart to Count Baldassare, can excite no astonishment; but the ambassador merits our pity rather than our blame. Indeed its complicated intrigues may well drive the historian and the critic to despair. Incidents, which, although attended by important consequences, seem sudden and unlooked for, might, upon more accurate scrutiny, be detected as results long aimed at, and patiently wrought out. Thus, some documents lately published by Lanz[1] prove that Charles, although disposed to yield much for a satisfactory accommodation with Clement, had authorised Moncada, early in the summer of 1526, to concert with Cardinal Pompeo Colonna a series of domestic insurrections, in order to embarrass his Holiness into a disposition for peace, the issue of which machinations we have seen in the first sack of Rome.

Although the acts of Charles and his generals during

[1] Lanz Correspondenz des Kaisers Carl V. See also the delightful and well-edited *Lettere di Castiglione* by SERASSI. Cf. also CASANOVA, *Lettere di Carlo V. a Clement VII.* (per nozze, Firenze, 1894).

1526-7 were uniformly and aggravatingly hostile to Clement, and prejudicial to the papacy, they must be regarded as in some measure forced upon him by the shuffling of his Holiness. His own position and prospects were not then by any means so secure as to render redundant the support still carried by the influence of the Keys; and the cherished aim of his manhood, which would have united Western Europe in one faith and under one sway, had not yet been abandoned as a fitful dream. By keeping in view these peculiarities in his situation, we may in some measure reconcile the obvious contradictions between his professions and his policy—between his language to Castiglione and the conduct of Bourbon; and we may appreciate in their true sense such apparently fulsome and false expressions as he thus addressed to Clement, on the 18th of September, 1526:—"And since God has constituted us two as mighty luminaries, it behoves us to endeavour that the globe should be enlightened by us, and to see that no eclipse occur through our differences; let us, then, take counsel together for the general weal, for repressing barbarian inroads, and restraining sectarian error." At a moment when the eastern frontier of the empire had been broken down by the victorious Crescent; when the crowns of Hungary and Bohemia were tottering on his brother's brow; and when, as he writes in 1526, the wars of Italy had extracted every ducat from his treasury, we may well suppose how sincere was his wish for a settlement of those protracted struggles within the Alps, and for a union of interests with the Holy See. That his measures little accorded with that object, and nowise tended to bring it about, arose less from want of sincere intention than from an ill-judged mixture of good words and hard blows, partly dictated by his own deficient judgment, partly by the misapprehension of his officers. Though therefore the pillage of Rome by the Colonna was a natural con-

Anderson

THE EMPEROR CHARLES V

From the picture by Titian in the Prado Gallery, Madrid

sequence of his own intrigues, the regret he expressed to the Pontiff that his people had been driven to it ["*que l'on ait donné l'occasion à mes gens que tel désastre soit advenu*"] was, no doubt, his real feeling.

Equally inconsistent in appearance, but natural in the circumstances, was his conduct in reference to Bourbon's outrageous proceedings. When news of the sack reached Madrid, he affected great indignation, and put his court into mourning. On the 25th of July, he addressed to the magistracy of Rome a letter defending his proceedings. After narrating his liberation of Francis, and the various other sacrifices made by him, preliminary to such a general pacification as might enable all Christian powers to unite their arms against the Infidel, he charged the Pope with defeating this scheme by suddenly, and without reason, instigating an attack upon him and the imperial dignity, whereby he was compelled from self-defence to march fresh forces upon Italy, in what he regarded as a worse than civil broil. Moreover, new alliances against him having been arranged by his Holiness, and the truce actually broken, his troops had no alternative but to adopt compulsory measures. That these should, by the blunders of his officers, have led to the siege of the city, without his knowledge, he deeply regretted, and gladly would shed his best blood to repair its disasters. But great as had been the sacrifice, he consoled himself with a hope of its paving the way for a general peace, which he would do his utmost to accelerate. In fine, he wound up with most sonorous professions of devotion to the grandeur of the Roman name.[1]

The Pontiff's natural dissatisfaction with his ambassador at Madrid was very plainly expressed in a letter of the 20th of August, which taxed him with undue reliance upon the Emperor's vague protestations, imputing gener-

[1] Vat. Urb. MSS. No. 1677, f. 36.

ally to him a want of foresight preceding the calamity of Rome, and a neglect of the proper remedies for that mischief. To this brief, Castiglione answered at considerable length, and with unnecessary diffuseness, as soon as it reached him in December.[1] The substance of his defence is that, on every occasion during the four years of his mission, he had laboured to establish a good understanding between his Holiness and Charles, and had been met with assurances, verbal and written, of his Majesty's anxious desire to meet these views; but that the great distance, and the delays of communication with Rome, not only rendered it impossible to provide for the successive exigencies as they arose, but left him entirely in the dark as to the most important movements until too late to avert impending mischief. Thus he had no intelligence of the truce arranged with Lannoy on the 15th of March, till he heard of its being rejected by Bourbon. These excuses ostensibly satisfied Clement; and, however inadequate they might be deemed in ordinary cases of diplomatic blundering, they may be allowed some weight in this instance; for, although the Emperor could scarcely fail to anticipate from the sack of Rome new facilities for domination in Italy, in consequence of the permanent humiliation of the papacy, history must acquit him of a preconcerted plan to bring about a catastrophe which incidentally resulted from Bourbon's disobedience and the disorganisation of his army. Indeed, had Charles been as much interested in the welfare of the Eternal City as Castiglione himself, he would have been powerless to arrest the destroyer, whose death had removed him from all reckoning on this side of the grave, and prevented his master from sacrificing him in token of good faith. It is, however, impossible to regard without contempt the hollow professions of an autograph letter addressed by the

[1] *Lettere de Principi*, I., 83.

Emperor to Clement, on the 22nd of November, wherein he congratulated his Holiness on his supposed liberation, thanking God for it "with joy as sincere as was the grief with which I heard of your detention from no fault of mine." Avowing himself his most humble and loyal son, ready to use every effort for the restoration and increment of the apostolic dignity, he besought the Pontiff to credit nothing to the contrary that might be inserted by false and interested suggestions.[1]

Such are the considerations which seem calculated, and not altogether inadequate, to account for the eccentric policy and hollow professions of Charles, in so far as we can gather from the strange events thus briefly sketched. But, if we are to rely upon a different view brought forward by the Sieur de Brantome in his anecdotes of Bourbon, the advance of the imperialist army was not dictated from Madrid. In his gossiping and often apocryphal pages is detailed a conversation held by him at Gaeta with a veteran, who in youth had been with the Constable, and who imputed to that renegade an intention of seizing upon the sovereignty of Rome. His overweening vanity and unbounded ambition countenance the idea, and the way in which he is there stated to have conciliated his soldiery, by pandering to their worst passions, gives colour to the charge. If it be credited, Clement's indignation was misplaced, and Charles might have defended his consistency at the expense of his pride, could he have demeaned himself to acknowledge having been baffled and betrayed by his own general.

Thus ended the Sack of Rome. No similar calamity had befallen the Holy City since the devastation of Robert Guiscard, who, four centuries and a half before, at the head of his Apulian Normans, laid in ruin and ashes the

[1] *Lettere de' Principi*, I., 71, 110.

most monumental portion of the imperial capital. On this occasion, fewer remains of antiquity were exposed to destruction, but the people suffered far more severely. From four to six thousand of them fell in the first fury of the barbarians, besides many who perished by more mature cruelties. Thirty thousand are said to have sunk under the famine and pestilence which, during many subsequent months, ravaged the devoted city, leaving only about as many more for its entire population, which, according to Giovio, had, ten years before, amounted to eighty-five thousand. The value of property pillaged and destroyed was supposed to exceed two millions of golden ducats; the amount extorted in ransoms has been stated at a nearly equal sum. So general a pauperism ensued, that regular distributions were long continued from the papal treasury, drained as it had been. But a great revival of religious observances followed, being inculcated by the clergy and government, and practised very generally among the inhabitants, whose oblivion of such duties, and addiction to debauchery, usury, and every grovelling pursuit, had hitherto been scandalously apparent. Through out all these scenes of misery, the Pontiff had bewailed the misfortunes of his subjects more than his own sufferings, and had penitently confessed himself their author. It was not till the 6th of October, in the following year, that he returned to his capital, pale and thin, languid and disheartened; and at the moment of his arrival, a preternatural storm burst over the city, succeeded by a most destructive flood. Nor were such omens out of season. In him had set the ancient glory of the papacy. From the moment that his predecessors, mingling in the arena of international strife, descended from arbiters to parties in the conflicts of Europe, their influence waned. When they had to canvass for the support of temporal sovereigns, they ceased to command them. But, after Clement was reduced to sue for personal protection to the successor of one who had knelt before a pontiff, the prestige of papal power was gone, its sceptre was shivered in the dust.[1]

[1] The name CLEMENT has been remarked as unlucky for the papacy: Under Clement V. the Holy See was translated to France; under Clement VI. the metropolitan church of the Lateran was burnt; Clement VII. saw Rome pillaged by an army of transalpine heretics, and capitulated to them.

CHAPTER XL

The Duke's mischievous policy—New league against Charles V.—A French army reaches Naples—The Duke's campaign in Lombardy—Peace restored—Siege of Florence—Coronation of the Emperor at Bologna—The independence of Italy finally lost—Leonora Duchess of Urbino—The Duke's military discourses.

WE must now return to the confederate camp at Isola, which the Duke of Urbino broke up, after having eased his conscience by sending to Francis I. the explanation of his views to which we have referred. The general feeling regarding his conduct was testified by a speedy withdrawal of many forces under his command, some deserting to the enemy, others retiring to their homes. On the 1st of June, he was at Monterosi, and thence fell back upon Viterbo and Todi, where he obtained some inglorious successes over the imperialist bands, as they fled in disorder from plague-stricken Rome. During the autumn his troops, which gradually diminished to a few thousands, led a life of disreputable pillage about the valley of the Tiber; and, after again embroiling himself in the affairs of Perugia with little credit or success, he interfered in the succession of Camerino in a way which we shall find eventually pregnant with mischief to his son. On the Pontiff's arrival at Orvieto, he hastened to wait upon his Holiness, and put forward the Venetian commissioner to make a laboured justification of his recent miscarriages. Clement, affecting contentment with what was beyond redress, received him cordially, and hinted at a union of his son Guidobaldo with Caterina, daughter of his late competitor, Lorenzo de'

Medici. But ere long he reaped the fruit of his feeble policy, by hearing that he was spoken of in the most disparaging terms by the gallant Francis I., and by the French general Lautrec.

Still more mortifying to him was the distrust shown by his Venetian employers. We learn from Sanuto's Diaries that, early in May, his Duchess had repaired to Venice, with the young Guidobaldo and a suite of forty persons, while the visits passing between her and the imperial ambassador soon became matter of unfavourable comment. On the 29th of June, a guard of barges was placed near her residence, to intercept any attempt at escape; and on the envoy from Urbino questioning this proceeding, the Doge said, in explanation, "We have much reliance on our Captain from past experience, but what has been done was to satisfy the vulgar." Hearing that his wife and son were thus under surveillance, as hostages for his good faith, the Duke, on the 9th of July, penned a remonstrance and justification, somewhat similar to that which he had transmitted to the French king. It will be found in the Appendix, No. III., and, though a most inconclusive defence, it was well received by the Signory, and his family were so far released from constraint, that, early in August, the Duchess was allowed to go for health to the baths of Abano. News of her departure from such a cause were little consolation to her lord, who declared that, were she to die, he should be in despair. Remembering, however, the fate of Carmagnola, he would not venture in person to Venice, until he had twice sent his confidential friend Leonardi to reconnoitre the state of feeling there. Reassured at length, by pressing invitations from the Signory, he in the spring took ship at Pesaro with a small suite, and was met upon landing by an escort of twenty gentlemen in scarlet, who conducted him to his lodging. Next day he was admitted to the interview which he had demanded, and was received at the top of the great stairs by the

Doge, followed by the principal senators. After mutual embraces, the Duke was led to a seat of honour, and had audience for an hour and a half. This being concluded, the public were admitted to see their Captain-general, who was richly decked in diamonds, with a massive bracelet of twisted gold on his left arm, and a jewelled device in his cap. On returning to his apartment, he had from the Signory the customary compliment of confections, malmsey, and wax lights. It would be hard to say how far he was indebted to his oratory for this happy extrication from his difficulties; but we are told by one of his suite that many of the nobility, who crowded to pay their respects, besought a sight of his speech to the senate, insisting that so eloquent an oration must needs have been written and committed to memory.[1]

Thinking it well to retire with flying colours, he next morning took his departure; and his party, being challenged by three of the patrol for riding armed, answered by beating them to death. The same intemperate behaviour brought him ere many days into a new dilemma with his employers. Gian Andrea da Prato, an officer of the Republic, having somewhat disrespectfully combated his opinion as to the defences of Peschiera, received from him a severe blow in the face, tearing it with a diamond ring he happened to wear, which was followed up by a severe beating with his baton of command; Leonardi adding that it was well for him the Duke was unarmed. The Venetian officers, protesting against this violence as an insult to the Signory, and as incompatible with due freedom of discussion in council, sent a complaint to the senate; but the Duke's resident minister succeeded in averting their indignation by explanations. Their satisfaction with his services under the banner of St. Mark was further testified by presenting him with a palace worth

[1] Leonardi's Memoirs, Vat. Urb. MSS. No. 1023, f. 85. Most of the preceding details have been gathered from Sanuto's Diaries.

10,000 scudi, which may fairly be taken into account as countervailing the strictures of Guicciardini and Sismondi.

The capture of Rome being known, a new coalition was hastily patched up, wherein France, England, Venice, and Florence were parties, and to which the free cardinals, in name of the Sacred College, adhered. Its avowed object was to check the exorbitant power of Charles in Italy, and to establish Francesco Sforza in Milan, then held by Antonio della Leyva for the Emperor. A powerful French army under Lautrec marched on the 30th of June, and, on its arrival in Lombardy, the Venetians recalled most of their forces from Central Italy. On the 4th of October Pavia was taken and miserably sacked, and Milan might have become an easy prey had not Lautrec preferred advancing for the Pope's liberation. But, having lost time in extorting contributions from Piacenza and Parma, he had only reached Reggio when he heard of his escape from durance. Clement, though avowing gratitude for these exertions on his behalf, declined committing himself by any overt act against the Emperor, whose troops still occupied Rome.

The year which now closed is justly characterised by Muratori as the most fatal and lamentable for Italy that history has commemorated. The horrors of war, which, during its course, were poured in accumulated measure upon the Eternal City, fell largely upon many other parts of the Peninsula. Four foreign armies were let loose upon her plains, to steep them in misery, and the enormities attending the sack of Rome were repeated at Pavia, Spoleto, and a multitude of minor towns in Lombardy and Central Italy. The furies of civil broil were meanwhile scarcely less rampant. The Campagna of Rome, the sunny shores of Naples, the towns of the Abruzzi, were ravaged or revolutionised by the arms and intrigues of the Pontiff. Florence, Siena, Modena, Rimini, Ravenna,

Perugia, and Camerino changed their governments, under pressure of foreign force or domestic violence. Nor were the elements more propitious. Incessant rains destroyed the harvest, and laid whole districts under water. With an unusual demand upon agricultural produce, the supply was greatly curtailed. Famine reigned throughout the land, and pestilence desolated the population. The inhabitants, reduced to general mendicity, beset the streets and highways with their squalid children. Their murmurs by day and their screams by night met with rare responses from passers-by as needy as themselves; and at length, worn out with suffering, they laid them down to die. It was during this year of general gloom that Machiavelli closed his life; and to it specially applies that passage in his *Principe* (whether then interpolated or written long before) describing the prostration of his native land. "Conquered, enslaved, divided—without leader or law—beaten, spoiled, partitioned, overrun, and in every way ruined—she lay half lifeless, awaiting some one to heal her wounds, to arrest the robbery, pillage, and forced taxation of her states, to heal her long-cankering sores."

To this hideous but faithful picture one finishing touch is wanting. Alarmed by Lautrec's advance upon Naples, the Prince of Orange at length, on the 16th of February, gave orders for the evacuation of Rome. But his army, now crumbled away to some thirteen thousand men, refused to march without an advance of pay, for which a final contribution of 20,000 ducats was wrested from the Camera. Not satisfied with this, the brutal soldiery redoubled their individual efforts, by every ingenuity of torture, to screw more treasure or ransom from the wretched inhabitants. But a summary vengeance awaited them. Such of the citizens as had arms secretly left the city, and, as their relentless foes straggled heedlessly across the Campagna, laden with spoil, they, by a succession of furious charges, recovered a vast quantity of the plunder, and, stripping the rapacious soldiery of their gala dresses and rich jewels, dismissed them naked. In this state the exasperated peasantry, headed by Napoleone Orsini, the warlike Abbot of Farfa, set upon and massacred them without mercy. So signal was these miscreants' fate that, in two years, scarcely one of them is supposed to have survived.

After delaying for some weeks at Bologna, to abide the issue of many intricate negotiations which followed upon the Pontiff's release, Lautrec advanced, by the eastern coast, to attack the kingdom of Naples. His army is estimated by Muratori at about fifty thousand, though stated by others at a much higher amount. On the 10th of February, he passed the frontier by the Tronto, and at Aquila, and elsewhere in the Abruzzi, was received with open arms by the remnant of the Angevine party. On the 12th of March, the two armies were in presence at Troia; but, neither of them being anxious for a decisive result, no engagement followed. After ravaging most of La Puglia and Calabria, the French troops sat down before Naples, on the 29th of April, and continued the siege during most of the summer. Once more did that delicious land, where the ancients placed their Elysian fields, and which is the terrestrial heaven of modern Italians, prove fatal to its spoilers. Its soil, fertile in nature's choicest products; its bright atmosphere, redolent of beauty; its climate, conducive to luxurious gratifications; its volcanic air, stimulating to sensual indulgences; its breezes, wafting perennial perfumes—all invited to an excess of enjoyment, enervating to the physical, as it was fatal to the moral energies of the invaders. Their cup of pleasure was drugged, and Naples was avenged on her destroyers by her own poisons, which they greedily quaffed. A contagious pestilence swept their ranks, and, on the 15th of August, carried off their leader. Weakened and discouraged, the remnant shut themselves into Aversa, but were soon forced to a capitulation, which being violated, most of them were cut to pieces.

To counterbalance Lautrec's expedition, the Emperor had ordered more troops across the Alps, and, in the beginning of May, Henry Duke of Brunswick brought fourteen thousand Germans through the Tyrol to the Lago di Garda. On the first alarm of their approach, the Duke of Urbino made the most of a handful of troops under his command, to protect the Venetian mainland territory; and his biographers give him great credit for defensive measures which ensured their towns from attack, and obliged the invaders to move upon the Milanese. Pavia having been, about the same time, surprised by della Leyva, Lodi alone remained in Sforza's hands, and before it the Duke of Brunswick drew his lines. But the destruction of his magazines by Francesco Maria reduced his army to great straits; and a virulent epidemic having carried off two thousand of his men, the residue broke up and made their way homewards, after their first assault had been sharply repelled.

In September, the Duke of Urbino's little army was reinforced by a strong body of Swiss infantry and French lances, led by St. Pol, and it was resolved to recover Pavia. Scarcely was the siege begun when news of the desperate state of the French before Naples induced St. Pol to propose withdrawing his contingent to the succour of Genoa, which, in consequence of Andrea Doria suddenly passing over from the side of Francis to that of his rival, was placed in great danger. A brief delay was obtained by the urgent representations of Francesco Maria, who, throwing aside his accustomed sluggishness, directed operations in person. On the sixth day he effected a breach by blowing up a bastion, which placed the city at its assailants' mercy, and it was again exposed to the horrors of a ruthless sack. This success was, however, counterbalanced by a revolution in Genoa, the city declaring itself independent of France, and was followed by the fall of Savona, on the 21st of October. It might have been saved by more prompt exertions on the Duke's part, who was unjustly blamed by his French allies for its loss, being, as Paruta assures us, interdicted by the Signory from leaving their frontier exposed.

During the weary wars of Clement VII., the fluctuations inherent in human affairs were rarely counterbalanced by high principles or commanding genius. Confederacies formed upon narrow views and selfish calculations were neither sustained with persevering energy, nor directed by men of enlarged views and gallant bearing. Indeed, courage itself faltered and zeal grew languid, in contests which seemed to demoralise officers and soldiery. It cannot therefore occasion surprise that all parties were equally ready to play fast and loose; that the great powers kept themselves ever open for new combinations; and that independent captains, true to old condottiere usages, readily transferred their services to the quarter whence most substantial benefits were likely to accrue. Thus, after the great discouragement resulting to the cause of Francis, from the loss of Lautrec's army and the desertion of Doria, his allies began to waver. The Pontiff, though scarcely recovered from the alarm in which his recent misfortunes had left him, displayed an unaccountable leaning towards their author; and even Sforza, having to choose between two claimants of his duchy, began to think that the best terms might be had from the Emperor. The Venetians were as usual waiters upon providence; but they so overplayed the temporising game, that the arrangements for a double treaty between Clement, Charles, and Francis found them still in the field, and they were left to make head single-handed against the imperialists. As such a contest was necessarily a defensive one, the Duke's dilatory manœuvres were at length well timed, and the

Signory preferred thus prolonging the struggle to restoring the territory they had gained during the war, as a preliminary condition of peace. The Emperor had landed in August at Genoa, with a powerful fleet and army, and new levies arrived from Germany. St. Pol, after drawing off his troops towards Genoa, was surprised and shamefully beaten ere he could be supported by Francesco Maria,[1] who had encamped at Cassano on the Adda, in a position that menaced Milan, and commanded supplies from the Bergamese territory, whilst it effectually protected the Venetian mainland from imperialist aggression. The Duke there resisted every attempt to dislodge him, until the senate had arranged the terms of a treaty with the Emperor, which was signed on the 23rd of December.

The ostensible motives of Charles in coming to Italy were twofold; to forward arrangements for a general league against the Turks, who, after overrunning Hungary, had laid siege to Vienna; and to have the imperial diadem and the iron crown of Lombardy imposed upon his brows by the Pope. Bologna was selected for the ceremony, whither his Holiness arrived in great state about the end of October, followed on the 5th of November by the Emperor. The two potentates were lodged in the public palace, and addressed themselves to the former of these objects with so much success, that on the 23rd of December a treaty was concluded, wherein were comprehended all the Italian states except Florence. The Lombard question was settled, Sforza being left in possession of his duchy, but hampered with ruinous payments to the Emperor in name of expenses; whilst the Venetians, besides paying heavy sums under the same pretext, had to resign their acquisitions about Ravenna and on the Neapolitan coast. Florence was not included, in consequence of its *de facto*

[1] In his *Discorsi Militari*, pp. 7, 8, the Duke minutely criticises the French general's tactics, which exposed him to this shameful reverse; but the details have now little interest.

government being in the hands of the democratic party, who, in 1527, had availed themselves of Clement's difficulties to expel the Medici; it was now, however, replaced under their sway by the combined arms of the Pontiff and the Emperor. After ten months of obstinate defence,—the final effort of its old republican spirit, which commands our sympathy and respect far more than the struggles of faction that used in earlier times to deluge its piazza in blood,—the city was surrendered on the 12th of August, 1530, and its chains were riveted by a base bastard, who seems to have had nothing of the Medici but their name. In this siege died Philibert Prince of Orange, one of the last survivors of the invaders of Rome. Like his comrade Bourbon, he was a renegade from the service of Francis I., in disgust, as was alleged, at being turned out of his palace to make way for the imperious Wolsey, and at the ridicule to which this slight exposed him in the French court. The title passed to his nephew René Count of Nassau, who carried it from Provence to Holland, and was grandfather of William III. of England. Their leader fallen, their occupation gone, a serious alarm spread throughout Central Italy, lest the victorious soldiery should re-enact the horrors perpetrated by Bourbon's sanguinary host. These fears, however, soon subsided; indeed a century and a quarter elapsed ere that fair land was again exposed to the devastations of foreign spoilers.

These diplomatic arrangements being thus satisfactorily concluded, preparations advanced rapidly for the coronation, and many princely feudatories of Italy flocked to witness that august function. Among these was Francesco Maria, who, though summoned as Prefect of Rome, had some cause to misdoubt his welcome from the Pontiff and the Emperor. The old family grudge still smouldered in the breast of the former, and he was alleged to have lately intrigued with Charles that the Prince of Orange, after re-establishing the Medici at Florence, should seize upon

Urbino for Ascanio Colonna, whose vague claims upon that duchy have been already explained.[1] Indeed, a rumour of that general's march upon his states in March, 1529, had suddenly recalled the Duke from Lombardy, in order to provide for their defence. To the Emperor he had been uniformly opposed, rather from the chances of war than upon any personal quarrel; yet he did not hesitate to repair to the coronation, arriving at Bologna about the 1st of November, and there met with an interesting incident.

As he approached the city with his suite he was met by about fifty German veterans, who addressed him in their rough transalpine tongue, and through an interpreter explained that they had come to pay to him their reverence, having served under his father in long past wars, inquiring where their old commander had died. They were told that it was himself that led them to victory; but, unaware how early he had commanded armies, they demurred to this, saying, that were their old leader alive his beard would be blanched. The Duke having assured them that their gallantry and attachment were well known and appreciated by him, they dismissed their doubts, crowding round to kiss his hands or mantle, and accompanied him to his lodging, a civility duly acknowledged by thanks and a suitable largess.

Several days having passed in visits of compliment, the Emperor arrived, escorted into the town by the Dukes of Urbino and Savoy, with their brilliant staffs. Mindful only of the renown which the former had acquired in recent campaigns, the monarch summoned him to his side, and conversed with him in friendly familiarity. He called him the first general in Christendom, and complimented his officers as worthy soldiers of a famous school, whose complexions bore the honourable scars and weather-stains of good service. Duchess Leonora became on her arrival

[1] Vol. II., pp. 420, 423.

equally the object of imperial favour, and received flattering testimony to her polished and princely manners. The purpose of these marked attentions was soon developed, in a proposal to confer upon Francesco Maria the baton, as captain-general of the imperial troops in Italy. This gratifying offer he gracefully declined, pleading an engagement to the Venetians, which prevented his listening to such proposals without consent of the Signory. To them Charles forthwith addressed his request; but received for answer that the same considerations which induced him to make it rendered them resolute in retaining the services of a leader who for many years had brought renown to their arms; but that, though unable to spare himself, they were ready to place him with all their forces at the disposal of his Highness. The Emperor had employed the Duchess of Savoy's intervention in this affair, who at his suggestion cultivated a great intimacy with the Duke and Duchess of Urbino, and her pleading was on one occasion enforced by Charles in person in a well-timed visit. The establishment of this lady is described by Leonardi, who was particularly struck with the easy elegance and graceful conversation of her six girlish maids of honour, seated on cushions of tawny velvet, and gaily decked in rich jewels, plumes, and streaming ribbons, chatting merrily with her guests. The Emperor, far from taking umbrage at his disappointment, sought Francesco Maria's opinion as to the person best fitted for commander-in-chief, who recommended the appointment of Antonio della Leyva. Indeed, Giraldi declares that Charles "never could have enough of his fine discourses or sententious remarks," and pressed him to name any favour he would accept of. The Duke, thus encouraged, urged the restoration of Sora, Arce, Arpino, and Rocca Guglielmi, which had been taken from him at the instigation of Leo X., a request to which Charles acceded about three years later, paying 100,000 scudi of compensation to a Flemish nobleman who had been invested with these Neapolitan fiefs.

On the 22nd of February, in the chapel attached to the Palazzo Pubblico, the brows of Charles were encircled with the iron crown of Lombardy, which, as Muratori observes, had not yet been rendered a sacred relic by the legend of its having been formed out of a nail of the true cross. Two days after, he received the imperial diadem in the church of S. Petronio, the Duke of Urbino, as Prefect of Rome, carrying the sword of state, with which the Pontiff had just conferred knighthood upon the Emperor. The populace were regaled in the Piazza with two bullocks roasted entire, whilst both the great fountains poured forth continued streams of wine, and silver largess was scattered at all hands. An accident from the fall of some scaffolding, which nearly proved fatal to the hero of the ceremonial, brought on a sharp altercation between the captain of the imperial guard and the chief magistrate of the city. To the threats of the officer, to treat the place as he had already done the larger town of Milan, the latter replied that in Milan they manufactured needles, but in Bologna they made swords. On the 22nd of March, Charles departed for Germany, in order to defend his Austrian dominions from the Turks; and, nine days later, Clement set out in a litter for his capital, where he arrived on the 9th of April, after spending the 6th at Urbino, on a visit to Francesco Maria.

From these transactions at Bologna there dated a new era for Italy. The long struggle of Guelph and Ghibelline was at length come to an end—the standard of her nationality was finally struck. Succeeding pontiffs were content to lean for support upon an authority which their predecessors had defied or resisted. It mattered little whether that paramount influence was held by an Austrian or Spanish imperial dynasty; so long as the two

Sicilies, Sardinia, and Milan owned its dominion, the freedom of the other states was merely nominal. The Peninsula was, indeed, no longer ravaged by European wars, yet the protracted struggle did not close until the victor had riveted on her his chains. She was seldom desolated by invading armies, but she was not the less plundered by licensed spoilers. Peace was restored to her, but independence was gone. The Reformation, too, which Leo left a petty schism, had in ten years changed the faith of a large section of Europe, and Rome was no longer the capital of Christendom. The results of this change in the Church it is not the province of these pages to notice, but, in common with other Italian feudatories, the Dukes of Urbino felt the altered aspect of their political relations. War was not now a profession demanding their services, and recompensing them with glory and profit. The trade of arms had come to an end, as regarded the old condottiere system and its frightful abuses, and was modified into the more orderly machinery of standing armies on a limited scale. We shall accordingly find these princes for the future little mixed up with the general affairs of the Peninsula, and scarcely ever taking the field, but left with ample leisure for the administration of their little principality, or the cultivation of their individual tastes. Had such been the lot of Duke Federigo or his accomplished son, their fame would scarcely have been dimmed, for theirs were virtues equally calculated to elevate a court or illustrate a camp. But it was otherwise with the two remaining sovereigns della Rovere; and the glories of the dynasty would suffer no diminution did we now draw our narrative to a close. Yet these Dukes were not commonplace men; and, making allowance for the age in which they lived,—when the fine gold of literature and arts had been transmuted into baser metal, and when genius had fled from a desolation which peace without freedom was powerless to reanimate,—they were not unworthy to rule in the Athens of Italy. Those readers, however, who have thus far followed our narrative must content themselves through its remaining chapters with characters less striking, views less general, events of narrowed interest; and must bear in mind that the niche in the temple of Fame appropriated to Urbino, as well as that enshrining the Italian name, was earned ere the coronation of Charles V. had closed the struggles of Italy, and consummated her subjugation.

After that time, according to one of the most rational as well as eloquent of the new dreamers after Italian nationality, "she underwent a rapid yet imperceptible decline; yet her sky smiled brightly as ever, her climate was as mild. A privileged land, removed from all cares of political existence, she went on with dances and music, happy in her ignorance, sleeping in the intoxication of incessant prosperity. Used to the scourge of invasion, the sons of the south took up again their guitars, wiped away their tears, and sang anew like a cloud of birds when the tempest is over."[1] This picture, drawn in bitterness, but not apparently in irony, paints the decline of Italy in colours more attractive than any we should have dared to employ; and we extract it chiefly for the sake of contrast with the same writer's ready admission that the liberty of the old republics was cradled amid convulsions of faction, which eventually exhausted their forces, or stifled their independence.

If the object of government be the greatest happiness of the masses, it seems, according to Mariotti, to have been more fully attained in Italy during the ages of foreign sway than in those of republican strife. Admitting in some degree, this conclusion, we accord a more hearty approval to the character he has elsewhere given of a state of matters worse, probably, in that land than either of

[1] Mariotti's *Italy*, II.

these alternatives,—"that slow and silent disease, that atrabilious frenzy—politics—which pervades all ranks, exhibiting a striking contrast with the radiant and harmonious gaiety of heaven and earth."

Our notices of the court of Urbino have been suspended during a long interval from lack of materials. Indeed, the military duties of its head too well accounts for this deficiency of incident, rendering his domestic life a blank. Even the brief intervals when he could steal from the camp to the society of his Duchess, were passed in some neighbouring town, where she met him, or at Venice, where she made a lengthened sojourn, partly as a safer residence during the alarm consequent upon Bourbon's invasion, but in some degree as a guarantee for her husband to the suspicious government he served. These circumstances occasioned him prolonged absences from his state, of which his consort availed herself to prepare for him an agreeable surprise.

Immediately north-west from Pesaro rises the fertile slope of Monte Bartolo, near the summit of which, but sheltered from the keen sea-breeze, Alessandro Sforza fixed the site of a villa called Casartole. The Emperor Frederick III., when returning from his coronation at Rome, in January, 1469, was magnificently entertained by that Prince, and here laid the foundation of a casino, which in compliment to him was named the Imperiale. Its dimensions were, however, unequal to that imposing name, for, on the death of Giovanni Sforza, in 1510, it was valued at only 8000 ducats. Having devolved upon the Duke of Urbino, with the lordship of Pesaro, it was selected by the Duchess for a compliment to him, which may be best explained by the inscription she placed upon the building:—"For Francesco Maria, Duke of the Metaurian States, on his return from the wars, his consort Leonora has erected this villa, in token of affection, and in compensation for sun and dust, for watching and toil, so that, during an interval of repose, his military genius may here prepare for him still wider renown and richer rewards." To carry out this idea worthily, she summoned Girolamo Genga, of Urbino, one of the best architects of his time; and under his able superintendence the casino of the Sforza, distinguished from moderate country houses only by heraldic devices and a lofty bell-tower, was rapidly transformed into a handsome palace, which the pencil of Raffaele Colle was employed to decorate with its master's triumphs.

The site of this villa was admirably adapted as a residence for the sovereign of those broad lands it overlooked. It commanded every dwelling in the little city of Pesaro, though perfectly secluded from contact with its busy streets. The vale of the Isauro or Foglia lay in verdure before it, beyond which were the gardenlike slopes of Novilara, terminating in a varied landscape of hill and dale, which carried the gazer to the blue mountains of Gubbio. To the left spread the coast of Fano and Sinigaglia; to the right the high lands of Urbino were bounded by the Apennines of Carpegna and the isolated heights of San Marino. In a word, the Imperiale scanned the whole duchy of Urbino, of which it might, not inaptly, be considered the eye. The attractions of this princely retreat have been described with enthusiasm by Ludovico Agostini, who enjoyed them in their prime, and whose eulogies remain unedited in the Oliveriana Library. But they owe to the pen of Bernardo Tasso a worthier and wider celebrity, in his letter to Vincenzo Laureo, which sums up the advantages of the Villa by declaring that no place in Italy united with a temperate and healthful climate so many conveniences and enjoyable spots.

Of many laboured and costly productions of human ingenuity little remains there but saddening ruins.

The lofty oaks celebrated by Agostini have yielded to

the axe; the grove which served as a game preserve has shared the same fate; the once innumerable pines and cypresses may be counted in units; the orange and lemon trees, the cystuses and myrtles have disappeared. Though even yet of imposing appearance, the building has undergone pitiable dilapidations. Almost every morsel of the marble carving has been carried off, and fragments may be purchased from the pawnbrokers of Pesaro. The frescoes, except that representing Francesco Maria receiving the adherence of his army, which seems the poorest in execution, are almost totally defaced. But that the saloons, where Bembo talked and Tasso sang, have been found well adapted for the culture of silkworms, the desolation, begun a century ago by Portuguese Jesuits, continued by a rabble soldiery, and permitted by its present proprietors the Albani, might ere now have been complete.

But while the works of man have thus by man been degraded, glorious nature remains unchanged. A few hundred paces lead to the summit ridge of Monte Bartolo, a spot rarely equalled even in this lovely land. To the vast prospect we have but now feebly described, there is here added a marine panorama, extending from the headland of Ancona to the Pineta of Ravenna, and including a boundless expanse of the sparkling Adriatic. A wanderer on that attractive coast, it has been my privilege to visit this unrivalled spot, and listlessly to survey the swan-like sails skimming the mighty mirror, wherein was reflected the deep indigo of an Italian sky, bounded along the horizon by that pearly haze gradually dissolving towards the blue zenith, which no painter but Perugino has been able to embody.

Of Duchess Leonora we know little.*[1] Unlike her predecessor, she had no courtly pen to transmit us her praises,

*[1] Cf. Luzio e Renier, *Mantova e Urbino* (Torino, 1893) and Julia Cartwright, *Isabella d'Este* (Murray, 1904).

no Bembo or Castiglione to celebrate the beauties of her person or the graces of her mind. She enjoys, however, one advantage over her Aunt Elisabetta; for in a speaking portrait by Titian, we may read much of her character, exempt from the vague flattery of such diffuse eulogists. Painted at that trying age when female beauty has exchanged its maiden charms for mature womanhood, the grave matronly air, the stiff contours and set features, with more of comely dignity than sternness in their general expression, attest fidelity in the likeness, and tally well with what we know of her temperament, and with the trials under which it must have been formed. There we may observe a composure calculated to moderate the fiery temper of her lord, a self-possession fitted to sustain him through his varied adversities. Her dress handsome rather than rich, her pose indicative of quietude, the spaniel watching by her side, the small time-piece on her table, are accessories adapted for one accustomed to pass the long intervals of her husband's absence rather in reflective solitude than in courtly pastimes.[1] To such a disposition the cares of maternity and her children's education afforded an ever pleasing resource, which she shared with the Dowager Duchess, an unfailing companion and friend, whose once lively spirits had been chastened by affliction into harmony with her temperament; but of this solace she was deprived by her death at Venice in January, 1526. In the autumn of 1529, Leonora, who administered the duchy in her husband's absence, received Clement at Pesaro, on his way to the coronation at Bologna, with a princely welcome and magnificent presents. In a letter which his Holiness took that opportunity to address to the Duke, he expresses gratitude for these, and for the attendance of the prince, "a youth of the highest hopes from his excellent disposi-

[1] Cf. Appendix XII.

tions, his modesty, and his natural inclination to literature, as well as his many estimable qualities." Whilst promising much favour to Guidobaldo, he compliments his father on the mild and equitable sway whereby the Duchess maintained his state in peace and tranquillity, and concludes with an apostolic blessing on him, his consort, and his son.

Returned to his state after so long a separation, Francesco Maria found, during the next two years, ample leisure to attend to its internal administration, and to watch the progress of his promising family. The eldest of these seems to have been Donna Ippolita, for whom he soon received, through the Marquis del Vasto, an offer of marriage from Don Antonio d' Aragona, son of the Duke of Montalto. At the nuptials, which were celebrated with suitable splendour, he had a very unlooked-for guest in Ascanio Colonna, whose intrigues to supplant him in the duchy we have lately noticed, but who, finding these hopelessly foiled by the Duke's establishment in the good graces of the Emperor, sought a reconciliation through the bridegroom, his cousin, whom he accompanied to Urbino. This frankness was met in a kindred spirit by his host, and their amity was cemented by a generous hospitality.

It was now, perhaps, that Francesco Maria took opportunity to dictate the results of his long experience of war, in a series of Military Discourses, which were published fifty years later, but which, being evidently printed from loose and unrevised notes, are not fairly amenable to literary criticism.[1] They are but desultory and disjointed obser-

[1] Discorsi Militari dell' eccellentissimo Signor Francesco Maria I. della Rovere, Duca di Urbino, nei quali si discorrano molti avantaggi et disadvantaggi della guerra, utilissimi ad ogni soldato. Ferrara, 1583. It was edited by Domenico Mammarelli, and dedicated to Signor Ippolito Bentivoglio. There is a transcript in the library at Newbattle Abbey, a. 3, 2, and a fragment of it in the Vat. Ottobon. MSS. No. 2447, f. 135. * Cf. also *I discorsi di F. M. I. della Rovere sopra le fortificazioni di Venezia* (Mantova, 1902). These were written 1537-38.

vations, carelessly jotted down, with little attention to order or style, and edited without emendation, or even intelligible punctuation. The matter abounds in truisms and common-places, displaying neither enlarged views nor knowledge of mankind: the style is garrulous, diffuse, and redundant. Yet, as on matters of military skill the Duke was considered a high authority, it may not be improper here to record some of his opinions.

This was his idea of a fortified town: "It ought to stand in a plain, its citadel commanded by no eminence. The rampart-wall should be three paces wide at base, supporting an earthern rampart of fifteen or twenty paces wide, with barbicans. This retaining wall should be in height about twenty feet, and have above it a curtain of nearly as many. The upper part, being most exposed to be battered, had better have an earthen facing. There ought to be a platform, rising sixteen feet over the curtain, placed half-way between each baloard and bastion. The baloards should have guns mounted only at the sides, and be of massive strength, from fifty to sixty paces in diameter, that the guns may be freely wrought. Should a baloard be taken, it will still be flanked by the adjoining platforms, a ditch drawn between each of which would in a night's time recomplete the defences. The fosse should be about twenty paces wide, and is best without water, so as to allow artificial fire to be showered down upon the enemy. There ought to be no counterscarp, seeing it generally serves as a protection to the besiegers; but, if there be one, it had better be only of earth, at a low angle of elevation. Above all, there ought to be provided many secret ports for frequent sallies, and for the easy return of the men." "It has been long noticed that no fortress was ever carried but by some oversight of its defenders, and everything depends upon a judicious selection of positions for defence. Unquestionably a single sin suffices to send a man to the devil, whatever be his other good works; and, in like manner, one oversight in fortification may lose the place, as happened when I took Pavia and Cremona. In short, it is all very well to play with plans and models, but one must see to everything on the spot."

"He said, in reference to the fortresses of Legnano and Verona, that it was very ill-judged in the Republic never to carry things out as they had been planned, in consequence of frequent ministerial changes, and the system of governing from day to day, and bit by bit, without reference to any general design. By adopting an opposite method, he had completed the defences of Pesaro much more efficiently, and at a third of the outlay it would have cost any one else, simply because he was the sole head and executor, and kept in view the entire works, not the individual gates, baloards, and details; and by so completing them that it must be attacked on two or three sides, whilst provided with ten or twelve concealed sally-ports." He contended that a fortress on a hill was difficult to defend, one on a plain less so; but that the easiest and most secure was one whose defences partly extended along the level, and in part rose upon steep ground, such as Verona, which he maintained could be more easily held by five thousand men against eighty thousand, than most towns by eight thousand against half that besieging force.

In conducting a siege, the Duke dwells upon the necessity of a choice infantry, in which German solidity should be happily combined with the active troops of Italy and Spain; yet he admits that men-at-arms, when dismounted, can be turned to excellent account in an assault, and that light cavalry are of obvious value. "Above all," he says, "you require a well-supplied commissariat, and regular pay, with sufficient artillery and military machines. After choosing the most eligible spot for encampment, just without range of the enemy's guns, the first thing is to provide your baggage and supplies against sudden surprise; next to open trenches for your artillery, securing your men by a ditch wide enough for their operations, but not so broad as to be commanded from the walls, and taking care not to let too many of them at once into the trenches, so as to embarrass each other. It is an immense protection to flank your trenches with lines drawn from your principal encampment close up to the city walls, which must be strongly defended against the enemy's guns, and must contain a force adequate to check their sallies, and, if necessary, to cover the trenches, or even succour your camp."

"Should you resort to a blockade, it is best to establish your army in one or two towns ten to fifteen miles off, taking care to secure every intervening place. At that distance your own supplies are more easily procured, and your light cavalry can readily intercept the enemy's convoys, whilst the garrison cannot attack you, except at every disadvantage, and without artillery."

As for artillery, we find a recommendation of battering guns carrying from thirty to one hundred pound balls, and of field-pieces and ship's cannon from fifteen to twenty pounds. The gunpowder in Italy being bad, fifty was the average of daily discharges; but the Turks, having very superior powder, could fire as many as seventy times, which was looked upon as a stupendous performance.

Animadverting upon those tardy tactics which never anticipated a movement of the enemy, the Duke compared them to a child applying its hand to the parts successively chastised, without attempting to ward off the next blow; yet, Fabius-like, he considered that a general's talent was more shown in his selection of suitable posts than in the conduct of a pitched battle. Popular risings he held very cheap, believing them utterly contemptible when not supported by disciplined troops, and instancing his own experience at Florence in 1527, when, with eighty soldiers, he put down an insurrection, and maintained the ascendancy of the Medici.

With reference to the respective merits of various nations whom he had seen in the field, he said that "a good Italian and a good Spanish soldier are equal. The Swiss at the outset are an excellent force; but, in a protracted campaign, they deteriorate, and become good for little. The Germans sustain an onset of men-at-arms most valiantly, and, during these Italian wars, have become in other respects expert, especially at skirmishes, either in cover or in the open country. The Turks, being unskilled in war, have hitherto owed their victories rather to the deficiencies of their opponents than to their own superiority. He ascribed the success of French armies against the Italians to an absurd practice of the latter, who always fought in squadrons of twenty-five men-at-arms, each squadron engaging another, so that the battle was made up of many separate skirmishes; and, in the end, the most numerous army generally carried the day. Charles VIII., on the contrary, formed in three battalions,—the van, centre, and rear,—and, with his force thus concentrated, bore down the detached tactics of his opponents. Yet the Duke did not consider this French disposition as invariably efficacious, preferring in many cases that an army should act in one body, even at the risk of leaving its baggage and artillery in the rear, and comparatively unprotected. But, on this and similar points, his maxim was not to adhere to any invariable rule."

Regarding the construction of an army, we find this passage:—"In preparing an expedition, the commander ought to imitate the process by which nature creates a living body, forming first the heart; then the vital members, such as the liver, lungs, blood, and brains; next the skin; and, finally the hair and nails. In like manner, the foundation of an enterprise should be the general, who is its heart, and in whom should be united varied capacity, with perfect rectitude and justice. Then his officers should be strenuous, experienced, and implicitly obedient, for such captains are certain to recruit soldiers of the same stamp. Next, let him look to his commissariat and military chest, and see that his arms and accoutrements are adapted to his enemy and the country. Lastly, let him regard all extraneous and casual aid as mere skin, hair, and nails, relying mainly on his own well-disciplined troops." The Duke considered that "men-at-arms are by no means so useless as they are sometimes regarded, and that, although infantry is the basis of an army, nevertheless it would not do to have only that force in the field; just as, although in the human body it is the eye alone which sees, the hand which works, the head which guides, yet man would not be so perfect or beautiful a creature with but eyes, hands, or head, as he is with all these various members. Hence he would wish to have soldiers of all sorts in his camp,—men-at-arms, light cavalry, a German brigade, and a full complement of Italians."

But whilst the theory of warfare thus occupied his thoughts, he was not neglectful of its munitions; and it was his special concern to provide for his veterans, horses, arms, and accoutrements of a quality which gained them general admiration. After nearly three years of peace the Venetians, fearing that their swords might become rusty, ordered a muster of their forces on the mainland, and an inspection of their frontier defences. The reviews were conducted by their Captain-general in person, who spent several months of 1532 in Lombardy with the Duchess, leaving the government of his state in the hands of his son Guidobaldo, now eighteen years of age. From thence he was called to Friuli, on the approach of a disorganised mass of Italian soldiery, who were returning home from the Turkish war, burning and plundering as they went. By firm and temperate measures he kept them in check, and constrained them to resume an orderly march. The only immediate result to the Peninsula from campaigns in Hungary was an alarm along the Adriatic coast of a Turkish descent, which was made a pretext by Clement for seizing upon Ancona, and annexing that republic to the papal states.

CHAPTER XLI

Italian militia—The Camerino disputes—Death of Clement VII.—Marriage of Prince Guidobaldo—Proposed Turkish crusade under the Duke—His death and character.

THREE nearly contemporary events had lately combined to extinguish the nationality of Italy, and those liberties which, shared in ample or more sparing measure by her many states, had till now crowned her military glories with intellectual renown. In the sack of Rome the power of the Keys had been shaken, the prestige of the papal city had passed away. The defence of Florence was the last effort of patriotism, and with it fell communal independence. The coronation of Charles V. laid upon the Peninsula an iron yoke of foreign despotism, which rendered her virtually a province of Spain. A necessary consequence of this sad change will be to limit the field of our investigation, and to restrict what remains of our work to the ducal family and their hereditary domains, which for the future were little more than an appanage of the Spanish monarchy. The Lords of Urbino had hitherto been prominent among the captains of adventure, and bore a part wherever engagements were offered, or hard blows to be had. But the condottiere system being now superseded, a new mode of warfare and machinery of defence became indispensable. Knight-service and the romance of war were swept away by artillery; the imposing *battaglia* of men-at-arms proved powerless when confronted by battalions of steady infantry, or out-manœuvred by the dashing cavalry of Dalmatia.

This lesson, first taught by the Swiss in their fastnesses, had been practically demonstrated to the Italians in every great action from the Taro to the recent Lombard campaigns, and had been adopted by most of their leaders. It now, however, became necessary to apply it in another sense, and, seeing that captains were no longer to be hired with their respective followings of efficient soldiery, to organise a militia of its own for the defence of such state, upon principles which Machiavelli was among the first to recognise and explain.

Before that system came into general use, the Italian infantry was notoriously incompetent to cope with transalpine levies, as Francesco Maria had bitterly experienced in the war of 1523–27. He therefore, in 1533, instituted a militia of his mountaineers, under the name of the Feltrian legion, which before his death numbered five thousand men, in four regiments, commanded by as many colonels. The object was to make them good soldiers without ceasing to be citizens; to maintain in readiness at small expense a military population, who were not men of war by profession. For this purpose lists were annually taken of all males from eighteen to twenty-five, learned professions and infamous persons being exempted, and to them arms were given. They were drilled and instructed in the necessary evolutions, and a proportion of them were called into active service when needed. On these occasions they were well paid; but, when kept on the reserve, their small stipend was rendered more attractive by a variety of political immunities and fiscal exemptions, including the exclusive privilege of bearing arms. The practical result was this,—the able-bodied population were, on the one hand, brought into a sort of direct dependence on the executive, and, on the other, were taught that the safety of the commonwealth was entrusted to their swords and sinews. It is scarcely necessary to add that this system has been generally adopted, and that on it are still based the military institutions of most continental nations.

In December, 1532, the Emperor returned to Italy, and was met near Vicenza by Francesco Maria, who welcomed him in his own name, and in that of the Signory. Dispensing with complimentary formalities, Charles received him at once to easy intercourse, and, requesting his continued attendance, spent much time in conversing with him on the art of war. At Bologna another congress was held by the Pontiff and the Emperor, in which were discussed the affairs of Italy, the proposed general council, and the matrimonial speculations of Clement for advancement of his house. The marriage of Alessandro de' Medici, now created Duke of Florence, was arranged with Margaret of Austria, natural daughter of Charles; but the hand of Caterina de' Medici, which the latter wished to be given to Francesco Sforza, was reserved by her ambitious uncle for a French prince. Charles left Bologna on the 28th of February, 1533, and embarked at Genoa for Spain, after giving some hope to Francesco Maria of a satisfactory settlement of his claims upon Sora. Clement in ten days after set out for Rome. The estrangement between these potentates, which at this meeting began to chill their intercourse, was greatly widened by the voyage of his Holiness in the following autumn to Marseilles, where he celebrated the nuptials of Caterina with Henry, second son and successor of Francis I. At this second congress of Bologna, Titian met the Emperor by special command; and it was perhaps on that occasion that he had commissions for portraits of the Duke and Duchess of Urbino, which now ornament the Uffizi gallery. The former is engraved as a frontispiece for this volume; of the latter we have lately spoken: both will demand further notice in our fifty-fourth chapter, and in the last No. of the Appendix.

In April the Duchess Leonora gave birth to a son at Mantua, who was named after Julius II., and was destined to holy orders. His father had at the same time a severe fit of gout; and, on his return home, the painful duty devolved upon him of providing against the visitation of a scarcity which then lamentably affected Italy. The close of the year found him a suitor with the Pope in the affair of Camerino, which we shall now briefly explain.

The small state of that name in the March of Ancona had been ruled for nearly three hundred years by the Varana family, some of whom we have occasionally mentioned in these Memoirs. Exaggerating the domestic atrocities, then too frequent among Italians of their rank, they became revoltingly notorious, in 1433–4, for a complicated fratricide. Bernardo, Lord of Camerino, jealous of his brothers Giovanni and Pier-Gentile, the offspring of his father's second marriage, had them put to death by the agency of his own sons. Ere many months passed, his subjects, loathing the foul deed, suddenly rose against its authors. With sweeping vengeance they slew him, his brother german Gentil Pandolfo, and his six sons, dashing the heads of the little ones against the wall. The succession was thus opened to Giulio Cesare, son of Giovanni, who, in 1451, married the only daughter of Sigismondo Pandolfo, despot of Rimini.*[1] He lived to see the usurpations of Cesare Borgia, and, falling into the hands of Michelotto on the capture of La Pergola, the old man perished by the bowstring of that monster in 1502, along with his eldest son Venanzio, and two natural children. Venanzio had, in 1497, married Maria, the only sister of Duke Francesco Maria, of whom we have already had to tell a tale of scandal, and left one son Sigismondo. He was born in 1499, and escaped the fate of his father and uncles, from having been sent in infancy to Urbino. There he was educated; and we have seen him defending

*[1] Cf. Edward Hutton, *Sigismondo Malatesta* (1906), p. 61.

S. Leo, when scarcely beyond boyhood. After years of imprisonment and exile, his uncle Francesco Maria made an ineffectual attempt, on the death of Leo X., to vindicate his hereditary fief, from the usurpation of his paternal uncle, Giovanni Maria, its *de facto* lord. Sigismondo sought consolation for his hard fortunes in low debauchery, until he fell in 1522 by the hand of assassins, at the supposed instigation of his usurping uncle, who, in 1527, had absolution of the foul deed, and to whose career we must now turn.[1]

Giovanni Maria, second son of Giulio Cesare Count of Camerino, was sent to Venice on Borgia's approach, and so avoided the fate of his family. On the death of Alexander VI., being then in his twenty-second year, he made a descent upon La Marca, and possessed himself of his father's seigneury, in defiance of his infant nephew's title to it. His authority was recognised by the Holy See, at a time when the hereditary principle was loose, and a strong hand constituted the best claim. He found a warm supporter in Leo X., through sympathy of their common hatred for the della Rovere race, and received from him the lordship of Sinigaglia and prefecture of Rome, on the deprivation of Francesco Maria, along with the additional dignity of Duke of Camerino. After the death of Leo, Sigismondo for a few months made good his authority at Camerino, until supplanted by the usurper, whose title was conveniently completed by his nephew's murder; whereupon he became *de jure* its sovereign, and continued in undisturbed possession of his ill-gotten honours.

On the death of Duke Giovanni Maria, in August 1527, the male heir of the fief was Ercole Varana, whose eldest son, Matteo, had been destined by the Duke's will to become husband of his infant daughter Giulia, then but

[1] Many details regarding these transactions have been given, vol. I., p. 411; vol. II., pp. 36, 317, 371, 419.

four years old. This arrangement was, however, resolutely opposed by his widow, Caterina Cibò,*[1] niece of Leo X.; and ere any steps could be taken to carry it into effect, the town was sacked by Sciarra Colonna, who, with his son-in-law, Rodolfa Varana, a bastard of its last lord, drove Caterina and her child into the citadel. Forgetting the double feud of Francesco Maria with her husband and her Medicean relations, she in her extremity besought his aid, offering to plight her daughter's hand to his son, Prince Guidobaldo. The proposal found him ingloriously inactive in Umbria, during the negotiations for release of Clement from S. Angelo, and, readily accepting it, he sent troops to relieve the suppliant lady, who continued for several years to administer the state in name of Giulia, with the passive countenance of her cousin the Pontiff. But the jealousy which rankled in the breast of his Holiness against the della Rovere princes, fretted at an arrangement so conducive to their aggrandisement, and at the first congress of Bologna he sought to break it off. The Duke's answer, as reported by Leonardi, was, that he would risk life and state rather than withdraw from the engagement, and that, if driven to defensive measures, the Pope should in the end bear the expenses of the war. With the recent and costly failure of Leo against Urbino in their recollection, the consistory would lend no sanction to the inclinations of their head, and so the matter rested until the return of Clement from France. Francesco Maria then formally applied for the papal sanction to a union of his son with the heiress of Camerino, but was put off on account of her tender age.

Meanwhile there occurred an incident characteristic of these lawless times. Like the other Italian commonwealths, Camerino had its exiles, expelled by faction or political convulsions, and Matteo, having rallied a body of

*[1] Cf. FELICIANGELI, *Notizie e documenti sulla vita di Caterina Cibò Varano* (Camerino, 1891).

these, surprised the city on the 13th of October, 1534, and seized the Duchess-Regent in her palace. His object being the abduction of Giulia, who had escaped into the fortress, he hurried her mother, in her dressing-gown, to its gates, and commanded her to summon the castellan to surrender. She, however, with extraordinary hardihood and self-possession, ordered him to fire upon the assailants; whereupon their leader drew his sword and threatened her with instant death. The heroic dame, after ejaculating a brief prayer, bared her neck and told him to strike; but Matteo, quailing before her daring spirit, and apprehensive of the infuriated populace, hastily withdrew, carrying her prisoner. He was speedily attacked by the citizens *en masse*, and the officer in charge of Caterina was glad to secure his own pardon by restoring her to liberty. A new inducement thus arose for placing the heiress in the hands of one competent to protect her; yet the redoubled instances made with the Pope for completion of her marriage were met by continued temporising, until the opportunity passed from his grasp.

On or about the 25th of September, 1534, Clement closed his life. Guicciardini, his countryman and protégé, tells us that he died hated by his court and suspected by princes, leaving a reputation rather odious than pleasing, and accounted severe, greedy, faithless, and illiberal. Muratori reviews his character more at length:—"He was a pontiff not destitute of political capacity; circumspect and dignified; dexterous in business, including dissimulation of every sort, and regarded by all his contemporaries as a man of double-dealing. Nature and experience had amply endowed him with many qualities befitting a temporal sovereign; but it would be less easy to detect in him those virtues becoming the Vicar of Christ, or to discover, amid the religious tempests of his times, what benefits he conferred upon the Church, what abuses or disorders he checked, though from him took its origin and pretext that terrible schism which yet dissevers so many nations from the true Church. He misapplied the papacy, its powers and resources, to instigate and maintain wars, which, besides many other mischiefs, brought upon Rome a dreadful sack, and upon his own dignity a shocking degradation. Still more did he turn these to despoil his native Florence of her freedom, and to aggrandise his own family rather by princely marriages than by honourable and discreet advancement. He died detested by the court for his avarice and close-fistedness, and still more loathed by the Roman people, who imputed to his policy all the miseries that befell their far-famed city." His versatile conduct has been fully exposed in these pages:

"With every wind that veered,
With shifted sails a several course he steered."

Finally, with him there originated national funded debt, that system which has so extensively affected the political, military, financial, commercial and monetary relations of the whole civilised world. Yet, though the results of his disastrous pontificate justified as they dictated these very sweeping charges, the testimony of the Venetian ambassadors, who describe the earlier portion of his reign, is much more favourable, at least to his motives. Whilst they represent him as timidly slow in adopting his measures, and as wavering and undecided in following them out, they commend his piety, his willingness to promote reforms, his conscientious observance of justice, the regularity of his habits, and the simplicity of his tastes. Possessing neither the liberality nor the epicurean propensities of his uncle, the contrast was unfavourable to his popularity; and those who had shared with Leo the pastimes of music and the chase sneered at discussions on engineering and hydraulics, which occupied the leisure of Clement.

As soon as the Pontiff's death was known to Francesco Maria, he sent his son to complete his nuptials at Camerino; but, within two hours after his arrival there, a courier brought from the Sacred College a protest against the marriage of the heiress during the vacancy of the Holy See.[1] This impediment was suggested by Cardinal Farnese in anticipation of his election, which took place as Paul III. on the 12th of October, the very day on which the bridal ceremony was completed. To balance this act of questionable fidelity to the See, the Duke, by well-timed movements, repressed attempts to assert the independence of Perugia and Rimini, and re-establish their hereditary seigneurs. But such zeal served him little with the new Pontiff, who at once made the Camerino succession a personal question, with a view to confer that state upon his own natural son. One of his earliest acts was accordingly to visit the contumacy of Caterina, her daughter, and son-in-law, with a stern monitory and summons to Rome, their disobedience of which was followed by excommunication, and by a movement of the pontifical troops to blockade Camerino.

Francesco Maria now interposed all his influence, backed by the imperial and the Venetian ambassadors, to induce Paul to a recognition of Giulia as heiress under the investiture given to her father, with remainder apparently to heirs general. Having vainly exhausted the expedients of diplomacy in this cause, he protested that the blame should not rest upon him of hostilities rendered necessary in his son's defence, and, sending provisions to Camerino, he marched at the head of ten thousand men to his support. At Sassoferrata he was met by a deputation of the citizens, laden with presents, who declared that though their walls were the Pope's, their hearts and substance were at his disposal. At Matelica he found his son and the ladies, before whom he passed his army in review, and marched home again without once encountering the papal

[1] Cuparini's account of the war of Camerino, Vat. Urb. MSS. 1023, art. 10. Leoni says the despatch arrived after the nuptials had been solemnised.

troops under Gian Battista Savello. In fact, it was a war of the pen rather than the sword, for at every step he renewed notorial protests of duty and obedience to the Church, and regularly paid the excise, as well as the price of all the stores which he took up for the use of the Varana party. Apprehending that, if too far provoked, he would be supported by the Venetian arms and by the Emperor, the Pontiff now suspended martial measures, and pressed the point of law on the Roman courts.

Thus relieved from immediate anxiety in this matter, the Duke of Urbino resolved to pay a visit of compliment to Charles V. at Naples. After reaching the Adriatic frontier of that kingdom, he dismissed the strong escort which had guarded him through the ecclesiastical state, and proceeded with a small suite. The Emperor received him with much courtesy, and sought his counsel in the invasion of Provence, which he was preparing. Francesco Maria would gladly have referred the Camerino affair to his arbitration, but this being rejected by the Nuncio, he obtained simply the imperial mediation, which proved unavailing. He on this occasion presented Charles with two swords of tried temper, and a finger-ring containing a repeating watch, the latter made at Pesaro. In returning he took the route by Benevento to the Adriatic, and halting for the night at the convent of Sta. Maria degl' Eremiti, near Troia, he allowed some of his attendants to examine into a curious tradition which then obtained general credit. It was said that Diomed arriving here with a company of attendants, he and most of them died within a few days, and were duly interred; but that their souls were transmigrated into a species of bird elsewhere unknown, which ever since had haunted the marshy grounds. These were seen but rarely of an evening, and towards morning uttered sounds like human lamentations. They flew on the approach of any one not of Greek birth, but allowed persons of that nation to visit their haunts familiarly. Three of the Duke's suite having volunteered to watch, they all heard mournful voices about three hours before dawn, a phenomenon which the narrator makes no attempt to explain.[1] Having crossed to survey the Venetian possessions at Zara, the Duke returned home in 1536, on board two galleys of the Republic. The rest of that year was chiefly spent by him at his post in Lombardy, protecting the Venetian mainland during the passage of some imperial levies; but his charge was no longer an important one, as the long contests for Milan had been finally set at rest in the autumn of 1535, by the death of Duke Francesco Sforza, after naming Charles V. heir of his state.

Apulia and the Venetian possessions in the Levant being menaced in the following year by Sultan Solyman, a general confederation was effected for the defence of Italy and its dependencies, at the head of which were the Pope and the Emperor. The Duke of Urbino as captain-general undertook to raise five thousand men for this armament, but, the danger suddenly passing away, distracted counsels prevailed among the allies. Finally, on the 31st of January, 1538, a new league was patched up, to carry into effect a suggestion of Francesco Maria, by diverting the war into the Infidel's territory. Considering, however, his impending difficulties with Paul III., the Duke obtained a joint guarantee of the contracting powers for maintenance in his state, in confirmation of papal brieves to the same effect dated in the preceding November. About the same time his services to the Republic were acknowledged by the present of a palace in the street of Sta. Fosca, valued at 16,000 ducats.

The views of the allies and their captain-general for this enterprise were vast, comprehending the siege of Constantinople and an invasion of Egypt: and the latter was indefatigable in his endeavours to put the armament

[1] Vat. Urb. MSS., 1023, art. 1.

upon a footing equal to such extensive designs, both as to its numbers and material. The enterprise was invested with the sacred character of a religious war; but whilst Francesco Maria concentrated upon it the energies of a mind in its prime, and the exertions of a frame renovated by new specifics against his hereditary enemy the gout, the hand of death was upon him. Returned to Venice from a comprehensive survey of her defences in Dalmatia and Istria, he was attacked by sudden illness on the 20th of September. Foreseeing its fatal termination, he had himself taken by sea to Pesaro, which he reached on the 8th of October. Next day he showed himself on horseback to his people, but feeling unequal to the exertion he took to bed, and gradually lost strength. On Monday, the 21st, a fit deprived him of speech, yet he continued sensible until near daybreak of the 22nd, when he expired in religious penitence, after receiving the sacraments.

All authorities agree in attributing his death to poison, but neither Leoni nor Baldi hint at the person whose "envy" dictated that base vengeance.*[1] Giovio speaks positively as to detection having followed upon a searching inquiry, and points at those interested in the Camerino question as authors of the crime. Sardi and Tondini charge it upon Luigi Gonzaga, Count of Sabionetta, surnamed Rodomonte, the nephew of Francesco da Bozzolo, a condottiere who commanded Bourbon's cavalry at the assault of Rome, and who facilitated Clement's flight some months thereafter. This assertion, which is adopted by various writers, receives some confirmation from a story in the gossiping MS. we have already quoted, that Gonzaga, having accused Gian Giacomo Leonardi, a doctor of laws at Pesaro, of instigating the murder, was challenged by the latter, who thereby gained the favour of Duke Guido-

*[1] Cf. VIANI, *L'avvelenamento di Francesco Maria I. della Rovere* (Mantova, 1902), and *La Morte di F. M. della Rovere*, in *Fanfulla della Domenica*, 23 March, 1902.

baldo II., and with it the countship of Monte l' Abate, near Pesaro.[1] On the other hand, this Rodomonte is stated in *Les Genealogies des Maisons Souveraines* to have died in 1528.

Whoever may have been author of the foul deed, it is agreed that the perpetrator was the Duke's Mantuan barber, who is generally said to have dropped a poisoned lotion into his ear. Baldi only mentions that he did it "in a new way," and gives no account of the medical examination of the body which, he asserts, took place. In an old chronicle of Sinigaglia, Guidobaldo is stated to have had the barber torn to pieces with pincers, and quartered in the streets of Pesaro.[2]

After a cast in plaster had been taken from his features, the body was dressed in a quilted doublet and hose of black satin, under his inlaid armour, over which was the ducal tunic, and, above all, the mantle of crimson satin embroidered in gold, which he had worn as Prefect at the coronation of Charles V. Next evening it was borne, with torches, by the principal courtiers, to the great hall, and there placed upon an elevated catafalque of black and gold, on which were arranged his ducal helmet, three magnificent head pieces, and as many silver batons of command; five standards which he had captured being set round with other trophies. It was watched all night, and lay in state till the following evening, when it was coffined in the dress just described. The same night it was taken on a litter to Urbino by torch-light, escorted by a vast following on horseback and on foot, under soaking rain. At the confines of the respective territories it was delivered over to the authorities and clergy of that city, preceded by mutes and mourners of various grades; among whom was led the Duke's favourite jennet, covered with black velvet, his ducal mail and morion being carried by a page in deep

[1] Relazione della Legazione di Urbino, Bib. Marucc. c. 308.

[2] Vat. Urb. MSS. No. 992. Gozzi's Chronicle, Oliveriana MSS., No. 324. Also Teofiles's MS. narrative, *penes me*.

weeds. Reaching the city at sunrise, the procession was joined by the chief magistrates, nobility, clergy, and citizens, and so arrived, through tearful crowds, at the church of Sta. Chiara, again to lie in state until evening, when it was stripped of its armour, and there committed to the dust at the left horn of the altar. It was subsequently deposited, by his grandson Francesco Maria II., in a tomb raised over the spot by Bartolomeo Ammanati, from the design of Girolamo Genga, which was eventually removed as inconveniently cumbering the church. The following epitaph, written by desire of the widowed Duchess, and ascribed to the pen of Bembo, is panelled into the wall:—

"To Duke Francesco Maria, endowed with the most comprehensive capacity for war and peace. His hereditary states, thrice lost by violence, he thrice by valour regained, and ruled them, when reconquered, with moderation; he commanded the Ecclesiastical, the Florentine, and the Venetian forces; finally, he was chosen general-in-chief for the Turkish war, but was cut off ere it opened. Leonora, his most devoted wife, placed this to her most meritorious lord, and to herself."

One more ceremonial was wanting to complete the measure of respectful duty to the deceased sovereign. On the 13th [or 22nd] of November, his obsequies were celebrated in the cathedral of Urbino. The church decorations, the catafalque, the vast concourse of clergy, of deputations, and of people of all classes, were such as the mournful solemnity required, and the sincere grief of his subjects dictated. The function was conducted by Federigo Fregoso, Archbishop of Salerno, whom we have formerly known at the court of Duke Guidobaldo I., and the funeral oration was spoken by Maestro Benedetto Milesio. Another, by Lorenzo Contarini, was pronounced at Venice, where the Signory ordered a celebration of his obsequies with unwonted splendour, besides voting him an equestrian statue in bronze. This was never executed, but another statue of him, made by Bandini for his grandson, the last Duke of Urbino, was presented to the Republic under touching circumstances, which we shall detail in the fifty-fourth chapter of this work.

The life of Francesco Maria affords a remarkable instance of the extremes of fortune. He was deprived of parental care at an early age, when it was peculiarly desirable as a restraint upon his naturally fiery temper. Soon after, he was hurried from his hereditary state, and compelled to seek safety in France. In the outset of manhood, his ungoverned passion involved him in the stigma of a sacrilegious murder. Twice was he deprived of the influential sovereignty to which he had attained, and recovered it only after years of exile, and at a ruinous pecuniary sacrifice. The lustre of a brilliant position, and of a distinguished military career, was veiled by his utter failure to save or rescue Rome. Finally, he was snatched from life just as a new and nobler field was opening for his martial glories. Reversing the picture, we find a youth of ardent temperament, born to princely sway, and becoming at eighteen the heir of one uncle in an important duchy, and the favourite of another, who, by virtue of his triple tiara, conferred upon him yet a third state. A military hero ere he escaped from his teens, his renown ever extended with his age. Thirty years after his star had set, a Venetian ambassador called him the light and splendour of Italy ; and notwithstanding some palpable blunders, he is still ranked with the first commanders of his native land. He died when his fame was at its height, and transmitted unquestioned to his son, that sovereignty which thrice had been wrested from him.

It is from posthumous influences that his reputation has suffered most severely ; and the three standard historians of his times, in Italy, England, and France, have meted him sparing justice. Without questioning the value of Guicciardini's narrative as the fullest exposition of the age in which he lived, and the most graphic portraiture of many of its features and incidents, we must demur to the "fearless impartiality" too hastily allowed him in modern times. True, he was not, like Machiavelli, a practised intriguer, acute to detect perverted purpose, or prone to assume its existence; nor did he, like Giovio, employ the iron stylus of vengeance, or the golden pen of flattery, as passion might prompt or venality dictate. But, born a Florentine, and favoured by the Medici, he was the partisan of that house in the closet as in the field; and no one thus shackled could write impartially of Francesco Maria della Rovere. Roscoe, with similar predilections, though far less biased, had no inducement to become champion of a sovereign whom Leo X. had twice expelled; whilst Sismondi, enamoured of nominal republics, is ever ready to echo taunts or calumnies pointed at an Italian prince. The examination of many less popular historians, and of numerous unpublished contemporary authorities, has, we trust, enabled us to place this Duke's character and conduct in a more true light, without extenuating the manifest errors of either.

Though small in person, Francesco Maria was active and well formed, with a manly air, a quick eye, and an engaging presence. His manner and address were mild and pleasing, and his conversation was seasoned with lively jests. He was strict in religious observances, an enemy to blasphemous language, and intolerant of those insults to female honour with which war was then lamentably fraught. In the regulation of his army, as in the government of his state, justice was his ruling principle. Of his unhappy violence of temper we have already had too much reason to speak; it was the bane of his life, the blot on his fame. Yet he was generous and forgiving, as he proved by putting his personal enemy Guicciardini on his guard against the designs of San Severino, Count of Caiazzo, who, having suffered from the Florentine's captious allegations, had resolved to assassinate him.[1]

A soldier by education, taste, and long habit, his character should be judged by a military standard; and perhaps the best tribute to his glory consisted in the public rejoicings ordered by Sultan Solyman on hearing of his untimely death. In following the narrative of his campaigns, we have unsparingly pointed out the faults which seemed to cramp his success. They were obviously systematic, arising from an excess of that caution, which his natural prudence and foresight prompted, and which the examples of Fabius Maximus and Prospero Colonna in some degree authorised. Yet we must not overlook an important element of consideration, in the quality of troops under his command from 1523 to 1528. His want of confidence in them was avowed, and in more than one instance it was justified, when their steadiness was put to the test. Nor was he less fettered by the faulty organisation of that army, made up of various contingents under their respective leaders, without a responsible commanding officer, and in which civilians were allowed a veto fatal to unity of action. The verdict of his contemporaries may, however, be admitted as conclusive upon his military reputation. Ruscelli tells us that he was, by common consent, called the father and founder of the art of war, as practised in the sixteenth century; and the opinion of the only dissentient, Guicciardini, a private enemy and no soldier, is amply balanced by that of Giovanni de' Medici, who ranked him in skilful tactics, and in the arts of command, as well as in foresight and activity, equal to the ablest generals. The testimony of Charles V. has been already given; and we are assured that after a public disputation in Padua, sustained by men of the greatest learning, he was voted

[1] Leoni, p. 386.

a match to any hero of antiquity, in judgment, experience, ingenuity, and military talent. Promis, with assuredly no friendly leaning, admits his great skill in military architecture, stating that he was often consulted by the principal engineers of Italy, and especially by Sanmichele, upon the fortifications of Corfu, regarding which that author attributes to him a Report to the Signory of Rome, now in the Ambrosian Library of Milan.[1] His opinion as to the defences of their lagoons, and principal garrisons on terra-firma, was, on various occasions, requested by that Republic, and during his command in Lombardy the towns of Lodi, Crema, Bergamo, Martinengo, and Orcinovo were all strengthened after his designs. Tartagli and Contriotto acknowledged their obligations to his suggestions; but Promis denies him the invention of baloards, as we have already seen, when writing of Francesco di Giorgio. The school of military engineering formed under his eye, during almost continual campaigns, numbered many distinguished professors of that art, among whom were Pietro Luigi Escriva, Gianbattista Bellucci, Nicolò Tartaglia, Girolamo Genga, Gian Giacomo Leonardi, and Jacopo Fusto Castriotto, the last three of whom were natives of his state.

But let us hear the evidence of contemporaries as to his character. Urbano Urbani, then his private secretary, thus describes him on succeeding to the dukedom:—"He was naturally low in stature, but well-proportioned, and of fine complexion. The short distance from his heart to his brain rendered his disposition choleric. Ever in movement, he was impatient of repose. Thoughtful, his ideas and discourse tended to lofty themes. Ready of hand, he dexterously managed, on horseback or afoot, the arms then in use. Of high courage, he invariably bent his mind to objects conducive to his honour and renown,

[1] *Trattato di Architettura di Francesco di Giorgio*, vol. II., p. 67. (Turin, 1841.)

especially in war. He was just, honest, averse to swearing, liberal, incorruptible, and no boaster. He loathed incontinence, and youthful excesses. In his household he was fond of splendour, and he generally entertained, in his almost regal court, a large attendance of distinguished gentlemen, such as Ottaviano Fregoso, Ludovico Pio, Gaspare Pallavicino, Giuliano de' Medici, Pietro Bembo, Baldassare Castiglione, Cesare Gonzaga (all of whom had been attached to his uncle Guidobaldo), Ambrogio Landriano, Febo da Cevi and his brother Gherardino, Filippino Doria, Benedetto Giraldi, and others conspicuous in arms, letters, or music; among whom Baldi names also Matteo della Branca, Carlo Gabrielli, Father Andreoni, Troiano and Gentile Carbonani, Count Gentile Ubaldini.[1]

Had his lot been cast in less turbulent times, it would have been his pride to maintain about him this goodly company, although he pretended not to his predecessor's literary tastes, and, if we may credit Sanuto, was unable to follow an oration delivered in Latin, on his arrival at Venice, in 1524. Yet, he was not indifferent to letters when connected with the engrossing occupation of his mind; and it was his habit, when time permitted, to have passages of ancient history read to him during several hours a day. This relaxation was varied by discussions arising out of these prelections, which he generally directed to military points, drawing out the opinions of his officers in attendance. Hence probably were suggested the Military Discourses, published in his name, of which we have already spoken; and various memorials of his conversation are preserved in a manuscript, which has supplied us with the anecdotes formerly quoted.[2] These were selected as illustrative of manners, from notes apparently made by a bystander; the others are almost exclusively

[1] Vat. Urb. MSS. No. 489, f. 61. See for many of these, vol. II.
[2] See Vat. Urb. MSS. No. 1023 art., 21.

upon military tactics and fortification, in which he was quite an adept.

Leonardi[1] confirms what we have stated of his character, dwelling much on his tendency to practical views. The sketch of Cristofero Centenelli must close these remarks:—"Though considered somewhat overbearing and hasty, he was at all times just. Even in youth, he was singularly self-denying of personal indulgences: guarding himself from the temptations of luxury and indolence, he sought daily occupation in the practice of arms, athletic sports, and equestrian exercises. He was liberal and magnificent, but grave and magnanimous; kind and affable to his friends, equitable and compassionate to his subjects. His courage was fiery and indomitable; of cold and heat, fatigue, watching, and privation, he was most enduring. He combined, to a rare degree, boldness in the field with prudence in the council-room, avoiding equally their extremes of temerity and timidity. To great skill in military discipline, he united uncommon perspicacity in discovering the snares of seeming friends or of open foes: astute with enemies, he was guarded with all. His eloquence commanded general admiration by its studied brevity, expressing the clearest views in fewest words."[2]

The Duke's constant and dutiful affection to his predecessor's widow deserves special notice. While she lived she shared his home, in prosperity or adversity, in sovereignty or in exile; and he occasionally availed himself of her prudence and popularity in the administration of the state during his absences. An interesting memorial of this filial affection is afforded by the following letter, which seems to have been written by Duchess Elisabetta.

"To the most illustrious Lord, my most esteemed Son, the Duke of Urbino, &c.

"The chair is so beautiful that neither words nor pen

[1] Vat. Urb. MSS. No. 1023, f. 85. [2] *Ibid.* No. 907.

suffice to express my thanks for this proof of regard; but most heartily, and with all the good will it merits, I accept so handsome and gallant a gift, and I shall use it for your sake as long as God pleases: it is not less beautiful than dear to me. I have seen the news sent by the Count: he would have done better to sacrifice something than to lose all by his imprisonment. We expect you in the morning. The Duchess kisses your hands and your mouth, and I commend myself to you with eternal thanks.

"YOUR MOTHER.

"The 8th of August."[1]

The widowed Duchess Leonora remained at Pesaro, stricken with grief, from which she slowly recovered to find a solace in her children. By her husband's will she had 28,000 scudi, besides the life-rent of his Neapolitan fiefs at Sora, which were left in remainder to their younger son Giulio. To each of the daughters were provided 20,000 scudi. She died at Gubbio, in 1543. Her devoted affection to her husband was accompanied by much sterling worth of character; but she was especially distinguished for that equanimity of temper which marks the expression of her admirable portrait in the Florence Gallery.

The children of Francesco Maria were these:—

1. FEDERIGO, born in March, 1511, and died young.
2. GUIDOBALDO, his successor, born 2nd April, 1514.
3. IPPOLITA, married in 1531, to Don Antonio d'Aragona, son of the Duke of Montalto, in Naples.
4. GIULIA, married in 1548, to Alfonso d'Este, Marquis of Montechio, son of Duke Alfonso I. From her descend the sovereign Dukes of Modena and Reggio.
5. ELISABETTA, married in 1552, to Alberico Cibò,

[1] Oliveriana MSS. No. 375. This may, however, have been addressed by Duchess Vittoria to Francesco Maria II.

Marquis of Massa, and died in 1561. From her descended the sovereign Dukes of Massa Carrara.

6. GIULIO, who was born at Mantua on the 8th of April, and created by his father Duke of Sora. He was educated for the Church, where his talents and application to business merited the shower of preferments which his high birth insured him, and which began by his nomination as Cardinal of S. Pietro in Vinculis by Paul III., when fourteen years of age. In 1548 he was made Bishop of Urbino, a dignity which he resigned three years later, on being appointed Legate of Rieti and Terni. In 1560 he had the see of Vicenza, but soon exchanged it for Recanati. In 1565, he was promoted to be Archbishop of Ravenna, to which was added, in 1570, the see of Tusculum; and, in 1578, when within a few months of his death, he became Archbishop of Urbino, having for some years previously been Legate of Umbria, and governor of Loreto. In these high posts he united to excellent business habits, and great energy in the discharge of his duties, a taste for magnificence, which made him popular with all classes. By his own family he was regarded as a valuable counsellor in every difficulty, and he greatly promoted the government of his brother and nephew, to whom he served as a sort of prime minister. His career of honour and utility was closed by a premature death, on the 5th September, 1578, when but forty-three years of age. Under his superintendence was drawn up a code of Regulations [*Riformazioni*] of Justice, which was published with his name in 1549. It does not appear in what way the dukedom of Sora and Arci passed from him, but, before the end of the century, it had been granted by Philip II. to Giacomo Boncompagno, natural son of Pope Gregory XIII.

From his descendants, the Princes of Piombino, that fief passed, about the end of last century, to the Neapolitan government; and its picturesque baronial towers at Isola, once the scene of their festive revels, are now degraded into a woollen factory. The Cardinal left two natural sons, who were both legitimated by Pius V.:—

1. Ippolito della Rovere, who had from his father San Lorenzo and Castel Leone above Sinigaglia, and was made Marquis of San Lorenzo in 1584, on his marriage with Isabella, daughter of Giacomo Vitelli dell' Amatrice, with 30,000 scudi of dowry. He had issue, 1. Giulio, who was disinherited for bad conduct; 2. Livia, born 1585, who became Duchess of Urbino in 1599; 3. Lucrezia, who married the Marchese Marc Antonio Lanti, and had issue.
2. Giuliano, Prior of Corinaldo, and Abbot of San Lorenzo.

BOOK SEVENTH

OF GUIDOBALDO DELLA ROVERE
FIFTH DUKE OF URBINO

CHAPTER XLII

Succession of Duke Guidobaldo II.—He loses Camerino and the Prefecture of Rome—The altered state of Italy—Death of Duchess Giulia—The Duke's remarriage—Affairs of the Farnesi.

THE course of our narrative seems to offer a not altogether fanciful analogy to that of the Tiber. Issuing from the rugged Apennines, this, with puny rill, is gradually recruited from their many valleys until it has gained the force and energy of a brawling torrent, and has absorbed a goodly portion of the Umbrian waters. So, too, the former has brought us past scenes of martial prowess and creations of mediæval policy. It has afforded us glimpses of townships where civil institutions revived, and letters were cherished, the petty capitals from whose courts civilisation was diffused. Carrying us across the blood-watered and time-defaced Campagna, it has conducted us to Rome at the moment of her lamentable sack by barbarian hordes. Henceforward our history, like the river, will decline in interest. The sluggish and turbid stream has little to enliven that dreary and degenerate land through which it must still conduct us. This contrast will be especially irksome in the life of Duke Guidobaldo II., who kept much aloof from the few events of stirring interest which then occurred in the Peninsula. We shall therefore hasten over it, in the hope that those who favour us with their company may find, in the incidents of his successor, a somewhat renovated interest, and may be gratified to learn by what means our mountain duchy came to be

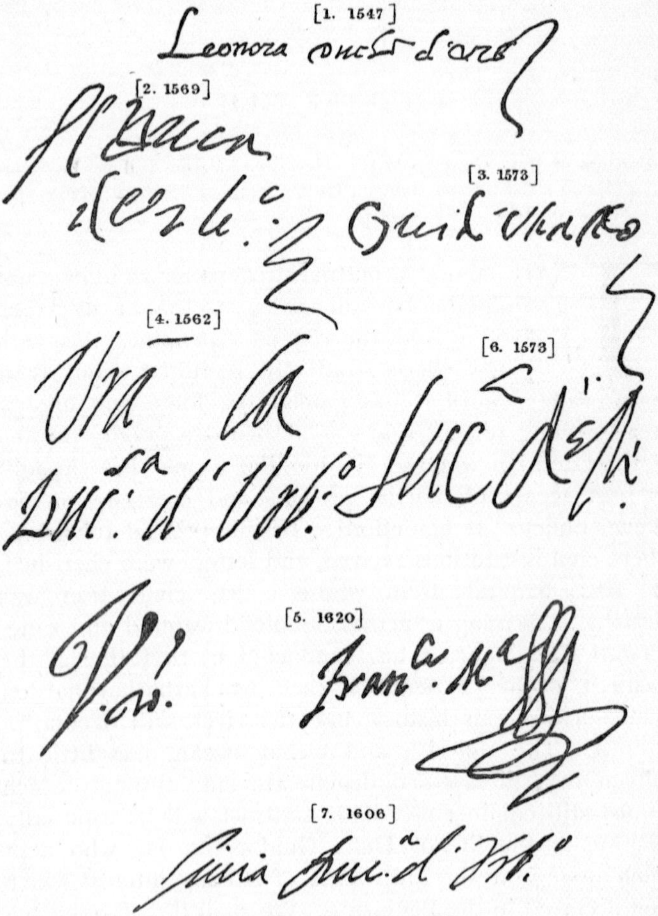

[1. 1547]

[2. 1569]

[3. 1573]

[4. 1562]

[6. 1573]

[5. 1620]

[7. 1606]

FACSIMILES OF SIGNATURES

finally absorbed in the papal dominions, just as the tawny river is lost in the pathless sea.

The birth-day of Guidobaldo II. has been variously stated; most authorities fix it on the 2nd of April, 1514, although the customary donative appears from an old chronicle to have been voted by the municipality of Urbino on the 17th of March. The Prince saw the light at a moment inauspicious for his dynasty. Under the fostering care of Julius II. it had attained its culminating point; and although his successor still smiled upon the far-spreading oak of Umbria,*[1] the intrigues of Leo X. were already preparing its overthrow. The infant had scarcely passed his second year, when the ducal family were driven from their states, and sought a friendly shelter at the Mantuan capital. Before their five years of exile in Lombardy had gone by, Guidobaldo is said to have been sent to the university of Padua. His early education was committed to Guido Posthumo Silvestro, who describes him as displaying, even in childhood, the spirit of his father, and of his grand-uncle Julius II., whilst his mild temper and sweet expression were those of his mother.[2] The preceptor, a native of Pesaro, was tempted by attachment to his early patrons, the Sforza, to avenge them with his pen, on the invasion of the Duke Valentino, upon whom and whose race he charged, in some bitter lampoons mentioned by Roscoe, all those crimes which have become matter of history. But years rendered him more pliant; for when another revolution came round, the attentions he had met with at the court of Urbino did not prevent his resorting, on Duke Francesco Maria's exile, to the protection of Leo, or lavishing eulogy and flattery upon that

*1 The Rovere were anything but an Umbrian family, as we have seen.

2 "Guidus Juliades, qui, quamquam mitis et ore
Blandus, ut ex vultu possis cognoscere matrem
Patrem animis tamen et primis patruum exprimit annis."

See as to Guido in ROSCOE's *Leo X.*, ch. xvii.

Pontiff. At Rome, he enjoyed the consideration there freely bestowed upon poets and wits, among whom Giovio assigns him a conspicuous place; but the life of luxurious indulgence to which he was tempted having undermined his health, he died in 1521.

Our authorities, barren of interest for the domestic life of Duke Francesco Maria,*[1] are altogether a blank as regards his children, and we know nothing of the Prince beyond the fact of his sharing his mother's virtual arrest at Venice in 1527. His early tastes seemed to have turned upon horses: in 1529, he ordered from Rome a set of housings for his charger, with minute instructions accompanying the pattern; ten years later, the Grand Duke Cosimo I. regretted his inability to find for him such horses as he had desired; and he appears to have paid 70 golden scudi for one from Naples. In 1843, I was shown, at Pesaro, the wooden model of a beautiful little Arab, which had long been preserved in the Giordani family, covered with the skin of his favourite charger, a fragment of which remained. We have seen Guidobaldo complimented by Clement VII. in 1529, and in that year he had a condotta from Venice, for seventy-five men-at-arms, and a hundred and fifty light horse, with 1000 ducats of pay for himself, 100 for each man-at-arms, and 50 for each horseman. In 1532, his father, on departing from Lombardy, left him regent of the duchy. The circumstances of his marriage, on the 12th of October, 1534, to Giulia Varana, then but eleven years of age, and her questionable succession to her paternal state of Camerino, have been fully detailed in our preceding chapter.[2] From 1534 till his father's death, in 1538, he

*[1] For certain details of Court life, cf. VERNARECCI, *Di alcune rappresentazioni Drammatiche nella Corte di Urbino* in *Arch. St. per le Marche e per l'Umbria*, vol. III., p. 181 *et seq.*, and ROSSI, *Appunti per la Storia Della Musica alla Corte di Francesco Maria I. e di Guidobaldo della Rovere* in *Rassegna Emiliana* (Modena, 1888), vol. I., fasc. 8; also VANZOLINI, *Musica e Danza alla Corte di Urbino*, in *Le Marche* (1904), An. iv., fasc. vi., p. 325 *et seq.*

[2] In the Harleian MSS. No. 282, f. 63, is a letter from Henry VIII. of

Anon. pinx. L. Ceroni. sculp.

GUIDOBALDO II, DUKE OF URBINO
From a picture in the Albani Palace in Rome

seems to have exercised the rights of sovereignty, with the title of Duke of Camerino, unchallenged by the Pontiff, who had recalled his censures. But no sooner was Paul III. relieved from the influential opposition of Francesco Maria, than his designs upon that principality were firmly carried out.

We possess from an eye-witness these ample details as to the ceremonial of investing Guidobaldo with his hereditary succession:—"On the evening of Thursday [25th of October], the day of the Duke's interment, his son the Prince arrived at Urbino about nine o'clock, attended by all the nobility, gentry, and officials, including Stefano Vigerio, the governor, and many more, who had gone out to meet him. Dismounting in the palace-yard, he proceeded to the ducal chamber, which, as well as the great hall, was hung with black. There he dismissed the strangers to lodgings provided for them in the town, and passed next day in grief and absolute seclusion along with his consort, preparations being meanwhile made to traverse the city.[1] Accordingly, on Saturday morning, mass of the Holy Spirit having been said by the Bishop of Cagli, who thereafter breakfasted in the palace, the citizens and populace crowded to the piazza, where the doctors and nobles assembled to accompany the priors. Thither also came a hundred youths of good family, in doublets of sky-blue velvet, with gilt swords by their side, followed by a vast many children bearing olive-boughs. The new Duke having been meanwhile dressed in white velvet and satin, with cap and plume of the same colour, Captain-general Luc-Antonio Brancarini marshalled the procession. The gonfaloniere marched first, in a jerkin of black velvet under

28th November, in his 30th year [1538], to Sir Thomas Wyatt, his ambassador to the Emperor, proposing a marriage of the Princess Mary either to the young Duke of Cleves and Juliers, or to "the present Duke of Urbyne," and desiring him to sound "whether he wold be gladd to have us to wyve with any of them." Guidobaldo had been already wedded for four years!

[1] *Correre la terra* is the usual phrase for taking sovereign possession, like "riding the marches" of Scottish burghs.

a long surcoat of black damask lined with crimson, begirt with a gold-mounted sword; his cap on his head and his mace lowered. He was followed by the nobility, the doctors, and citizens; and on entering the palace they halted in the basement suite towards the garden, which were all hung with tapestry, the windows of the great hall being occupied by the Duchess and her ladies in magnificent attire. When all was ready, the Prince issued forth into the Piazza, and advanced to the cathedral, followed by the officials and train. At the top of the steps he knelt on a rich carpet and brocade cushions, whilst the bishop, chapter, and clergy came out, and with the usual ceremonies brought him into the church, and to the high altar, before which other ceremonials were gone through, and he offered an oblation-coin of ten Mantuan ducats. Meanwhile his charger was brought to the foot of the steps, covered to the neck with a housing of silver tissue, and other trappings, including a white plume. It was led by seven lads of the chief Urbino families, Bonaventura, Peruli, Passionei, Cornei, Corboli, and Muccioli, all richly apparelled, and two of them holding goads. There was also a horse for the Gonfaloniere with velvet harness, led by two lads. The fore-mentioned hundred youths and numerous children having ranged themselves around, the Prince and Gonfaloniere descended the steps and mounted their steeds, and the latter, drawing his sword, proclaimed aloud 'THE DUKE, THE DUKE; FELTRO, FELTRO; GUIDOBALDO, GUIDOBALDO!' the cry being taken up and repeated by all. The cortège, making a circuit by Pian di Marcato, Valbona, Santa Lucia, and Santa Chiara, returned to the palace, where the Duke dismounted. His charger and mantle were then seized, as their perquisite, by the youths, who, mounting one of their number, Antonio dei Galli, again went through the city crying and making merry. The Duke, having taken his seat with his consort, received the gonfaloniere, priors, and citizens to kiss hands.

Alinari

? GUIDOBALDO II DELLA ROVERE
From the picture by Titian in the Pitti Gallery, Florence
(Probably once in the Ducal Collection)

"On the following morning, there came in envoys from various places to offer their condolence, wearing mourning robes that swept the ground. The first who had audience were the gonfaloniere and priors of Urbino, and then those from San Marino. After breakfast, the other communities were admitted without order, in consequence of a wrangle for precedence between Gubbio and Pesaro, Cagli and Fossombrone, and this continued till seven o'clock in the evening. Next Monday being the festival of San Simone, the oath of allegiance was administered on Tuesday. A stage covered with black was erected between the two windows of the great hall, on which stood a bench with a coverlet of black velvet, and thereon an open missal, with a miniature of the crucifixion. After breakfasting, the Duke seated himself on this stage, with Messer Stefano, one of the judges; and the deputies from communes being assembled, with their commissions in their hands, Messer Stefano called upon the magistrates of Urbino with about a hundred of the citizens, desiring them to swear fidelity, as was right and customary, which they did, formally placing their hands on the crucifixion. Thereafter, the envoys of other communities were brought up and sworn; but on account of the aforesaid wrangling, those of Pesaro, Sinigaglia, Fossombrone, and Cagli were sent back to take the oaths at home. Next day, however, on their humble petition, those of Cagli and Fossombrone were received, along with some other highland deputies who had come in late; but Pesaro, Sinigaglia, and the vicariat, took the oaths before the vice-dukes in their respective cities. On the following Tuesday, there arrived four envoys from Fano, and two from Città di Castello, to offer condolence, who were honourably received; and next day came those of Camerino and Rimini, men of high station. On Thursday, Messer Quaglino, ambassador from the Duke of Ferrara, dismounted at Pesaro, to condole with the dowager Duchess, and thence proceeded with a suite of five to Urbino, where he was lodged for three days in the Passionei Palace, and had audience. At the same time, the like formalities were discharged by Vicenzo Schippo, who came with an escort of ten, as representative of the Duke of Mantua. On Sunday, deputations from all parts of the duchy went to offer their duty at Pesaro to the widowed Duchess."

The smouldering embers of the Camerino quarrel soon burst forth, when Paul III. found that the Emperor's influence and the arms of Venice were no longer arrayed against his grasping pretensions, and that the weight of the struggle had devolved from a renowned warrior to an untried youth. In order to supplement the legal deficiencies of his case, the Pontiff had in 1537 conferred certain estates upon Ercole Varana, on condition of his claims upon the succession of Camerino being assigned to his own grandson Ottavio Farnese; but the death of Francesco Maria having released him from the necessity of temporising, he at once sent a body of troops into that duchy, under Stefano Colonna or Alessandro Vitelli. The young Duke, relying on the support of Venice and the Medici, was at first disposed to resist, but finding himself deserted, soon abandoned the idea. He had in the history of his family too many examples of the perils of papal nepotism; and it was obvious that the times were past when church feudatories had anything to hope from single-handed contests with their over-lord. In the certainty that to provoke this would be to hazard all, he made up his mind to an unwilling compromise, surrendering his wife's rights to Camerino for a full investiture of his own dukedom, and the sum of 78,000 golden scudi as a poor compensation for her inheritance. This transaction was completed on the 8th of January, 1539; nor was it the only mortification he was destined to undergo from the ambition of the Farnesi. The Prefecture of Rome, although held by his father and grandfather, was a personal dignity at the disposal of the new Pope, who conferred it upon his own grandson Ottavio. In the end of 1538, he also married that youth, then but fifteen, to Margaret of Austria, natural daughter of Charles V. and widow of Duke Alessandro de' Medici, who had been slain by his cousin Lorenzino, within a year after his marriage. That imperious dame, who brought Ottavio a handsome dower in lands about Ortona on the Adriatic, wrought upon the weakness of Paul, until in 1545, she obtained for her husband's father, Pier-Luigi, natural son of his Holiness, the sovereign duchy of Parma and Piacenza. In order to put a gloss upon this dismemberment of the ecclesiastical states, and to accommodate the whole arrangement to the modified nepotism of his age, the Pontiff stipulated for a resurrender by Ottavio to the Holy See of Camerino and Nepi. These remained part of the papal temporalities, whilst their Lombard duchy gave to the Farnese family an important position among the sovereign houses of Europe.

Although the altered circumstances of Italy which humbled her pride had also arrested her convulsions, these untoward events, at the outset of his reign, proved to Guidobaldo that her few remaining principalities were far from secure. To strengthen his position became therefore a natural policy; and although neither the Emperor nor the Venetian Signory had lent a willing ear to his representations on the subject of Camerino, he sent to remind the former of his promise to give him a company of men-at-arms, whilst, with the Pope's permission, he accepted from the latter a two years' engagement. The terms of this condotta, which was dated in 1539, and continued in force until 1552, were one hundred men-at-arms and as many light cavalry, with 4000 ducats of *piatto* or yearly pay, and an obligation to have in readiness ten of his father's veteran captains, whose monthly pay was fixed at 15 scudi in peace, and 25 in war. Four years later he was requested by the Republic to serve them in another capacity, by complimenting Charles V. in their name on his passage into Germany, on which occasion he was accompanied by the vile sycophant Pietro Aretino.

In our fourteenth chapter, we had occasion to consider the change which military affairs underwent in Italy about the time of the first French invasion, and we have seen in Duke Federigo of Urbino one of the last condottieri of the old sort. But it was not until the fall of Rome and Florence had extinguished Italian independence, that military adventure was entirely abolished; and it is curious to find in his grandson Duke Francesco Maria I., not only the latest captain who gathered laurels under that system, but to see him joining with the Pope and the Medici to exterminate those armed hordes which survived its mercenary armaments, and which, like the restless spirits of a departed generation, troubled the repose of their degenerate sons.[1] Their occupation was indeed gone. Tamed by invaders whom they were powerless to resist, domestic broils no longer demanded their services. Their forays were become intolerable in a land where peace was the price of freedom. How far the earlier adoption of Machiavelli's plans of defence might have availed against ultramontane hosts were now a vain speculation; they were only destined for trial after the sacrifice had been consummated. The national militia suggested by him was not enrolled until there was no longer a nationality to defend—until it was needed but as an armed police under foreign control.

This new force had been embodied in our duchy under the name of the Feltrian Legion, by a proclamation dated 1st of March, 1533, and it so fully satisfied the late Duke's expectations that he gradually increased his militia to five thousand men in four regiments. Such was the description of troops which henceforward maintained order at Urbino, or were subsidised on foreign service. But

[1] Ricotti, IV., p. 129, quoting Adriani Storie, lib. II.

their sinews, hardened by a rude climate and rugged homes, maintained for them the reputation gained by their ancestors; and although Duke Guidobaldo II. lived in quiet times, and pretended to no heroic aspirations, we find him accepting of commands offered chiefly for the sake of securing his hardy mountaineers.

The abject position in which Italy was left after the wars of Clement VII. has already been noticed. Her internal conflicts were at an end. Of those states whose struggles for independence or for mastery had during long ages convulsed her, the lesser had been absorbed by the more powerful, and these in their turn had bowed to foreign dominion or foreign influence. She was tranquillised but trodden down, pacified but prostrate. Her history became but a series of episodes in the annals of ultramontane nations, on whom her few remaining princes and commonwealths grew into dependent satellites. Even the popes, no longer arbiters of European policy, sought a reflected consequence by attaching themselves to the interests of France, Spain, or the Empire. Nor were they losers by the change to the same degree as other Peninsular powers. The papacy was indeed shorn in part of its temporal lustre. It no longer directed the diplomacy of Christendom, nor did it waste its resources upon bloody and bootless campaigns. But as its energies were gradually weaned from general politics, they became more concentrated upon ecclesiastical affairs. The small speck on the horizon towards which Leo X. had scarcely directed a look or an anxiety, was now rapidly overspreading the sky, and already excluded the rays of Catholicism from a large portion of Central Europe. His successors, threatened with the loss of spiritual as well as temporal ascendancy, had the wisdom to make a stand for maintenance of the former, leaving the latter to its fate. The spirit of popery from aggressive became conservative; its military tactics gave place to theological weapons. It was by Paul III. that a vigorous opposition was first made to the Reformation, the primary steps taken towards that Catholic reaction, which Paul IV. and Pius V. afterwards so successfully promoted, as not only to check the rapid progress of Protestantism, but to regain a portion of the lost ground. Seconding the zeal of the old monastic orders, which had been revived in the Theatines,*[1] he, in 1540, recruited to it the cold clear-sighted cunning of the Jesuits. Two years afterwards he re-established the Inquisition,*[2] and in 1545 opened the Council of Trent, whose sittings were not finally closed until eighteen years later, when it had completed that bulwark which still constitutes a stronghold of the Roman church. Extirpation of heresy henceforward became the pervading principle of the papacy, and the engrossing dogma of its zealots; the object for which councils deliberated, pontiffs admonished, legates intrigued. For an end so sanctified no means were accounted base. When argument failed threats were at hand. From reason an appeal lay to the rack. Thus was the wavering power of the Keys restored or confirmed over much of Europe, and an alliance was effected between political and spiritual despotism for their mutual maintenance and common defence. The success which crowned these new efforts far exceeded any that mere mundane aims had ever attained. The re-influx of Catholicism was in some instances more signal, as it was

*[1] The Theatines were a congregation of Clerks Regular, founded by Gaetano Tiene, a Venetian nobleman, in 1524. They are under the rule of S. Augustin. S. Gaetano Tiene died in 1547. In 1526 Matteo di Basso of Urbino founded a reform of Franciscan Observants, giving his followers a long-pointed hood, which he believed to be of the same shape as that worn by S. Francis. These friars became known as Cappuccini or Capuchins. At first they were merely a company of hermits devoted to the contemplative life. They remained, in fact, under the Observants till 1617. They are now a separate order governed by a general. They live in absolute poverty.

*[2] The Inquisition was revived by a Bull of Sixtus IV. in 1478. Two years later it was reinstated in Spain by the Catholic kings. In 1526 it was established in Portugal; but it was only introduced into Italy in 1546, at Naples, and came into Central Italy only with many restrictions.

more inexplicable, than had been the recent spread of the Reformation.*[1] Although fatal to freedom of thought, its influence proved highly favourable to morals. The revival of religion was attended with a happy reformation of manners, after examples emanating from high places. The sins, or at least the scenes, that had disgraced the Borgian and Medicean courts no longer met the eye, but were replaced by a semblance of ascetic virtue. The new religious orders, being of more rigid rule, tended by precept and example to restore discipline, and to purify, at least externally, the cup and the platter. Prelatic luxury was curtailed, brazen vice retired from public view, and the free exercise of papal nepotism was finally restrained by Pius V., who, in 1567, prohibited the alienation by his successors of church property or jurisdictions. But in these themes our narrative has no part. The battles of orthodoxy were chiefly fought beyond the Alps; the reformed morality of the papal court was exampled in its own capital: in neither had Urbino any near interest.

Guidobaldo's condotta from the Signory being renewed in 1546 upon more favourable terms (namely, 15,000 scudi of pay for his company, and 5000 of *piatto* for himself), he was invested about midsummer, by an imposing ceremonial pompously described in the letter of an eyewitness among the archives of Urbino. His jewelled cap and diamond collar are mentioned as superb, and his sword is valued at 700 scudi. After high mass in St. Mark's, the great standard being unfurled and supported by three bearers, and the baton of wrought silver placed in his hands, the Doge thus addressed him: "Lord Duke, we presented to your Excellency this standard of our St. Mark the Evangelist, in the wonted form, and in token of supremacy; and we pray the Lord our God that it tend to the weal and service of all Christendom, but

*[1] It might seem that those parts of Europe securely within the Roman Empire of antiquity eventually remained Catholic.

especially to the defence of this state. We give it to your Excellency, confiding in your loyalty and prudence, well assured that you will use it with courage and faith conformable to your deserts. And we hand to your Excellency the baton, therewith designing you head and governor of our forces, and transferring to you the obedience of all our military: it is our will that you be obeyed, honoured, and respected by our several condottieri and soldiery, as representing our Signory itself. May it please the Divine Majesty that all be well ordered, to the well-being and furtherance of the Christian community, and of this our serene Republic." The Duke replied, "I most willingly accept, most Serene Prince, the distinction granted me by your Serenity, and with the sure hope of maintaining the good opinion you repose in me, which shall be nowise disappointed. I shall ever pray our Lord God graciously to vouchsafe me an early occasion of honourably serving your serene government, that I may thereby prove my good will. And I feel sure that your Serenity will have cause to be well satisfied at giving me this rank, which, without reserve of life or fortune, like one aware of his obligation to your Serenity, it will be my care so to hold as to augment my claims upon your favour." The function being over, the Duke was escorted by an imposing military pageant to his palace, where a splendid banquet was set out, of which, however, the jealous regulations of the Republic did not permit her officials to partake.

The court having gone to spend Christmas of 1547 in the mild climate of Fossombrone, the Duke, in January, 1548, again repaired to Venice, intending to return home for carnival. On the frontier he was met by news of his consort's serious illness, and immediately sent expresses to summon from Padua and Ferrara, Frigimiliza and Brasavolo, two famous physicians. Under them and her own doctors, the Duchess rallied for a time, but died on the 17th of February,—"a very religious, charitable, and lettered lady, and a great loss to the state." Her body was borne by torchlight to Urbino with the usual solemnities, and, after lying in state, was entombed in Santa Chiara on the 19th. The funeral service was performed at Urbino the 24th of March, with due pomp, and a ceremonial preserved by Tondini. The procession consisted of the Duchess's household, twenty-two in number, with thirty-nine of the Duke's; Guidobaldo and his brother; the ambassadors of five friendly states; twenty-two principal nobility of the duchy; forty captains; the municipality of Urbino, with seventy leading citizens; deputies from thirty-six other towns; in all, about three hundred and sixty persons. The obsequies were celebrated in the cathedral, which was illuminated by a hundred and eighty-six wax lights of four pounds each, and above two hundred torches. The funeral oration was pronounced by Sperone Speroni, and is published among his works.

Although, in somewhat startling contrast to these details of death, we here introduce a letter written by the Duchess, which may interest our lady readers. It is addressed to Marchetti, her steward of the household, then at Venice, and is printed in his life by Tondini:—

"Master Steward, our well-beloved,

"This is to inform you that, on your return with his Excellency, our Lord and Consort, you must by all means bring as much of the finest and most beautiful scarlet serge, such as is made on purpose for the cardinals, as may suffice to make us a petticoat, taking care that it be at once handsome, good, and *distingué*. You can ascertain the necessary quantity. Here they tell us that if the stuff be two *braccie* [a yard and a quarter] wide, at least eight *braccie* will be required, and more if narrower, say nine or ten. See that you get full measure, and let the quantity be ample rather than deficient, so that we may not have to mar it for want of cloth. And if you cannot find such serge, bring some beautiful, good, and thin Venice cloth, being careful that it be light in texture, and that the colour be of the most bright and lively scarlet that can be found. Use all diligence that we be well suited and satisfied, if you would do us a grateful service. Bring also some of those books and rosettes, as they are called, which are commonly made there of thin white wax tapers; and so good health to you. From Fossombrone, the 6th of October, 1541.

"JULIA DUCHESS OF URBINO."

The Duchess had given birth to a son in 1544, but was survived only by a daughter Virginia: her marriage had been interested, and her lord lost no time in contracting another from similar motives, on the excuse of requiring a male heir. In August he went to kiss the Pope's feet at Rome, on occasion of negotiating a new matrimonial alliance with his grand-daughter, Vittoria Farnese. On the 30th he returned home, and next month again met his Holiness at Perugia. The nuptials were interrupted by the assassination of the bride's father, Duke Pier-Luigi, whose son had supplanted Guidobaldo at Camerino, and whose tyranny in his new state of Parma sharpened the daggers of his outraged nobles. The ceremony, however, took place on the 30th of January, 1548, when Vittoria, who had been previously affianced to Duke Cosimo I., was twenty-eight years of age. On the 2nd of February she visited Urbino, amid many demonstrations of respect, among which was a muster of forty lads in her livery of yellow velvet, to each of whom an allowance of seven scudi had been voted by the city; but it was the Duke's pleasure that they should pay for their own dress. Art, too, had contributed its honours, and Vasari narrates how Battista Franco aided in decorating the triumphal arches designed by Girolamo Genga for her reception. Similar welcome was given her at Gubbio, where the youths wore purple velvet with white sleeves and white lilies.*[1] Coincident with, and in consequence of, this marriage, the Duke received from Paul a new investiture of his states, and a cardinal's hat, with the title of S. Pietro in Vinculis, for his brother Giulio, who, though but in his fifteenth year, was soon after named Legate of Perugia. On the 20th of February, 1549, there was born a prince, who succeeded to the dukedom as Francesco Maria II., and the grateful people manifested their loyalty by customary congratulations and donatives.[2] These happy events were, ere long, interrupted by the death of Paul III. on the 10th of November, followed by that of the dowager Duchess of Urbino, on the 14th of February, thereafter.

The little state of San Marino forms a solecism in the polity of Europe, having preserved its petty limits and its purely popular government during many centuries, whilst all the other republics of Italy successfully yielded to personal ambition or foreign conquest.*[3] For its independence during the ceaseless changes of the fifteenth and sixteenth centuries it was debtor to the Dukes of Urbino, whose aid was ever at hand when their name proved an inadequate safeguard. The nature of the protection which they accorded to that republic is shown in the subjoined document, which seems worthy of insertion from its resemblance to those letters of maintenance usually granted about the same period by the greater barons of Scotland, in favour of less powerful neighbours and friends, among the minor nobility, and even the burgh communities.

*[1] Cf. PELLEGRINI, *Gubbio sotto i Conti e Duchi d'Urbino* in *Bolletino per l'Umbria* (Perugia, 1905), vol. XI., p. 236 *et seq.*

[2] Vat. Urb. MSS. No. 934, is an elaborate exposition of the devices and mottoes displayed on this august occasion.

*[3] Cf. FATTORI, *Delle cause che hanno conservata la Repubblica di S. Marino* (Bologna, 1887).

"Protection under which, at the instance of the Liberty of S. Marino, pressed by its envoys, the Lord Duke Guidobaldo II. assumes the aforesaid Liberty, its men and territory, following therein in this the course adopted by Duke Federico, Guido I., Francesco Maria his father, and others of his house: promising to the best of his ability, and at all times, to defend, protect, and guard it against all persons whatsoever who may seek or wish to injure it, whether in respect to its possessions, subjects, state, or pre-eminence, holding its enemies for his enemies, and its allies for his allies; and further, undertaking to accord to it all possible aid and favour in the maintenance of its independence and freedom: the said envoys, on the other part, obliging themselves to the Lord Duke, in name of the foresaid, with all their exertion and power to assist, uphold, and preserve the subjects, state, honours, and dignity of the said Lord Duke, against whatsoever person, state, or potentate who may make attempts against him; promising to hold the friends of his Excellency as their friends, and his foes as their foes, and to pay him at all times the respect due to a faithful and good protector. At the requisition of Ser Bartolo Nursino, 20th May, 1549."

It was Guidobaldo's policy to maintain with the Holy See those amicable relations which his second marriage had established, and he had accordingly, on the death of Paul III., sent some troops to Perugia, in order to secure the quiet succession of Julius III. This being effected, he went to Rome on a visit of congratulation to the new Pontiff, accompanied by Aretino, whose venal appetites were ever on the watch for opportunities of bringing his sycophancy to a good market. The Pope disappointed him of the anticipated guerdon, but, aware of the ready transition from adulation to slander, disarmed his tongue of its venom by a gracious accolade, kissing the forehead of this "scourge of princes." The first token of favour bestowed on the Duke by his Holiness was his nomination as governor of Fano in 1551. In the following year he spent some time at Verona with the Venetian army, accompanied by his boy, who there had an illness which occasioned him much anxiety. This command was a somewhat anomalous one, with the title of Governor of the Republican forces, which he vainly negotiated to exchange for that of General. Disgusted by this refusal, he listened to an overture from his brothers-in-law for transferring his services to the French King. Ottavio Farnese, now Duke of Parma, apprehending some hostile intentions from the imperialists, had applied, in 1551, to the Pope for succours, in order to guarantee his possession of that state; but, unable to spare reinforcements or money, Julius had recommended him to take his own measures for defence. Acting on this advice, he had recourse to Henry II., from whom he accepted a condotta, on condition of Parma being supplied with a French garrison. Such a step could not fail to alarm the Emperor, who, representing that Ottavio had, in fact, made over his duchy to France, brought upon him the thunders of the Vatican. The inducement offered to Guidobaldo by the Farnesi for following them into Henry's service was that the King should renounce the supposed claims upon Urbino competent to his wife Caterina de' Medici, in right of her father Lorenzo, its usurping Duke. But the decided measures adopted by the Pontiff cut short this negotiation, and we hear no more of pretensions which were doubtless vamped up to serve a temporary purpose. Although the Pontiff was nominally a party to the petty war which ensued in Lombardy, it was, in fact, but a chapter in the prolonged struggle between the houses of Hapsburg and Bourbon, with which our narrative has no concern. Another episode in the same contest was more alarming to Central Italy, and, when Tuscany became involved in the strife, it seemed well for Julius to stand on the defensive. Accordingly, in January, 1553, he named

Guidobaldo captain-general of the Church, who, in April, proceeded to Rome for his installation; and accompanied by a brilliant staff, reviewed the pontifical troops.

Siena, originally Ghibelline, had, during the recurring convulsions of a nominally democratic government, remained in some measure devoted to the imperialist party. But, irritated by the licence of their Spanish garrison, and alarmed at a rumoured intention of Charles V. to seize their state, and exchange it with the Farnesi for that of Parma, the citizens, in 1552, foolishly listened to the intrigues of French emissaries, and, with the Count of Pitigliano's aid, ousted their oppressors. In the campaign which followed, Siena was under French protection, whilst Florence efficiently co-operated with the imperialists against her, the Pope maintaining an armed neutrality. The duties of Guidobaldo were thus limited to an occupation of Bologna, in order to protect the ecclesiastical territories and his own state, on the passage of French troops into Tuscany. That his wishes favoured the independence of Siena appears from his having, at the election of Marcellus II., in April, 1554, recommended an intervention in its favour; but it was too late, as the city had already capitulated, and was soon after finally annexed to Florence.

The successor of Julius III., who died in march, 1555, was Marcello Cervini, Bishop of Gubbio; and the Duke of Urbino congratulated himself on seeing a personal friend mount the throne of St. Peter. But his satisfaction was transient. Popular superstition awarded an early death to any Pontiff who should take for title his Christian name: the fate of Adrian VI. had verified the omen; and, after a reign of but three weeks, Marcellus was carried to the tomb. Guidobaldo immediately took armed possession of the Roman gates for protection of the conclave; but the election of Cardinal Caraffa as Paul IV. passed off satisfactorily, and his energy was rewarded by a confirmation in his command, and the restoration of the Prefecture of Rome, with reversion to his son, an honour which, though long held by his father and grandfather, had been enjoyed for the last seventeen years by the Farnesi.

CHAPTER XLIII

The Duke's domestic affairs—Policy of Paul IV.—The Duke enters the Spanish service—Rebellion at Urbino severely repressed—His death and character—His children.

THIS somewhat barren portion of our narrative may be appropriately enlivened by the marriage of Princess Elisabetta, sister of Guidobaldo, to Alberico Cibò, Prince of Massa. The bride left Urbino on the 26th of September, accompanied by the Duke and Duchess, and remained at Castel Durante for two days. She was convoyed for some miles farther by the court, and parted from her family with copious tears on both sides. That night she slept at S. Angelo, and next day reached Città di Castello, escorted by an immense train of the principal residents to the Vitelli Palace. There she was entertained at an almost regal banquet, with about fifty gentle dames, each more beautiful than the other, and all richly dressed; after which there followed dancing, to the music of many rare instruments and choruses, till near day-break. Travelling in a litter by easy journeys, she reached Florence in four days, and was welcomed with magnificent public honours. She entered the city in a rich dress of green velvet, radiant with jewels, and passed two days there, the guest of Chiappino Vitelli, who spent 2000 scudi upon four entertainments in her honour, including a ball and masquerade. On going to court, she was received by the Grand Duke and Duchess as a sister, with much kindness, and a world of professions. Near Pisa she was met by her bridegroom, at the head of a cavalcade which resembled an army marching to the assault of the city ; and his mother, though almost dying, had herself carried to the bed in which the bride had sought repose, to embrace her with maternal affection. More acceptable, perhaps, than this singular visit, was the present received from her in the morning, of two immense pearls, and a golden belt studded with costly jewels. The pair entered the capital next day, amid a crash of artillery, martial music, and bells, preceded by fifty youths in yellow velvet and white plumes. The festive arches delighted the narrator, but still more the palace furniture, "where nothing was seen but armchairs brocaded in silk and gold, and one everywhere stepped on the finest carpets." The community offered six immense vases, and a donative of bullocks, fowls, and wax. "But all this is nothing to the excessive affection which the Lord Marquis bears to his most illustrious consort: he does not merely love her, he adores her. May God continue it, and maintain them in happiness."[1] This kind wish had scanty fulfilment, for the Princess died nine years later, her husband surviving to the patriarchal age of ninety-six.

In 1556, Guidobaldo finished the citadel and fortifications of Sinigaglia, which had occupied him during ten years, and which were considered an important bulwark against Turkish descents on the Adriatic coast. There also he instituted a college for the study of gunnery; and he commemorated the completion of these establishments by striking four medals, of which three are described by Riposati; none of them, however, merit special notice, the beauty of Italian dies being already on the wane. The court was now for the most part resident at Pesaro, a situation excelling in amenity and convenience the original capital of the duchy. Among its attractions may be numbered the palace-villa of Imperiale, which has

[1] TONDINI, *Memorie di Franceschino Marchetti*, App., p. 16.

been described; but it became necessary to provide a town residence, that in the citadel, which had sufficed for the Sforza, being far too restricted for the demands of growing luxury. Of the palace at Pesaro, Guidobaldo II. may be considered the entire author,*[1] and if it seem scarcely suited for the accommodation of so famed a court, we must recollect that the golden days of this principality were already passing away, that the military qualities of its sovereigns and people had become less gainful, and the devotion of its dukes to letters and arts was beginning to languish. Although extensive, the aspect of this residence is mean, its buildings rambling. It exhibits no appearance of a public edifice except the spacious *loggia* or arcade. Over this, its single external feature, is the great hall, measuring 134 by 54 feet, and of well-proportioned height. Here we find some interesting traces of the della Rovere, in those quaint and significant family devices which it was their pride unceasingly to repeat. The manifold compartments of its richly stuccoed ceiling contain their heraldic badge, the oak-tree; the ermine of Naples; the half-inclined palm-tree; the *meta*, or goal of merit, and similar fancies.[2] These recur among delicately sculptured arabesques on the internal lintels, and ornament the imposing chimney-pieces, varied by figures of Fame strewing oak-leaves and acorns. This palace was later the winter residence of the cardinal legates of Urbino and Pesaro, of whom portraits, from the Devolution of the duchy to the Holy See, in 1626, surround the great hall. In 1845, Cardinal della Genga was the forty-eighth of this long succession.

Paul IV. was seventy-nine years of age when he assumed

*[1] It was probably the work of Girolamo Genga (1476–1551) and his son Bartolomeo (1518–58). It is now the Prefettura. It has never struck me as "mean," but rather as being a somewhat imposing building.

[2] See these devices explained in No. V. of the Appendix to Vol. I. The respective importance of the ducal residences is marked by their colloquial epithets,—the *corte* at Urbino, the *palazzo* at Pesaro, tbe *casa* at Gubbio.

the triple tiara. His life had been one long exercise of holy zeal and ascetic observance, and the Romans, again sunk in those habits of luxury and indulgence from which Bourbon's army had roused them, saw with little satisfaction the accession of one so intolerant. But they were ill-prepared for a turbulence unparalleled during many years. His policy leaned to the once favourite, but long dormant, idea of expelling the Spaniards from Lower Italy; while, to the astonishment of mankind, the almost abandoned pretensions of nepotism were revived with unflinching fierceness by this octogenarian founder of the strictly devotional order of Theatins. A trumpery outrage on the French flag by the Sforza of Santa-fiore,*[1] in which the Colonna were alleged to have participated or sympathised, supplied a pretext for putting the latter to the ban; and their vast possessions, which in the ecclesiastical states alone numbered above a hundred separate holdings, were conferred upon the Pope's nephew, Giovanni Caraffa, Count of Montorio. The Colonna flew to arms, and, being under the avowed protection of Spain, were supported by troops from Naples, against whom the Duke of Urbino was ordered to march; but fortunately the ashes of civil broils were nearly cold, and peace would have continued undisturbed, had not Paul, in the following year, issued his monitory against Philip II. Although the Spanish intervention in behalf of the Colonna formed an ostensible ground for this aggression, its true motives are traced by Panvinio to more remote and personal considerations, dating from the viceroyalty of Lautrec, by whom the Caraffa, always adherents of France, had been harshly treated. Reverting to the papal policy of half a century before, Paul sought to avenge this quarrel through French instrumentality, and although a pacification of unusual

*[1] For all that concerns Santa Fiora and the Sforza-Cesarini, see a forthcoming work by EDWARD HUTTON, with notes by WILLIAM HEYWOOD, entitled *In Unknown Tuscany* (Methuen). It deals with the whole history of Mont' Amiata and its castles and villages.

solemnity had been concluded in February of this year between Charles V. and Henry II., preparatory to the former retiring from the cares of sovereignty, he contrived, by successful intrigues, to bring the two great European powers once more into hostility, and to revive in the Bourbon King those ambitious projects which had formerly brought his predecessors across the Alps for the conquest of Naples.

Anticipating this threatened danger, the Duke of Alva marched an army of fourteen thousand men into the Comarca, which he overran in September, occupying Tivoli on the one hand, and Ostia on the other, whilst Marc-Antonio Colonna scoured the Campagna, to the gates of Rome. Guidobaldo, who appears to have been about this time superseded, and his truncheon of command transferred to the Pontiff's favourite nephew, contented himself with sending a contingent of two thousand troops, under Aurelio Fregoso, for his Holiness's support. The efforts made on all sides to conclude a harassing and useless war, were rendered unavailing by the Pope's obstinacy and ambition; the only terms he would agree to including an investiture of his nephew as sovereign of Siena, in compensation for the Colonna estates.

During the winter months, a horde of northern barbarians were once more mustered to invade unhappy Italy. Fourteen thousand Gascons, Grisons, and Germans, under command of the Duc de Guise, marched early in the spring upon Romagna, which, though a friendly country, they cruelly ravaged. Faenza having escaped their brutality by denying them entrance, its citizens testified their gratitude for the exemption, by instituting an annual triduan thanksgiving, and dotation of two of their daughters. The Duke of Urbino did his best to secure his people during the transit of this army, which crossed the Tronto in April. It would be tedious to follow the fortunes of a campaign in which he took no part, and which, whoever gained, was the scourge of Italy. On the 26th of August, the Duc de Guise placed his scaling ladders against the San Sebastiano gate, and Rome had nearly been carried by a coup-de-main. At length the representations of Venice and Florence, which had remained neutral, prevailed with his Holiness, and, on the 14th of September, peace was restored, leaving matters much on their former footing. Riposati assures us that during this war the French monarch would gladly have secured the services of Guidobaldo, now free from his engagements to the Pontiff, but that Duke Cosimo of Florence interested himself to procure for him an engagement from Spain. This was at length arranged, in the spring of 1558, previously to which Charles V. appears to have bestowed on him the Golden Fleece, the highest compliment at his disposal.[1]

The terms upon which the Duke took service under Philip II. are thus stated in a letter of Bernardo Tasso. The King guaranteed him protection for his territories against all hazards, and bound himself to supply and maintain for him a body-guard of at least two hundred infantry, besides a company of a hundred men-at-arms, and another of two hundred light horse. He further engaged to pay him monthly 1000 golden scudi for his appointments as captain-general, besides maintaining for him four colonels and twenty captains. In return, the Duke took an oath to serve his Majesty faithfully against all potentates, the pontiffs alone excepted. The political results of this arrangement were strongly and painfully felt by Bernardo, who regarded it as establishing the tranquillity of Naples, the security of Tuscany, and, in a word, the Spanish domination in Italy. Inclined to the French interests (for there was no longer an Italian party in exist-

[1] Some authorities represent him as receiving this Order eleven years later from Charles V., but that Emperor died in this very year. He is said to have had knighthood from the Pope in 1561.

ence), he would have gladly seen the sovereign of a highland population, whose warlike sinews were not yet quite relaxed, preserve his neutrality, or rather, like his father, attach himself to the republic of Venice, which still possessed much external power and internal independence. Indeed, he laments the short-sighted policy of the Signory, in omitting this opportunity of securing, as an available check upon Spanish influence, an able confederate, and corn-growing neighbour; a blunder which was the more unaccountable, as, in the opinion of Mocenigo, who was Venetian envoy at Urbino many years later, the prepossessions of Guidobaldo were even then in favour of a connection which had hereditary claims upon his preference. On the first days of May the convention was published at Pesaro, after solemn thanksgiving to the Almighty for a dispensation so acceptable to the Duke.[1] The importance to Spain of this condotta may be understood from a fact mentioned by Riposati, that Gubbio alone sent forth, between 1530 and 1570, three captains-general, two lieutenants-general, six colonels, and sixty-five captains of note. Mocenigo says, there were in 1570 twelve thousand soldiers in the duchy, ready at call.

Our notices of Guidobaldo become ever more barren. In 1565 the armament of Sultan Solyman against Malta spread consternation throughout Western Europe, and, by desire of Philip II., the Duke of Urbino sent four or five thousand troops to aid in the defence of the knights. Prince Francesco Maria asked leave to accompany the expedition, but his father, considering his time better bestowed in visiting courts, sent him in this year to Madrid, with commission to recover a long arrear of his own military allowances. In this he was successful, but the sum

[1] From an account of this engagement preserved among the Oliveriana MSS., and slightly differing from that by Bernardo Tasso (II., letter 166), we learn that the pay of officers was from 15 to 40 scudi a month, that of cavalry privates 5, and of infantry 3 scudi. It appears to have been worth to Guidobaldo in all about 35,000 scudi a-year, but to have been irregularly received.

scarcely sufficed to clear the expenses of his journey. Particulars of this visit, and of his marriage in 1571, will be told from his own pen in next chapter. But there was no lukewarmness on his father's part on the question of the Cross against the Crescent. After the Prince returned from the naval action off Lepanto, which will also be narrated from his Autobiography, Guidobaldo prepared a Discourse on the propriety of a general war against the Turks, the means of conducting the proposed campaign with due regard to the security of Italy, the preparation of adequate munitions, and the best plan for carrying the seat of war into the enemy's country. It is unnecessary to dwell upon a matter now so completely gone by: the paper emanates from a mind capable of enlarged views, and fully conversant with the belligerent resources and general policy of his age, as well as experienced in military operations.[1]

The *Relazioni* of the Venetian envoys supply us with some notices of Urbino about this time, and prove that the Duke's expenses were very great, partly from frequent calls upon his hospitality by visitors of distinction, but still more from his maintaining separate and costly establishments for himself, the Duchess, the Prince, and the Princess.[2] Mocenigo estimates his income from imposts, monopolies, and allodial domains, at 100,000 scudi; adding that, "should he think proper to burden his people, this sum might unquestionably be greatly augmented, but, choosing to follow the custom of his predecessors, in making it his chief object to preserve the affection of his subjects, he is content to leave matters as they are, and live in straits for money."[3] He also tells us that, though poor in revenues,

[1] Vat. Ottob. MSS. No. 2510, f. 201.

[2] That of Mocenigo, 1570, is printed by Vieussieux, second series, vol. II., p. 97, and in the *Tesoro Politico*, II., 169; that of Zen or Zane, 1574, in the same volume of Vieussieux, p. 315.

[3] Of several statements as to the ducal revenue and expenditure which I have seen, none is distinct or satisfactory. The most detailed is in a MS. in the public library at Siena, K. III., No. 58, p. 240, but the sums have been inextricably blundered by the transcriber. See Appendix VIII.

he was master of his people's affections, who on an exigency would place life and substance at his disposal. The accuracy of these impressions is in some degree impugned by what we are now about to relate.

The most remarkable incident in Guidobaldo's reign was an outbreak of the citizens of Urbino, dignified in its municipal history by the name of a rebellion, which acquires a factitious importance as the only symptom of discontent that troubled the peace of the duchy, from the death of Oddantonio in 1443, to the extinction of its independence in 1631. We shall condense its incidents from the contemporary narrative of Gian-Francesco Cartolari, who designated himself agent of the Duke, and who, notwithstanding his official position, writes with apparent frankness and impartiality.[1]

In August, 1572, the Duke intimated to the council of Urbino that he had received authority from Gregory XIII. to impose a tax of one quatrino per lb. on butchers' meat, and of two bolognini upon every *staro* of grain and *soma* of wine;[2] and in October he made proclamation throughout the duchy of these new imposts. It being rumoured that the envoys of Gubbio had obtained for that community a suspension of the obnoxious duties, discontent began to prevail, and on the 26th December one Zibetto, a cobbler, in an inflammatory harangue, at a public assembly dignified with the name of general council, declared that these were exactions under which the poor could not exist.*[3] On his proposal, forty delegates were

[1] Vat. Ottob. MSS. No. 3142, f. 165, and Oliveriana MSS. No. 390, p. 63.

[2] The *staro* or *stajo* corresponded to a bushel; the amount of a *soma* is doubtful. A *quatrino* is $\frac{1}{8}$ of a *bajoccho*, that is, of a halfpenny in present value. A *bolognino* was about $7\frac{1}{8}$ farthings. See vol. II., p. 259.

*[3] In 1562 Guidobaldo had augmented the tax on grain by leave of Pius IV. Cf. UGOLINI, *op cit.*, vol. II., p. 28, and PELLEGRINI, *Gubbio sotto i Conti e Duchi d' Urbino* in *Boll. per l' Umbria*, vol. XI., p. 239 *et seq.*, and esp. CELLI, *Tasse e Rivolluzione* (Torino, 1892), p. 39.

chosen from the nobility, and sworn to represent the matter to the Duke in person. They repaired to Pesaro, and, on the 29th, had an audience to present the memorial agreed to by the council, which Guidobaldo received, and desired them to go home, promising that an answer would be transmitted when he had considered their statement. They, however, stayed a week, vainly looking for his reply, during which the council met daily at Urbino, and at length they were recalled by an express from the Gonfaloniere. Meanwhile a vice-duke had been sent thither, who, on the 1st of January, 1573, published a suspension of the new imposts throughout the whole state. This concession, however, did not satisfy the discontented, who, in another general council, accredited two envoys to Prince Francesco Maria, begging his intervention to procure an answer to their memorial. Having failed in this object, and finding that troops were being secretly organised to garrison their city, the people of Urbino rushed to arms, closed the gates, and, having mustered above a thousand men, began to strengthen the defences and lay in stores. The Vice-Duke being thereupon recalled, the general council assembled daily in such numbers, that adjournments to one of the largest churches were found necessary, and the inhabitants, setting aside private rivalries, co-operated with one mind for the public safety, mounting guard, and making every exertion to render their city tenable. The impossibility of doing so against the Duke's military levies being however quickly apparent even to the insurgents, an embassy of six was despatched to Rome to beseech the Pope's mediation. Nor did the reaction stop there; a general cry rose for the Prince, or his brother the Cardinal, the opportune arrival of either of whom would have ended the *emeute*. On the 29th, however, the Duchess came with a small suite, and was received with cries of "Long life to the Duke, but death to the *gabelle!*" The efforts of the magistracy and popular leaders to make their peace were unavailing, in consequence of their having sent representations to the Pontiff, and, on the 3rd of February, the Duchess departed without effecting any arrangement, to the infinite annoyance of all parties. The envoys could get no other reply from his Holiness but that they must go home and make submission, and they were followed by a brief from him, enjoining them to lay down arms and seek his Excellency's unconditional pardon. As soon as this had been publicly read by the Gonfaloniere, the people piled their arms in the piazza, and the peasantry dispersed to their country homes.

Notwithstanding this surrender, Guidobaldo advanced upon the city, quartering his troops in the surrounding villages, so as to blockade it, and all the public functionaries were superseded. Dreading a sack, the citizens rushed to the monasteries with their valuables, and, about the middle of February, sent fifty of the nobles to crave pardon of their sovereign. After waiting at Pesaro for three days, these were admitted to tender submission on their knees. and were then placed under arrest at their inn for twenty days, notwithstanding incessant petitions from their fellow citizens for their release. Six of them were then committed to the castle, and from time to time other leaders were brought from Urbino to share their imprisonment. So terrified were the insurgents by these measures, that those most compromised fled from the duchy, and but few remained in their houses; a proclamation was therefore issued that all exiles should return home within two months, under penalties of rebellion. The property of the prisoners and exiles was confiscated; the city was disarmed; public assemblies were prohibited; and the magistracy were discharged from their duties.[1] Such rigorous measures having inspired a general panic, the

[1] The magistrates of Urbino were four in number, a gonfaloniere chosen from the city nobles, a prior to represent the merchants, and two priors of the trades. The general council seems to have been open to all citizens.

imposts were again proclaimed at Easter, to include retrospectively the previous year. These severities were perhaps scarcely beyond the exigencies of the case; at all events, they cannot be justly regarded as an extreme exercise of the despotic authority which the Duke undoubtedly possessed; but those which ensued must be viewed with abhorrence, alike from their own enormity, and from their prejudicial influence in confounding vengeance with justice.

A judge was brought from Ferrara to sit upon the prisoners, and on the 1st of July nine of them were beheaded in the castle at midnight; their bodies, after being flung out and exposed beyond the city, were huddled together into an unconsecrated pit, until some days later they were taken up by order of the Bishop of Pesaro, and received Christian burial. Nor was the indignation of their sovereign appeased by these revolting cruelties: others implicated were sent to the galleys or died of hard usage. A commission sat at Urbino for two months to realise the estates of those attainted, whose widows and children were deprived of their dowries, and in some instances their very houses were razed to the ground. The results were fatal to the whole community, for magisterial business was suspended, the schools were left without teachers, the town without medical practitioners, trade of every sort at a stand. At length, in December, permission was obtained to hold a general council, at which it was determined once more to send ambassadors to intercede for mercy. For this purpose about eighty of the principal nobility were selected to accompany the Gonfaloniere and priors to Pesaro, their cavalcade amounting to above a hundred persons on horseback. On the 27th of December, they were admitted to an audience in presence of the whole court, and the Gonfaloniere, after a very judicious speech, presented to his Excellency a petition couched in the following terms :—

"Most illustrious and most excellent Lord Duke, our especial lord and master! Inspired by a most ardent desire for your illustrious Excellency's favour and good will, and having ever felt the utmost grief and regret for the recent events, the city of Urbino, with entire devotion and alacrity, has resolved to send to your illustrious Excellency its magistrates, and the present numerous embassy, in order that with every possible humility, they in our name, and we likewise for ourselves, may supplicate you, with all reverence and submission, to accord us grace and pardon, entirely forgetting the provocations received, and, as our clement father and master, full of charity towards us, to deign willingly to comfort us, and receive us again, and restore us to your love and benign grace; assuring your most illustrious Excellency, that this your city will never, in fidelity, love, and obedience towards your most illustrious person and house, yield to any other in the world, and that it is, and ever will be, most prompt at all times and occasions to expose our lives, and those of our children, and our whole goods and possessions, in your service and honour; so that, in the event of our receiving, as we desire and hope, forgiveness from your infinite bounty and magnanimity, we, the humblest and most faithful of your servants, thanking God with sincerely joyful hearts, may return, singing in chorus—'Blessed be the Lord God of Israel, who hath visited and redeemed his people,' and may ever keep in remembrance this trusted day of grace, and render it a gladsome festival in all time to come."

To this petition the Duke returned the following gracious answer:—"I hear with much good will and satisfaction the duty which you pay, the free pardon which you ask, and the penitence which you exhibit, all which induce me to confirm to you, as I now do most willingly, the forgiveness I already have accorded: and the promise which you make, of being ever faithful and loyal to me, proves you ready to second your words with good purposes, as I readily believe you will do. I also promise you from henceforward entirely to forget the past, and to receive you into my pristine affection; and had it pleased God that the warnings and persuasions which you received from my lips had been taken by you at first, you would have been spared many evils, annoyances, and losses, and I much displeasure. Nevertheless, take courage, and, as I have already said, so long as you do your duty, you will find me as loving in time to come as I have ever been, all which you will report to your city."[1]

This reply gave great satisfaction to the deputation, and after being suitably acknowledged by their head, all of them knelt to their Sovereign, the Duchess, and the Prince, kissing the hems of their garments in humble attitude. Next day they returned home, and summoned a general council, to which there was read a letter from Guidobaldo, reinstating the city in its former privileges, and removing the obnoxious imposts. Four deputies having been commissioned to thank his Highness for these demonstrations of returning favour, they were honourably received and entertained at Pesaro. The council next voted a peace-offering of 50,000 scudi towards paying the Duke's debts, which had been the primary root of the evil; but, in consideration of their recent sufferings, he accepted of but 20,000, payable in seven years. Although there remained some symptoms of smouldering sedition, the Duke on the 14th of June suddenly started for Urbino, and was welcomed by a deputation, and such other marks of respect as the short notice would permit. During a residence of twelve days, he renounced 8000 scudi of the donative, and conceded several privileges to the community, whom he did not again visit during the brief residue of his life.

The Urbino rebellion holds a place in the history of that state which neither its incidents nor its issue deserve.

[1] Vat. Ottob. MSS. No. 3141, ff. 160, 165, dated December 27, 1573.

It originated in a sore of old standing, the Duke having for years comparatively deserted the ancient capital of his duchy, and transferred his residence to Pesaro. Influenced by this grudge, its citizens, instead of, like the other communities, resting satisfied with his remission of dues in January, 1573, kept up an agitation, and finally piqued their sovereign by carrying their grievances to the papal throne. On the whole, these transactions were in all respects most unfortunate, and it was long ere the duchy recovered from the heart-burnings they left behind. The Duke then forfeited the popularity of a lifetime, and his fame continues blackened by the scurrilous traditionary nickname of Guidobaldaccio, a usual diminutive expressing contemptuous disparagement. Grossi says that, when too late, he regretted the harshness of his after measures; and some doubt as to his good faith in regard to an amnesty is hinted in the following letter from his cousin-german Ludovico Gonzaga, Duke of Nevers and Rethel, which I found among the Oliveriana MSS. at Pesaro.

"Most illustrious and most excellent Lord,

"Your Excellency's letters of the 15th of June and 9th of July reached me together, at the forest of Vincennes, only on the 10th instant, along with another addressed by you to the most serene King of Poland, which I have not failed to deliver in person to his Majesty, with such expressions as seemed suitably to convey your Excellency good wishes. With these his Majesty was much satisfied and pleased, and he returns to your Excellency many thanks. I have not as yet been able to obtain his answer, as he went off suddenly to Fontainbleau, whither I now am on my way, and on my arrival shall get it sent you as soon as possible.

"I have read the summary of the trials of these rebels, of whom your Excellency advises me you had nine beheaded, as to which matter I have been glad to be informed, in order satisfactorily to answer those who occasionally speak of it; and also being at all times glad to learn that your affairs go on well and to your contentment. It is my conviction that you have acted most justly, and done everything for clear reasons; yet, I do not omit telling you that some people are perplexed at these events, saying, that your Excellency having granted a general pardon to all the conspirators, they cannot see by what right you afterwards let justice take its course against them. This I mention purposely that you may be informed of everything.

"It only remains to beseech that you will deign command my willing services, in whatever respect you consider me useful, as this is my ardent wish; and so I sincerely kiss your hands, praying God to grant you all happiness. From Paris, the last of September, 1573. Your Excellency's most devoted, and most obliged cousin,

"LUDOVICO GONZAGA."

The account of these disturbances, given by the Prince in his Autobiography, is as follows: "His father having by great liberality and magnificence deranged his finances, found it necessary to augment his revenue, and his subjects, unused to such burdens, began to offer resistance. The Duke, not to let himself be thwarted in that way, prepared to use force; but at last matters were restored to quiet, by their humbling themselves, and receiving his pardon, not without the punishment of some, as an example to the rest. At this juncture Francesco Maria contrived so to conduct himself, that his father had reason to be well satisfied with his services; and the people had no cause to be discontented with him, his uniform endeavour having been, to the utmost of his power, to mollify the one and moderate the other, which was in the end effected."

Of this dull reign little remains to be told. In the

words of the same Memoir,—"Guidobaldo went to Ferrara in the autumn of 1574, to visit Henry III. of France, who was on his way from Poland, on the death of his brother Charles IX. Returning to Pesaro during great heats, he fell ill, and passed to a better life on the 28th of September, aged sixty. On hearing of his illness, Francesco Maria hastened to Pesaro from Castel Durante, where he generally stayed for the hunting season, and finding his father in great suffering, he attended him assiduously through the fatal malady. The funeral ceremonies were performed with much pomp, in presence of many deputies and ambassadors; and Giacomo Mazzoni pronounced a long and elaborate oration, commending his clemency, liberality, bravery, prudence, and other princely virtues." We are told by a contemporary chronicler that his illness was a quartan, which became a putrid fever, but that he bore it with patient and pious resignation, supported by the aids of religion. His funeral took place in the church of Corpus Domini, at Pesaro, in conformity with his own wish, mindful perhaps, in his last moments, of his recent quarrel with Urbino, where the ashes of his ancestors were laid.

The character of this Duke, drawn by the Venetian envoys, is quite as favourable as the few notices given us by Urbino writers. His habits were free and social, and his liberality to friends and favourites gave him a popularity at court which extended to his subjects and soldiery. In affairs of honour his judgment was often sought, and his decisions generally admitted. Though seldom in the field, he was considered an authority on military affairs, and, without rivalling the literary tastes of his son, he was a patron of letters, and especially of music.*[1] The device

*[1] Cf. a letter from Angelo Colocci to the Duke, printed by MORICI, *Due Umanisti Marchigiani* in *Boll. per l'Umbria*, vol. II., p. 152; and for Music, ROSSI, *Appunti per la Storia della Musica alla Corte di Francesco Maria I. e di Guidobaldo della Rovere* in *Rassegna Emiliana* (Modena, 1888), vol. I., fascicolo 8, and *supra*, p. 88, note *1.

which he selected was a goal or winning-post, with a Greek inscription, "To the most devoted lover of worth"; and Ruscellai informs us that he acted up to the sentiment in encouraging merit. His hospitality is alluded to by Ariosto in Rinaldo's journey to Lapidusa, and Count Litta ascribes to him the institution of the Pacieri, an association of both sexes for the purpose of preventing litigation. It is true that his failings of character or temper were neither gilded by the military renown of his father, nor redeemed by the pious philosophy of his son; but so far as the meagre materials within our reach have enabled us to judge, no great faults have been brought home to him either as a sovereign or as a man. Indeed, we are enabled to adduce one satisfactory instance wherein, under circumstances peculiarly irritating to a person of impetuous disposition, his conduct was marked with great forbearance and gentleness. His favourite undertaking of fortifying Sinigaglia had been thwarted in 1556, from the obstinate refusal of money by a Jew, who, though sent to him for the purpose of effecting a loan, resisted his urgent persuasions to conclude it.*[1] After mentioning the circumstance in a letter to his confidential favourite Marchetti, he thus continues: "We avoided all expressions which might seem to approve of his discourse, and so left him. However, to you we shall just say that if they won't lend, may they meet with the like.[2] We shall seek some other course, and obtain by other means what is required for the operations. You may, therefore, after doing your best for this purpose in Sinigaglia, proceed first towards La Pergola, and then to Fossombrone, but there is no occasion to employ in this matter threats or severe language. On the contrary, you are only to seek out the people, to exhort and civilly urge them to what is wanted,

*[1] Cf. Celli, *Le fortificazioni militari di Urbino, Pesaro e Sinegalia* (Castelpiano, 1896).

[2] "Tal sia di loro," a phrase which may perhaps only mean "be it so."

but of their own free will, and by no other means; and if they will not agree, you need not break out upon them, but let it stand over, that we may see what can be effected in some other way."

In absence of any contemporary estimate of this Duke's character, we may cite one from the pen of a modern writer, himself a citizen of Urbino, and an enthusiastic student of its history. "Although possessing not the marvellous sagacity, the untainted justice, the quick intelligence in public affairs, nor the other brilliant and rare virtues of his ancestors and of his son, which have rendered their names great, their authority respected, their memory dear and popular; he had good sense, military experience, and much fondness for all liberal acquirements. He protected and honoured the first geniuses of his time; and his beneficent actions were splendid even beyond his means. Could one page be blotted from his life, too fatally memorable from its unjust and slippery policy, too detestable and disgraceful to his name; and had his manners been more affable, his nature less impetuous and violent, his temper less overbearing, and his resolutions less inflexible; the people of Urbino would probably have attempted no revolutionary movement, and he would have acquired much of the reputation left by his great-grandfather, and by his estimable son."[1]

For the fine arts he seems to have cared little, and his memory has suffered in consequence of this neglect. Angelo Bronzino is said to have painted him during the life of his father, but the only original portrait I have ever found of him is a miniature in the Pitti Palace. Bernardo Tasso was the laureate of his court, and we shall mention, in chapter L., the friendly welcome extended to that fortune-stricken bard during part of his life-long struggle. Bernardo Capello and Pietro Aretino were among his guests; and Ludovico Domenichini of Piacenza, having

[1] Padre Checcucci, Professor of Rhetoric in the University of Urbino, 1845.

dedicated to him an Italian translation of Plutarch's *Lives*, visited Urbino in 1555 to present the work to his patron.

Guidobaldo left by his first wife one daughter,—

VIRGINIA, married in 1560 to Count Federigo Borromeo, whose premature death is said to have frustrated a project of his uncle, Pius IV., for investing him with Camerino. She afterwards married Ferdinando Orsini, Duke of Gravina, and, dying in childbed, left to her father about 180,000 scudi.

The children of his second marriage were,—

1. FRANCESCO MARIA, his heir.
2. ISABELLA, married in 1565 to Nicolò Bernardino di Sanseverino, Prince of Bisignano, a Neapolitan nobleman, with a fine fortune, but greatly encumbered. She was a princess of generous and attractive character, and died in 1619 without surviving issue.
3. LAVINIA, said in the Venetian Relazione of Zane to have been betrothed to Giacomo Buoncompagno natural son of Gregory XIII., but the nuptials never took place. She afterwards married Alfonso Felice d' Avalos d' Aquino, Marquis of Guasto, son *[1] of the famous Vittoria Colonna, and died in 1632, aged seventy-four.

   (From similarity of name, this princess has been confused with her second cousin Lavinia Franciotti della Rovere, wife of Paolo Orsini, whose intimacy with Olympia Morata is well known to those who trace the quickly smothered seeds of Protestantism in Italy.)

Guidobaldo left also two natural daughters,—

1. ——, married, first, to Count Antonio Landriano of Pesaro; secondly, to Signor Pier-Antonio da Lunà of Castella, in the Milanese.
2. ——, married to Signor Guidobaldo Renier.

*[1] This is a mistake. Vittoria Colonna had no children. There was, however, a Marchese del Vasto, a cousin of her husband's, whom she adopted as her son, and to whom she frequently alluded in her poems; one of her sonnets bewails his death.

BOOK EIGHTH

OF FRANCESCO MARIA II. DELLA ROVERE SIXTH AND LAST DUKE OF URBINO

CHAPTER XLIV

Autobiography of Duke Francesco Maria II.—His visit to the Spanish Court—His studious habits—His marriage—Is engaged in the naval action of Lepanto—Succeeds to the dukedom.

IN following the history of his father, we have details of the early life of Francesco Maria. Upon these we now turn back, and shall avail ourselves to the utmost of the Memoirs he has left behind him, which, though brief and incomplete, afford a valuable illustration of his character, and an interesting addition to our few autobiographies of sovereigns. From the introductory sentence, we learn the motives by which they were undertaken:—"As it is very usual for people to blame the actions of others, and especially the proceedings of those who have long directed the affairs of government, it has hence seemed to me right to narrate simply, truly, and briefly, the incidents that have occurred to Francesco Maria, second of that name and sixth Duke of Urbino, in order that those who read this abstract may be aware of the actual and candid truth." Upon a narrative thus modestly prefaced it is unnecessary to make any critical remarks. Ere we close this Book, their abrupt termination, before the marriage of Prince Federigo, will be sadly but sufficiently accounted for.[1]

[1] For the life of Francesco Maria II. our materials have been ample. His own Memoirs, extending from his birth to the marriage of his son, have been nearly all quoted verbatim. The autograph of this MS. I have examined in the Oliveriana Library (No. 384, folio 219 to 229), but have made my translations from the only printed edition, in the twenty-ninth volume of the *Nuova Raccolta d' Opuscoli*, known by the name Calogeriana, and published at Venice in 1776. There too will be found an account of the Devolution

"To them [Duke Guidobaldo II. and Duchess Vittoria] was born at Pesaro, on the 20th of February, 1549, a son, who was named Francesco Maria. Cardinal Duranti was sent by the Pope to perform the ceremony of his baptism, which was celebrated with great splendour on the 1st of May, Giacomo Soranzo acting as godfather in name of the republic of Venice. He was in infancy brought up with becoming care, and at three years of age was carried to Venice by his father and mother. Guidobaldo was then general in the service of that state, and their troops were chiefly stationed at Verona, whither Francesco Maria was taken, and where he had a dangerous illness, recovered from which he returned home. There, as he grew up, he was taught all fitting exercises of mind and body, under the successive superintendence of Muzio of Giustinopoli, Antonio Galli of Urbino, and Girolamo Simonetta of Cagli: his masters in grammar were Vincenzo Bartoli of Urbino, and afterwards Ludovico Corrado of Mantua, of literary note. After some years, the Duke and his brother the Cardinal, having resolved to amuse themselves with a visit to Venice, at the fête of the Ascension, they took with them Francesco Maria, who was received with great favour and much made of, being admitted into the company delle Calze." This was in 1564, and even thus early his taste for painting was

of Urbino to the Holy See, from the pen of Antonio Donata of Venice, by whom that negotiation was concluded on the Duke's part. In the Magliabechiana Library at Florence (class 25, No. 76) is the autograph Diary of Francesco Maria from 1583 to 1623, which I have closely searched. The rich MS. collections of the Oliveriana are stored with original correspondence and other documents illustrative of his reign, most of which have been looked into with scarcely remunerative labour, but among the matter there gleaned, his instructions to his son may be deemed of especial importance. From a vast mass of such correspondence in these two libraries, a general insight into his character and position, and those of his son, has been acquired, as well as many minute traits of both; but the Prince's brief and unhonoured span has been illustrated in a great measure from collections made by Francesco Saverio Passeri, of Pesaro, nephew of the naturalist Gianbattista Passeri, and printed in the twenty-sixth volume of the Calogeriana Collection. * Cf. also SCOTINI, *La Giovinezza di F. M. II.* (Bologna, 1899).

noticed by Titian, and celebrated in a sonnet by Verdizzotti. An establishment was maintained for him at Venice apart from that of his father and uncle, and he gave many sumptuous entertainments.

"Having returned to Pesaro, and completed his sixteenth year, he had a great wish to go forth and see the world and its usages, and made much interest that his father should send him to some court, preferring that of the Emperor, who was then at war with the Turk. To this his father was pleased to agree, but desired first to consult the Catholic King (Philip II.), in whose service he was, and who in reply commended the plan, but desired that it might be carried into effect at his own court, where the Prince would be welcomed and treated as a son. His intentions being thus necessarily altered, at the close of 1565, after the marriage of his sister Donna Isabella with the Prince of Bisignano, he took his way to Spain, accompanied by many knights, particularly by Count Francesco Landriani, and Pier-Antonio Lonato. Choosing the route by Genoa, he passed through Ferrara to Mantua, where he stayed fifteen days by his father's desire, who in youth long inhabited that city; and hearing of his uncle the Duke of Parma's return just then from Flanders, he went to see him. On his arrival at Genoa he was lodged by Count Filippino Doria, his vassal in the castle of Sassocorbaro, and, after being visited and much distinguished by the Signory, he embarked in a war-galley of the Duke of Savoy, which, with another fully armed, had been sent on purpose for him, under the command of Admiral di Leini. In it he went to Savona, the native place of his family, where he was received into the house of Vigeri, who were his subjects, and being storm-stayed during eight days of the carnival, was entertained with festivities and serenades, as is customary in that country.

"When the weather cleared, he re-embarked, and after a pleasant voyage of a few days reached Palamos in Spain, whence he went by land to Barcelona. In that city he passed most of Lent, to give time for an apartment being prepared for him in the palace, but got to Madrid for Easter week. He was met by the whole court and by many grandees, especially by the Marquis of Pescara, who manifested singular courtesy, attending to him as his own son; whence a most intimate and enduring friendship arose between them. He got the same quarters which the Prince of Florence had occupied shortly before, and his treatment was precisely similar. Next day he waited upon the King, Queen, and Prince Royal, the Princess of Portugal, and the two sons of the Emperor [Maximilian II.], who were being educated there. By all he was received with distinguished favour, which continued during the two years and a half he spent at Madrid. He occupied himself in all those noble exercises which there, more than anywhere else, were attended to, practising military games on foot and horseback in public, and also privately under superintendence of the Marquis of Pescara, who was then considered unequalled in them. He frequently went out hunting with Don Carlos, by whom he was received into much intimacy; and enjoyed a close friendship with Don John of Austria, afterwards the famed commander by sea and land. He also paid court to the ladies, and learned the sports of the jennet as practised there, from Don Pedro Enciquel, afterwards Count of Fuentes and general in Flanders.

"Some movements having occurred in Flanders, the King gave orders to proceed there, and the court, including Francesco Maria, made preparations to attend him. But the latter, wishing to see France, asked permission to take that route by land, and so to rejoin his Majesty, who was to go by sea. The King, desiring his attendance on his person, refused his request, and so the opportunity was lost, to his great mortification, and perhaps to the no small loss of his Majesty. Subsequently occurred the imprisonment of Don Carlos, which was thus effected by order of his own father. An hour after midnight, the King, in his dressing-gown, holding a candle in his hand, having gone down to the Prince's room with his council of state and but one gentleman of his chamber, found him in bed. The Prince on seeing them tried to reach the corner, where were his sword and a pair of arquebuses, which he kept there always ready; but this was prevented by the Duke of Feria, who had already secured these arms. Then, rushing to his father, he exclaimed, "So you are come to kill me?' To this his Majesty replied, 'Not so, but because you must live as becomes you, so be calm;' and never addressed him again. The Prince then said, 'I see that I am taken for a madman, which I am not, though a desperate one.' The King, having seen the doors and windows nailed up, leaving only a shutter open for light, and having desired the arms and all such things to be taken away, returned to his apartment, leaving with Don Carlos his major-domo Ruggo Mez de Silva (?) with several chamberlains and other officers of his household, a guard of Germans being stationed outside of his door; and the court was greatly vexed thereat."

These details are curious, in illustration of the mysterious fate of Don Carlos, eldest son of Philip II. It seems agreed that he was of a most unhappy temperament, perverse, wilful, and violent, possibly insane. The immediate cause of the unnatural scene here described has never been satisfactorily explained. It is generally stated that he was discovered in treasonable correspondence with the Dutch; though others have attributed the behaviour of his father to jealousy of an old attachment between his wife Elizabeth of Valois, and the Prince, to whom she was said to have been previously promised. The Prince's arrest occurred in January 1568: it was followed by no trial or public investigation, but in the following July he ceased to live. His death was understood to have taken place under some judicial sanction, but whether by poison or the sword was never known. The entombment of his head separate from his body renders the second supposition more probable.

We may here mention that, before embarking for Spain, the Prince had, from his Cardinal uncle, the dukedom of Sora, yielding an income of about 4000 scudi, which, however, proved quite inadequate to his expenditure. Zane, the Venetian ambassador, asserts that the large arrears of pay due to his father, which he was commissioned to recover from the Spanish government, were more than absorbed by his extravagance, and that this was the reason of his recall. His own narrative, however, is entirely silent upon this subject.

"Francesco Maria, having been at length recalled by his father, who was anxious for the marriage of his only son and heir, took leave of the King and Queen, and the royal family, and proceeded by Saragossa to Barcelona, where he embarked in a galley with the Marquis of Pescara, then going as viceroy to Sicily. After a prosperous voyage of eight days, he reached Genoa, where he lived with Giovanni Andrea Doria, with whom he had become intimate at the court of Spain. Thence he went to Milan for some days, and was welcomed with distinction; and then visited Madame of Austria at Piacenza; and at Parma stayed with the Duke and his son, towards both of whom he maintained the best intelligence and cousinship. He next passed through Bologna to Ravenna, where his uncle, the Cardinal of Urbino, was archbishop, and accompanied him to Pesaro. He arrived on the 11th of July, 1568, and was received with the greatest joy by all classes.

"After a few months, seeing that his father made no movement in the affair of his marriage, he returned to his studies, interrupted during his absence from Italy. He read mathematics with Federigo Comandino, and

Franz Hanfstaengl

ISABELLA D'ESTE

After the picture by Titian in the Imperial Museum, Vienna

afterwards philosophy with Cesare Benedetti (subsequently Bishop of Pesaro), Felice Pacciotti, Giacomo, Mazzoni, and Cristofero Guarimone. At the same time he kept up active exercise in arms, riding, hunting, ball, and racket." About this time Mocenigo, the Venetian ambassador, praises his fine dispositions and pleasing manners, as well as his progress in various pursuits, especially mathematics and fortification; but says that his eager exposure to fatigue gave rise to apprehensions for his health, which were sadly realised. He adds that, since his return from Spain, something of the hauteur which characterised that nation was noticed in his manner.

"Finally the Duke decided upon his marriage with Donna Lucrezia d'Este, sister of Alfonso, the last Duke of Ferrara, which took place, though little to his taste; for she was old enough to have been his mother. He went for this purpose to Ferrara, where the nuptials were celebrated with great splendour, and with chivalrous games and other festivities."

Such is all that we learn from the Memoirs of Francesco Maria regarding one of the most eventful moments of his life. Passeri, in his collections for the life of Prince Federigo, mentions a rumour of his attachment to a lady at the Spanish court as the immediate cause of his recall home, and of the match with Princess Lucrezia being concluded; indeed, I have seen, in the correspondence of the Oliveriana Library, that a certain Donna Madalena Girona was the supposed object of that early affection. That he made no secret to his father of his distaste at the connection laid out for him, is stated on the same authority, as well as the Duke's answer, that his people's welfare was to be considered rather than his son's fancies, whose youth made it the more requisite to mate him with a princess of tried prudence and staid manners. How far these epithets were borne out by Lucrezia's subsequent conduct will be presently seen; meanwhile, the following letter, to one who long after continued an especial friend and favourite, will show that the bridegroom gave no outward signs of his discontent.

"To Camillo Giordani.

"My most magnificent and well-beloved,

"I am confident that you feel the pleasure which you express at the conclusion which it has pleased God to vouchsafe to my marriage with Madam Lucrezia d'Este, and at all other like occasions of joy which happen to me; and the duty you have in this instance paid me in your letter has been most truly acceptable, and has my best thanks. God ever bless you! From Pesaro, the last day of [15]69. "THE PRINCE OF URBINO."

The ceremony took place at Ferrara on the 2nd of January, 1571, and on the 8th the bride was brought home to Pesaro. The people hailed her with enthusiasm, and spent largely in shows and rejoicings to welcome her arrival, besides giving to the Duke a donative exceeding 10,000 scudi. Yet Mocenigo, the Venetian ambassador accredited to the marriage, while lauding the handsome and gracious Princess, admits an early prepossession against her, on the part both of her new subjects and her lord. It was the hope of a heir to the dukedom that preponderated with the former; and, as she was many years older than her husband, a chill of disappointment naturally mingled even with their congratulations.[1] The same observer states it as the general impression that, the Prince having compromised himself with a lady in Spain, his father thought the best way of getting him out of all difficulty with that court was to match him suddenly with a princess of high rank, whose dowry of 150,000 scudi

[1] Tesoro Politico, II., fol. 169. Relazioni Venete, serie II., vol. II., p. 105. Litta says she was born the 16th December, 1535, making her thirteen years and two months his senior. Her sister, Tasso's Leonora, was born the 19th of June, 1537.

was by no means unacceptable. Zane, another envoy from the maritime Republic a few years later, describes the Duchess as below par in good looks, but well-dressed: adding that difference of age accounted for the absence of affection between her and her husband.

The following letters from the Duke and Duchess of Urbino, Prince Francesco Maria and his bride, were written in answer to congratulations sent them on occasion of the marriage, by the Cardinal de' Medici, who afterwards became Grand Duke of Florence, by the title of Ferdinand I.[1] They have been introduced here as an index to the feelings of the respective writers regarding a union which turned out so unsatisfactory to all parties; but, still more, as a specimen of the epistolary style then prevalent between personages of exalted rank, and of the general formality and barrenness of interest which characterise such documents.

"My most illustrious, most reverend, and most respected Lord,

"The Marquis of Villa Franca has discharged towards me the duty with which your most illustrious Lordship was pleased to entrust him, and he has represented your gracious sympathy towards our wedding in a manner most acceptable to all. For the satisfaction we, and myself especially, have derived from this, I do most heartily thank your most illustrious Lordship, praying you to lend a willing ear to the assurances of my affection, and of my wish for frequent opportunities of correspondence, which I have given to the Marquis, and which I do not doubt he will, without fail, in compliance with my desire, fully repeat to you. I kiss your most illustrious Lordship's hands, praying for you all happiness. From Pesaro, the 15th of January, 1571.

"Your most Illustrious Lordship's servant,

"THE DUKE OF URBINO."

[1] Bibl. Riccardiana, MSS. No. 2340, art. 116–19.

"My most illustrious, most revered, and most respected Lord,

"The proof which your most illustrious Lordship has deigned to give me, in your most kind letter, of the pleasure you take in the marriage of the Prince my son, I esteem a great favour; for not only do I desire your sympathy in all my happiness, but I am also anxious in every circumstance to find occasion of serving your most illustrious Lordship. Thus will all my present and future occasions of joy be valued by me in proportion as they may become subservient to that object, and to the affection I bear your most illustrious Lordship, whose hands I kiss, praying the Lord God of his grace to vouchsafe you a happy accomplishment of all your desires. From Pesaro, the 15th of January, 1571.

"Your most illustrious and most reverend Lordship's most humble servant,

"THE DUCHESS OF URBINO."

"My most illustrious and most reverend Lord,

"The Marquis of Villa Franca, who has handed me your most illustrious Lordship's letter, will likewise report to you my unceasing desire for your service, and the pleasure wherewith I have received the courteous duty you have been pleased on this occasion to send me, for which I certainly am under many obligations, as the Marquis will more fully show you. I, however, pray your illustrious Lordship to afford me frequent opportunities of effectually proving to you my good will; and I kiss your hands, beseeching for you from our Lord God all the happiness you may desire. From Pesaro, the 15th of January, 1571.

"Your most illustrious and most reverend Lordship's most affectionate servant,

"THE PRINCE OF URBINO."

"Most illustrious and most reverend Lord,

"Whatever pleasure my affairs may afford your most illustrious Lordship is only the consequence of your great kindness and courtesy; and as regards the expression of it, which you have thought fit to communicate to me by the Marquis of Villa Franca, and by your own letters, I can but say that I kiss your hand for all your affection, assuring you that every occasion of happiness you may enjoy will afford me cause for quite as much congratulation as I now have received from you: and referring you to whatever more that gentleman will say in my behalf, I remain, praying God to gratify you in all your desires,

"Your most illustrious Lordship's very obedient,

"Lucrezia d' Este.

"From Pesaro, the 16th of January, 1571."

Renée of France, mother of Princess Lucrezia, had embraced the doctrines of Calvin, who visited Ferrara about the time of her daughter's birth, and Francesco Porta da Creta, preceptor of the young Princess, was discovered to be tinged with the same principles. Alarmed for the orthodoxy of his daughters, Duke Ercole dismissed their instructor, and secluded his escort, in a wing of the palace, from all intercourse with the children. A cloud of mystery hangs over these transactions.

"Soon after his return to Pesaro from his marriage, the Pope, the King of Spain, and the Venetians having [on the 20th of May] leagued together against the Turk, Don John of Austria came into Italy as commander-in-chief, and Francesco Maria, with his father's permission, set out on the 8th of July, to join him at Genoa. There he embarked in the *Savoyard* frigate[1] that had carried him to Spain, commanded by the same Monsignor de Leini,

[1] The word which I thus translate means literally a ship or galley commanded by a captain.

who had orders from the Duke of Savoy to receive him with that affectionate courtesy which both he and his sovereign ever displayed towards him. Having touched at Naples, he was there welcomed with the utmost favour and distinction, and passed his time most agreeably. From thence the fleet sailed to Messina, where he assisted at a general council of war, as indeed he often subsequently did.[1] Leaving Sicily, the expedition in a few days arrived at Corfu, and on the morning of the 7th of October fell in with the Turk. Don John drew up the Christian fleet in order of battle, the Proveditore Agostino Barbarigo, of Venice, having the landward squadron, and Giovanni Andrea Doria the opposite and heavier one, with Don Alvarez di Bassano as a reserve; the centre he kept for himself, where was also Francesco Maria, in the foresaid frigate. Here was the thick of the fight, as at this point the two admirals met. The Turkish at first selected the frigate in which was Francesco Maria, whom he well knew, and who warmly received his attack; but as soon as he distinguished the flag-ship, he turned to engage it: and, after fighting for two hours, the Turks struck, their admiral, Pacha Ali, having been killed by an arquebus; the others were all put to the sword; and so was this long very doubtful victory secured to the Christians. Meanwhile the *Savoyard* frigate fought two galleys, one ahead and the other astern, and had enough to do, most of her company being killed or wounded. The squadron under Barbarigo drove on shore many galleys, sinking and taking others; but he was wounded by a splinter in the eye, of which he soon after died. Doria had at first run out to sea, fighting all the while; but seeing the wing exposed, he returned and made good use of the opportunity, cutting up several galleys, and getting off uninjured. Such is an abstract of this battle, wherein

[1] The muster-roll of the armament at this time will be found in V, of the Appendix,

Francesco Maria acquitted himself becomingly, for which Don John distinguished him with many marks of regard, and assigned him, among other favours, twenty-four Turkish slaves. The Admiral bearing for Sicily, he sailed from Corfu in a Venetian galley to Otranto, and returned home by land in November, to await orders, and rejoin the fleet the following year."

The naval engagement of which Francesco Maria has given the preceding sketch was that of Lepanto or Curzolari, where Passeri states that he had with him a large body of his father's subjects, a fact which, although passed over in his own account of this his only military service, is confirmed by Armanni, who tells us that there were in the fleet above fifty from Gubbio alone, thirty of whom were officers, a circumstance on which the Prince was complimented by Don John. It is unnecessary here to add to the Prince's details. The general result of the engagement was most conclusive: the enemy's loss has been calculated at thirty thousand killed, ten thousand wounded, and fifteen thousand Christian slaves rescued from bondage, besides the destruction or capture of six hundred sail, and a vast booty. The Christian fleet consisted of above two hundred war-galleys, besides many other vessels of various sorts.

"On bringing his wife from Ferrara to Pesaro [in January, 1572], they were magnificently received, and passed a gay carnival. In Lent he repaired to Rome, after visiting the holy house of Loreto, and was there entertained by his uncles, the Cardinals of Urbino and Farnese. Pius V. insisted upon very graciously admitting him to an audience, notwithstanding an illness of which he soon died.[1] . . . . Francesco Maria was also distinguished by his successor, Gregory XIII., but, on suddenly being re-

[1] Particulars of those intrigues in the conclave, by which Cardinal Buoncompagni prevailed over his rivals Morone and Farnese, are omitted, having no reference to our immediate subject.

called by his father, he at once, though reluctantly, obeyed. Soon afterwards, he was attacked by a severe illness, which lasted for three months, aggravated by a false rumour of another naval engagement."

The part taken by the Prince in the unhappy disturbances of Urbino has been already shown from his own pen, and that of other narrators, as well as his attendance upon his father's death-bed.*[1] We have now, therefore, to enter upon his reign, and here again we have recourse to his memoirs:—"The new Duke departed from Urbino, where he showed himself at the archiepiscopal palace in his robes of sovereignty, and then, as was usual, rode through the streets, on a milk-white steed, dressed in white, and under canopy, thereafter receiving the oaths of allegiance in the great hall of the palace: all this he repeated at Sinigaglia." Among the Oliverian MSS. is this account of the ceremonial, curiously illustrative of the manners of the age:—"After mass of the Holy Spirit had been sung, the Archbishop, Felice of Cagli, advanced to the door of the cathedral, and thence, accompanied by the Gonfaloniere, the three priors, and the people, went to bring forth the Prince from the palace. He wore a riband and scarf of white damask; on his head a crown of pearls, from behind which there hung some bands; and on his shoulders a short cloak of white fur. When he reached the head of the stair in the archiepiscopal palace, on which was a carpet and a cushion, the Archbishop held the Cross for him to kiss. He then entered the church, and approached the high altar, on which was the Holy Sacrament, where, after the usual devotions, accompanied with beautiful sacred music, the Primate read certain prayers and pronounced the benediction, and his Highness made offertory of a piece of ten scudi. He then retired to an adjoining chapel, and, changing his dress, put on

*[1] Cf. Celli, *Storia della Sollevazione di Urbino contro il Duca Guidobaldo, 1572–4* (Torino, 1892).

a mantle of white, with cap and feathers, in which he issued from the church, and mounted a handsome charger. The Gonfaloniere preceded him on horseback, his drawn sword in his hand, calling aloud, 'Long live the Duke of Urbino!' and the people followed, repeating the cry. Thus they went through the city and returned to the palace. The populace then took off his cloak; and M[aestr]o Antonio Fazino asked his cap, and received it. In like manner he was stripped of his spurs; and his Highness then presented his horse to the city youths, and Mo. Calber Galler mounted it. Mo. Antonio Corboli and the Cavaliere Guido Staccoli next put him on his spurs, Mo. Flaminio Bonaventura his mantle, and Mo. Antonio Fazino held his horse. Having been by this formality elected, he went into the great hall, where the Gonfaloniere and priors, with all the deputies of other cities, by a formal instrument gave their oaths of allegiance, whilst he, in a letter read in his presence by Mo. Giulio Veterani, his secretary, promised to be to them a loving sovereign; after which, all the people came one by one to kiss his hand. All this was done with much rejoicing on the part of the public, and of his Highness, to whom may God grant grace to rule his subjects to the contentment of all."

The following letter, to the young Duke upon his succession, is printed in the correspondence of Girolamo Muzio, his preceptor, whose advices, though somewhat long, well merit attention, totally opposed as they are in spirit to then prevailing principles of government, and anticipating opinions even in our day charily developed in Italy. It is, above all, interesting to discover, on such satisfactory evidence, the political views which must have been inculcated on Francesco Maria from his early years, and which bore some seed in after life, notwithstanding the natural defects of his temper, and the crotchets imbibed from a false philosophy. Had such counsels been generally given and followed, constitutional government in Italy would now have been neither a mockery nor a bone of contention.

"Men tried by difficulties and crosses nerve themselves to endure them; yet, knowing how your Excellency has long suffered from many troubles and annoyances, I shall undertake no vain task in wishing to offer consolation in this your new vexation and trial. I need not now say with what grief I have heard of the late sad event, knowing as you do how true a servant I was of his Excellency our Sovereign. On the contrary, I shall address myself to talk of certain considerations which appear to me beseeming the succession you have obtained, through a long and noble ancestry, meaning to speak to you with the freedom and loyalty which a servant should display when his master's interests are at stake; and upon this understanding I shall begin.

"I remember more than once, while conversing with the illustrious Duchess your mother, to have lamented the manner in which I observed the government of the state conducted, praying the Almighty to protect you from the risk of being expelled from it, as there would have been no reasonable hope of the people recalling you again; a fact of which her good sense was fully aware. It would be long and irksome were I to repeat the various matters that I disapproved of, but from them I can deduce certain rules which it seems to me you ought to adopt for regulation of your authority, and the maintenance of justice, so as to reacquire and preserve the affection of your subjects. But, Sire, permit me to drop ceremonious designations, in order more readily to express my views.

"Let it be your first care, then, to endow the magistrates and city authorities with the ample jurisdiction which their duties require, enjoining upon them to execute justice without respect to persons; command also your courtiers not to interfere in private suits, and do you in like manner yourself forbear meddling with such, leaving the judges to proceed therein by the usual course. Further, should the judge be suspected by either party, let the cause be remitted to another, or let an assessor be named; and, to such alleged suspicion, it is no sufficient answer that any one may be doubted by anybody. In short, it is enough that the judges proceed to pronounce sentence in the regular way; and for such as feel aggrieved, the common and appropriate remedies are open. In my time the custom was abolished—I know not at whose recommendation—of sending causes to be inquired into by a council of skilled persons [a jury?]; it was an excellent and much approved mode of judging, and on that account it would be more advisable to return to it than to leave it off. Statutory penalties have also been changed to arbitrary ones, which has effected great alterations; for where the statutes condemned ten, caprice has multiplied by hundreds, with what justice I know not. This was, indeed, by advice of certain doctors, who declared that the Prince's will ought to be held as law,—a diabolical sentiment, since it is not the absolute will, but the virtuous and upright opinion of the Prince that should be deemed law; nor do I see how any virtuous and honest opinion can contravene statutes confirmed by mutual agreement, and sanctioned by oaths.

"Be specially attentive in hearing those who bring complaints of oppression or injury received from your ministers or courtiers, and refuse not to listen even to such as accuse those most dear to you; on the contrary, lend them all your ears, for in proportion as your favourites can reckon upon you, they are likely to consider themselves safe in committing outrages and insults. Think not you can have about you persons who will never make a slip, whether from love, or hatred, or dishonesty. Hear, therefore, by all means hear, and punish him who has either done amiss, or who has brought a false charge. And such audiences you may give at all seasons and places, even when going to mass, or in your moments of recreation, without engaging yourself for a future day; for quarrels may arise requiring prompt remedy, and which cannot wait a future day or hour. By these means you may easily secure the execution of justice, because there will eventually not be many such disputes, when once, by a few examples of severity, you have brought your magistrates, your court, and consequently the rest of your subjects, into such discipline that you will have few complaints to listen to, and will be able to govern your state with little trouble. But see in the commencement to give proof of your vigour, that matters may subsequently proceed favourably.

"When others have suffered injury or offence, do them justice, punishing offenders for the general satisfaction; for you may be sure that to visit offences committed upon others protects yourself from the like, whilst impunity gives security to offenders. In the matter of third parties, clemency need not be thought of, forgiveness of a fault being a favour bestowed, which affects the interest of the party offended; thus, he who pardons injuries done to me, disposes of what I alone should dispose of, which is unjust. It may be well to remit injuries done to yourself, for that is your own affair, and it is worthy of a magnanimous prince to pardon when he might punish; but a sovereign ought never to forgive offences against others without their special consent, which cannot be freely given if he intimates such to be his desire. Should disputes arise among your people involving individual honour, you must be judge of this, as much as of charges touching their life and property. Indeed, you ought to decide judicially as to whose reputation is intact and whose compromised; and by chastising any unworthy action, you will at once promote justice and give satisfaction to the injured party. I am touching briefly upon matters which require ample consideration, but it is enough that I moot certain points, knowing well that you have good sense to weigh and decide them. And now to pass to another topic.

"You ought to calculate the amount of your revenues, and so proportion your expenses that at the end of the year you have rather a surplus of ten than a deficiency of one; for a short-coming of one to-day, and another to-morrow, and another the day following, will bring you to ruin. Surround yourself with a court more distinguished by the qualities than the number of its members; let it not be larger than you can support, and see that you maintain the mastery, letting none there gain an ascendancy over you. Let each have his department, and be satisfied to do his own duty well, the chamberlain not interfering with the counsellor, nor the sewer with the secretary. See that all have their allowances punctually. Never aggrieve merchants, citizens, nor peasants, by laying hands upon their effects. True generosity will satisfy first those who have rightful claims, not squandering upon gamblers or buffoons; and when these are satisfied, will give to the needy, and to other works of charity. Do not, to gain an empty name for liberality, lavish your means on costly hospitalities towards great personages: those who have hundreds of millions do not so, while you who scarcely have tens would do it! Entertain the master at dinner or supper with yourself, but let the rest go to the hotel at their own expense, and so will you avoid vast trouble and great expense.

"In towns all innovations are unpopular and annoying, but especially new imposts; you cannot do anything more generally offensive than to raise them, nor more acceptable than to replace on their original footing those which have been augmented. New taxes and extraordinary escheats seem at first sight useful, but by a providential dispensation they absorb ordinary revenues, making these incomprehensibly to disappear. Let all keep their own; resort to no compulsion of property nor of person; interfere not with marriages; seek not to reward friends or benefit servants out of other people's means: and be it ever graven on your memory, that princes are sent for the people's weal, not people for the benefit of princes.

"These few observations have occurred to me, most excellent Sire, for your remembrance. And I have to observe generally and in fine, that you should render yourself amiable to your subjects, being kind, considerate, affable, and doing your utmost to recover their pristine affection, which appears to a great degree lost. You could not by force maintain this state against a powerful foe: let the attachment of your people then supplement your strength; and it can only be acquired by justice, equity, mildness, and clemency. In the present juncture, you might by a single act gain, confirm, and augment the good will and devotion of all your subjects. That act is a grand amnesty, and restoration of exiles and emigrants, embracing all as your children, forgetful of the past. Ah, do this, Sire! do it; it will be a welcome favour to your people, to your friends, to your servants. On the strength of such generosity, you will gain the name of a benign and a magnanimous prince; and, besides having to hope from the Almighty an eternal reward, I can ensure your receiving from the Pope thanks and approbation.

"I pray God that this letter of mine may be received by your Excellency with the same feelings as those which dictated it, and that He would vouchsafe you a long life and happy reign; and I kiss your hands. From Rome, the 11th of October, 1574."

Let us now see from his own narrative what effect these blunt but precious counsels, and the prudent advices of

Alinari

DUKE FRANCESCO MARIA II RECEIVING THE ALLEGIANCE OF HIS FOLLOWERS
After the fresco by Girolamo Genga in the Villa Imperiale, Pesaro

his uncle Ottavio, Duke of Parma, had upon his early measures. "His first act on assuming the government was to raze those fortifications at Urbino which had been made during the insurrection, and to reduce the impost laid on by his father in his necessity; and this although the late Duke's liberality had imposed upon him many burdensome expenses to which his revenues were scarcely equal, besides heavy debts at interest. He was thus obliged to restrict himself to the unavoidable state expenses.

"Further, he was disappointed of those aids he looked for from the kindness of his Catholic Majesty, in whose service his father had died, at whose court he had himself been brought up, for whom he had fought in the battle of Lepanto, and to whose service he had ever professed his intention steadily to adhere. But, during eight long years his hopes dragged on without any result from that quarter, and thus was he compelled to attend closely to his private affairs, and prevented from carrying into execution an intention he had always entertained of following the career of arms, which he was on the point of commencing in Flanders, where he was already looked for when he lost his father. He, however, succeeded in contenting his subjects, and in effacing from their minds whatever bitterness remained in consequence of the recent measures; and this chiefly from their being aware that these events had been displeasing to him, and that he had studied to assist their cause in so far as his parental duty permitted."

The moderate and self-denying measures to which the Duke thus modestly alludes are the subject of more detailed commendation by Zane, who was commissioned by the Venetians to congratulate him upon his succession. At the moment of receiving the oaths of fidelity, he abolished those imposts which had occasioned the recent discontents. They were five in number, all upon exciseable commodities, yielding about 16,000 scudi to the revenue. This course he followed up by various grants and immunities to the respcctive cities, but especially to Urbino. Even before his father's death he had obtained a commutation there of the duties on casking wine and cheese, and of the quatrino per lb. upon butcher-meat, for an equivalent of 20,000 scudi payable in ten years; but he now remitted entirely this contribution. He restored to their property and privileges most of the outlaws and their families; he recalled the proclamations disarming the district; and, by destroying the fortifications erected after the rebellion, he at once relieved the people of a garrison, and demonstrated his renewed confidence in their fidelity. But what had still happier effect, was his repeatedly visiting that capital with but one or two attendants, in full and well-placed reliance upon the affection of his subjects, of whom he ever spoke in public and private with the most affectionate regard. Himself deeply imbued with sentiments of religion, it was his aim to encourage the same among his people. Nor was he indifferent to personal accomplishments, or to the reputation which his predecessors had established, and which Castiglione has immortalised. "There are ever at his court some persons distinguished in arms or in letters, and it is the taste for all to cultivate a refined urbanity of manner, and to be in every respect perfect courtiers, a fashion of old observance there, yet more than ever in repute since the Prince visited Spain." But it is time to resume the Autobiography.

"Notwithstanding this state of affairs, he discovered a conspiracy against his person, originating with men who had reason to apprehend the consequences of their former proceedings. These were Pietro Bonarelli of Ancona, on whom the late Duke had bestowed the countship of Orciano, with other estates and great wealth, and Antonio Stati, Count of Montebello. Orciano saved himself by flight, and was condemned in absence; the other was put

Alinari

DUKE FRANCESCO MARIA II RECEIVING THE ALLEGIANCE OF HIS FOLLOWERS

After the fresco by Girolamo Genga in the Villa Imperiale, Pesaro

upon trial, and at length, in due execution of justice, he was beheaded, and some of his accomplices hanged.[1] Francesco Maria, nevertheless, laboured for the good government of his people, with due economy of his time. In the morning he gave audience to his counsellors and secretaries, and in the evening to all who desired it, dismissing these with despatch; and thus business went on well and rightly." We are told by Gozze,[2] who seems to have been a contemporary, that at this period he occupied himself much with criminal police, and exerted himself to repress brigandage, and to reform the abuses arising from privileged sanctuaries. His rigorous perseverance in such measures, and his stern demeanour towards the nobility, acquired for him, with many, a reputation for severity, which the infirmities of his temper must have served to confirm. The only other reference to his system of administration which the Autobiography contains, is as follows:—"He attended assiduously to the government of his state, maintaining peace, and administering justice with integrity and impartiality. He passed the summer at Urbino, the winter between Pesaro and Castel Durante. At intervals he visited his other residences, and when he omitted doing this in person, he despatched one of the judges on a sort of circuit, who in one year went to Gubbio, Cagli, Fossombrone, and La Pergola; in another to Sinigaglia and Mondavio; and in a third to the province of Montefeltro."

[1] The object of this plot is stated to have been the Duke's assassination at a hunting party in the manors of Orciano, to which he was invited by the conspirators.

[2] MSS. Oliveriana No. 324.

CHAPTER XLV

The unsatisfactory results of his marriage—He separates from the Duchess—His court and habits—Death of the Duchess—He remarries.

HAVING thus thrown together all that the Duke has thought fit to detail regarding the principles of his government and the early events of his reign, we now proceed to narrate in their order, from his Diary and from other sources, the few incidents afforded by those peaceful and monotonous pursuits wherein many subsequent years were passed. The first of these was of a painful domestic character, arising out of the unsatisfactory terms upon which he had during several years been with the Duchess. That love formed no ingredient in the match has been already shown, and perhaps his speedy and voluntary departure on a distant military expedition may be taken as a proof that his indifference did not diminish after wedlock had riveted his chains. In 1573, Lucrezia was laid up at Novilara with a feverish cold, and was attended by her husband, who with great reluctance consented to her return to Ferrara, on the excuse of change of air being requisite for re-establishment of her health. The truth seems to have been, that her marriage appearing unlikely to give an heir to the family, the Prince was confirmed in his original distaste, and this is said to have occasioned some disagreeable scenes with his father, whom he blamed for having forced upon him so unfortunate an alliance. The scandal to which these probably gave rise, and the example of coldness towards her which he most assuredly set, had, no doubt, rendered her position sufficiently unpleasant, and, after exchanging it for the freedom of her brother's elegant court, it is scarcely to be wondered that she hesitated to return, even after her husband had succeeded to the sovereignty of Urbino. That rumour was busy with gossip and conjectures is pretty obvious, and the countenance which Muratori gives to an allegation of Lucrezia's jealousy of his supposed infidelities may be taken as the version current at Ferrara of their mysterious non-adherence. Of this suspicion the life and character of Francesco afford an ample refutation, but its existence induced an endeavour on his part to bring about a better understanding with his wife.

In 1577, accordingly, he employed the Bishop of Pesaro and Father-general del Carmine to persuade her to return to his home. In a paper of instructions for their guidance, preserved among the Oliveriana MSS., he declares that the excuses she pleaded were of no weight, and could not be the real motives of her absence. In reference to pecuniary arrangements, he urges the great economy and self-denial which his father's embarrassments imposed upon him, but offers her the same establishment as his mother enjoyed, besides Novilara and its dependencies, in all about 6000 scudi a-year. But, in consideration of the slanderous and groundless imputations against himself to which her absence had given rise, he intimates his intention to select for her a suitable suite of respectable persons, leaving her, however, to choose eight or ten from them to be more immediately about her person. This negotiation having failed, the affair was next year submitted for the decision of Cardinals Farnese, Sforza, and d'Este: it would appear that an amicable separation was then determined upon; at all events, the Duchess returned no more to her husband's state.

The notice of this disagreeable topic in the diary of Francesco Maria is as follows:—" Meanwhile the Duchess wished to return to Ferrara, where she subsequently chose to remain, a resolution which gave no annoyance to her husband; for, as she was unlikely to bring him a family, her absence mattered little. Her provision was amicably arranged, and their intercourse continued uniformly on the most courteous terms." In support of this last statement the following letter from Lucrezia is conclusive.

"To the most serene Lord my Consort the Duke of Urbino.

"My most serene Lord and affectionate Consort,

"I could not have heard any message with more satisfaction than that which Count Alessandro della Massa has brought me in your Highness's name, on presenting your affectionate letters, nor could any present have been more gratifying than the picture which you were pleased to send me: both on account of its subject, and as coming from your hands, it will be ever the most valued that I possess. On all accounts, therefore, do I kiss your Highness's hand, recommending myself to your goodness; and I pray the Lord to preserve you ever in all happiness. From Ferrara, 28th of May, 1586.

"Your most loving and obedient consort and servant,

"LUCREZIA D'ESTE."

The Oliveriana MSS. contain many other letters from Lucrezia; but, as usual with such princely documents, they are more rich in mannered phrases of compliment than in those natural sentiments which form the charm of epistolary composition, and afford a correct index of individual character. Most of them are commendatory introductions of priests and friars, a class of acquaintances more congenial to her husband's disposition than her own, the chief foible in her character being an immoderate addiction to those festive and exciting pleasures, which, although the business of her brother's court, met with

Anderson

FRANCESCO I DE' MEDICI
After the picture by Bronzino in the Pitti Gallery, Florence

little encouragement at that of her consort. Her intercourse with Tasso will fall to be noticed in our fifty-first chapter, when describing the sorrows of that wayward genius. After her return to Ferrara, she interested herself in establishing at San Matteo an asylum for wives, who, like herself, were separated by incompatibility of character. Soon after his separation from the Duchess had been arranged, Francesco Maria paid a visit to the court of Tuscany, where he met with a distinguished reception, and spent fifteen days very agreeably amid the many attractions of Florence, varied by comedies and amusements of the chase. During the ensuing carnival he introduced unwonted gaiety at Pesaro, holding a tournament, at which he entered the lists in person. About this time, too, his finances were recruited by a donative of 10,000 scudi granted to him by that city.

The Duke's autograph Diary, from which we have recently quoted, and to which we shall frequently refer, having been carried to Florence with his other personal effects in 1631, remains in the Magliabechiana Library (Class xxv., No. 76). It is a narrow folio volume, like an index book, containing about two hundred pages entirely in his own hand. The entries are limited to a bare notice of facts without comment. The topics most frequently registered are the passage of remarkable strangers through Pesaro; the births, marriages, and deaths of persons of rank; his own periodical movements to his various residences, and visits to other parts of the duchy; his frequent hunting parties in autumn and winter, chiefly from Castel Durante; his taking medicine, including regular semestral purgations in spring and autumn. His taste for the physical sciences is illustrated by noting the occurrence of earthquakes, unusual storms, or other phenomena of nature, the recurrence of frost and snow, of the cigala and the nightingale, of mosquitoes, and similar signs of the seasons; also the appearance of any rare animal or monstrous production of nature. The Journal commences in April, 1583, and is continued without interruption until March, 1623, when it terminates abruptly.

The disappointment felt by the Duke at the fruitlessness of his family friendship with the crown of Spain was removed by receiving, towards the close of 1582, a military commission from his Catholic Majesty. This was the only relic of the condottiere system that survived the changes of the sixteenth century upon the political and military aspect of Europe. It was the intervening link between mercenary bands of the middle ages and standing armies of modern times. No plan could have better suited all parties. The great powers were thus enabled to command on sudden exigencies an ample force, without waste of time or treasure. The petty sovereigns by it eked out their inadequate revenues, without further burden to their subjects than an occasional call upon the military services of those who regarded arms as a pastime, and whose restless spirits, if not thus employed, would have been dangerous at home. The people, without abandoning the arts of peace, reaped a portion of the fruits of war. These benefits were, indeed, purchased by a surrender of the last vestige of independence, for the salary paid to the princes in name of stipend was, in fact, the price of their political subserviency. Yet it was but a nominal compromise, to sell the shadow when the substance had long departed; and we find the example of Spain in retaining friends throughout La Marca, for pecuniary considerations, recommended for the imitation of Venice by one of her ambassadors about this very time. The conditions of the Duke's service were an annual pay of 12,000 scudi, which, in 1599, was augmented to 15,000, a company of men-at-arms in the kingdom of Naples, and ample protection in all his undertakings; in return for which he was bound to provide, when called upon by Philip II., three thousand militia, and to take the field with them when his Majesty appeared there in person. The amount of troops thus actually raised in the duchy for the Spanish service during the next thirty years has been calculated at seven thousand two hundred men, a sufficient proof that the benefits accruing from the arrangement were mutual. The Pope now granted Francesco Maria the honourable prefix of "Most Serene" to the title of Highness, which he had enjoyed in common with other minor sovereigns, a distinction said to have been accorded with difficulty, and after long entreaty. The establishment of a Swiss guard is another illustration of his partiality at this period to pomps which he subsequently little esteemed.

In the following year, the court of Pesaro was enlivened by the Princess Lavinia's nuptials with Felice d' Avalos, Marquis del Vasto, when twelve poetesses were said to have tuned their lyres at the Imperiale, in honour of the joyous occasion. His marriage presents to his bride, mentioned in her brother's Diary, consisted of a necklace of jewels, a bag or muff of sable skin—the head and feet studded with precious stones, called a *zebellino*, and similar to that represented in Titian's beautiful portrait of her grandmother, Duchess Leonora,—a set of fan-sticks, a gem mounted as a sun, two pearls for ear-drops, a diamond cross and eagle, and an order for 3000 scudi: the whole was valued at 10,000 scudi. The happy pair spent some months at the court of Urbino, while the Marquis often joined the hunting parties from Castel Durante. But the sun that rose thus brightly was soon clouded by his wretched and tyrannical temper, which embittered his consort's life. Many years after, she married, in her widowhood, the gallant Marquis of Pescara, her brother's long-tried friend, and, finally, with her two daughters, sought repose and peace in the convent of Sta. Chiara at Urbino, where she died in 1633. In the end of 1583 the Duke began to build the Vedetta, on the most commanding eminence of Monte Bartolo, which he had obtained for this purpose from the Gerolimini convent. Of this casino only the foundation remains, but it would seem to have been an appendage of the Imperiale palace, whither the court ascended in the summer heats, to inhale gentle breezes from the blue Adriatic, which sparkled some hundred feet beneath. For such a purpose no spot could have been better chosen, and the magnificent prospect, which we have elsewhere noticed without attempting to describe, renders it probably the most attractive site in all the fair duchy.

As a further mark of favour, Philip II. of Spain sent him, in 1586, the decoration of the Golden Fleece; and in order to confer it in manner at once honourable and complimentary to his personal feelings, his Majesty requested the investiture to be given him by his uncle the Duke of Parma. That Duke was then suffering from gout, and drawing towards his death, which occurred in the following autumn; so Francesco Maria showed respect at once for the King and for his relation, whom he revered as a parent, by proceeding to meet him at Bologna. The two princely guests were magnificently entertained by the authorities of that city, as well as by the Cardinal Legate Salviati and the Archbishop Palotta: they were lodged in the palace of the latter, who performed high mass in the cathedral at the investiture. The collar and girdle of the order were set with brilliants, and were accompanied by a rich present of jewels to the Duchess, consisting of four hundred and twenty-six pearls, and a handsome necklace, girdle, two pendants, and sixty buttons, all enamelled in red and white upon gold, and studded with diamonds.

Although, on the whole, a more popular sovereign than his father, we have seen Francesco Maria subjected, in the early years of his reign, to seditious movements on the part of some discontented nobles. Of a similar attempt in 1586, few particulars have been preserved; but this notice of it in his Diary exhibits him as a stern dispenser of justice. "Count Giovanni de' Thomasi was beheaded in the fortress of Pesaro for homicide, sedition, and bad service towards his master: he died as a Christian and a brave man, and may God pardon his sins." But, though of hard, and even stern manners, the Duke retained the affection of his household, most of whom remained long in his service. From a catalogue of the chief officers at his court, compiled by Lazzari, we learn the emoluments belonging to the principal places.

	Scudi.
The superintendent of the household had yearly	1000
The master of the chamber	400
The master of the household	200
The gentlemen cuirassiers	250
The chamberlains	224
The sewer or carver for visitors	250
The philosopher or dilettante of poetry	300
The physician	250
The chaplain	150
The auditors or judges	500
The eight counsellors	400
The chief secretary	400
The secretary of justice	350
The treasurer	250
The fiscal advocate	350
The captains of the guard	232
The commandants of garrisons	300
The castellans, besides perquisites	150
The ambassador to Spain	1000
The ambassador to Venice	400
The agent in Rome	100

Francesco Maria had now reached the flower of manhood, and this may be considered the most fortunate period of his reign. During the next twelve years no untoward incident interrupted the smooth current of his life, or the prosperity of his government. The healthful exercise of the chase constituted his favourite relaxation from the cares of state, and his Diary preserves more minute information on this than on any other topic. He had within reach of Pesaro eighteen preserves, stocked with roe-deer, goats, foxes, hares, pheasants, and partridges, all of which were, in those days, considered fair game. The more exciting sport of wild-boar was found in greatest perfection near Mondolfo, and the following entry occurs in January, 1588. "Hunted in the chase of S. Costanzo, and, in three hours, killed nine wild boars, weighing 2580 lbs., besides offal. The largest one weighed overhead 917 lbs. We cut off its head close behind the ears, and hung it in the castle window over the great street of Mondolfo; its weight was 59½ lbs."

But red deer were the Duke's noblest and favourite sport, which, being only found in the highlands of his duchy, was his original attraction to Castel Durante, whence the best forest coverts were easily accessible. It was on that account selected as his chief residence during his father's life, and continued his annual resort in autumn so long as he could follow the game. When increasing years precluded such pastimes, we shall find that he there provided other appliances more befitting his circumstances, and that these preserved for Castel Durante a partiality which increased to the latest hours of his life. He was in use there to spend the autumnal months, returning to Pesaro before the carnival, and moving to Urbino towards midsummer. In the interval from the 7th of September, 1588, till the end of the following January, twenty-eight hunting parties are mentioned in his Journal, at some of which wolves and smaller game were killed. Red deer must have been in great abundance: thus, November, 1587, "We killed a dozen, six of them males, the largest weighing 464 lbs., besides 380 lbs. of offal. We left Castel Durante about noon, and returned at dusk, after losing nearly an hour in watching a hind which took refuge in the broken ground of the Lady's Park, when fell dead the famous hound Box-cur, the only British one I had. The twelve deer weighed 2914 lbs., without offal." In the subsequent season, "hunted red deer in the valley of S. Martino with greyhounds, but without canvas or nets. Saw twelve, and chased five of them; but, though the dogs came up with them, they were not able to hold any." The park which he had inclosed in the beautiful vale of the Metauro, just out of Castel Durante, was stocked with fallow-deer: which, however, seem to have been kept chiefly for ornament, though occasionally resorted to for greyhound coursing, when age had relaxed his limbs for the rougher mountain sport. The last hunting party he mentions was in 1615.

Though reserved in manner, and little apt to indulge his court in amusements uncongenial with his own unsocial temperament, he sometimes relaxed so far as to have dancing fêtes at the Imperiale, where he mentions three hundred ladies as having on one occasion been present. The representation of comedies was a frequent carnival pastime. The manner of conducting these theatricals, and the methodical punctuality of the Duke's character, are at once illustrated in the following extract. In February, 1589, "a comedy by the late Maestro Fabio Bagnano was recited in the great hall of Pesaro, beginning at 4 p.m. The first act lasted an hour and ten minutes; after which came an interlude for twenty minutes, from the fable of Ulysses hearing his wanderings foretold by Tiresias; then act second, in fifty minutes, with a musical interlude for ten minutes; then act third, in half-an-hour, with, for interlude, the marriage of Eolus and Deiopeia, in twelve minutes; then act fourth, in forty-eight minutes, and its musical interlude, in seven minutes; lastly, act fifth, in thirty-eight minutes, with its interlude of the gods allotting their various dominions; but this was not finished in consequence of a cloud which, by some mismanagement, did not descend properly." Among the performances noted about this period are the comedies of *I falsi Sospetti* by Pino; another by the Cavaliere Ludovico Odasio, *I Suppositi;* and an eclogue entitled *La Myrtia.* The interludes between the acts were frequently moresque dances or ballets representing mythological subjects, such as the fable of Prometheus, that of Calisto, the birth of Venus; varied by more familiar themes, as hunting the owl. In 1597, we find noticed, among other gay doings during carnival, a tournament in the great hall of Pesaro, wherein ten or twelve knights ran each three courses, and which was followed by an exhibition of various pleasing conceits.

Of Francesco Maria's literary pursuits we have various pleasing memorials. Not satisfied with the valuable library of MSS. that had descended to him from the Feltrian dukes, he formed another of standard printed works. Indeed, he became an assiduous book collector; and the letters of his librarian Benedetto Benedetti, in the Oliveriana Library, are full of lists which his agents in Venice, Florence, and even Frankfort are urged to supply. In his own voluminous correspondence, we find constant offers from authors of dedications or copies of their productions, the tone of which is highly complimentary to his taste for letters. In 1603, the Archbishop of Monreale, in Spain, transmits him the regulations he proposed to prescribe in bequeathing his library to a seminary he had founded in his diocese, expressing a hope that they might prove useful to the Duke's collection, "at this moment without parallel in the world."[1] Instead of quoting the vague testimony of courtly compliment, as to the use which this philosophic Prince made of these acquisitions, let us cite the brief records of his studies, preserved in his own Diary. In 1585, "terminated an inspection of the whole works of Aristotle, on which I have laboured no less than fifteen years, having had them generally read to me by Maestro Cesare Benedetti, of

[1] Bibl. Oliveriana, No. 375, vol. XI., p. 204.

Pesaro." But his reading was not limited to such speculative topics, and we presently find him imbibing knowledge from a purer source. In 1587, "I finished my examination of the whole Bible, with various commentaries, on which I have spent three years and ten months." Again, on the "15th of December, 1598, completed my second perusal of the entire Bible, which I read this time with the commentary of Dionysio the Carthusian, occupying upon it eight years." A curious inference of the contemplative character of his mind may be drawn from the devices he successively assumed as emblematic of his feelings. In youth he used a flame vanishing into air, with the motto *Quies in sublime*, "There is rest on high:" after he succeeded to the dukedom, he took a terrestrial globe with the legend *Ponderibus librata suis*, "Self-poised."

The position of Pesaro, on the principal high road to Loreto and Rome, exposed it to the constant passage of travellers of all ranks. The former was the habitual resort of Roman Catholics, to whom holy impulses, the hope of any specific blessing, or gratitude for mercies vouchsafed, suggested an unusual devotional observance. The annual functions of Easter, St. Peter's day, and Christmas, besides the great occasional jubilees, attracted to the latter crowds of pious pilgrims from all Christendom. The dukes were thus laid open to frequent calls upon their hospitality, which the state maintained by passing visitors often rendered most onerous. Thus, in 1589, Duke Alfonso II. of Ferrara, on his way to and from Loreto, spent four days at Pesaro, with his suite, consisting of fifty carriages, and one hundred and fifty mounted attendants, at an expense to his host of 3000 scudi. All royal pilgrims did not, however, thus mingle worldly pomp with religious duties: ten years after, Ranuccio, Duke of Parma, arrived incognito, in company with three others, who wore red sack dresses, and travelled on foot. After passing the night at Pesaro, they proceeded to Sinigaglia, on their way to the opening of the holy door at Rome, in the jubilee of 1600. Eighteen years later, Francesco Maria's Diary thus notes a more interesting visit: "9th June, 1618, the Galileo arrived at Pesaro, on his return from Loreto to Florence." The philosopher was then resident at the Villa Segni, near his native capital, and suffered much from the effects of a chronic illness caught in Lombardy some years previously, while sleeping with an open window. Perhaps his pilgrimage to the holy house may have been influenced by this circumstance.

> "'Twas he who, risking life and fame to crush
> The idol-worship that enslaved mankind,
> Restored its native freedom to the mind."

In October, 1597, the direct line of the dukes of Ferrara closed on the death of Alfonso II., whose object had been to secure to his cousin Cesare, Marquis of Montecchio, the succession of his states, as well as his private heritage. He had been able to obtain from the Emperor a new investiture in his favour of Modena, Reggio, and Carpi, but failed in procuring the like boon from Gregory XIV. as to the Ferrarese holding. Immediately upon the vacancy, Cesare assumed the dukedom, with full consent of his people, who dreaded the descent to provincial rank which must have followed upon their annexation to the papal state. Clement VIII., who then filled the chair of St. Peter, answered a conciliatory embassy sent him by the claimant, with a summons to appear at Rome, and, on his non-compliance, thundered excommunication against him and his abettors. These decided steps were followed up by a levy of nearly thirty thousand men, but ere they could be brought into the field, Cesare d' Este gained some partial successes near Bologna. Finding, however, that his position was hopeless, he availed himself of the mediation of Lucrezia Duchess of Urbino, who succeeded in reconciling him with the Legate. The devolution of Ferrara to the Holy See was harmoniously completed in February; but the lady has been accused of sacrificing the interests of her cousin to an old grudge against his father, and to a promise of the fief of Bertinoro. She did not, however, live to receive the bribe, and her death is thus dryly noted in her husband's Diary:—

"February 14th, I sent the Abbé Brunetti to Ferrara, to visit the Duchess, my wife, who was sick.

"—— 15th, Heard that Madame Lucrezia d' Este, Duchess of Urbino, my wife, died at Ferrara during the night of the 11th.

"—— 19, The Abbé Brunetti returned from Ferrara."

In his Memoirs she is the subject of still more brief remark:—"Her death occurred after some years, leaving him [the Duke] executor by her will of many pious bequests." Considering that the largest bequest was in his own favour, a less chilling notice might have been bestowed! The sum she left him was 30,000 scudi: to her various attendants and servants she gave 12,000 in small legacies, and 20,000 among several convents, in masses for her soul. There was also a fund to be mortified for the endowment of poor girls, half at Ferrara and half at Urbino, and Cardinal Pietro Aldobrandini, the Pope's nephew, was named residuary legatee, a selection which has been ingeniously ascribed to the countenance bestowed by his family on Tasso, in the closing scenes of that minstrel's troubled life.

The anxiety which had long been generally felt on the prospect of a failure of the ducal family began to show itself after the death of Lucrezia. The impediment of a childless marriage having thus been providentially removed, men's hopes were again awakened, and their wishes were not long in finding a unanimous expression. When Francesco Maria appeared in public, his ears were greeted with murmurs from the populace, which at length broke out in enthusiastic demands for his marriage, and *Serenissimo, moglie*, "A wife, your Highness," became the universal cry.*[1] The ferment thus created was greatly increased by a circumstance which at first sight does not appear much connected with the welfare of the duchy. In the spring of 1598, Clement VIII., on his passage to take possession of Ferrara, paid a visit to the court of Pesaro, where the magnificent reception accorded him, and the long confidential interviews he had with the Duke, were construed by popular jealousy into preparatives for political changes. The extinction of the reigning line would infer a lapse of their sovereignty to the Pope, similar to that which had just degraded Ferrara: Francesco Maria's disinclination for state-toils had already begun to show itself: the readiness of his Holiness to secure so valuable a reversion, or even to anticipate it by providing for the Duke an honourable retreat from duties which he considered onerous, scarcely admitted of a doubt, an appetite for annexation being naturally whetted by the recent acquisition of territory. These ideas became a theme of discussion among the multitudes who crowded from all quarters of the state to witness the courtly shows at Pesaro; and when the Duke returned to the city from escorting the Pope towards Ferrara, he was met at the gate by a host of his subjects, whose loyalty and patriotism burst forth afresh in tumultuous shouts of "*Serenissimo! moglie.*"

That the object of Clement's visit had been faithfully construed by the general voice seems more than probable from the document we are about to quote; but upon this point the Memoirs throw no light. They merely notice his reception of the Pontiff with all distinction, and the remarkably friendly bearing of his Holiness towards himself and the Duchess mother during a day spent at their

*[1] Cf. CALOGERÀ, *Memorie concernenti Franc. Maria II.* (Venice, 1776).

court: mutual presents passed between them, and Clement dwelt on the good service which his father had afforded to Duke Guidobaldo. From the Duke's Diary we learn that after meeting his Holiness on his southern frontier, and again escorting him out of Sinigaglia, where he had slept with a suite of sixteen cardinals, he took boat and hastened to Pesaro. Next morning he proceeded to meet his visitor, who had spent the night at Fano, and welcomed him to his capital. Passing back to Rome in the end of the year, the Pope halted at Pesaro only to say mass in the cathedral; and on both occasions he was preceded one day by the Holy Sacrament. In the following year the Pontiff, in acknowledgment, perhaps, of these hospitalities, accorded to his host a dispensation, whereby the indulgences, to which the use of certain rosary prayers and ave maria's entitled him, were united and concentrated in a single *cavalliere*.[1]

The predominant feeling of Francesco Maria, even at this period of his life, appears to have been a selfish attachment to solitary habits and pursuits, tempered by sincere anxiety to discharge his public duties for the benefit of his people. An argument addressing itself to both motives readily occurred to the wily Pontiff. An immediate abdication would secure to the Duke personal ease, and the consequent devolution of his government to the Camera Apostolica might be guarded by stipulations for the public weal, which such voluntary demission alone could entitle him to dictate. The art with which these considerations had been urged, and the impression they made upon the Duke, may be best gathered from a circular he addressed to the magistrates of each city in

[1] Rosaries, *corone*, and such were helpmates or promptuaries to prayer, differing in form and varying in supposed efficacy, according to the special privileges and indulgences bestowed on them by ecclesiastical gift. A specimen of the nature and powers of such indulgences will be found in the description of a corona belonging to the Grand Duke of Tuscany in 1666, See Appendix VI,

his state, curiously exemplifying him in that character of royal philosopher which it seems to have been his ambition to attain.*[1]

"Most magnificent and well-beloved,

"Ever since we understood that you so affectionately long for the continuation and maintenance of our house, we have had no wish more urgent than to conform to your desires; and although for some time past we have been always anxious to facilitate this resolution, yet the more we consider it, the greater do the difficulties daily appear, not only by reason of our age and infirmities, but much more from the obligation laid upon us to take no step that might turn to your prejudice, as we know this would do: for, upon weighing the advantages that would accrue to you by being placed after our death immediately under the sway of the Church, there cannot, in our opinion, be a doubt that this would be most beneficial; since, besides being rid of the present inconvenient restrictions on trade in grain, salt, oil, and similar commodities, you might well hope, from a sovereign so powerful as his Holiness, many exemptions and facilities which we, however well-disposed, cannot, with due attention to the suitable maintenance of our rank, accord you. Wherefore, we exhort and pray you, to take all this into your most serious consideration; and, along with it, those suggestions which your affectionate devotion may prompt, in conjunction with our delicate and advanced age, as these might, at all events, render vain the hope of a succession, or at least might occasion you to be some day left under a minority (ever a judgment of God upon a nation), and us to die with such pain as you may conceive the predicament of leaving a minor would occasion us: whereas, on the other hand, were we to remain in our present condition, looking, so long as God

*[1] Cf. Reposati, *Della Zecca di Gubbio*, vol. II., p. 220 (Bologna, 1772–3). The date of this letter was June 7th, 1598.

may vouchsafe us life, for no other children than yourselves, we might the more diligently apply to the cares of our government. It is therefore our desire that you satisfy yourselves in this matter, and, after having prayed in all sincerity to our Lord and Saviour for His inspiration, that you convoke a full meeting of your usual council, excluding all officers of our government, and that, after reading to them this our letter, they should decide by ballot what they judge most fitting for the common weal, having sworn the consuls to conceal nothing of the resolution they come to; and you shall report their decision to the Bishop of this city, who, keeping it secret from us and all others, shall declare only the general result of this appeal to you and to the other principal places of our state, to whom we write in similar terms: and the opinion so expressed we shall, in accordance to our love towards you, endeavour to carry into effect even at the hazard of our life, thus appealing to the faithful attachment you have ever displayed towards our house and ourselves, as is well known to all, but chiefly to us.—May it, therefore, please the blessed God so to inspire you, that these our exhortations and commands may be executed so as to bring about the best results, and may He preserve you. From Pesaro, 7th June, 1598. "FRANCESCO MARIA."

The consequence of this singular appeal was a unanimous and urgent resolution in favour of the Duke's immediate marriage; indeed nothing else could well be looked for, the alternative contemplated by the people being loss of their independence, and the substitution of a foreign legate, changed every few years, for a hereditary and popular sovereign. Passeri conjectures that this result was in fact less distasteful to Francesco Maria than the tone of his letter might infer; and that the whole expedient was adopted in order to obtain a satisfactory answer to the importunities of the Pontiff, whom the stern measures lately adopted towards Ferrara had rendered the Duke peculiarly averse to thwart, by opposition to his scheme. From the Memoirs so often quoted, we learn nothing beyond the obvious facts, that the marriage was undertaken in compliance with urgent entreaties of the Duchess mother and of the people of Urbino, and that the bride was his own choice.

Of Cardinal Giulio della Rovere's two natural sons we have already spoken.[1] In the correspondence of Francesco Maria, there occur some proofs of a bad understanding between him and these cousins, the origin and circumstances of which it is unnecessary to examine. To Ippolito Marquis of S. Lorenzo, there was born in 1585, of his marriage with Isabella Vitelli, Princess dell' Amatrice in the Abruzzi, a daughter Livia, who was educated in the convent of Sta. Caterina at Pesaro; and on her fell the choice of Francesco Maria, as announced in the following extract of a letter to the Archduchess Maria of Austria. A selection so obviously ineligible may have been dictated in part by that shrinking from close contact with strangers which his reserved habits were calculated to generate, and partly too by the sad experience he had already reaped of a marriage of state policy.

"Moved by the unremitting entreaties of my subjects, I have been forced to establish myself by a new alliance: yet as my age and other considerations would have prevented me from taking this resolution but for their satisfaction, I have chosen to combine with their wishes a due consideration for my own, by selecting one of my proper blood, and brought up in this country, in whom are combined many of the qualities suited to my views."

Of the domestic life of Francesco Maria after his second union no record has been preserved to us. The circumstances in which it was effected were not such as to promise a high degree of matrimonial felicity, to which

[1] Above, p. 82.

his cold nature, advanced age, and reserved character were virtually impediments. Nor could the monotonous seclusion of his habits be attractive to a youthful bride, transported from a convent to the rank of sovereignty with few of its gauds. That she had the good sense simply to conform to her position may be inferred from the rare occurrence of her name in the documents which I have inspected. The brief notices of her in her husband's Diary merely prove that they were seldom apart, and in one instance she is mentioned as accompanying him to his favourite pastime of deer hunting. Regarding preliminaries for their marriage, that record is silent, and the only allusion to it is in this concise phrase: "26th April, 1599, I married the Lady Livia della Rovere." But letters of the Duchess, written long subsequently, to her grand-daughter, of which a specimen will be introduced below, exhibit her character in a light so amiable as to warrant our regret that it has not been more prominently brought into view, in the few materials which we possess for this portion of our narrative.

Francesco Maria's affection to his mother would have been beautiful in any rank. Besides anxiously providing for her comfort by a suitable establishment, he made her his friend and confidante through life; and during his first marriage she filled at his court the place which in happier circumstances would have been occupied by his wife. The ailments of her advancing years he tended with affectionate anxiety, and thus notices her decease on the 13th December, 1602, after a long indisposition. "Most deep was the public grief for the loss of this excellent and sainted Princess. She was beloved by all, but most by her son, who felt her death as no common sorrow, and testified both in public and in private the sincerity of his feelings. Her funeral oration, pronounced by Leoni, was very fine, though his praises necessarily fell far short of her real merits." The Venetian Relazioni from the della Rovere court bear witness to her sound judgment and business habits, to her generous disposition and beneficent charities, as well as to the piety of her character, and the exemplary conduct observed by her household.

Her remains were interred by those of her husband, with an epitaph which will be found in No. VII. of the Appendix, and her son appears from his Diary to have worn mourning for her for upwards of a year.

CHAPTER XLVI

Birth of Prince Federigo—The Duke's retired habits and aversion to business—His constitution-making experiments—His instructions to his son—The Prince's unfortunate education and character.

ALTHOUGH the patriotism and loyalty of his people had been gratified by the gracious manner in which he had assented to their eager desire for his marriage, yet was there wanting somewhat to the full fruition of their cherished hopes. The health of the Duchess was watched with anxiety, and when months had passed away without the promise of an heir, apprehensions more restless than before spread over the land. In a matter beyond the limits of human will, recourse was had to the Dispenser of all events. Prayers were offered up in public and private. Vows were solemnly registered by all the towns, by confraternities, even by village communities and private individuals, for the erection and dedication of churches and altars, especially to S. Ubaldo, once bishop of Gubbio, who had been assumed as special protector of that city and of the race of Montefeltro. About the beginning of 1605, it was announced that these devotional appeals had been crowned with success: the gloomy anticipations of the citizens were turned to joyous hope; and so formidable to the public tranquillity did the reaction of enthusiasm appear, that orders were issued for transporting into the fortress of Pesaro all the state archives, in case any tumult or conflagration might endanger their safety.

As the Duchess's confinement drew near, the subject seemed exclusively to engross men's minds, and when her hour was reported to have arrived, the piazza in front of the palace was crowded with an impatient multitude, who remained a day and night in eager expectation. At length, on the morning of the 16th of May, the festival of the patron saint Ubaldo, to whom their prayers had been addressed, about nine o'clock, the Duke appeared at a window of the great hall, and announced with a loud and clear voice, "God has vouchsafed us a boy!" The cheer of joyous triumph which rang through the palace-yards was but an inadequate expression of the general exultation, and the precautions taken to preserve the peace proved but too limited; for the insensate popular excitement vented itself in an attack upon the Jews' quarter, and succeeded in sacking and burning their synagogue and shops, in spite of exertions by the military, who had been held in readiness to quell the outbreak. Meanwhile salvoes of artillery proclaimed the Prince's advent; and in grateful acknowledgment of his good fortune, his father proclaimed pardon to many prisoners, and favours to various classes of his subjects. At the same time, with due regard to good order, he checked the longer continuance of noisy and tumultuous festivity, and in particular prohibited discharges of fire-arms under the heavy penalty of 100 scudi.

Any scepticism which might have been secretly entertained of the infant being truly a *dieu-donne*, in special answer to the thousand prayers that had been proffered to or through S. Ubaldo, was removed or silenced by his arrival on the fête of that saint whose hold on the devotional feelings of the people was thus marvellously riveted. Among the couriers speedily despatched over the duchy to bear boot and spur the happy news, one directed to Gubbio, the city and diocese of S. Ubaldo, was charged with a special letter from Francesco Maria.*[1]

*[1] Cf. PELLEGRINI, *op cit.*, in *Boll. cit.*, vol. *cit.*, p. 506 *et seq.* There seems always to have been an antagonism between Gubbio and Urbino, and

Arriving in hot haste, he found the whole population assembled in arms in the piazza, with the magistrates at their head, to whom he delivered the welcome missive; after publication of which the multitude formed a solemn procession to the cathedral, to render thanksgivings to S. Ubaldo, its and their protector. In that church the community of Gubbio lost no time in erecting a new chapel commemorative of the occasion, and placed on the altar a picture, in which the Madonna and Child smile benignantly on the suppliant saints, John Baptist and Ubaldo (the former their original patron), whilst in the lower part is seen the courier's arrival with the ducal despatch. Other places were scarcely less enthusiastic in redeeming their pious pledges, though enthusiasm seems to have been occasionally tempered by meaner considerations. Thus, in the communal records of S. Angelo in Vado, I found appeals from the Duke to quicken the tardy contribution of 500 scudi towards the erection of a votive church to S. Ubaldo; and months were spent in discussions among the magistracy how that sum was to be raised, by an assessment upon the artisans, and a duty upon butcher-meat. I know not whether we are to regard as an economical solution of the difficulty an altar picture in the church of S. Filippo there, in which S. Ubaldo is represented as introducing to the Madonna and Child the young Prince, led up by S. Crescenzio, the patron of Urbino, while St. John Baptist intercedes in his behalf. Federigo seems a child about five years old, in a very richly embroidered dress, and strongly resembles a portrait of him which came into my hands from the Vatican Library, and which is here introduced.[1]

now Gubbio could certainly crow. She appears to have done so. See note 2, p. 506, of work quoted. The country was not quiet after the rejoicing till May 30th, the festa being kept in all the cities. CORRADI, *Feste per il nascimento di un Principe nel sec XVII.* in *Il Giornale di Foligno* (Foligno, 1887), No. 28 *et seq.* describes the rejoicing in Cagli.

[1] In 1843–6, a variety of duplicates and objects of art belonging to the Vatican Library were exchanged away, with the sanction of Gregory XVI.,

According to the religious usages of the age, the measure of gratitude due by the sovereigns of Urbino for their long desired heir would have remained incomplete without a pilgrimage of thanksgiving to the Madonna of Loreto. Benedetto Benedetti, librarian to the Duke, writes, on the 20th June, 1605,[1] that the Duchess was to set out next day on this holy mission, "carrying with her a plate of solid gold, the size of a half sheet of writing paper, on which was portrayed in oil by a young pupil of Baroccio the infant Prince, who is one of the most lovely babes I should wish to look upon; fat, of good complexion, and comely features, his eyes large and black, unlike those of the Duke, and his mouth resembling his mother's." It appears, however, from the Diary of Francesco Maria, that he had already acquitted himself of this pious debt by attending the festival of the Corpus Domini at Loreto on the 9th of June. On the 29th the Duchess carried her son to Urbino. At the gate they were met by twelve youths in blue damask trimmed with gold, and twenty-four children in white and gold; and the Prince, with his nurse, was borne by these youths in a close chair to the palace, through streets embellished with fountains and other ornaments.

Three days after the child's birth he had been privately baptised by the Bishop of Pesaro on Ascension Day, and named Federigo Ubaldo Giuseppe. His public baptism took place on the 29th November at Urbino, on which occasion his father, in deference to the loyal joy of his subjects, broke through his wonted habits of quiet and retirement, and celebrated the solemnity with a pomp more congenial to the pageant observances of Italian

whilst my lamented friend Monsignore Laureani, the librarian, was forming, by that Pontiff's order, from very limited resources, a most interesting series of early panel pictures illustrating the progress of Christian painting. The portrait of Prince Federigo now belongs to my friend Andrew Coventry, Esq., Edinburgh, and appears the production of a scholar of Baroccio.

[1] Oliveriana MSS. No. 375.

courts than to his own tastes. Every community of the duchy, by special invitation, sent their deputies, expensively arrayed, and bearing costly gifts. The states of Italy likewise were there, represented by ambassadors rivalling each other in magnificence. But chief among all was the Marquis of Pescara, envoy of Philip III. of Spain, who, before its birth, had promised to stand godfather to the infant. We pass over the ceremonial with which he was welcomed, but must pause for a little upon the spectacle of the baptism, as described in a contemporary narrative.[1]

From the houses in front of the Duomo were displayed those rich and many-tinted hangings which add so much to the effect of an Italian pageant. The short space from the palace was closed in by an awning of green, red, and white, the ducal liveries. The whole interior of the church was hung with magnificent decorations, in which were mingled tapestries and brocades, pictures and heraldic blazonry. The high altar was profusely furnished with statues, vases, candlesticks, all of solid silver. Into the cathedral thus prepared was seen advancing, about two hours before mid-day, under a bright and genial sun, a most imposing procession. The principal public functionaries, and the most distinguished of the nobility, were followed by twenty-five pages of high birth, dressed in Damascus blue. Then came representatives of the seven principal cities, bearing the massive silver vessels to be used in the ceremony. At their head walked Count Alessandro Tiane, Gonfaloniere of Urbino, conspicuous not less by his handsome person than by the rare splendour of his costume. He wore a close-fitting dress of white, brocaded with gold and silver; his flowing mantle of purple velvet was lined with violet and gold; and on his neck and cap was displayed a profusion of costly jewels. A scarf embroidered with pearls and

[1] Vat. Urb. MSS. No. 818, f. 444.

precious stones suspended from his neck a white cushion, whereon lay the babe in "toys of quaint apparel," which the writer attempts not to describe. The nurse, attended by sixty noble matrons arrayed in gala, closed the cortège, amid the clang of artillery and martial music. The sacred rite was administered by the Bishop of Fossombrone, and the religious function having been auspiciously ended, the company proceeded to a ball, followed by a supper, where the grotesque taste and elaborate ingenuity of Italian confectioners were lavishly displayed in the table-ornaments.

About seven in the evening, the guests were summoned by trumpet to the windows and balconies to witness a triumphal representation of the glories of Duke Federigo, whose name had that day been revived in the infant Prince. The space in front of the palace was fitted up as a vast stage laid out with woodland scenery, in the midst whereof rose a mountain, emblematic of the Apennines. Near its summit a cavern exhibited antique trophies and elephants, among which was a broken bust of Asdrubal, allusive to the defeat of the Carthaginian army near the Furlo pass. The whole was overshadowed by two vast oaks personifying the Duke and Duchess, under which were grouped shepherds playing on their national instruments. Across this mimic representation of the duchy of Urbino a gorgeous procession passed with military music, in the following order. The car of Fame advanced, glittering with the precious metals, and drawn by winged horses. On its front, amid garlands of flowers, was perched a black eagle crowned, the monarch of birds, and heraldic bearing of Montefeltro; and it contained figures of Fame, Time, and Truth. Fame stood winged upon a globe, to which were yoked two dolphins; her robe of gold and silver tissue was *semé* with countless eyes, ears, and mouths, and in her hand she held a golden trumpet. Before her sat old Time, with his hour-glass; behind, Truth chanted stanzas in compliment to the hero of two mottoes which were displayed over the car:—

"TO THESE AND EARTH'S MOST DISTANT LANDS ARE SHOWN
OUR FREDERICK'S GLORIOUS DEEDS, HIS HONOUR AND RENOWN."

"BY MARTIAL VALOUR WERE HIS TITLES WON."

In the procession which followed, were borne the armorial insignia of Duke Federigo, and of the sovereigns in close alliance with him; his various decorations of knighthood, the golden rose, the sword and baton of the Church, and similar badges of his dignities. Then came another car, drawn by four horses, and magnificently ornamented with cornucopias of public prosperity, intermingled with devices used by the various Dukes, amid which sat Justice, Bravery, and Prudence. Next marched by, an imposing military pageant, with the banners and ensigns of those states and cities over which Federigo had been victorious, and with the batons of command entrusted to him by the different powers whom he had served. To these succeeded a third car, still more magnificently decked out, which was dedicated to martial glory, and bore a figure of Pallas copied from the antique; it was laden with pictures and mottoes, allusive to his principal triumphs; and over a mass of books was the legend,—

"MINERVA'S LIBERAL ARTS HIS VICTORIES DID CROWN."

This lengthened procession having all passed, the various figures who had performed in it assembled upon the stage and executed a melodramatic ballet, which lasted till about 10 p.m.; and the ceremonies of the day were wound up by a splendid display of fireworks.[1] It has been

[1] A comparison of this stately entertainment with the ceremonial at the baptism of Prince Henry of Scotland in 1594, as given in the *Lives of the Lindsays*, vol. I., 382, from a rare contemporary pamphlet, shows how Italian revels influenced the courtly displays of our ancestors, due allowance being made for the difference of climate and the somewhat more material attractions of the northern festivity.

stated in most accounts of the baptism, that the Golden Fleece was conferred on the infant by the Marquis of Pescara in name of his master Philip III. But, from the Diary of Francesco Maria, we learn that this decoration had been transmitted to himself some weeks before, that he, as a knight of that order, might invest the Marquis with it, which was duly done on the 1st of December.

The Duke's advancing years had by this time considerably modified his personal habits. To the pleasures of the chase succeeded the less fatiguing interests of a large breeding stud. His partiality for animals and natural history had long induced him to give his attention to improve the race of horses, and he notes in his Diary frequent arrivals of stock of all sorts from various quarters, purchased or received in presents. Thus, in 1588, he had fifty-four young horses at one time from the Duke of Savoy, and he mentions paying 300 to 500 ducats for stallions. After his second marriage, entries of this sort became more frequent, and details of hunting less so. The great breeding establishment was maintained on Monte Corciano near Cagli, where the young stock ran at grass during the summer months; in winter they were brought down to Mirafiori, where those which were sufficiently advanced went into the hands of breakers. This was a casino just without the walls of Pesaro, so called from a flower-garden the Duke had made there, whither rare and beautiful plants were brought from all parts at great expense. In it too was preserved a very rich armoury collected by him, which is mentioned with admiration by Scotti in his published travels, and which afterwards passed to the grand-ducal family of Tuscany.

But the most marked alteration of his character was his growing aversion to public business, and increasing proneness to gratify his secluded and selfish habits by devoting an undue portion of time to his private relaxations of study and books. The tendency to solitude which had been gradually stealing upon him was checked for a season after the birth of his son. This joyous occasion seems to have in some degree revived the elasticity of his youthful feelings: his visits to Pesaro were more frequent, and, in 1606, the Comedy of *L'Ingannata* was repeatedly performed in the palace there. Ere long, however, his mind gradually relapsed into a sort of morbid abstraction which was constitutional to him, and the retirement of Castel Durante became more and more attractive. It would indeed have been difficult to find a spot more congenial. Known originally as Castel del Ripa, a title appropriate to its position on a peninsula, formed by the rugged ravine of the brawling Metauro, it had been destroyed about 1277, in a foray of the people of Urbino, whence it is distant about nine miles. Pope Martin IV. ordered it to be rebuilt by his Legate in Romagna, Guglielmo Durante, a noted canonist, who gave it his own name. Having subsequently passed in seigneury to the Brancaleoni of Mercatello, it was obtained, under the title partly of conquest, partly of inheritance, by the Counts of Montefeltro, in 1429. After that dynasty had been extinguished, it owed to papal munificence a second re-edification in 1636, when Urban VIII. raised it to the rank of a city, suffragan to the Bishop of S. Angelo in Vado; and the improvements he made upon it are commemorated by his statue erected in the town, and by another change to its present name of Urbania.

Its situation is singularly beautiful. Surrounded by wooded hills, it occupies the nearest point of the upper valley of the Metauro, which extends to the Mercatello in a stretch of rich alluvial land that pleasingly contrasts with the rest of this highland province. Adapted equally for the sports of the chase, and for a peaceful retreat from the busy world, it was in all respects suited to the wants of Francesco Maria, in youth and in advancing years. His usual residence was a large palace which, entering from the street, overhangs to the back the romantic river; and which, like many more of the ducal possessions, has passed to the Albani, and is doomed to the neglect consequent upon absenteeism and protracted litigation. It was here probably that he built a library, to which in 1609 he transported from Pesaro the many books which he had collected, leaving at Urbino those which had been amassed by his predecessors. On the opposite bank he enclosed an extensive park, and stocked it with fallow-deer and smaller game. Within that enclosure, on the slopes of Monte Berticchio, he built, after his second marriage, another palace, and surrounded it with a delightful garden. The park walls also included the convent of Franciscan Observantines, which still stands about a mile to the west of Urbania; and to them perhaps may be attributed the beginning of that monkish influence which tinged his latter years. But they were eventually superseded in his regard by the Minims, for whom, in 1617, he purchased the church of the Madonna della Neve, just beyond the park gate, and changed its name to that of the Crucifix. He there built for them a small convent, and invited to it twelve monks, distinguished for learning and acquirements in those philosophic pursuits which chiefly occupied his mind. Thus, as years advanced, did he become more and more inordinately attached to Castel Durante, where, leaving in his capital the trappings of sovereignty, he surrounded himself with a small and select suite, and sought in books and philosophic discussions, those gratifications which, since the chase had lost its charms, were most conducive to his humour. Here accordingly we find him corresponding with Isaac Casaubon, as to a MS. of Polybius, which, by desire of Henry IV., he had forwarded for an edition then in preparation at Paris, and urging its restoration, on the plea that MSS. of such value were not removed from the library, even for his own use.[1] It was doubtless the same

[1] Brit. Mus., Burney MSS. No. 367, f. 64.

Polybius which Giunta tells us was returned by that monarch under a military escort.[1]

It being the whim of Francesco Maria to unite in his person the opposite characters of monarch and philosopher, manifold inconsistencies were the natural consequence. In the address to his subjects, which we have quoted in reference to his second marriage, we have seen him dwell on the government of a minor as the greatest evil that could befall a people. Yet scarcely had he obtained the blessing of an heir than he began to devise steps for devolving prematurely upon his child the responsibility of sovereignty, and thereby releasing himself from those cares of state which reached him even at Castel Durante, and jarred upon his morbid love of seclusion and books. To this motive, at least, seem attributable the measures which we are now to detail, although he apparently excused them to himself as a wise precaution, in anticipation of his own death ere his son should have attained maturity. But, whatever may have been his real inducement, the scheme, so novel in that age, of imparting to his subjects a share in the government, was obviously calculated to gratify his love of philosophic speculation, while it threw upon others those duties and anxieties from which the prevailing desire of his advancing years was to escape.

His first step towards this plan was taken in 1696, by ordaining that the episcopal cities of Urbino, Pesaro, Gubbio, Sinigaglia, Fossombrone, Cagli, and S. Leo, with the province of Massa Trabaria, should send him a leet of their inhabitants most qualified for the administration of affairs. Selecting one from each, he constituted them into a council of state, to sit permanently in Urbino: on this body he conferred the most ample powers to govern in his name, and, in the case of his death, to become the regency. In order fully to explain this project, we quote

[1] MS. Albani Library at Rome.

the state documents relating to it, which have been printed by Marini in his *Saggio di S. Leo.* These will be rendered more intelligible by premising that the inhabitants of towns were then divided into four classes,—the nobility, the merchants and wealthy citizens, the master artisans, and the operative artisans. Each of these chose their own prior, and the prior of the nobles was the gonfaloniere, to whom, among other duties, was confided the standard in battle. These political rights did not extend to peasants, menial servants, nor mechanics of the baser callings.

"To the magnificent and our well-beloved, the Gonfaloniere and Priors of S. Leo, and to the Four, and the Parliament of the province of Montefeltro, THE DUKE OF URBINO.

"Magnificent and well-beloved,

"Ever since the birth of the son whom God has vouchsafed to us, it has been our fixed intention, in consideration of the age we have attained, to leave behind us such a form of government as may, during his minority, secure your welfare, and be in conformity to your wishes; and the desire increases with the affection which we bear to you, and to which you are so well entitled. For this end nothing seems more suitable than that you should govern the commonwealth and him also. To carry our design into execution, your council of S. Leo, uniting with the Four and the Parliament of the province of Montefeltro, will elect three or four well-qualified persons, without reference to their rank or station, or to their being members of council or parliament. From these we shall select one, who, together with those from the other seven communities, may represent our whole state, and give their undivided attention to such important matters for the general weal as shall be impartially proposed by us, with a view to your own benefit, and that of our house. The enclosed draft is sent to you as a foretaste of this plan of government. Be careful, therefore, to complete the election as soon as possible, as it is our intention to make trial during our life of this mode of government, and so to introduce it that, after us, it may proceed with the more facility, and in better order, in the name of the Almighty. From all this we feel assured that you must perceive the great confidence which we have in you, and which we firmly hope will much contribute to those good results of our plan so strenuously desired by us and by you. May the Lord God protect you.

"From Urbino, the 24th of August, 1606.

"FRANCESCO MARIA."

[*Draft enclosed in the preceding letter.*]

"The form of government by the persons elected shall be as follows. All the Eight shall reside at Urbino, with the same absolute rules as I myself enjoy, attending with all diligence and loyal fidelity to the guidance of the state and of their pupil. And, further, each of them shall make oath before the auditors to exercise their functions in the manner prescribed, and, in due time, to execute to the letter my testament, and all such written memoranda as I may leave behind me.

"They shall have two secretaries, one for foreign affairs and correspondence, the other for those of the interior, and shall assemble with them twice a day, or oftener if necessary. They shall take their seats at the same side of the table in their respective order; and those whose rank may have been matter of dispute shall decide by lot who is to take precedence at first, and shall thereafter enjoy it by turns, changing each succeeding month. They shall observe the same order in voting and on all occasions of meeting for public business, but at other times they are to have no sort of rank. And this rule shall be observed as to all questions of precedence that may arise, until it be modified by consent or legal authority, always without prejudice to the rights of individuals; and, if any one be discontented therewith, the others shall be entitled to administer the state with unimpaired authority.

"They shall enjoin the secretaries to make minutes of all that occurs, writing them afterwards into a book for the purpose. The Eight, or whatever be their number, shall discuss verbally all motions, and ballot upon them, the resolutions supported by most balls being carried; and this shall be specially minuted, with the signature of both secretaries. In case of an equality of votes, the president of the bench of auditors shall be called upon to decide the point.

"All their resolutions, letters, and documents shall run in name of the sovereign, with the ducal seal, and with signatures of the first in rank, and of the two secretaries.

"In absence of one or more from illness, or the like lawful cause, the others shall continue vested with the same authority, provided there be a quorum of five; but, if fewer, the auditors must make up that number. And, should one die, or become permanently disabled, his place must be forthwith filled up by election of another leet as at first.

"The courts of law [*udienza*] shall continue to enjoy the same authority as heretofore, but subject to the first of the eight deputies, to whom shall be submitted memorials of all cases for pardon, in the same way as has been hitherto observed. By these courts shall be named the officers of justice for the state, who, in absence of cause shown to the contrary, shall be confirmed by the deputies, on whom shall depend absolutely all the other officers of the household and state.

"And, in order that these deputies may give undivided attention to their official duties, they shall each receive from the treasury 300 scudi a year."[1]

[1] Vat. Ottob. MSS. No. 3184, f. 154. The salary of 300 scudi was increased to 400.

Four days after date of the preceding letter, the provincial parliament of Montefeltro, and the council of S. Leo, met to deliberate thereon, by summons from the commissioner of the province and the podestà of the town. The parliament consisted of four delegates from the landward districts, and twenty-nine others from as many townships; the council was composed of the gonfaloniere, three priors, and twenty-nine citizens. They elected four deputies by ballot, excluding, by a majority of black beans, two of those proposed; and, from these four, one whose election had been unanimous was selected by the Duke as deputy to the council. Similar forms having been observed by the remaining cities, the council entered upon their duties on 22nd of January, 1607, and Francesco Maria resigned himself more than ever to the selfish ease of his solitary and abstracted life at Castel Durante, flattering himself (to use his own words) that "they would inform themselves fully of all matters of internal policy and foreign relations, and would direct these for the service of God, and to the benefit of his subjects, and of his heir."

It would be tedious and unnecessary to notice all the minute instructions issued from time to time to the Eight on matters of police, of patronage, or of trade. The following memorandum, however, written out by Francesco Maria himself for their guidance, in 1611, affords some insight into his views of general policy:—

"In order to continue hourly more fully satisfied with you, I give you the following suggestions, which seem to me called for at this moment. Ever have before your eyes the three objects which I have often enforced upon you—plenty, peace, and justice. The first of these will be secured if the old plan for plenty be not re-established, which, indeed, might be more appropriately called perpetual scarcity, as it was adopted solely for enriching six or eight of the worst citizens who managed it; and should it become necessary to purchase grain, let an advance from my funds be made to the public, always endeavouring to clear off such loans as remain undischarged. And never permit the local councils to meddle with matters that concern them not, seeing that I, by adopting the contrary plan for their satisfaction, fell into errors which turned out ill.

"As to maintaining peace among my subjects, this may easily be done by chastising the riotous and sowers of dissension and discord, whose punishment ought to be public and severe; above all things preventing persons of whatsoever rank to pretend to or maintain retinues of followers, or to domineer over others.

"Justice will be observed by insuring the prompt issue of suits, and by punishing judges when they fall into error; but especially by enforcing an inviolate observance of all orders, decrees, and proclamations; by rarely, and only from necessity, suspending the prosecution of outlaws; and by receiving few fugitives from other states. Prevent so great an increase of lawyers and notaries, and offer obstacles to their admission. Show no undue favour to parties in suits. Vigilantly defend our authority, ever covertly assailed; but do this by fair means, avoiding if possible open ruptures. Eschew partiality and prejudice, rigorously maintaining justice and your duty.

"In the despatch of business promptitude is requisite, avoiding arrears, which occasion oversights, and lead to a wholesale transaction of affairs, without the accuracy necessary to their being done well; and although full consideration and discussion be required, there are few matters which cannot be exhausted by employing on them one's entire energy during two hours; after which they should be carried into effect quickly, without further discourse, but with secrecy. Provided you do all these things with that affection upon which I rely, I doubt not of their happy issue; but I again, and for the last time, remind you that your chief care should be the punctual execution of all my injunctions and commands."[1]

Whatever may have been the immediate effect upon the management of public affairs of the Duke's wayward conduct, its mischievous influence on the character of the young Prince was not long dormant. His education was entrusted, in 1607, to the Countess Vittoria Tortora Ranuccio Santinelli, whose husband was major-domo to the Duke; but the anxiety felt for a life so precious was unduly exaggerated by certain symptoms of childish delicacy, and the system adopted was that of unbounded indulgence, balanced by no obligation to apply himself to anything. Before he had completed his second year, Philip III. settled upon him in reversion his father's retaining pension of 15,000 golden scudi, and company of men-at-arms in Naples, assuring him of ample protection. That the Duke was sensitively anxious to prepare his mind for the duties of manhood thus crowded prematurely upon him, is interestingly shown by a paper of instructions, written in the anticipation of his being left an early orphan. To find in it maxims directly opposed to the writer's own practice may afford scope for saddening speculation to a philosophic moralist, and must have greatly detracted from their influence upon the boy to whom they were addressed. The length of the document, and its interruption to our narrative, will be excused from its importance as illustrating the character of Francesco Maria.

"Believing that at my advanced age I cannot be much longer with you, I have resolved to write down certain memoranda which I consider it most necessary that you should remember, preserving them not merely under your eye, but impressing them deep on your heart; for by none can they be offered you with more affection, or perhaps

[1] Vat. Ottob. MSS. No. 3134, f. 158.

with greater experience, from the affairs which I have conducted.

"I would, therefore, desire you chiefly to endeavour with all your might, to live in the favour of our Lord God, devoutly honouring His holy name, and being careful never to offend Him, firm in His most holy faith without superstition. As to priests and monks, after securing them in the position which is their due, do not establish with them much familiarity beyond what your devotional duties call for; but leave them to look to their proper business, whilst you attend to yours without their assistance, further than their prayers in your behalf.

"Be not merely faithful to his Holiness the Pope, but also obedient, doing all that in you lies for his service, and with sincere attachment seeking to exalt the Holy See.

"In the service of his Catholic Majesty show yourself at all times most zealous, performing it with constancy, and never quitting it until it becomes inconsistent with your honour, which I feel assured it never will be. And further, be ready to display your devotion in a befitting manner; and should his Majesty take the field in person, fail not to be there also, and to identify yourself with him, from which you cannot fail to derive great reputation: remember also, to treat all Spaniards with amiable courtesy. With other sovereigns and princes cultivate the most friendly terms, obliging them when opportunity offers, especially neighbouring powers.

"Maintain towards all, sincerity and truth with mildness; but beware of being deluded, and for this purpose be slow to credit any one.

"When called upon to form any important resolution, examine both sides of the question, and attach yourself to that which seems safest.

"Remember that you leave not for the morrow what can be done on the instant; and so will your affairs generally succeed according to your wishes. When just, your undertakings will ever be forwarded and directed by the Almighty; and thus will the labour be less to yourself than if they are allowed to go on accumulating.

"In the government of your subjects and dependants be most decided; to your associates and well-wishers be gracious and pleasing; towards others just and strict.

"At the hour most convenient to yourself give daily audience to all who seek it, hearing them patiently and without interruption, and tolerating them even while trifling a little. Leave the judges free from interference in the lawful execution of their duties, dispensing mercy where it is justly merited, and reluctant to the punishment of death. In all but aggravated cases, commute it into a minor penalty, especially by sending culprits to the Venetian galleys, since this is an old usage in our family, and as these protect our seas from pirates.

"Choose for your service faithful and prudent nobles, neither selfish, greedy, nor partial.

"See that your ministers and counsellors be men who, as the proverb goes, take the cart road, and boast not themselves inventors of new theories, which, however specious and fine at first sight, are most difficult in practice, and in their issue full of mischief. Show no favour towards rash ventures or novel expedients, but give your attention rather to forward measures that have been determined on. Be not anxious to make many new laws, but, on the contrary, endeavour to condense the old ones.

"Encourage not your relations to meddle in the affairs of your government, lest they should in consequence arrogate to themselves undue influence; but contrive to keep them in good humour by honouring them yourself, and by taking care that others respect them.

"Visit in person, annually, your whole state; or, when prevented from doing so, send one of your judges.

"Be courteous to ecclesiastical dignitaries, giving them

such honours as are their due, and exacting the like in return.

"See that your household be discreet and in nowise quarrelsome, and divide annually among the most deserving of them some donative from escheated property; but I recommend you to keep hold of all castles, and never alienate them, unless to those who have done you some signal and most important service.

"Be liberal in your expenditure, but never exceed your revenues, managing so that every year you may have something in hand; for if you do not attend to this, you will probably find yourself tempted by necessity to seize upon what belongs to your subjects,—a thing you must ever guard yourself from, as well as from any attempts upon the honour of their wives, especially those of the nobility.

"Be to all benignant and affable, entering freely into conversation with men of letters or military acquirements, and, above all, with those skilled in politics and affairs of state.

"Do not be too anxious to devote yourself to scientific studies, which both preoccupy the mind from more important subjects, and sadden it. Be satisfied with a thorough knowledge of your native tongue, so as to read in it all old and modern histories, and at fit times some devotional book; but trust to acquiring knowledge of the sciences from the discourse of their respective professors. It is advisable to learn other languages; indeed, Spanish is necessary, as you are in the service of his Catholic Majesty.

"Practise all heathful exercises, especially, ball, hunting, and the manège. In the first of these you may indulge almost daily; for the second, once a week is sufficient, as it loses the entire day, and when too frequently followed is apt to render one coarse. Make use of the third when you feel inclined, maintaining a small breeding stud, for which your country is admirably adapted, with about thirty fine horses always at your disposal. I warn you, however, not to over-exert yourself in this or similar exercise, for excessive fatigue brings on many infirmities, as has happened to myself. Fencing is likewise most needful, especially that called wide fighting, for close-quarters are dangerous, and of little real avail. Instrumental music and singing are excellent recreations, as well as dancing to give the body freedom. Swimming is also an excellent preservative, especially in travelling.

"Do not indulge too much in sleeping. Eat and drink of everything indifferently, without reference to diet such as is recommended by physicians, of whom keep aloof while you can, never calling them in until you are ill; but when really so, obey them strictly, committing yourself first to God, and secondly to their skill.

"Remember, as soon as convenient, to complete your marriage with the sister of the Grand Duke of Tuscany; for no alliance could be found better or more entirely suitable for this state, for our house, or for yourself. To her, as your wife, be ever most affectionate; yet see that she meddle not in the affairs of government, but more particularly that she does not interfere in matters regarding the administration of justice. Endeavour always to maintain a most friendly footing with her family, paying to the Grand Duke the deference due to a father, and consulting him on every incident of importance.

"Should God grant you more than one son, purchase for one of them a fief, however small, in the kingdom of Naples, and other property, yielding in all 12,000 scudi of revenue, but give him no lands in your own state: by this means you will found a second house, and avert the danger in which our family was at the time of your birth. Your other sons you may provide for by making one a churchman with the Pope's assistance, and by giving to the rest such savings as will in that case be very requisite. Forget not to treat your eldest son like a brother, admitting him to share with you the government and administration, which, if God grant me life, I shall certainly do towards you.

"Lastly, I assure you, that those who have been faithful and attached to me will, if you avail yourself of their services, be the same to you; others you may seek to attach to you, but abandon not these.

"Such is the little I would impress upon you, not without difficulty and much consideration; but take courage, and the execution of it will become easy. I give you my paternal benediction, praying the blessed God to confirm it."[1]

But though it seems agreed that the seed thus kindly and carefully sown fell upon a soil not naturally ungenial, and though to much childish beauty the Prince is stated to have joined a fine temper, a remarkably quick apprehension, and an uncommon memory, he was destined sadly to verify a remark of Dante, that,—

> "Rarely into the branches of the tree
> Doth human worth mount up."

The good fruit of almost spontaneous growth was speedily and entirely choked by rank weeds, fostered under an erroneous system of early discipline. An only child, he was deprived of playmates of his own rank, and even of the companionship of the higher nobility, for whom were substituted those whose flattery and indulgence provoked and pandered to all the worst passions of a spoiled brat; and so early and fatally was this perversion effected, that he had scarcely passed the years of infancy ere the people, who had hailed him as a gift of Heaven, ominously deprecated his accession to power. On his eighth birthday, he was sent by the Duke, with a suitable attendance, to

[1] Bibl. Oliveriana.

pay his vows at the shrine of his patron saint in the cathedral of Gubbio, and to offer there a small bust of himself chased in gold. On this occasion the aged courtiers, who assembled to do honour to his reception, were heard to draw the most melancholy forebodings, on observing the overbearing and fiery temper which he was at no pains to control or conceal.*[1]

*[1] Cf. PELLEGRINI, *op cit.*, in *Boll. cit.* vol. *cit.*, p. 509 *et seq.*, who gives two contemporary accounts of the visit of Federigo in 1618.

CHAPTER XLVII

The Prince's marriage—The Duke entrusts to him the government and retires to Castel Durante—His dissolute career and early death—Birth of his daughter Vittoria—The Duke rouses himself—He arranges the devolution of his state to the Holy See—Papal intrigues.

THE anxiety of Francesco Maria for continuance of his line, and for the maintenance of his state against the risk of a minority, led him to select a match of policy for his son while yet a mere infant. In October, 1608, he sent a confidential adviser, Count Francesco Maria Mammiani, to attend on his behalf the marriage of Cosimo Prince of Tuscany; and during its prolonged festivities, a negotiation was happily concluded for the betrothal of Princess Claudia, youngest daughter of the Grand Duke Ferdinand II. to Prince Federigo. The death of her father, soon after, did not delay the ratification of an engagement so advantageous to all parties, and on the 24th of April following, it was publicly announced,—the united ages of the childish couple amounting to eight years and a half, and the Princess being the elder by eight months. In November, she sent to "her husband" the appropriate presents of a nicely accoutred pony, a poodle taught to leap, a jackdaw, and an inkstand in the form of Mount Calvary containing various conveniences. In honour, probably, of the same auspicious occasion, was a gift of jewels from Philip III. of Spain to the Duke and Duchess in 1609, consisting of a girdle, necklace, and brooch of gold; the girdle containing twenty-eight, and the neck-

FEDERIGO, PRINCE OF URBINO
From the picture once in the possession of Andrew Coventry of Edinburgh

lace eighteen links, studded with a hundred and twenty-six diamonds; sixty gold buttons enamelled in white and red, each with three diamonds; and a string of two hundred and twenty-six pearls of various sizes.[1]

The long and friendly intercourse of the Dukes of Urbino with the crown of Spain had moulded their court to a tone of Spanish gravity, and a certain severity of manner, which the cold character, reserved habits, and strict morals of Francesco Maria had served to confirm. To this the conduct of the youthful Prince soon offered the strongest contrast. Wilful in all things, and impatient of control, he endured no constraint upon his gratifications. These were generally of the most trifling and childish description; and in one respect alone, and that an unfortunate one, did he exhibit any manly quality. His precocious gallantry was a scandal to the staid manners of the court, and proved ruinous to his own constitution. Too late was his father made aware of follies and vices which he had allowed to attain a dangerous height; and to the counsels of his advisers, that even yet a decided check should be applied, he weakly replied, in the subtleties of a false philosophy, that restraints now imposed would but irritate his son, and surely lead to greater excesses so soon as they could be removed or burst. In truth, the old man shrank from the exertions which his interference would require, and selfishly calculated on being removed from the scene ere the mischief was fully matured. But, whatever may have been the Duke's motives, his refusal to interfere was quickly reported to the Prince, who, thus secured against control, was emboldened to new excesses.

Finding that years only confirmed those vicious symptoms which the Prince had manifested from childhood, and which a bad education had not even attempted to eradi-

[1] Oliveriana MSS. No. 375, vol. XXXI., p. 62.

cate, his father thought fit to try the experiment of sending him forth to see the world, where, in the intercourse of courts, and in contact with men of distinction, he might observe those qualities which mankind deem worthy of honour, and might learn the reputation acquired by his ancestors. This plan, which had more good sense than most of those which Francesco Maria was in the habit of forming, unfortunately failed, and brought about results exactly the reverse of those which had been anticipated.

On his journey through Romagna towards Florence, Federigo's evil genius brought him into the company of some strolling comedians returning from Venice. Delighted with their loose manners, he threw himself among them without reserve, and a taste for their pursuits was formed at first sight, which disgracefully occupied the few remaining years of his life. Such is the account given by Passeri; and two entries in the Duke's Diary mention that the Prince set out to visit Florence on the 1st and returned on the 22nd of October, 1616. During the following month the Grand Duke Cosimo II. arrived from Loreto on a visit to Pesaro, with his brother the Cardinal; they travelled with a large suite partly in coaches and six, partly in litters, or on horseback, escorted by a guard of cuirassiers, being in all not less than six hundred persons. The Prince met and welcomed them at the head of a hundred mounted gentlemen, and accompanied them on a hunting party. They stayed six days at Pesaro, and thence proceeded to Rimini, leaving many presents, among which the Grand Duke gave Federigo a beautiful little office-book in a case, worth 1000 golden scudi. Regarding his youthful irregularities the Journal maintains a uniform silence, and the few notices of amusements at court scarcely afford us any index of his tastes. It would seem that up to his marriage he rarely left his parents' residence. During that time we find but two theatrical representations mentioned. In the carnival of 1617 nine couples of knights fought within a barrier, where there were also two chariots, one of Pallas, the other of Venus. The following year a wild boar, caught near Mondolfo, where it had attacked various peasants, was baited in the palace-yard at Pesaro with large dogs and spears; and some days thereafter the Prince, with five others of his age, held a mimic tourney in the great hall.

The melancholy turn which the Prince's folly had taken determined his unhappy parent at once to conclude his marriage, which, even should it unhappily fail in rescuing him from a disgraceful career, might at least secure the continuance of his family. The Princess had a character for high spirit, not free from hauteur, but accompanied with decided talent; qualities that seemed likely to influence her destined husband, or, at all events, to maintain his dignity against the debasing tendency of dissolute habits. An intimate alliance with so powerful and so close a neighbour was in every view politic, but especially at a time when the duchy of Urbino had become a more than ever desirable adjunct to the Papal States. If any further inducements were wanting to render this the most advisable marriage for the Prince, it was supplied by the dowry of 300,000 crowns of gold. But an arrangement so eligible seemed fated at every step to be thwarted by the unsparing hand of death. When all was ready for publishing the betrothal, the bride's father was, as we have seen, called away; just as the nuptials were on the eve of celebration, thirteen years later, her brother, the Grand Duke Cosimo II., died on the 28th of February, 1621. The urgent and advantageous circumstances of the connection again superseded the formality of court etiquette, and an early day was fixed for the marriage.

On the 19th of April the Prince sent on a confidential envoy with the following letter to his bride[1]:—

[1] Bibl. Oliveriana MSS. No. 396, p. 131.

"To the Princess Claudia, Consort of the Prince of Urbino.

"Most serene Highness, my Lady, and most affectionate Consort,

"Giordani precedes me, and will give your Highness certain assurance of my arrival next week, by the favour of God. I beseech your Highness to accompany me on this journey with the favour of your good wishes and prayers; and meanwhile I, with all my heart, kiss your hands. From Pesaro, the 16th of April, 1621.

"Your Highness's most affectionate servant and husband, who loves you more than himself,

"THE PRINCE OF URBINO."

The same day Federigo went to visit his father, and on the 22nd left Castel Durante. At the Alpine frontier he was met by a guard of honour, under whose escort he arrived on the 25th in Florence, where, after a pompous entrance into the city, the Villa Baroncelli was assigned for his reception. The ceremony was performed on the 29th, the respective ages of the parties being sixteen and seventeen.*[1] The public joy felt in the duchy at a step which promised to secure the continued succession of the ducal house, and with it the nationality of the state, was proportioned rather to the importance of those objects than to the merits of Federigo. As yet, however, his faults had been shown to but a limited extent, and by most of those who were cognisant of them were generally believed the exuberant but passing growth of boyish folly, which time, and, above all, a respectable marriage, would surely eradicate. The Duke was willing to second the manifestation of these feelings, and the festivities wherewith the event was celebrated at Pesaro were consequently very elaborate.

*[1] The ceremony was performed on the 28th February without any pomp. Cf. UGOLINI, *op cit.*, vol. II., p. 437.

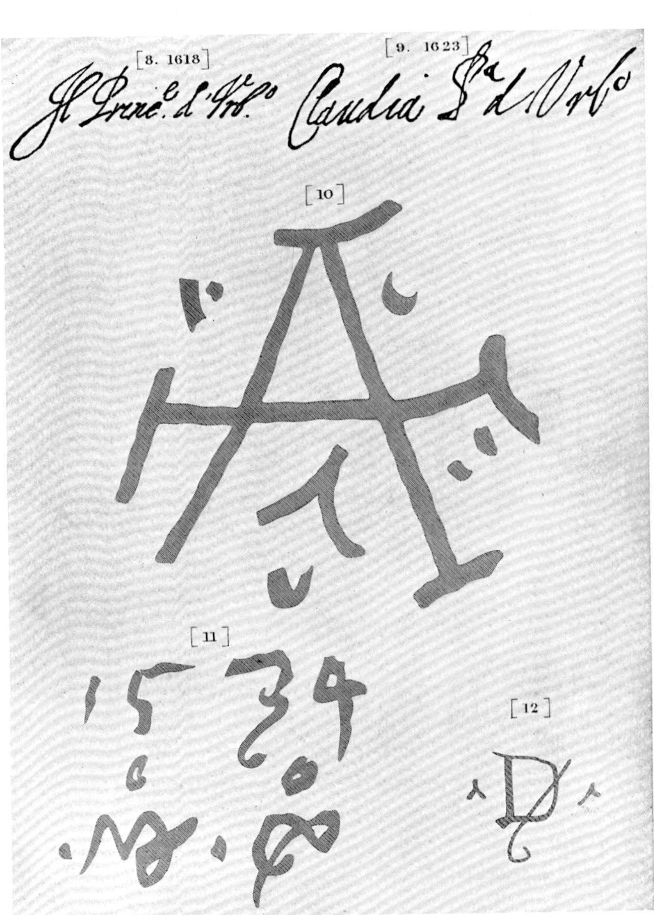

FACSIMILES OF SIGNATURES AND MONOGRAMS

Among the most striking novelties was a device by which discharges of artillery were so regulated as to harmonise, or rather to beat time with the military bands, and the great hall of the palace was fitted up as a theatre for the performance of entertainments similar to what we have lately described.[1]

The Prince preceded his bride, and, after passing a day with his father at Castel Durante, reached Pesaro on the 15th of May. On the 21st, she set out on her ill-fated journey, and on the 26th was met at Lamole by her husband. Although it is only within the last few years that the Apennine range has been there opened up by a road equalling in convenience any of the celebrated Alpine passes, a hasty effort was made to render her route practicable for a carriage from the frontier to her new capital. In the communal records of S. Angelo in Vado, I noticed an instruction that the town should bear its portion of the repairs of the way from Borgo S. Sepolchro, preparatory to her passage, and should contribute towards the public rejoicings, triumphal arches, and other complimentary demonstrations. Among the ingenious devices adopted in honour of the occasion, was the construction in wood of a colossal equestrian figure of the Prince on horseback, part of which still remains in the public hall of S. Angelo. Tradition ascribes it to Frederico Zuccaro, but his death in 1609 places him beyond the suspicion of executing what seems to have been little creditable to the artistic skill of his townsmen. The bridal party, after sleeping at Mercatello, proceeded by easy journeys to Pesaro, spending only a forenoon at Castel Durante with the Duke, who, unequal to the journey, had deputed his principal courtiers, escorted by a hundred gentlemen on horseback, to receive the Princess on the Apennines, and conduct her home. Among the deputations which on this occasion attended to welcome her to her future dominions,

[1] See p. 177.

was one from S. Leo, the ancient capital of the original fief of the Feltrian race, bringing a donative of twelve silver cups valued at 500 scudi, to whom she returned the following answer :—

"To the most magnificent and my much loved the Gonfaloniere and Priors of the city of S. Leo.

"Most magnificent and well-beloved,

"On entering this state, I brought with me a firm resolution impartially to favour all, but this I shall especially observe towards you; for I have particularly to acknowledge your affectionate devotion, and gratefully to accept the duty you have expressed towards me by the mouth of your deputation, and by the compliment of plate you have given me in token of your attachment. I shall ever cherish towards you the like good will, and a desire of usefully testifying it. May God preserve you. From Pesaro, 19th December, 1621.

"Your most loving,

"CLAUDIA, PRINCESS OF URBINO."[1]

With infatuation unequalled perhaps in the long catalogue of parental errors, Francesco Maria now gave the finishing stroke to a system which had trained up his only child to become the scourge of his people and the ruin of his house. We have seen him deprecate a minority as a national misfortune; we have now to witness him anticipating all its evils, by voluntarily entrusting the reins to one whom youth, education, inexperience, and follies combined to render utterly inefficient for their management. That this plan had long been cherished as a favourite speculation, may be gathered from those instructions to his son which have been already quoted; that its most attractive feature was the escape it secured to him from the business and duties of his station, admits not of a

[1] MARINI, *Saggio di S. Leo.*

doubt. Flattering himself that, in providing the Prince with an honourable and eligible match, he had done his utmost to retrieve past errors and secure a prosperous future, he hurried the execution of his scheme, apprehensive perhaps that delay would render its absurdity more glaring, or bring to light some new disqualification in Federigo. In absence of any rational explanation of such a step, it has been supposed a secret stipulation with the Grand Duke at the time of the marriage, but of this there is not a shadow of evidence. The motive imputed by Gozzi, that it was a device of the Duke to prevent his son from longing for his death and for the delights of sovereignty, seems quite reconcileable with the false philosophy by which he so perversely regulated his general conduct. We turn with interest to the Diary at a moment thus important to his history and that of his state, but find it here more than usually meagre, alluding neither to the fact of his abdication, its manner, nor its motives.[1] Like King Lear, the old man already felt—

> "How sharper than a serpent's tooth it is
> To have a thankless child,"

and his Memoirs abruptly conclude with the negotiation for the Prince's marriage. From Passeri's investigations, we only learn that he one day called round him his son and principal officers, and, after addressing to both a long exhortation on the new duties about to be devolved upon them, made over to the former the reins of government.[2]

[1] As a specimen of the style of this most disappointing MS., and in proof of its small historical importance, I extract all the notices for August 1621, the month in which, according to Passeri, this transaction took place.

"6. News arrived of the death of the Archduke Albert, which happened at Brussels on the 13th ult.

15. Vespers began to be performed in the church of S. Rocca of Castel Durante.

21. A stag was killed, weighing fully 530 lbs.

26. Four large English dogs coursed in the park, which belong to the Prince; they killed two fallow deer."

[2] It appears that on the 25th of July the Prince arrived from Urbino, and stayed two days, during which probably this scene took place.

Reserving for his own use one-third of the private revenues of his family, which from various documents seem to have amounted to about 300,000 crowns, he shut himself up more closely than ever in his—

> "Boasted seat
> Of studious peace and mild philosophy."

Among the Oliveriana MSS. I found a list of his court taken to Castel Durante, which, though undated, probably refers to the arrangements made at this period.

1 counsellor, 1 secretary, 5 gentlemen of the household . .	7
4 captains, 5 chamberlains, 4 assistant chamberlains . .	13
1 dwarf or hunchback, 1 watchmaker, 1 barber . . .	3
1 master of the wardrobe, 2 porters, 4 pages and their 2 servants	9
1 physician, 1 apothecary, 2 chaplains, 3 readers . . .	7
18 household servants, 10 stable servants . . .	28
Total . . .	67

Yet the theoretical tendencies of his mind had not prevented him from establishing, in the early portion of his reign, many practical regulations conducive to the acceleration of business, and to the due order of public affairs. His sway had been upon the whole a mild one; and on a retrospect of two centuries, the government of his predecessors must be pronounced to have promoted, in a degree rarely paralleled, general happiness and public decorum, and at the same time the true glory of their state. But all this was now to be changed, and the brilliant dynasty of Urbino was doomed to expire, exhaling a vile and loathsome odour. That court which the refined tastes of the Feltrian Dukes and the polished pen of Castiglione had rendered a model to the world, which the literature and conduct of its later sovereigns had maintained in like honourable distinction, was about to present a melancholy spectacle of unexampled degradation. To enumerate the debasing excesses successively introduced by Federigo is a sad and sickening task, which it were well briefly to go through. His fancy for music was indulged, to the exclusion of more serious avocations. His casual acquaintance with the company of Venetian comedians was ripened into an intimacy, which gradually monopolised his time and thoughts, and was followed out with frenzied enthusiasm. These persons, belonging then to the vilest classes, and treated accordingly, became the Prince's associates in public and in private. Conforming his morals to theirs, he admitted the actresses into his palace in daring defiance of decency, and openly established one, named Argentina, as his mistress, fêting her publicly in Pesaro, and lavishing upon her large sums. Advancing from one extravagance to another, this petty Nero of a petty court delighted to bear a part in their dramatic representations before his own subjects, generally choosing the character of a servant or a lover, as most congenial to his degraded capacity. His people, imbued with respect for the traditionary glories of their former Dukes, and accustomed to the gravity of Spanish manners, stood in consternation at such spectacles. But they scarcely dared express their feelings or hope for redress, for, whilst he thus

> "Moiling lay,
> Tangled in net of sensual delight,"

the Prince had adopted the most severe precautions to prevent his father becoming cognisant of what was passing.

But, however he might succeed in blinding one who was probably too happy to shut his eyes and ears against all that occurred beyond the limits of his favourite park and convent at Castel Durante, those who owed the youthful tyrant no allegiance of apprehension carried rumours of his doings to Florence. The family of the Princess anxious to interrupt a career so disgraceful to her husband, so miserable for herself, invited Federigo to visit them; and we find from the Diary so often quoted, that he went to Florence on the 12th of September, and returned on the 3rd of December, 1622.

The Princess still fondly hoped (for women's hopes when fed by their wishes die slowly) that the case was not desperate; she accordingly received her husband with the joy and affection of a faithful wife, and ordered a salute of a hundred cannon to welcome him back. But her trust was doomed to a grievous disappointment. The recent restraints of a foreign residence were speedily compensated by new indulgences, more scandalous, if possible, than before. The buffoonery he had learned on the stage was carried into the streets, through which he sallied in some low disguise, insulting all and sundry, and striking them with the flat of his sword, till frequently obliged to discover himself to the astonished spectators. The time which he could spare from such ribaldry, and from his comedians, was devoted to the stable. Besides driving his own horses, an occupation in those stately days exclusively menial, he performed about them the vilest offices of farrier and stable-boy. At length, in executing a feat, unattempted, perhaps, by subsequent Jehus, that of driving eighteen horses in hand, he galloped over a poor child. This outrage, having reached his father, provoked him, in a fit of passionate indignation, and in forgetfulness of his abdicated powers, to pronounce sentence of exile from Pesaro against the Prince,—an order which, of course, was not enforced. The reserved inanity of the Diary throws no light whatever on the Duke's knowledge or feelings in regard to such occurrences, though the following notices are scarcely reconcileable with his ignorance of one excess of his son's headstrong career.

"1623, February 24. The Duchess went to Urbino for the comedy represented there the following day, and returned on the 26th.

"——, —— 27. The comedy was performed in Castel Durante."[1]

[1] The succeeding entry abruptly concludes the Journal:—"March 7. The Prince arrived about 10 A.M., having left Pesaro the preceding day, and returned there the 10th;" probably his last meeting with his father.

Resuming Passeri's Memoir, to which, although incorrect in many details, we are mainly indebted for this portion of our narrative, we find that the Prince moved to Urbino early in the summer, the company of actors forming the strength of his court, and there nightly performed with them, amid the acclamations of a rabble audience. With a view to conciliate his mother-in-law, the Grand Duchess of Tuscany, whose interference in behalf of her insulted daughter he had too good reason to anticipate, he prepared a magnificent coach and six costly horses as a present to her. On the 28th of June he acted as usual on the stage, the part which he sustained on this occasion being (according to Galuzzi) the degraded one of a pack-horse, carrying about the comedians on his back, and finally kicking off a load of crockery with which he was laden. About midnight he retired to rest, worn out by this buffoonery, after giving orders for a chasse next day at Piobbico near Castel Durante. At dawn, hearing the clatter of the horses which were setting out for Florence, he rose and gave some orders from the window in his night dress. In the morning his attendants, surprised at not being summoned, and fearing he would be too late to attend mass before noon, knocked in vain at his door. Three hours passed away in doubts and speculations, and at length two of the courtiers burst open the door, exclaiming "Up, your Highness, 'tis time for the comedy!" But for him that hour was past; the well-known and welcome words fell on an ear whose silver cord was broken. His body was under the icy grip of death; his spirit had fled to its awful account.

The body was discovered on its back, bleeding at the nose and mouth, the left hand under the pillow, one leg drawn up, and the mattress much discomposed. The Prince always slept alone, and locked himself in, without retaining any attendants in the adjoining apartment. Six strangers, with the Tuscan accent, had been observed about the palace the day before. From these circumstances, and from his odious character, suspicions of foul play were entertained; but most of the accounts which I have seen attribute his death to apoplexy, resulting probably from premature and excessive dissipation. The body was opened, and no traces of poison were detected; but a small quantity of water was found upon the brain, which the medical report attributed to over indulgence in athletic sports, and to the bushy thickness of his hair, which he greatly neglected. The most probable explanation of this catastrophe was that of the astrologer Andrea Argoli, who, after an elaborate calculation of the Prince's horoscope, pronounced him to have died of an epileptic fit, induced by the chill of the morning air; a conclusion dictated, no doubt, by medical experience, rather than by the study of those malignant planetary influences which the quack thought fit to quote as decisive of the question.

On the first alarm the Princess had rushed to the room, breaking through all opposition, and exclaiming, "What! my Lord is ill, and am I not to see him?" but finding him dead, she fainted. The chief anxiety of all was how to break the dire news to the "way-worn and way-wearied" Duke, who was suffering from a severe fit of gout, in his wonted retirement. At length, the Bishop of Pesaro, nominally head of the court, undertook the painful mission. Having arrived at Castel Durante, he sent in by a chamberlain a sealed note, containing the words "The Prince is dead." This the Duke at first desired to be laid aside till later, with his other letters; but on being told that the Bishop was in attendance, he read it without emotion, and exclaimed in Latin, "The Lord gave, the Lord hath taken away; blessed be the name of the Lord." This Christian stoicism might seem inexplicable, but from the context of the narrative, which states that to the lamentations of his attendants, he without a sigh or tear supplied consolation, assuring them that the event was irremediable, and one for which he had long been prepared; and adding, with Sancho Panza-like resignation, "He who lives badly comes to a bad end, and one born by a miracle dies by violence." He then with perfect self-command gave directions necessary for the funeral, and for the exigencies of the government; and at supper ordered the reading of Italian and Spanish books of edification to be continued as usual.

In an age when omens were observed with a heathenish superstition, the people began to take note of these before they considered the recent event in its practical and political bearings. It was now recollected that the journey of the Prince and Princess, on their return from their marriage, had been interrupted, before they reached Pesaro, by an extraordinary tempest, which flooded their capital, and delayed their public entry. On the day month preceding Federigo's death, a flight of brown moths passed over Urbino towards the sea, darkening the air for hours. Again, during the fatal night, a strange and threatening cloud was seen by many to cast its gloomy shadow over that city, and, after successively assuming the forms of the eagle of Montefeltro, and the tree of Rovere, to disperse and vanish in the direction of Rome. Others saw serpents and similar monstrous apparitions wrestling in mid-air, and contributed their quota to the strange saws and marvellous instances which fed the popular craving for prodigies. It is scarcely necessary to observe that these facts, or at all events their application, had called for no remark until men's minds were filled with the catastrophe of which they were then interpreted as the precursors. But it may be thought singular that those who busied themselves in finding out ominous coincidences omitted to note a circumstance chronicled by the often-cited Diary, that, on the 21st of August, 1604, nine months before the Prince's birth, lightning struck the Duke's chamber at Castel Durante. Thunder on the left was hailed by the Roman augurs as lucky, but this visitation seems too violent for a good omen.

The honours of a royal sepulture were lavished on one whose life had been thus unworthy of his station; and such was the magnificence displayed in the trappings of death that, besides many overcharged narratives of the funeral, portraits were multiplied of the Prince laid out in his richly-silvered robes. He was deposited in a tomb which Francesco Maria had destined for himself in the grotto or crypt of the metropolitan cathedral, with an inscription to the following purport:—

In this tomb,
Prepared for himself by
Francesco Maria II., Last Duke of Urbino,
Rest the ashes of
His son Federigo,
Who was cut off by a sudden death,
On the 29th June, MDCXXIII.,
Aged XVIII. years.

On a tablet in the church of Sta. Chiara, his fate is thus touchingly commemorated:—"The waning day saw Federigo Prince of Urbino, in whom sank the house della Rovere, sound in health, and pre-eminent in every gift of fortune; the succeeding dawn beheld him struck down by sudden death, on the 29th of June, 1623. Stranger! pass on, and learn that happiness, like the brittle glass, just when brightest is most fragile."[1]

The first year of the Prince's marriage had given him a daughter, born at Pesaro, on the 7th of February, 1622, whose advent, as we learn from her grandfather's Diary, was marked by the appearance of three suns in the heavens. She was baptized Vittoria, and was hailed by the Duke and his people with joyful anticipations of a fruitful union,

[1] See these and other monumental inscriptions of Urbino sovereigns, Appendix, No. VII.

which were destined never to be realised. Francesco Maria's age and infirmities cut off all hopes of a new alliance, and the male line of the Rovere race, to whom were limited the ducal dignity and state, was obviously doomed to extinction in his person. It was true that a similar failure of rightful heirs had, in the preceding century, been supplied by a substitution of the heir-general to this very fief; but that transaction was, in fact, a new investiture, dictated by papal nepotism, and scarcely veiled under the guise of a heritable title. The spirit of the papacy had, since then, been greatly changed in the ordeal of the Reformation; and the ambition of its successive heads, purified from selfish motives, had been long concentrated upon advancing the spiritual and temporal supremacy of the Holy See. But here the question rested not merely on such general principles of law and policy. The foresight of Paul V. had interposed a barrier clause in the marriage contract of Federigo, whereby the Grand Duke's solemn renunciation of all pretensions in behalf of the female issue of that union was distinctly recorded.

As soon as the widowed princess had rallied a little from an advent which, however shocking to her nerves, could not be supposed very long to weigh upon her feelings, she despatched a courier to Florence with the news, and soon prepared to leave for ever a country which she had adopted with bright hopes, quickly turned to bitter experience. After paying a brief visit to the Duke, in whose hands she left her child at Castel Durante, she returned to her family, to forget the troubled dream of the last two years. That she succeeded in banishing it from her thoughts may be presumed from her remarriage, three years after, to the Archduke Leopold of Austria; and it is interesting to notice that the latest jotting in the Diary of her former father-in-law, long after its regular entries had ceased, runs thus:—"On 26th March, 1626,

Count delle Gabiccie was sent to Florence to visit Donna Claudia, Archduchess of Austria."

The situation into which Francesco Maria found himself thrown by the Prince's death was one requiring the support of all that philosophy which it had been the chief pursuit of his life to attain. His house was desolate; his line suddenly extinguished; his sovereignty about to lapse. But these crushing blows were accompanied by aggravating circumstances, which called for immediate exertion. The brief reign of Federigo had proved equally detrimental to his state and ruinous to himself. The government was falling to pieces, the finances were in hopeless confusion. Thus was the literary retirement which the Duke had thought to secure from the residue of his life rudely interrupted, and the cares of sovereignty he had shaken off were thrown back upon him, more inextricable than ever. The good order at home and influence abroad, from thirty-seven years of prudent and popular sway, had, in two brief years, been scattered, and there remained to the old man but the choice of recommencing the labours of a lifetime, or abandoning the reins of government now thrust back into his unnerved hands. Judging from his dispositions and past history, it would not be difficult to conjecture which of these alternatives had the greater attraction; yet at this juncture, sense of duty for a time triumphed over the dictates of inclination and Francesco Maria showed himself every inch a monarch.

After consulting for a few days with the Bishop of Pesaro, Count Francesco Maria Mammiani, his favourite and Count Giulio Giordani, a friend of forty years' tried service, he thus matured his measures. The papal chair being vacated by the death of Gregory XV., on the 8th of July, he sent to the College of Cardinals an official intimation of his son's death, and a full assurance o dutiful devotion. He accompanied the like notification to his subjects with an injunction for the election of a new council of eight, to whom he proposed to commit the administration of civil and criminal justice, for the burden of which his years were incompetent. To the widowed Princess he made every overture which affectionate sympathy could suggest. Finally, he resumed the ducal mantle, and the functions which he had so unfortunately devolved; and, dismissing the whole administration which his son had employed, he entered upon the government, with the assistance of a small but select cabinet. His first thoughts were bestowed upon the destiny of his orphan grand-daughter, and, notwithstanding the suggestion of his counsellors, that he should keep her as an instrument whereby the policy of neighbouring powers, who would doubtless aspire to so eligible a match, might be made subservient to strengthen his relations abroad, he insisted upon some immediate arrangement, which would relieve him from the apprehension of leaving unprotected a prize so tempting to papal or princely ambition. The question was brought to a speedy solution by a well-timed offer from the Grand Duke Ferdinand II. of Tuscany, to receive and educate in his family his niece, and eventually to make her his consort, on condition of her being declared heiress of all the Duke's allodial and personal property. To secure the intimate alliance and support of the Medici had, as we have seen, long been the cherished policy of Francesco Maria, and the importance of a connection sufficiently powerful to maintain the rights of the Princess, in that revolution which must succeed immediately upon his death, was self-evident. But there was another consideration equally cogent, for, on the extinction of her father's family, nature and law pointed out her maternal cousin as the most suitable guardian of her childhood and education. Having decided in favour of a proposal at once advantageous to his grand-daughter, and releasing him from one of the greatest anxieties of his position, the Duke lost no time in sending her to the court of Tuscany, under protection of Count and Countess Mammiani. Indeed, these arrangements were all concluded within four months of his son's death.

On the 6th of August, the conclave elected Cardinal Maffeo Barberini, of a family originally Florentine, who had only attained his fifty-fifth year; a man respectable at once from his talents, his habits of business, and his moral character. It was observed that, during the sittings of the conclave, a hive of bees swarmed under one of their windows, an incident rendered notable from the Barberini carrying that insect in their arms. On ascending the chair of St. Peter, the first business which occupied Urban VIII. was the important accession to the ecclesiastical state promised by the Prince of Urbino's death. There was no legal doubt that the fief, limited to the male line of Guidobaldo II., must lapse on that of the old Duke; but the struggles whereby church vassals had formerly supplied, by steel or gold, similar defects of constitutional title, were not forgotten, and the College of Cardinals looked upon the infant Princess as a subject of keen interest.*[1] It was, therefore, not without jealousy that they learned her sudden betrothal to so powerful a sovereign; and the Pontiff's remonstrances, though avowedly grounded on the conclusion of that important transaction without enabling him to display his friendly respect for the parties, were probably intended to keep the arrangement open for after cavil. A brief interval supplied new grounds for anxiety, on the arrival of a messenger from Francesco Maria with tidings of an overture on the part of the Emperor Ferdinand II., directly at variance with the pretensions of the Holy See. Ferdinand had accompanied his condolence with a proposal that the

*[1] Cf. *Memorie istoriche concernenti la devoluzione dello stato d'Urbino alla Sede Apostolica* (Amsterdam, 1723).

Duke should recognise the imperial title to the countships of Montefeltro and Castel Durante on his death, as being original fiefs of the empire, and offered to renew the investiture of these in favour of the infant heiress. But, faithful to his ecclesiastical allegiance, the Duke courteously declined availing himself of a favour which seemed more likely to reawaken the slumbering controversies (though scarcely now the conflicts) between Guelph and Ghibelline, than to secure any available benefit to Princess Vittoria. Pleading a disinclination to open up questions that might disturb the peace of his declining years, he left it to the Emperor, when these should close, to transact any such arrangement directly with the Holy See; a reply which pleased neither him nor the Grand Duke.

The Emperor being uncle of the Grand Duke, his proposition could not be viewed in any other light than as an attempt to establish a legal basis for whatever claims on the states of Urbino it might suit the husband of Vittoria hereafter to make. It was accordingly met by Urban with very decided measures. He delegated three prelates of tried fidelity to the circumjacent provinces of the Church, with instructions to watch closely the affairs of the duchy, and, in case of any movement adverse to the ecclesiastical interests, to march troops at once across the frontier. He then made a formal appeal to the Duke, as the faithful and devoted adherent of the Holy See, to resign into its safe custody S. Leo, which, besides being considered the most impregnable fortress in Italy, was capital of the countship of Montefeltro, and formed part of the mortgage assigned by Clement VII. to the Medici, in security for alleged debts, still unsettled since the usurpation of Lorenzo de' Medici. This unceremonious proposition was accompanied by a distinct avowal of the Pope's resolve to make sure of the devolution to the ecclesiastical state of every morsel of the dukedom; and an intimation that any refusal would necessitate military demonstrations at Rimini and Città di Castello. So decided, indeed, was his Holiness to abate nothing of the renown which he anticipated from effecting this important accession to the pontifical temporalities, that he is said to have avowed his resolution to fall under the walls of Urbino, or be hanged on its battlements, rather than yield one tittle of his demands.*[1]

But this precipitation failed in its object. The Duke was startled by what seemed at best a harsh return for the leal and true faith towards his ecclesiastical over-lord which had actuated his conduct. His suspicions thus aroused placed him on the defensive in his interviews with the legate Pavoni, whose persuasions were coldly repelled, and whose tone of menace called up all the old man's pride. He briefly and indignantly replied that death alone should deprive him of a sovereignty which he was fully able to maintain ; that the extinction of his family was a dispensation of God ; but that the Pontiff's demand was an insinuation against his good faith, which was far beyond question ; finally, that his Holiness would do well to await the close of his few remaining days, when he would obtain everything in the due course of nature. To show that he spoke in earnest, he the same night despatched a reinforcement to the garrison of S. Leo ; and his jealousy being thoroughly awakened, he refused to perform the alternative which the Legate had, with modified tone, suggested as a satisfactory solution of the difficulty, by writing a formal acknowledgment that his entire state was held under the Church, and a promise to do no act that might compromise or prejudice her rights over it. Monsignor Pavoni, interpreting some hasty expression of the Duke into a dismissal, was about to set out for Rome the same night ; but, having remained

*[1] It is curious to note the shameless zeal, astuteness, and cunning of the papacy in this matter. I believe a work on the subject is promised by Professor C. Scotoni. The Pope could not have proved his right to Urbino in any tribunal. His claim was really more absurd than the claim of the Emperor.

till morning to allow time for cooler consideration, he obtained, under the hand of his Highness, such a declaration as he had suggested. On his return, he met Cardinal Cennino, another ambassador whom the impatient anxiety of Urban had despatched to insist with still greater urgency on the original terms. It were useless and irksome to follow the thread of diplomatic intrigue now brought to bear on the poor bereaved Duke. He felt himself demeaned even by the document which he had consented to give; but when he found it was but a prelude to new demands,—when he ascertained that a war establishment was ready along the ecclesiastical frontier to pounce upon his territory on the slightest pretext,—and when he was actually called upon to administer to the governors of his principal fortresses, and to the officers in command of his militia, an oath ensuring their allegiance to the Pope from the day of his own death, accompanied with a promise on his part not to appoint any one to those situations who had not taken a similar oath, indignation brought on an attack of illness which had nearly put an end to all difficulties by carrying him to the grave. This new misfortune, far from obtaining for the old man relief from these persecutions, stimulated the papal emissaries who surrounded him to fresh importunities. Urban's apprehensions were augmented by measures which Francesco Maria had taken for garrisoning his principal fortresses with troops from Tuscany and Naples, and by rumours of a new intrigue for transferring the hand of Vittoria to Leopold, son of the Emperor, thus giving to the latter a direct interest in this already involved dispute, which Philip IV. of Spain, jealous of the prospective aggrandisement of the Church, showed every disposition still further to complicate. The Pope, in order to forward his views upon the duchy, had, without consulting the Duke, promoted Monsignor Paulo Emilio Santorio from the see of Cesena to be Archbishop of Urbino, a man of violent temper and coarse manners, whose nomination was regarded as an insult by Francesco Maria, and who injudiciously substituted threats for conciliation in his intercourse with the Duke. This example was followed by subordinate agents who surrounded his sick bed, and wore him out by alternately working on his irritable disposition, his avarice, and his superstitious belief in astrology. Every turn of his malady was watched, and reported to Rome as matter of hope or fresh anxiety, whilst his palace was beset by troublesome and meddling spies.

Nor were his negotiations with the Pontiff the only sources of irritation which daily accumulated upon the unhappy Francesco Maria. The cares of state, from which he had of late escaped, returned more irksomely than before. The brief misgovernment of the Prince had thrown upon him a greatly aggravated burden of anxiety and labour in the direction of these affairs; and his old favourites and tried counsellors were dropping around him, just at the crisis when he most required their services. His constitution, impaired by years and broken by gout, gave way under his agony of mind, and a paralytic seizure made fresh breaches upon his system. With a frame thus enfeebled, a mind thus disgusted, he sent for Antonio Donato, a noble Venetian long resident at his court, who had been at various times employed in political affairs, and addressed him in words which his Narrative of these events has preserved to us:—

"Your Lordship sees to what a condition God has reduced me. My house he has left unto me desolate: he has taken from me my dominion, my health, and my honour. I have sold myself to one skilful in profiting by my misfortunes: I am reduced to the shadow of sovereignty, and continually exposed to new inroads. To await death in so miserable a plight is impossible, to anticipate it were a crime: unable to recover what is gone from me, all now left me is to die without disgrace, after living for seventy-six years with nothing to regret. To you I would impart my ideas, that we may consider whether, by surrendering what remains, I might mitigate my vexations. I think of entreating the Pope to send me any one he pleases, who may govern this country, dependent upon me and by virtue of my authority, which I shall delegate to him as fully as it is vested in my person. Thus may his Holiness more effectually secure the return of these states after my death under the sway of the Church, and thus will he be enabled to liberate me from the restraint of obligations and oaths, no longer necessary when his own deputy is invested with the government, leaving me, in these my last hours, time to think of death, and to prepare myself suitably to meet it, as I well know it cannot be distant. . . . And perhaps this plan, which I own is hard to digest, may be less irksome in practice than it now seems in discussion; for in truth, I am no longer what I once was, nor ought I at this juncture to think but of my people's peace and my own. After all that has occurred, this ecclesiastical governor may prove the least annoying expedient; at all events it will free me from the irritation and slavery which past events have brought upon me."

After having at first argued against the measure thus suggested, Donato was at length induced to carry the proposal formally to the Pope, without previous consultation with any one else. Suspicious perhaps of so sudden a change in the sentiments of Francesco Maria, the Sacred College raised difficulties in order to gain time for deliberation; but when, with his wonted impatience, he proposed to recall Donato and reconsider the matter, with a view to some other measure, the proffered devolution was accepted without further delay. The papal brief to that effect was dated the 10th December, 1624, and on the 20th, the Duke executed a blank warrant, making over his whole sovereign authority to the governor who might be named, and reserving only the empty name of his subject's allegiance.

The Devolution was effected on the following terms. Along with all sovereign rights, there were conveyed to the Holy See the various fortified places in the duchy, and the residences at Urbino, Pesaro, and S. Leo. The Camera was allowed a preference in purchasing such warlike instruments, ammunition, and stores, as these places might contain, and was to pay to the Duke 100,000 scudi in name of expenses and ameliorations. To him and his heirs were reserved the furniture and movables in these three residences, and the whole allodial possessions of the family, including the palaces of Castel Durante, Sinigaglia, Gubbio, Cagli, Fossombrone, Novilara, and Della Carda; the *palazzetti* or villas of Imperiale, Montebello, Monte Berticchio, Mirafiori, Velletta, and Barchetto, the three last being at Pesaro; many parks, forests, vineyards, houses, and particularly thirty-two mills. The Grand Duke of Tuscany was a party to the deed of devolution, which was executed on the 30th April, 1624, and he therein specially renounced for himself and his family all claim to the dukedom and states.[1] The assertion of Muratori, that Francesco Maria often regretted this step is not borne out by any authorities I have consulted.

In these arrangements the party most immediately interested had no voice, for the consent of the governed was then little studied in such transactions. Though the eloquent historian of the Italian republics maintains, upon true Guelphic principles, the blessings of the ecclesiastical sway compared with that of the petty seigneurs,*[2] those

[1] Oliveriana MSS. No. 324. Many documents regarding these transactions are printed in Riposati, vol. II.

*[2] Here I heartily agree with Dennistoun. If the people preferred the ecclesiastical sway to that of the Signori, why was the whole state of Urbino so eager to get Francesco Maria II. married? And if we want another example from more recent times, why, in 1860, did the people of Perugia

who have read the preceding chapters may hesitate ere they apply this doctrine to the duchy of Urbino. Four times have we seen the people throw off the transient rule of the Church, and recall their native princes to maintain that microscopic nationality which, to an Italian, is far dearer than personal liberty. Guicciardini admits that those who, under the princes, were maintained in ease with little personal exertion, generally hated papal domination. But under the popular dynasty of those dukes whose lives we have endeavoured to sketch, the loyalty implanted by selfishness was watered by affection, until its mature growth overshadowed the land. The extinction of their race was therefore bewailed by a grateful people, whose degradation to provincialism was felt as a still greater, and, in the circumstances, an irremediable misfortune.

It is but justice to Urban to contrast his conduct on this occasion with the eagerness displayed by many of his predecessors for the aggrandisement of their own houses, by investing them with the lapsed fiefs of the Church. The obstacles to such an arrangement were no doubt increased by the altered spirit of the age, by the curtailed influence of the papacy, by the watchful jealousy of the great powers, and by numerous bulls directed against such alienations. Yet other ambitious pontiffs had trampled upon parchments, had braved public opinion, and had deluged Italy in blood for less tempting baits, and Muratori hints that such an attempt might, in the present case, have been sanctioned by Spain. Whilst, therefore, we blame the discourteous manner in which his Holiness made the aged Duke feel, with unnecessary acuteness, his bereaved and enfeebled position, we give

turn out *en masse* and tear down the papal fortress, leaving a desert, which they still gloat over, in its place? The temporal rule of the Church has been bad everywhere at all times and in every way. That is why we have beggared her.

him credit for a self-denying policy becoming the head of a Christian church.*[1]

The first governor delegated by the Pope was Monsignor Berlinghieri Gessi, Bishop of Rimini, who took possession on the 1st January, 1625. The Duke assigned to him his palaces, and a salary of 2000 scudi, paying also the other officials, and the only internal change in the government was the dismissal of the council of Eight. Indeed, the deference shown by the people for those forms under which they had long been governed, obtained a guarantee for their continuance during ten years; and we are told that the chief innovation upon them consisted in an extension of literary academies, which had been discouraged by Francesco Maria on an apprehension of their taking a political tendency.[2] In January, 1626, the Bishop received a scarlet hat, and was succeeded as governor three years subsequently by Monsignor Lorenzo Campeggi, Bishop of Cesena, afterwards of Sinigaglia who held that office until the death of Francesco Maria.

But, though happy to escape from the personal superintendence of the government,

> "The old man, broken with the storms of state,"

did not consider himself exempted from all concern in the welfare of his subjects. We accordingly find, in a collection of his letters made by his secretary Babucci,[3] a very long remonstrance addressed to Cardinal Gessi regarding certain malversations in the management of public affairs. His complaints were directed against abuses of patronage,

*[1] This is amusing of Urban VIII., of whom Pasquino said—

> "*Quod non fecerunt Barbari*
> *Fecerunt Barberini.*"

[2] Brit. Mus. Lib. Add. MSS. Ital. No. 8511, art. 3.

[3] Dr. Antonio Babucci transcribed for the press a number of letters written by the Duke after the Devolution, and dedicated them to the Grand Duchess Vittoria. The MS. is preserved in the Magliabechiana Library, class xxv. No. 77, and fully bears out the commendation we have given to his epistolary style at p. 213.

by conferring places of trust upon young and inexperienced persons, especially in the army, where many officers were rather children than soldiers; against a laxity of manners and conversation among the women, extending even to the nunneries; against the indiscriminate bearing of arms, which had already led to numerous homicides, and to the extirpation of game in the preserves. To Campeggi, the next governor, he complains, in 1628, of an increasing expenditure with impaired revenues.

CHAPTER XLVIII

The Duke's monkish seclusion—His Death and Character—His Portraits and Letters—Notices of Princess Vittoria and her Inheritance—Fate of the Ducal Libraries—The Duchy Incorporated with the Papal States—Results of the Devolution.

AFTER his release from the cares of state, and from all anxiety as to the fate of his subjects and of his grand-daughter, Francesco Maria was left to employ his unimpaired powers of mind on more congenial topics. His few remaining years were passed in the society of those monks of the order of Minims,*[1] whom he had brought to the new convent, and who had been selected for their literary acquirements. He made them the companions and aids of his studies, and discussed with them such subjects as his reading suggested. Though ever respectful of the doctrines and observances of religion, fanaticism had no part in his character; and it is clear from his last will, and other evidence, that, in circumstances peculiarly favourable to an undue exercise of priestly influence, he kept himself free from its thraldom. Yet was he exemplary in pious preparation for the change which his sinking frame, as well as his philosophy, taught him to regard as at hand. To blighted hopes, parental anguish, and a desolate old age, were added great bodily sufferings. Gout, to which he had been subject from his thirty-fourth year, had by degrees so twisted his limbs that he was fed like a child, and a fresh

*[1] An order not of monks but of friars, founded by S. Francis of Paola in Calabria in 1436. The rule is based on the Franciscan, and the religious are mendicants.

paralytic seizure at length completed his decrepitude. Still, amid

> "The waste and injury of time and tide,"

his mind continued unclouded. To the end his letters maintained their clear and graceful style ; and the frequent correspondence he kept up with his grand-daughter, a child in years rather than in ideas, formed the latest link that connected his thoughts and hopes with mundane objects. Of this correspondence, so creditable to the hearts of the writers, a few specimens will be found at p. 220.

The registers of the Roman convent of Minims of S. Lorenzo*[1] enable us to trace the closing scenes of the old man's feeble existence. During the autumn of 1630 a change took place, and he was chiefly confined to bed during the subsequent winter. The rapid decay of his digestive organs was accelerated by rigid fastings during Lent, in which he persisted despite of his confessor's remonstrances. From the debilitating effects of this discipline, exhausted nature could not rally; but life ebbed so slowly, that four days elapsed after extreme unction had been administered, ere his flickering pulse was still. At length, on the 28th of April, 1631, he passed away, bewailed by his subjects, regretted by all Italy. To the citizens of Castel Durante his death was an especial bereavement. "They wept for a beloved father, the chastener of the bad, the rewarder of the good, the stay and advocate of the poor, the protector of the orphan, the support of the weak and oppressed, the consoler of the afflicted, the benefactor of all."[2] Thus deprived of the glorious and desired shade and shelter of their goodly OAK, which, transplanted from the Ligurian shores, had branched out so boldly in their mountain soil, his people

*[1] This I know not. Their present *Casa generalizia* is at S. Andrea delle Fratte. The basilica of S. Lorenzo is now in the care of the Franciscans.

[2] CIMARELLI, *Istoria dello Stato d' Urbino.*

saw their independence extinguished, and their position in provincial insignificance riveted for ever.

He lay in state during two days, arrayed in the ducal mantle of silver tissue lined with purple taffetas; on his head a coronet of gold surmounted the velvet cap of maintenance; the collar of the Fleece was on his neck, the ring on his finger, the sceptre in his hand. In these trappings of sovereignty, a last tribute to the station which he had quitted for ever, and which none remained to fill, he was by his own desire interred. Seven years before, he had prepared for himself an unornamented tomb under the holy-water vase in the church of the Crucifixion, at Castel Durante. There he chose his final resting-place, amid sites endeared as the scene of his youthful sports, the relaxation of his busy manhood, the retreat of his chastened age. Thither he was escorted by a procession of five hundred gentlemen, besides a numerous attendance of priests and monks. Each of the latter received a scudo and a pound of wax; and by one of them, Padre Ludovico Munaxho, the funeral oration was pronounced. At his own desire, this prayer, from the liturgy of his church, was inscribed under the front, in lieu of epitaph:—"O Lord, incline thine ear to our prayers, wherein we supplicate thy mercy, and that thou wouldst establish in peace, and in the realms of the elect, the soul of thy servant Francesco Maria II., Duke of Urbino, which thou hast summoned from this life, and that thou wouldst ordain it to be received into the company of thy saints, through Christ our Saviour. Amen. He died in the year of God MDCXXXI., and of his age LXXXIII."

The character of Francesco Maria presented many strange contradictions. The manifold inconsistencies of his precepts and practice have already been pointed out; and the opinions of his contemporaries varied, not only from the estimate with a perusal of such memorials as I have

FRANCESCO MARIA II, DUKE OF URBINO
From a picture once in the possession of James Dennistoun

discovered of his reign would lead one to form, but also from each other. It may be well to give the judgments of those who had best opportunities of forming just conclusions, leaving the reader to reconcile their discrepancies. Donato, his chief counsellor in the Devolution of his state, whose experience was chiefly of his latter years, writes of him as follows:—

"For sixty years did he enjoy his dukedom, ever loved but ever feared by his subjects, and highly esteemed by foreigners. Having had always about him the most famous literary characters of his time, having himself mastered many sciences, and read a multitude of books, it would be difficult in a few words to do justice to his finished knowledge, to his acute genius, to his profound memory, to his elegant and unaffected style in speaking and in writing, to his intimate acquaintance with natural history and geography, as well as with the political relations of states. Nor was he less skilled in the more important acquirements of theology and sacred subjects, upon which he was accustomed to dispute with those whose business it was to teach these doctrines. He was a prince of great piety, of exemplary manners, of austere address. He lived as a sovereign, but spoke like a simple gentleman. His modesty veiled the pride of his station; his strict justice obtained for him the respect due to a king; his conduct was on all occasions exemplary. Fond of despatch, he was impatient of dilatory measures and superfluous discussions. He would have been a paragon for princes, and worthy of undying fame, had not the irritability which unaccountably swayed his temper, and his violent fits of passion in matters regarding himself, hurried him unrestrained by his many virtues into numerous excesses and errors. Among such may be accounted his throwing up the reins to his son, his abandoning himself to the guidance of favourites, his credulous adherence to first impressions, his abhorrence of those who had once alienated his regard. Timid and suspicious from his solitary habits, he was averse to generosity, cautious in his expenditure, but, punctual to his promises, was fully to be relied upon for an exact performance of his word. In person he was well-proportioned, neither stout nor thin. He was a good knight, skilled in arms and equestrian exercises; he was devoted to the chase and all manly exercises; attached to persons of accomplishment and high birth."

Thus speaks his courtier Donato; and he is in the main confirmed by a somewhat less favourably coloured testimony from Gozze, who seems to have been a contemporary, and whose narrative is contained in No. 324 of the Oliveriana MSS. According to it, he was singularly active, skilful in all manly exercises, and particularly fond of racket and of hunting. He was hasty in temper and in speech; impatient of contradiction, and obstinate; so cunning that one scarcely knew when he was in favour. He had much practical good sense, but was wayward, choleric, discontented, selfishly inconsiderate of those about him, and, having taken offence, was apt to brood over and resent it. He was most exact in business, and habitually regular in its duties; punctual in payments, but most strict in accounting with those who managed his affairs. He was fond of magnificence, and maintained a numerous court, though less brilliant than his father's. He had but one favourite at a time, keeping all others at a distance; indeed, his stern manner overawed even when his words were gracious. He was handsome, in person scrupulously nice, but neither effeminate nor extravagant in his habits. His disposition was retired and melancholy, and he indulged it much by reading, writing, or walking in solitude. He was ostensibly devout, and was regular in the observance of religious duties. He spoke and wrote very well and solidly, studying a terse and simple style. His tastes were decidedly literary, with a partiality for the graver sciences, and he ever maintained about him persons distinguished in letters and art.

Writing at an interval of nearly a century and a half after his death, but with the advantage of access to many original documents, Passeri thus characterises Francesco Maria II. "In him military skill, intercourse with courts, and scientific studies, combined to form the rare instance of a sovereign philosopher. No prince of the day was more wise, more courtly, or more attached to his people; and his systematic government by means of excellent ministers might be adopted as a model. To men of letters he paid the greatest honour, and he willingly sought their converse; none such ever passed through Pesaro whom he did not receive with distinction. It was his desire to introduce all sorts of manufactures, that his subjects might have no occasion to send their money abroad for the purchase of necessaries; indeed, they exported silks, woollens, leather, and majolica, which produced a large balance over their imports. The improvement of agriculture shared his anxious care, and the means he adopted to effect this merit high encomium. He wrought to advantage the iron mines of Lamole, and those of copper at Gubbio. Thus did his state become populous and wealthy, while lightly taxed, for the expenses of his court were nearly limited to the income of his private estates, and to the profits derived from the importation of grain out of the dominions of the Church. He maintained a sort of standing militia of thirteen thousand men in the pay of Spain, who, in peace, pursued their occupations at home, but, in war, were placed under the command of that power. From this arrangement great benefit resulted; for thus had the military spirit, for which the country had always been remarkable, an ample and safe outlet, whilst the talents so developed often led to individual distinctions and promotion."

From a narrative of Urbino, compiled in 1648,[1] we

[1] Maruccelli MSS. C. No. 308.

gather one or two anecdotes of this Duke. When irritated he used to apply contemptuous epithets to his various cities, founded upon the temperament he had discovered in their inhabitants. Thus he called the people of Urbino proud and foul-mouthed; those of Pesaro, cowards; of S. Leo, Mantuan sheep; of Cagli, bum-bailiffs; of Fossombrone, tax-gathers; for the citizens of Mondavio alone he reserved a compliment, saying that they were born courtiers. Though fond of letters, he ever set his face against the establishment of academies, alleging that they might degenerate into revolutionary conventicles. To the just views which guided his political arrangements the best testimony is supplied by the fact above mentioned, that his people interceded for a prolongation of all his government institutions during the ten years succeeding the Devolution, and that, Urban having consented, these were found so well adapted to the well-being of the province, that they remained undisturbed after that period of probation had expired.

In person, Francesco Maria was handsome, and, from being puny and stunted in childhood, grew up active and graceful, but with a complexion of almost effeminate beauty. He was, therefore, fortunate in having for his court painter one whose men and women, as Sir Joshua Reynolds has happily remarked, seem nourished by roses. Although it is improbable that Baroccio executed the swaddled effigy of him in the Pitti Gallery, there can be little question that the four portraits we shall now mention are by that artist. One of these, in the Tribune of the Uffizii at Florence, with a repetition of equal merit in Baron Camuccini's choice collection at Rome, represents to perfection a strikingly elegant youth in the gorgeous uniform worn on his naval expedition in 1571.*[1] There is in my possession a half-length, with one of

*[1] No longer in the Tribuna, but in the Sala di Baroccio. It is the painter's masterpiece [Cat. No. 1119].

Ambrogio Baroccio's curious time-pieces upon the table, which came from the Durazzo Gallery at Genoa; and the head introduced above, at p. 151, done in full manhood, when the cares of sovereignty had begun to furrow his features with "lines of anxious thought," was purchased by me at Pesaro, in 1843. In the Antaldi Palace there, I saw a head of this Duke ascribed to Baroccio, but evidently done some years after his death. It is a slight sketch, thrown off at a sitting, and painfully preserving features whereon age and sickness, sorrow and anxiety, have set their seal. Portraiture can show no contrast more startling than that time-worn figure, with glassy eye and ghastly visage, offers to the glowing cheek and gallant bearing of the richly accoutred hero of Lepanto. But still more melancholy the change that had come over the man, then gladsome in youthful beauty, rising fame, and chivalrous hope, burning to enjoy the advantages of high station, to maintain and transmit the respect and popularity of a long-honoured name.

We have referred to letters of the Duke written during his last years, as interesting expressions of his state of mind. Besides the collection of Babucci already quoted, a considerable number of these are preserved in two other MSS. in the same library; also many others, addressed by her relations to the Princess Vittoria, with her answers, dated between 1627 and 1632.[1] The whole exceed two hundred in number, and form a series of royal correspondence equally remarkable for Christian sentiment and domestic affections. In the following pages we give literal translations of a few of them, which pleasingly illustrate these virtues in the Duke and Duchess, in their daughter-in-law, now remarried to the Archduke Leopold, and in the young Princess herself. By the first letter, the Archduchess announces to her daughter the birth of a brother; by the second, Francesco Maria intimates his confidence

[1] Magliabechiana MSS., class viii., Nos. 60, 61.

in the husband he had chosen for his grandchild. In Nos. 3 and 6 the warmth of his attachment to her is gracefully tinged with the pious resignation of a dying Christian. Nos. 4 and 5 relate to his making over to her his family jewels, a precaution, perhaps, against any difficulties that might arise after his decease. No. 7 was his last letter, dictated about a month before his release from sufferings. The remaining four refer to that event, and to the affliction of his nearest relatives.

1. *The Archduchess Claudia to the Princess Vittoria.*

"My most serene and beloved daughter,

"Now that you have obtained from God your little brother, after, as you tell me, having prayed for him (who, when he is grown tall, will love you well), it remains for you to thank the same God, who is the giver of all good. You say that you wish to have this little brother for yourself; and I agree to humour you under these conditions: First, that your prayers obtain for me another next year; second, that you come hither yourself to take him, so that you may have the pleasure of seeing me, and I you; third, that, in the meantime, you in everything obey Madam [the Dowager Grand Duchess] and your other superiors, and that you often pray for the health of the Lord Duke, to whom you owe so much. And now I and my Lord your [step] father [the Archduke Leopold] give you our blessing, beseeching for you a divine one much more ample and perpetual. 3rd June, 1628.

"Your most affectionate mother,

"CLAUDIA."

2. *The Duke Francesco Maria to the Princess Vittoria.*

"Your Highness having now attained the age of seven, his serene Highness the Grand Duke, your betrothed husband, has intimated to me that, the better to secure his intentions in your behalf from the speculations and gossip of the public, he will forthwith voluntarily contract with you the sacred rite of marriage. But, as I have adopted my measures, after taking every conjuncture into account, I cannot allow myself to suppose any purpose of drawing back in the mind of a prince of his station, endued with virtues which must ever render him estimable to posterity, and a worthy grandson of the great Ferdinand. I have, therefore, declined his request, and have offered my consent that the contracts already executed and concluded between us should be carried into effect when most agreeable to himself. And, though I should not be then a party to these arrangements, as, surely, I am little likely to be, considering the years and ails which, lame as I am, hurry me with long and great strides towards the tomb, yet is it my hope to behold from heaven the comfort of your Highness, which I pray God may be perpetual, and uninterrupted by any misfortune. I have informed you of this that you may be aware of what is going on, and I salute you," &c.

3. *The Duke Francesco Maria to the Princess Vittoria.*

"Most serene Lady, my grandchild,

"Your Highness has much reason to send me happiness, for, as I am so closely united to you, and love you so much, it will all return to you for your own benefit. But, feeling myself reduced to such a state that I can no longer find it in this world, I shall take it as a great favour that your Highness pray God Almighty to grant me, instead of such enjoyments as are prized in this life, patience amid the great sufferings wherewith he visits me, and to account these as meritorious for my glory in the next. Keep yourself well and joyous; love me as always; and command my paternal benediction: and I kiss your hands. From Castel Durante, 7th January, 1630.

"Your Highness's servant, and grandfather, who loves you from his heart, THE DUKE OF URBINO."

4. *The Duke Francesco Maria to the Princess Vittoria.*

"I send to your Highness all the jewels remaining in this house after its many calamities, and I consign them to you during my life, since God knows what may happen after my death. Your Highness will accept them in token of my sincere affection towards you, and in good time will ornament with them your person, forgetting not first to adorn your mind with those virtues which become ladies of your station, and which may render you more and more dear to your most serene husband. And so I salute your Highness." [9th April, 1630.]

5. *The Princess Vittoria to the Duke Francesco Maria.*

"Most serene Lord, my most respected grandfather,

"I know that I ought always to pray God more for your Highness's health and long life, seeing how, for affection to me, you never cease to consider what may be for my benefit. On Saturday morning I received your Highness's letter of the 9th, by your master of the wardrobe, and had the greatest joy in hearing that your Highness has been pleased to send me the jewels. Yesterday too, after breakfasting at the palace with Madam my most serene grandmother, and the Lady Princess Anna, I had such delight in seeing them all in presence of the most serene Grand Duke my spouse. And as they are already brought to this convent, your Highness may rest assured that they will be kept in safe custody, and will serve to adorn me as I may choose, as well as the others of the most serene Archduchess my mother, which also I willingly believe she will reserve for me. The thanks I shall render to your Highness are my prayers for your behalf, which I shall continue devoutly to offer several times a day, having no other way of doing you a service; and I give you my most humble duty with all my heart. From Florence, 15th April, 1630."

6. *The Duke Francesco Maria to the Princess Vittoria.*

"Most serene Lady, my granddaughter,

"I am sorry to trouble your Highness with so many of my letters, but the love I bear you, and the news I have from your city so contrary to my wishes, compel me to this. Your Highness must therefore bear with it, and believe that in writing I fancy myself with you, and find in this a satisfaction even beyond what I derive from knowing that you are settled where no demonstration of courtesy and affection will ever be wanting to you. I pray God to send a change of weather, that so I may feel assured your Highnesses are exempt both from danger and from its consequent anxieties. I augur for your Highness a continuance of health and every good; and I endearingly kiss your hands. From Castel Durante, 29th November, 1630.

"Your Highness's servant, and grandfather,
who loves you from his heart,
"THE DUKE OF URBINO."

7. *The Duke Francesco Maria to the Princess Vittoria.*

"Most serene Lady, my granddaughter,

"My usual ailments have for the last several days so harassed me, that the prayers which your Highness addresses to God for me have been most appropriate. For these I heartily thank you, and since His great goodness gives me a hope that the Almighty listens to them, I beg of you to continue them for that divine assistance of which we all have need, but I in particular, who in age bear so many additional ills. I hear from the letters of your most serene spouse, that he, your Highness, and all his most serene house are in health, and that the prevailing epidemic may be considered extinct. On this I heartily congratulate your Highness, of whom I would daily learn some new good fortune and happiness, and by such would esteem myself fully recompensed for the sufferings to which my few remaining days must be subject. And with all my heart I kiss your Highness's hands. From Castel Durante, 2nd April, 1631.

"Your Highness's servant, and grandfather,
who loves you heartily,
"THE DUKE OF URBINO."

8. *The Duchess Livia to the Princess Vittoria.*

"Most serene Lady, my beloved granddaughter,

"As, by connection of blood and of affection, our consolations are in common, so also are our griefs and afflictions. We have lost, by the death of the most serene Lord Duke, more than I am able to express on paper, but I know that your Highness's ready comprehension will be sensible of this. It pains me to have to send you the sad and mournful tidings of his death, which took place last Monday, about half-past three o'clock; but since I could not give you such news without sorrow, I pray you to excuse me and console yourself, as I myself do in so far as possible. And I affectionately kiss your hands, only adding that to ensure your receiving it I have sent a duplicate of this. Castel Durante, 2nd May, 1631.

"Your Highness's servant, and most affectionate
mother, who loves you more than herself,
"LIVIA DUCHESS OF URBINO."

9. *The Princess Vittoria to the Duchess Livia.*

"My most serene Lady, and respected grandmother,

"I feel deeply the bad news of my grandfather, and though they do not say he is dead, I much fear it, for they do not speak plainly. Should it have pleased God to call him to glory after such sufferings, I cannot but pray for his soul in my devotions. And in the extreme grief which I shall feel under so great a bereavement, and so heavy a loss, I shall beseech your Highness to consent to come and stay in this serene family, where I know you are much wished by all their Highnesses, for this will be the utmost consolation I could have. Meanwhile I await that of your Highness's letters and commands, and I make you my reverence, praying God to grant you every happiness. From Florence, 3rd May, 1631."

10. *The Princess Vittoria to the Archduchess Claudia.*

"My most serene Lady, and respected mother,

"The most serene Lord Duke my grandfather is at length dead, to my infinite sorrow, and I seem to stand abandoned by all; for I never knew other father but him; and your Highness, though my mother, is so far away, that I feel not the warmth of your affection, as I in some measure felt that of my Lord grandfather, by his proximity and the frequent comfort I had from his loving letters and other tokens. Your Highness will therefore sympathise with me, whilst I condole with you on so great a loss and severe a misfortune, and I beseech you to give me what consolation you can. And I make you my reverence, praying God ever to increase your happiness. From Florence, 10th May, 1631."

11. *The Archduchess Claudia to the Princess Vittoria.*

"Princess, my beloved daughter,

"The regret has been universal for the departure of your grandfather, the Lord Duke of Urbino, to a better life, and for the loss of a prince who maintained the superiority of his rank by that of his merits; no wonder, therefore, that it has been so great in you, for this is just by the laws of blood, and due as a debt of gratitude. I too have found it bitter, partly on your account, partly from my own obligations. But considering that the good Lord has gone from us at an age when life began to be a burden, and death desirable, I resign myself to the divine will, conforming to that which He had from eternity ordained. This surely you also have done, after the first bursts of feeling, to which, rather than to your reason, I ascribe your lamenting to me your bereavement of him as a loss of all support, and your entire abandonment. And, my daughter, I should be much distressed, did I not believe that by this time you have changed that view, so injurious to the affectionate solicitude your Lord grandfather took in so well providing for your future. Though distant from you, I bear you in my heart, and your little brothers grow up with a thousand inducements to love and serve you, prompted by nature and my suggestions. Their Highnesses, too, are always most disposed to caress and honour you, in particular Madam my Lady [Dowager Grand Duchess], who will fill my place in administering with watchful affection to all your sympathies and wants. You have likewise your lady grandmother, whom you should ever most affectionately respect, and from whom you may expect a lively interest in your welfare and success. You have, lastly, what is still more important, the protection of the Lord God, provided you fail not to deserve it, by acquiring those virtues, which, if displayed by you, will prove to the world that the glory of our race is not entirely extinguished. Be careful, then, to grow up cheerfully; and be it your aim to fulfil the expectations generally entertained of your good abilities, assured that the greater your attainments the more will be my comfort in you. Humbly kiss in my name the hem of your serene grandmother, and beseech the blessed Lord our Saviour that he would listen to my prayers and longings, the first of which are for your prosperity and happiness. From Inspruck, the 24th May, 1631.

"Your most affectionate mother from the heart,

"CLAUDIA."

Princess Vittoria seems to have merited the affections of her relations, so warmly expressed in these and many similar letters. On arriving at her future capital, she had been placed for education in a convent, where her progress was so rapid that before she was eight years old, she composed as well as penned her letters, and within two other years could write them in Spanish. From the period of her betrothal, she was always addressed as Grand Duchess, and her marriage was privately celebrated in 1633, when she was under twelve, her husband being then double her age. Four years later, the public celebration of this union took place with suitable demonstrations of joy, and in due time it produced two sons, Cosimo, afterwards Grand Duke, and Francesco Maria, Cardinal de' Medici. In her grandson, the Grand Duke Giovanni Gaston, the male line of the Medici expired in 1737, when their state passed to the house of Lorraine. The portraits of Vittoria preserved in the Pitti Gallery represent her as an overgrown but comely matron, of good-humoured expression. Her matured character did not realise its early promise. Proud, vain, suspicious, and weak, she inherited her grandfather's predilection for the society of priests; and her bigotry, increasing with her years, so contrasted with the frank and lively temperament of her husband, that a separation became advisable. These faults she transmitted to her favourite son Cosimo, under whose reign they bred many public evils. She died in 1694, after twenty-four years of widowhood, disliked by her subjects as much as her husband had been esteemed. The Duchess Livia retired a few weeks after her bereavement to her paternal estate of Castel Leo, near Sassoferrato, where she lived in great retirement, and in religious exercises, varied by visits to Assisi and Loreto. She left her whole property to her grand-daughter the Grand Duchess Vittoria.

The Duke must have taken great pleasure in will-making, as his Diary frequently mentions his being employed in that way. At his death it would seem that more than one valid testament was found, the general provisions of which, as stated in a contemporary abstract,[1] were as follows:—He desired to be buried in the church of the Crucifixion at Castel Durante, and that two thousand masses should be said for his soul. He instituted his grand-daughter Vittoria his universal heir and executrix, burdened with these legacies: To his Duchess Livia, 50,000 scudi, and an annuity of 4000 scudi; to his sister, the Marchioness del Vasto, the palace and garden at Montebello, in which she was living; to the Marquis of Pescara, a jewel, a gold watch, and 2000 scudi; to the Duke of Modena, the Marquis del Vasto, and the Cardinals Farnese and de' Medici, each a gold watch; to the Zoccolantine monastery in the park of Castel Durante 50,000 scudi; among his servants 12,000 scudi; to the community of Urbino, the library of MSS. and printed books in his palace there, with the Campo dei Galli under the fortress for maintenance of a librarian; to the convent of Minims, at Castel Durante, the library he had at that residence. In case of the death of his grand-daughter without issue, he substituted the Dukes of Parma, Modena, and Aiello, to his succession.

The inheritance thus conveyed was immense. The lowest estimate I have seen states its amount at 2,000,000 of golden scudi, though probably somewhat impaired by a litigation which arose with the Camera Apostolica, in consequence of involved questions, as to what were public and what allodial rights of the late Duke. It included lands in Naples worth 50,000 scudi, and estates in the duchy which, in 1648, were computed to yield 15,000 scudi a year, besides the residences and their dependencies, worth 4000 more.[2] The personal property was valued at 340,000 ducats, exclusive of family jewels previously sen

[1] Magliabechiana MSS., class viii., No. 74.
[2] Maruccelli MSS. C. No. 308. Mercurius Gallicus, 1624.

to the Princess, and of the libraries otherwise bequeathed.[1]

The fate of the two famous Urbino libraries deserves more special inquiry, and it is very disappointing to offer but a meagre result. Those who have glanced over our eighth chapter will be aware that the collection of MSS. made by Duke Federigo was the wonder of his age, and the admiration of all who have celebrated the glories of his lettered dynasty. The circumstances under which it was amassed, the accommodation provided for it in the palace of Urbino, and the most beautiful of its contents, have already been introduced to the reader. The losses it had sustained during the Borgian usurpation by plunder and accident were, we are assured by Paulo Maria, bishop of that metropolitan see, nearly supplied by the anxious care of succeeding Dukes; and, though none of these appear to have been bibliomanes, literary as they were in taste, and ever surrounded by men of high acquirement, it may be supposed that their library was from time to time recruited with works issuing from the press. But this casual supply was inadequate to the wants of the studious Francesco Maria II. Instead of disturbing the old library at Urbino, he drew from all quarters to his residence at Pesaro a numerous and choice store of printed books which he eventually transported to Castel Durante, for the amusement of his leisure hours.

Such were the two libraries separately bequeathed by the Duke's will, to which we have just referred. He left "to the community of Urbino his library of MSS. in that city, as well as all MSS. and drawings in that of Castel Durante, as soon as they can be transported thither; and, in order that the said community may maintain a person to take charge thereof, he conveyed to them certain lands for his support; expressly enjoining that the said library

[1] Such particulars of the wardrobe inventory as relate to objects of art are included in the last No. of the Appendix.

shall never be removed from the place where it then was, nor be diminished by a single volume, under forfeiture of their right thereto, in favour of the company Confraternita della Grotta of Urbino." The library remained under charge of Vittorio Venturelli, a man of some literary note; but ere many years had elapsed, the destination by Francesco Maria was defeated. In 1657, the community had formal notice from Alexander VII. of his wish to transport the collection to the Vatican, "for the increase of its splendour, and the benefit of Christendom." After some delay and hesitation, this proposal was reluctantly acceded to by the magistracy, who took the opportunity of stipulating certain favours and immunities for the public. The chief of these were a diminution of the contingent of interest payable by Urbino on the state debt; exemption from certain imposts; the establishment there of educational institutions under charge of the Jesuits; the removal thither from Urbania of the Minims, with the other library left to them by the late Duke; an annual sum for repairs of the ducal palace; the preservation of their library in the Vatican under its proper name, and the perpetual appointment of a native of their city among the librarians there; lastly, a surrender to the community of the property bequeathed for the support of their librarian. The Pope's interference seems to have been suggested, or perhaps only excused, by a rumoured intention of the community to sell the collection to some foreign prince. The MSS., numbering 1793 volumes, were finally sent to Rome in sixty-three cases; and a tradition is still current in Urbino that they were removed secretly, and during night, to the bitter mortification of the inhabitants, who regarded this as the last relic of sovereignty and independence remaining to them, and who probably esteemed it more as a monument of better days than from a just appreciation of its real value. The MSS. were assuredly worth a far higher ransom than was obtained by the citizens, but there can be little doubt that their safety and utility were enhanced by the transfer. They were deposited in a section of the vast corrider at the Vatican, where an obscure lapidary inscription informs us that "in 1658, Alexander VII. added to the Vatican collection the ancient MSS., of all sorts and in all languages, which formed the library of Urbino, thereby insuring their preservation and proper treatment, after compensating those who assigned over the boon."[1] The printed books of this library, in number 233, were retained in Urbino.[2]

It remains to trace the library at Castel Durante. In the archives of the Convent of Minims at S. Lorenzo in Lucina, at Rome, I discovered a copy of a settlement by Francesco Maria, dated 1628, in which he leaves the Minims of the Crucifixion, at Castel Durante, "all the library of printed books which may be in Castel Durante," with the room in which they are, and the shelving, etc.; but under an obligation "that before taking possession thereof, they shall without delay send to the library of Urbino, at the expense of the heir, all such MSS. and books of designs as may be among them." There is also a special condition that, if these monks permit any part, however small, of the collection to be removed from thence or transported elsewhere, the bequest shall lapse to the Confraternità della Grotta, at Urbino; and a small provision is made for maintaining a librarian. The active interest taken by Urban VIII. in Castel Durante (now Urbania) did not overlook the benefit which such a public library was likely to afford to that town, and he provided for its perpetual security by proclaiming ecclesiastical

[1] Alexander VII. Pont. Max.
Antiqua omnis generis omniumque linguarum
Urbinatis bibliothecæ manuscripta volumina
Repenso cedentibus beneficio
D. tutiorem custodiam atque proprietatem
Vaticanæ adjunxit an. sal. MDCLVIII.

[2] Most of these particulars have been gleaned from the communal archives at Urbino, R. No. 30.

censures against such as should dilapidate or carry it away.

About twenty-seven years after the Duke's death, Alexander VII., being at a loss how to furnish with books the library of his newly-erected university, the Sapienza, at Rome, bethought himself of the collection at Castel Durante; and on the assumption of its very limited utility there, and of the excellent purpose to which it might be made subservient at the Sapienza, transported it thither. He had previously obtained a sort of forced consent on the part of the monks of the Crucifixion to this arrangement, by promising to the convent of their order at Rome the custody of the new library, and other favours: the opposition of the Confraternità della Grotta he had also neutralised, by purchasing their reversionary interest in the bequest. The transaction was enveloped in great secrecy, in anticipation of opposition from the grand-ducal family, or from the citizens of Castel Durante; indeed, when the removal of the books was begun, the latter manifested such indignation and discontent, that about five hundred volumes were allowed to remain for their use. Notwithstanding this concession, and their unwillingness to agree to the arrangement, the monks were for a long time greatly persecuted by the people; their Provost fled in terror of his life, and nothing but dread of papal censures would have induced their compliance. Upon the pretext that persons bound to reside in a cloister, at some distance, could not be efficient guardians of the new library at Rome, even the promised boon was withheld from their brethren of S. Lorenzo, who received in compensation the lectureship of moral philosophy at the Sapienza, along with certain exemptions affecting the internal discipline of their order.

The consulting catalogue of the Vatican Urbino MSS., now used by the librarians, was compiled in 1797 by Mauro Coster, and being alphabetical, does not show the number of MSS.; but the numeration of articles exceeds

4000. In it, at No. 1388, will be found another catalogue by Stefano Gradio, wherein the numeration of volumes, many of them containing several articles, amounts to 1361; but in the general catalogue for reference, the volumes are only 1026. Under the regulations prohibiting indiscriminate access to the Vatican catalogues, I have not been able satisfactorily to reconcile these discrepancies, nor to pronounce upon the accuracy of any of these calculations; they, however, afford sufficient data to estimate the extent of the Urbino MSS. Their value is probably greater in reference to their number than that of any other component portion of the Vatican collection; indeed, than any existing library except the Laurentian; but this point, too, must remain unresolved, so long as the present restrictions are maintained.*[1]

As soon as the Duke's demise seemed to be certainly approaching, Urban had directed his nephew, Prince Taddeo Barberini, general-in-chief of the ecclesiastical troops, to occupy the frontier, who, on that event, marched through the state to receive its allegiance, and thus secured its unopposed Devolution to the Holy See, to the infinite satisfaction of the Pontiff. Another nephew, Cardinal Antonio Barberini, was soon after named Legate, under whom the ancient Dukedom passed at once into its new position as a province of the papal state. But after a few months he resigned the appointment, and it was bestowed upon his brother, Cardinal Francesco, who, preferring Rome as a residence, governed the province for many years by a vice-legate. The Pontiff, in proof of his paternal affection for his new subjects, conferred a Cardinal's hat on the Bishop of Gubbio, and established in that town a branch of the Inquisition!

*[1] I am not able to state more accurately than Dennistoun the number of volumes from the Urbino collection now in the Vatican. Unhappily there is not a library in all Italy that possesses a catalogue fit to use. For the MSS. to-day existing in the library of the University at Urbino, see *Le Marche*, An.iv., p. 212.

The revenue drawn by the Camera from the state of Urbino, in the years immediately subsequent to the Devolution, fell considerably short of the expenses; but after the imposts had been augmented, the income, in 1648, exceeded 40,000 scudi, leaving a balance at the credit of the government. The population was then above two hundred thousand. The change from independent to provincial rank had already become painfully manifest. The vaunted fidelity of the natives was degenerated into servility of demeanour. Everywhere their eyes rested on some symptom of departed grandeur. The palaces of their dukes were falling into neglect, crumbling and grass-grown; the gardens, overrun by rank weeds, sadly recalled days of past festivity; the degraded castles testified to an impoverished and absentee nobility. The glories of Urbino were gone.[1]

But the cup was charged with a bitterness beyond these humiliations. Surrounded by ecclesiastical provinces, the inhabitants of the duchy had long a foretaste of their coming fate, which amply accounted for the exultation with which they had hailed the promised continuance of the ducal line, and their sullen despair on witnessing its inevitable extinction. The Venetian Relazioni, quoted by Ranke, supply us with the opinion of disinterested contemporaries as to the condition of the papal state during the seventeenth century. In 1600, its "nobles and people would gladly cast themselves upon any sovereign whatever, to escape from the hands into which they had fallen." Ten years later, the very blood of the inhabitants was wrung from them by excessive taxation, and their enterprise was crushed by commercial restrictions. "The foreign traders had quitted Ancona, the native merchants were bankrupt, the gentry impoverished, the artizans ruined, the populace dispersing." A year or two after

[1] Maruccelli MSS. C. No. 308. See App. No. VIII. for statistical notices of this period.

the last Duke's death, his people are described as grumbling much at the change, calling the new government a tyranny, and sneering at the priests as interested solely in accumulating wealth, and aggrandising themselves. In 1666, we have this calamitous but probably overcoloured picture:—"It is palpably evident that the ecclesiastical realm is quite overburdened, so that many landholders, unable to extract enough from their possessions to meet the extraordinary public imposts, resort of necessity to the abandonment of their estates, in order to seek fortune and sustenance in less rapacious communities. I speak not of duties and customs, from which nothing eatable is excepted; because the taxes, donatives, subsidies, and other extraordinary extortions would excite pity and astonishment, even if the terrible commissioners sent from Rome into these cities, with absolute authority to inquire, sell, carry off, and confiscate, did not exceed all belief; no month ever passing without a flight of griffins and harpies, in the guise of commissioners, either of the fabric of St. Peter's, or of pious bequests, or of movable goods, or of archives, or of some five-and-twenty other Roman courts, by all which the already drained purses of the helpless subjects are tortured to the last degree. And thus,—setting aside Ferrara and Bologna, to which some consideration is extended, and which are favoured by nature and art with excellent soil, and with manufacturing industry,—all other cities of Romagna, La Marca, Umbria, the Patrimony, Sabina, and the Campagna are utterly wretched; and, to the disgrace of the Roman government, in none of them do woollen or silk factories exist, nor even of gold stuffs, except in a few such little towns as Fossombrone, Pergola, Matelica, Camerino, and Norcia, although the abundance of wool and silk might afford a most advantageous trade. The ecclesiastical territory is merely an estate leased out to tenants, who give no thought to its improvement, but only to extract the greatest possible amount of its produce from the unhappy land, whose scourged and arid soil will be unable to yield more than very barren crops to succeeding occupants. . . . The more hateful and abhorred they find themselves, the more merciless do they become; and dragging their hats over their brows, they look no one in the face. They glean all sorts of corn into their sheaves, intent wholly upon their own interests, without the smallest regard to the public." By the end of the century, matters had become worse, the country being "depopulated and uncultivated, ruined by extortions, and destitute of industry." The duchy of Urbino, which, according to the preceding extract, was the last refuge of the silk trade, had then fallen into deep decay, and the corn commerce of La Marca was clogged by export dues and injudicious restrictions.[1]

These plaintive notes might still [1859] find not a few echoes along the papal coasts of the Adriatic—the focus of Italian discontent,—over-taxation to maintain a distant government being ever the burden of their song. But the question is not, in truth, one of financial administration. However open to stricture the fiscal details may be, when tested by sound principles, the amount of revenue raised is moderate in consideration of the wealth there lavished by beneficent nature, in a degree denied to other not less burdened districts of the Peninsula. Nor can the papal sway, however objectionable, be in fairness regarded as otherwise than mild. But centralisation is necessarily alien to the spirit of a people long broken up into miniature communities, as it was formerly uncongenial to

[1] The state of feeling in the duchy, even under the comparatively beneficent sway of its native pope, Clement XI., may be inferred from an incident of trifling moment. Having obtained trace of a petition or remonstrance addressed to that Pontiff among the MSS. of the Bibliotheca Borbonica at Naples, I was refused a sight of it by the Archbishop then at the head of that library, on the ground of its injurious allegations against the authorities. Verily such overcaution may defeat its own end, by leaving an exaggerated impression of the mischief it would veil. So Gergorovius was turned out of the Vatican Library.

Anderson

VITTORIA DELLA ROVERE, GRAND DUCHESS OF TUSCANY
From the picture by Sustermans in the Pitti Gallery, Florence

their ancestors, whose personal pride, political influence, and hopes of promotion, equally turned upon the continuance of a sectional independence. Hence the popular dissatisfaction rests as much upon traditional evils as upon existing and obvious misgovernment. Four centuries ago there were above a dozen capitals, flourishing in the balmy atmosphere of as many gay courts, and basking in patronage and prosperity, all within the circuit of that province where now a few priestly legates perform the functions of sovereignty without either the taste or the means for indulging its trappings, and dwell in princely palaces without the habits or the popularity of their ancient lords.

But these are not matters for casual discussion. From the accession of Count Guidantonio in 1404, till the Devolution by Duke Francesco Maria in 1624, this little state had enjoyed two hundred and twenty years of a prosperity unknown to the neighbouring communities. Her sovereigns were distinguished in arts and arms, respected abroad, esteemed at home; her frontiers were comparatively exempt from invasion, her tranquillity unruffled by domestic broils: within her narrow limits were reared or sheltered many of the brightest names in literature, science, and art; her court was the mirror of refinement, her capital the Athens of Italy. Since the Devolution, she has passed an equal number of lustres in provincial obscurity and neglect. It has been the object of this work to portray somewhat of the splendours of that former period, though the subject would require colours more brilliant, and a hand more skilled. Here our task must close, for to follow her destinies to their decline and fall were one of few attractions.

> "Kingdoms are shrunk to provinces, and chains
> Clank over sceptred cities, nations melt
> From power's high pinnacle, when they have felt
> The sunshine for a while, and downward go!"

BOOK NINTH

OF LITERATURE AND ART UNDER THE DUKES DELLA ROVERE AT URBINO

CHAPTER XLIX

Italian literature subject to new influences—The academies—Federigo Comandino—Guidobaldo del Monte—The Paciotti—Leonardi—Muzio Oddi—Bernardino Baldi—Girolamo Muzio—Federigo Bonaventura.

"FOR a long lapse of years, Italy had been an organised body of highly civilised states, different in their origin, laws, and constitutions, divided by local jealousies and opposite interests, constantly engaged in their endeavours to establish a political equilibrium by the manœuvres of a wary and even unprincipled diplomacy, baffled oftentimes in their ambitious schemes, and brought into sudden collision, but still deriving new energies from their very rivalry, and promoting, with their own, the interests of social progress."[1]

It was in a state of things thus happily described that letters and art attained their zenith of glory in the Peninsula. But the close of the fifteenth century had introduced elements of change, which a fatal policy permitted to spread. Those foreign aggressions and domestic convulsions which we have seen extirpating nationality and crushing independence were not less destructive to mind and its efforts. A struggle of thirty-five years against her ultramontane invaders,—a series of unavailing because ill-directed and discordant efforts,—closed with the coronation of Charles V., and left Italy for nearly two centuries at the mercy of Spain. The states which escaped the direct miseries of that iron domination, and retained a nominal

[1] MARIOTTI'S *Italy*, II., p. 177.

independence under the papal sway or their native dynasties, sank unresisting before an influence affecting at once their politics, their manners, and their literature. The pride of the Spaniard had long been proverbial, and was little susceptible of modification even in a new country. The conquered race quickly conformed to fashions which they could neither shake off nor exclude. They aped a pompous bearing that sat with singularly bad grace upon a vanquished people, and the affectation which at first loaded their language with fulsome epithets, soon corrupted their writings by elaborate adulation. It is difficult for those whose taste has been formed upon the models of a less copious language to judge fairly of Italian ornamental literature, for its authors, in availing themselves of the resources at their command, are prone to lavish them too unsparingly. When tried by such a standard their prose may seem tedious or tumid verbiage, their epics may teem with overstrained hyperbole, and even their lighter poetry may appear to substitute subtle conceits and elaborate epithets for graceful ease and flexibility. But these idiomatic peculiarities are but echoes of the national genius, and ought not perhaps in fairness to be subjected to canons of criticism unknown to their authors. Yet it cannot be denied that facilities such as the language of Italy affords to flowery composition are virtually premiums on feebleness, and that decorations of style afford a tempting disguise for indolence of mind or poverty of matter. The influence of petty courts was peculiarly and fatally favourable to such qualities. Trifling incidents there assumed an importance that justified magniloquence befitting loftier themes, whilst the narrow views common to limited circles found ample scope in exaggerated phrases of metaphor and hyperbole. Thus came abundance without fertility, exuberance yielding only redundancy.

Associations and clubs for political or social objects

being then incompatible equally with the spirit of governments and the habits of the people, men readily formed themselves into religious confraternities or literary academies. But these academies acted as drags upon the progress of that literature which they were instituted to promote; they clogged its chariot wheels with devices originally dictated by pedantry, and soon degenerating into puerile verbiage. From the draughts of inflated poetry and corrupted rhetoric which they manufactured, every stimulating ingredient was gradually withdrawn, while opiates were freely introduced in their stead. They thus lulled to sleep what little public spirit had survived the subjugation of the Peninsula; and the governments of the new régime, quickly aware of their emasculating tendencies, lavished upon them patronage until they deluged the land, and stifled the energies of the national mind in all-prevailing mediocrity. The classic spirit of the fifteenth century had originated this mischief, by diverting letters from the sphere of popular sympathy, and nourishing that affectation to which an almost exclusive study of the dead languages must ever lead. But the evil was aggravated by Spanish influence. Ingrafting frigid forms and stately phrases upon the lively intercourse of a naturally light-hearted people, it did for the manners what pedantry had effected for the letters of Italy. Nature and originality were replaced by imitation and servility. Parodies suppressed inspiration, compliments chilled cordiality. In both cases genius languished, epithets multiplied, and terse and vigorous diction passed with independence to happier lands.

In all histories of Italian literature the academies occupy a conspicuous place, and we have already noticed the Assorditi of Urbino, for whom municipal vanity has asserted an origin in the reign of Duke Federigo.[1] They appear to have occasionally met as early at least as that

[1] See vol. II., p. 112.

of his successor, although not formally constituted until about 1520. Their name, like that of most similar associations, being probably adopted from some foolish whim, the next step was to invent a badge suited to the humour of the times, so they assumed "the ship of Ulysses surrounded by sirens"; and for motto, playing at once on sound and sense *Canitur surdis,* "They sing to the deaf." The word *assorditi* properly means "the deafened," but its signification might be stretched by punning to include absurdity, niggardness, or filth, none of them very flattering qualities to connect with the epithet. The rolls of this fantastic association included many authors who were harboured at Urbino, but it is in no way identified with their reputation. Having fallen into neglect, it was revived in 1623, and, after nearly a century of provincialism, was once more reconstituted in 1723.

As these literary associations rose, their predecessors, the scholastic academies, declined. That which Lorenzo the Magnificent had founded at his villa of Carreggi, was closed in 1522, and Platonism having consequently waned, the Stagirite philosophy was once more master of the field. But another and more deadly struggle awaited it. When men began to study nature and base their reasonings upon her laws, the deficiencies of their old guide were detected, and its authority was impugned. Yet the peripatetic system was too deeply founded to be at once dismissed, and the ingenuity of its disciples was long directed to accommodate its dogmas to modern discoveries,—a vain effort which only divided their ranks and led them into inextricable dilemmas, until Galileo appeared "to furnish forth creation," and conduct them clear of the labyrinth by a silver thread of truth. But though a new light had dawned, new snares beset the way. From bold investigation and speculative inquiry, ecclesiastical authority and civil despotism had much to lose, nothing to gain. Their side was therefore soon chosen. War was declared against thought, backed by the whole armoury of oppression. Where prevention failed, persecution followed, and the censor's veto was enforced by rack and faggot.

Thus was it that the Reformation had but an indirect influence on the Italian mind. The scanty seeds wafted across the Alps fell upon stony ground, and ere long withered away. But the great reaction of the papacy was not only directed against the new truths; it waged war upon every thing calculated to afford them a disguise under which they might become dangerous. The policy of pontiffs and the duty of the Inquisition tended to exclude all light, lest any rays of Protestantism should reach the faithful During three centuries have these efforts been continued; and when we consider the talent by which they have been directed, the stern ministers by whom they have been carried out, we well may wonder that the Italian mind has not been utterly debased by foreign tyranny and priestly domination. They have sown the wind; it remains to reap the whirlwind.

The fashion for classic imitation was succeeded in Italy by an age of rhetoricians, with Bembo at their head, and the academies as their strongholds. But they either encouraged or inadequately repressed a too fluent facility which has ever since been the blemish of their mellifluous language. In Boccalini's satirical *Ragguaglio di Parnasso*, some prolix writer is condemned to a perusal of Guicciardini's narrative of the Pisan war; but, after a brief essay, he avows his preference for the galleys to pursuing, through dreary details, the siege and capture of a pigeon-house. This biting jest is applicable in a far greater degree to other writers of the sixteenth century, whose cumbrous grandiloquence is often diluted by trivialities, or tinselled with factitious pomp. Yet there were some authors of purer taste, who resisted such extravagance, and it is curious to find Caro, della Casa, and Bernardo Tasso concerting measures for curtailing the use of superabundant compliments. The two principal points of their attack were the recent substitution of the feminine pronoun in the third person singular for the second person plural in addressing any one, and the indiscriminate use of Lordship, Excellency, Gentility, as courteous phrases, to the entire exclusion of Master and Madam. Against the former of these abuses Caro and Tasso declare open war; but, although they unite in condemnation of the latter as still more fatal to vernacular purity, and avow themselves ready to support any onset, each shrinks from leading the charge. "This age of ours is altogether given up to adulation. Every one, in inditing a letter, bandies 'lordship'; all expect it when addressed. And not, forsooth, our grandees alone, but even the middle classes and the very plebeians aspire to such distinctions, taking affront if they receive them not, and noting as blunderers all who do not offer them the like. Most silly and revolting does it seem to me that we should have to speak to one person as if he were another, always talking to a sort of ideal abstraction, quite different from the individual himself. Yet this abuse is now established and general." Thus far Caro, to whom Tasso replies, "Oh the wonderful charm of Italy, which every one seeks to destroy! It sufficed not that the Goths, the Vandals, and other strange and barbarous nations have sought, and still seek, to possess thee, and that multitudes flock hither from earth's farthest corners; even Lordships, never previously seen or known here, quitting their native Spain, are come in swarms to sojourn among us, and have so mastered our vanity and ambition that we cannot shake them from our shoulders." In a subsequent letter to Claudio Tolomei, Bernardo congratulates him on having applied the lash to such empty titles, and promises to follow his example by retrenching them all when he revises his own letters for the press.[1] But these attempts met with little success; redundant

[1] *Lettere di Bernardo Tasso*, edit. 1733; vol. I., pp. 14–22 and 427–30.

superlatives still lead Italian literature, and an Italian letter is little more than a tissue of exaggerated epithets, from its address to its signature.[1]

Few branches of human knowledge more flourished during the palmy days of Italian literature than the exact sciences, especially in connection with military affairs, and the elegant arts. Their application to both objects was received with marked favour by the successive Dukes of Urbino, who, for a century and a half, combined the pursuit of arms with the patronage of art. We have seen this done by Federigo and Guidobaldo I., for the defence of their duchy and the decoration of their capital; we now have to mention the progress of similar studies under the della Rovere princes. During the latter epoch, pure mathematics were brought into fashion by numerous translations of standard Greek works into Latin or Italian, a labour shared by various literati of Urbino, but especially by Comandino, Baldi, and Alessandro Giorgi. This, however, but served to facilitate their practical development in pursuits more congenial to those martial dispositions for which the inhabitants of Romagna have in all ages been noted. Whilst the revived literature of Greece and the philosophy of Plato flourished on the banks of the Arno, the exact sciences were cultivated in the highlands of Umbria, and took the practical turn of strengthening those fastnesses with which nature had provided that mountain-land. Francesco di Giorgio, of Siena, was less in request by Dukes Federigo and Guidobaldo as architect of their stately palaces, than as the most famous military engineer of his time. Events which made their duchy the seat of repeated invasions early in the sixteenth century, as well as the warlike character of Francesco Maria I., maintained a demand for fortifications, and, from the school which

[1] In proof of this I give in IX. of the Appendix a letter of introduction, of which I was bearer, from one of the most accomplished *professors* of Rome.

thus grew up in his capital, there issued a series of military architects whose fame and services extended beyond the Alps.

The first of these whom we shall mention was FEDERIGO COMANDINO, born at Urbino, in 1509, of a noble family. His grandfather was secretary of Duke Federigo, whose last confidential instructions he received, when death surprised that veteran general in the fens of Ferrara. Baldi has claimed the invention of those bulwarks in fortification called *baluardi* for his father, Gian Battista,[1] who built the walls at Urbino in the beginning of the sixteenth century. After a liberal education, Federigo passed several years at the court of Clement VII., nominally as a privy chamberlain, but really to amuse with learned disquisitions the Pontiff's leisure hours, on whose death he repaired to Padua, where he devoted ten years to the study of philosophy and medicine. Having graduated, he settled for clinical practice at Ferrara, but seems soon to have abandoned the healing art for mathematical research. He accompanied his sovereign, Guidobaldo II., to the camp at Verona when in the Venetian service, and, having gained his confidence by successfully treating him in a severe illness, he was selected to instruct him in astronomy and cosmography, as well as in military tactics and engineering. Soon, however, resuming his more abstruse studies, under the patronage of Cardinal Ranuccio Farnese, brother of Duchess Vittoria, he was carried by him to Rome, and introduced into the society of Annibale Caro, Fulvio Orsini, Baldassare Turrio, and Cardinal Cervini, the last of whom was cut off too quickly after his election as Marcellus II. to be able to benefit his friends. But for Comandino ambition offered few temptations, and courts had no charm. In studious retirement he devoted to the exact sciences the

[1] This has also been imputed to Francesco di Giorgio, to Sanmichele, and to Bartolomeo Centogatti of Urbino.

matured powers of a comprehensive and most retentive mind. He explored all that classical authors were known to have left on these subjects, and rendered again accessible much that lay forgotten among the rubbish of by-gone learning. He translated, and copiously edited, Ptolemy's treatise on the planisphere, which was published at Venice, in 1558, and, four years afterwards, gave to the world a work on the analemma, founded upon the same author's previous and imperfect discoveries. His labours were then transferred to the writings of Archimedes, several of which he printed for the first time, as well as the dissertations of Serenus and Apollonius upon conic sections, all with elaborate commentaries.

After spending the prime of life in these pursuits at Rome, he returned to his native duchy, where his instructions in mathematics were sought by Prince Francesco Maria, with whom he read and expounded Euclid's *Elements*; and afterwards, at the request of his pupil, published a Latin translation of them. It was about 1569 that he was visited there by a young Englishman named John Dea, whose love of the exact sciences induced him to seek so distinguished a professor, and who supplied him with some Arabic MSS., hitherto unknown.[1] Six years thereafter he was surprised by death, with many unfinished works on his hands, part whereof saw the light under the superintendence of the Marquis Guidobaldo del Monte. The life of a hard student is rarely one of varied incident; and even the voluble pen of his pupil Baldi has failed to illustrate that of Comandino with interest, beyond his scholiast labours.[2] Yet severity formed no part of his social character, and he was ready at all times to relax his toils by Epicurean indulgences, which are said eventually to have curtailed his life. To the last, however, his engrossing pleasure was

[1] GROSSI, *Uomini Illustri di Urbino.*

[2] It is printed in the Raccolta Calogeriana, XIX., 149.

in books; and, although his works number more translations than original compositions, he is ranked by Montucla among the most able and judicious of commentators.

One of the pupils whom Comandino left in his native state was GUIDOBALDO, MARQUIS DEL MONTE, who was born of distinguished lineage, in 1544. Tiraboschi has cited, as a singular proof of the engrossing nature of his studies, the fact that his life offers a nearly total want of incident. So tranquilly did his days flow on at his castle of Monte Baroccio, amid abstruse occupations, that he seemed to have forgotten a world unconscious of his very existence, and the only memorials of his life are his works. His treatise upon Perspective successfully carried forward what had been indicated by Pietro della Francesca in the preceding century, and he was afterwards engaged upon the doctrine of Planispheres, the correction of the kalendar, and the solution of astronomical problems. But though thus devoted to abstruse science, he spared a portion of his thoughts for its practical branches, working upon mechanics, and translating from Archimedes. It is unnecessary here to go into an examination of results which modern discoveries have left far behind; the ground has been well sifted by Montucla, whose work indicates whatever is still of value in this class of now somewhat superseded labours. The Marquis was addressed by Torquato Tasso in a sonnet beginning *Miserator de' gran celesti campi*, and died early in the seventeenth century, survived by a younger brother, Francesco Maria, who had been made cardinal by Sixtus V.

Among the names distinguished in Urbino for mathematical talent, that of PACIOTTI was conspicuous. Jacopo Paciotti, who held several situations of trust under the two first Dukes of the Rovere dynasty, was father of three sons, all eminent proficients in the exact sciences. Felice was one of those commissioned to rectify the Gregorian Kalendar, and invented an instrument for constructing dial-plates. Orazio became a military engineer, and erected fortresses for the States of the Church, for Savoy, and for Lucca, with such reputation that his services were sought for Poland and for the Emperor Rudolph. But the most remarkable of the family was Francesco,[*1] who, after enjoying a liberal education, and thoroughly grounding himself in architecture under Girolamo Genga, went to Rome, where, in 1550,[*2] he was named engineer-in-chief by Julius III. Next year, he was employed to fortify Ancona against the dreaded descents of the Turk; but, leaving this undertaking to be completed by Fontana, he passed in 1551, to the service of the Farnesi, and thence to that of Emanuel Duke of Savoy, with 60 scudi of monthly pay. He soon afterwards published a plan of Rome; but his attention was chiefly devoted to military architecture, in which his reputation rapidly spread. In 1558, he was employed by Philip II. to survey, and report upon, the principal defences of the Low Countries, for which he was remunerated with 6000 scudi, and a massive gold chain.

Paciotti was now on the ladder of royal favour, and, having accompanied Duke Emanuel to Paris, for his marriage, was decorated by Henry II. with another magnificent chain worth 1000 scudi. The gorgeous compliment, however, nearly cost him his life, for, while wearing it next day, he was set upon by two robbers, one of whom he slew, and wounded the other, a feat which procured him new marks of favour. The next ten years of his life were chiefly spent in the service of Savoy; but he was at various times summoned for engineering purposes to

[*1] Cf. MADIAI, *Il Giornale di Francesco Paciotti da Urbino* in *Arch. St. per le Marche e per l' Umbria*, vol. III., p. 48 *et seq.*

[*2] This is the year in which the journal begins. In 1551 he tells us he left the service of the Pope to enter that of the Duke of Parma.

Spain and Flanders. The warm personal regard in which he was held by Philip II. was proved by his winning a bet, that he would make that proud monarch hold a light to examine his plans, and was more substantially shown by many rich presents which he carried from that court. In consequence of recommendations from his Catholic Majesty, he had from the King of Portugal the order of Jesus Christ; and in 1578, at the Duke of Savoy's request, the Castle of Montefabri was erected into a countship in his favour, by Francesco Maria II. of Urbino. After for several years superintending fortifications in the papal states, and those of the Grand Duke of Tuscany, he retired to his native place, and passed the remainder of his life in honourable ease, enjoying from various sovereigns pensions of above 3000 scudi a year. He died in 1591, aged seventy, leaving behind him a European reputation, and three sons, in whom the mathematical talents of the family were hereditarily developed, all being military engineers of some note; one of them, Federigo, became a Knight of Malta, and Guidobaldo was blown up by a mine, while in the service of Charles V.

Gian Giacomo Leonardi is mentioned by a recent writer[1] as "one of those extraordinary men, so abundant in Italy during the fifteenth and following century, who have left little fame to posterity, and who, though universally known in their day, were after death forgotten, and overlooked by subsequent writers." Nor is this surprising in his case; for his distinction, gained in the camp, was spread still wider by his diplomacy. He was at one moment referred to on delicate points of honour between knights and sovereigns; at another consulted on questions of legal intricacy; whilst his writings have remained unedited and unknown. They are all upon fortification

[1] *Trattato di Architettura da Francesco di Giorgio*, edited by C. Promis, Turin, 1841.

and engineering, and are enumerated by Promis in his elaborate compilation upon these subjects. His services, though eagerly sought by great monarchs, were affectionately devoted to his native princes, being long companion in arms of Francesco Maria I., and ambassador to Venice from Guidobaldo II. He was born at Pesaro, near which he had from the latter the countship of Monte l' Abbate in 1540, with permission to bear the name and arms of della Rovere, and died about 1560.

Although we have been led to mention engineers in connection with mathematical science, they were in these days usually architects, and regarded as belonging to the class of artists. Ricotti informs us that no vocation was more varied or laborious. Uniting the practice of arms with an intimate knowledge of design, their services were sought for in every part of Europe, either to plan fortresses, build palaces, cast statues, paint frescoes, execute hydraulics, or command troops. Lazzari, in his *Uomini Illustri del Piceno*, enumerates sixteen such as conferring lustre upon Urbino, but of these we shall only name one more. MUZIO ODDI was nobly born there, in 1569. In 1595, he accompanied, as military engineer, a contingent sent by the Duke into Burgundy; and, three years after, employed his architectural skill for the festive decorations in honour of a visit by Clement VIII. to his native city. He had less success in placing a cupola upon the cathedral there, in 1604, which was said to contain 100,000 pounds of iron-work and 80,000 of lead, the weight of which brought it down in 1789. On some indistinctly recorded charge, he was thrown into the citadel of Pesaro, and there detained many years in a loathsome dungeon. Denied the use of books or writing materials, he made for himself ink of charcoal and candle-soot, mixed with water in a walnut-shell, and, by pasting together shreds of paper with bread-dough, contrived to jot down mathematical treatises on sundials and the square, using for compasses a couple of twigs tied together. On his liberation, in 1609, he passed into Lombardy, and spent above twenty years of exile in sighing for his country; nor was it till within two years of the close of life that he was appointed mathematical professor at Urbino. He died at seventy, leaving a Treatise on Mathematics, in two volumes 4to.

BERNARDINO BALDI*[1] has a double claim upon our attention, as the most prolific writer whom the duchy has produced, and as one who devoted a large share of his literary labours to the illustration of his native state. He was born at Urbino in 1553, of a family which, during several generations, had held with credit various important situations in the magistracy. By force of that extraordinary diligence, which continued to stimulate his entire life, his youthful studies advanced with precocious success; yet it is singular to find him confessing that his early inclinations were all towards painting, and that his preference of his pencil to his grammatical exercises often brought him into intimate acquaintance with the birch. We cannot echo the observation of his biographer Affò,*[2] that this discipline may have deprived Urbino of a second Raffaele; but though he assuredly was gifted neither with the lofty genius nor the pervading sense of beauty which characterised his countryman, a deep devotional feeling would doubtless have inspired his paintings. The peculiar connection which existed at Urbino between the exact sciences and the liberal arts frequently attracts our notice; and this it may have been which led the thwarted painter to turn with his accustomed energy to mathematical studies, under Federigo Comandino, for whose edition of

*[1] Cf. ZACCAGNINI, *La vita e le opere edite e inedite di B.B.* (Modena, 1903); UGOLINI, *Versi e prose scelte di B.B.* (Firenze, 1859); see also MADIAI, *Pierantonio Paltroni e B.B. biografi di Federigo da Montefeltro* in *Le Marche* (1902), vol. II., pp. 5–6.

*[2] Cf. AFFÒ, *La Vita di B. B.* (Parma, 1783).

Euclid, published in 1572, he is said to have drawn the diagrams. It was about this time, that, urged by his parents to choose between law and medicine for a profession, he preferred the latter, rather, as he tells us, from its analogy with philosophical inquiries than with any special liking for the healing art. With these views he was sent to the University of Padua, where he brought his vast application successively to bear upon logic, and ethical and physical philosophy, varied by his favourite mathematics, and by a comprehensive cycle of Greek literature. To that seat of learning there then resorted the youth of ultramontane lands, whose harsh language so piqued Baldi's curiosity, and developed his prodigious philological talents, that in an inconceivably short time he mastered French and German. But these multifarious pursuits did not suffice his versatile mind, so he enlivened them by draughts of the Castalian spring. There may seem something ludicrous in an epic, entitled "Artillery," and illustrative of gunnery practice; but a theme so ponderous for poetry was suited to the spirit of the age, as well as congenial to its author's thoughts. A visit to the mountain home of Petrarch, at Arqua, gave, however, a lighter turn to his muse, and taught his number to flow in madrigals, to the honour of some nameless Laura of his love or fancy, containing more borrowed classicism than inspired passion.

In 1575 he returned home, to share the last labours, and watch the death-bed, of his friend Comandino, and to encounter from his parents many a remonstrance as to his neglected professional acquirements, of which, in the various food with which he had appeased his literary craving at the university, he seems entirely to have lost sight. But their efforts were vain. The Eugubinean tables, that philological enigma, having attracted his attention, he boldly encountered their solution, and studied Arabic as a stepping-stone to the lost dialects of Central

Italy. His biographers insert Etruscan in the catalogue of his polyglot acquirements, but the tables of Gubbio remain a puzzle to antiquaries. Those who made literature a profession, before there existed a "public" to remunerate their exertions, looked for maintenance to princes or private patrons; and in 1580 Baldi gratefully accepted the offer of Don Ferrante Gonzaga, Lord of Guastalla, to instruct him in mathematics, on an allowance of ten scudi a month, besides board for himself and a servant,—an appointment which made him favourably known to Cardinal (afterwards St.) Carlo Borromeo, uncle of that prince, and to many persons of literary reputation who frequented his miniature court. There his time was divided between mathematical and poetic compositions, until, in 1586, a sudden change took place in his position by his adopting a clerical habit, at the request of Don Ferrante, in order that he might hold the Abbacy of Guastalla, the emoluments of which yielded him about 320 golden ducats. This promotion brought out a curious feature in the character of so hard a student, and we find him immediately repairing to Rome, to canvass for the higher honours of a titular bishopric, on being refused which, he struggled for permission to wear some trifling distinction in his canonical robes with pertinacity befitting a worldling rather than a philosopher. Neither was it from such a character that we should have looked for a zeal in the maintenance of ecclesiastical discipline, which led him beyond the bounds of prudence in wielding his inquisitorial powers.*[1]

Those theological studies which usually precede ordination were in his case followed out with his wonted energy, after obtaining the preferment to which they are generally intended to lead, and it was probably then that he added

*[1] In Rome he pursued too his artistic studies; it was this sojourn which inspired the *Sonetti Romani*. He seems to have passed the years 1592–1609 between Rome, Urbino, and Guastalla.

Hebrew and Chaldee to his accomplishments. But his first great undertaking, after thus gaining a position of leisure and independence, was a General Biography of famous mathematicians. This he never completed for the press; but a sort of vidimus of the three hundred and sixty lives, which it was intended to contain, was printed after his death, with the title *Cronica de' Mathematici*, Several minor works in science and literature at the same time occupied his pen, among which were his Description of the Urbino palace, his Eulogy of that state, and his History of Guastalla. Nor were his poetic inspirations neglected, and, besides a variety of occasional effusions, his *Nautica*, or the Art of Navigation, was printed at Venice in 1590. We may include among his lighter labours an Essay on History, dedicated in 1611 to the Duke of Urbino, and lately published by Cardinal Mai.[1] Although, like most similar essays, some of its observations are trite and even trivial, the various topics are well handled, and many useful suggestions are offered as to the best method and style for history, the qualities requisite in its author and desirable for its students. It would have been well had Baldi attended, in his historical biographies, to his own recommendation, that the prolix and copious diction of Livy should be chastened by that terse and sententious manner found in Tacitus and Sallust. Nor were it amiss that he had construed less literally the maxim by which Pliny the Younger pleads for mediocrity, Content yourself to do much indifferently, if it be beyond you to do a little well.[2]

Although Baldi appears to have entered the Church rather from temporal considerations than any spiritual vocation, no priest was ever more tenacious of rights and privileges; and it was his misfortune to find, in the exercise of his

[1] *Spicilegium Romanum*, I., xxviii., from Vat. Urb. MSS.

[2] Satius est plurima mediocriter facere, si non possis aliquid insigniter. Lib. V., Epist. 5.

ecclesiastical functions, ever-recurring misunderstandings with his clergy or the civil authorities, and even with the superior tribunals at Rome. Through these we shall not follow him. As early as 1590, the Duke of Urbino interfered as a friendly counsellor to recommend him moderate measures; but new jars from time to time recurred, and in 1609 he carried into effect a step which he had proposed seventeen years before, by resigning his benefice, under reservation of two-fifths of its income. But these wranglings penetrated not within the portal of his study, where his active mind and adamantine pen laboured assiduously, through good report and bad, upon the most incongruous matters.

The Abbot renounced his preferment on the plea of family matters, requiring his presence in his native city, and, faithful to this domestic duty, declined an offer from Cardinal d'Este of a situation in his household. His own sovereign received him with that friendship he ever extended to men of piety and literary merit, and, in 1612, sent him on a mission to congratulate the New Doge of Venice.*[1] The remainder of his life passed in peace, amid the varied resources of an ever-busy mind, interrupted only by those occasional bereavements, whereby, as years wear on, death warns us that our turn will also come. Besides sad breaches in his domestic circle, Baldi had to mourn his long-attached friend Baroccio, the painter, who died in 1612. Prepared by such proofs of human frailty, he resigned his spirit on the 10th of October, after a lingering but lenient malady, and was carried to the tomb amid the sincere regrets of many friends and admirers.*[2] It was remarked that, in his long and minute will, he left no instructions regarding his multifarious unpublished works, most of which passed into the library of his relations, the

*[1] Cf. Zaccagnini, *Un' ambasceria di B.B.* in *Rassegna Crit. d. Lett. Ital.*, vol. VII., p. 201.

*[2] He died in Urbino, October 10th, 1617.

Albani, where they remain at Rome. His epitaph reckons his compositions at forty-eight,*[1] and the languages he knew at twelve, which Crescimbeni increases to sixteen—substantial testimony to that avidity of application which is said to have been habitually appeased by perusing the the Fathers whilst at table, and by conning over Euclid in Arabic, as an aid to digestion. To detail and criticise the results of labours as Protean as Herculean is a task which we cannot attempt. His diligent biographer Affo' enumerates about thirty printed works, running to above two thousand 4to pages, and seventy left in manuscript, some of which have been since published. They may be thus classed :—

	Printed.	MSS.
In Theology and biblical criticism		13
„ Mathematics	7	14
„ Philosophy		2
„ Geography		2
„ Law		2
„ History	1	8
„ Topography and antiquities	4	4
„ Poetry	10	8
„ General literature and philology	4	16

*[1] I record the more important. In 1575 he wrote a poem on *Artiglieria*, and in 1579 another on the *Invenzione del bossolo da navigare ;* this was published by CANEVAZZI (Livorno Giusti, 1901). Cf. concerning it, PROVASI in *Le Marche* (1902), and ZACCAGNINI in *Rass. Crit. d. Lett. Ital.*, vol. VII., p. 166. His masterpiece, *Nautica*, written between 1580–85, is a didactic poem in four books imitating the Georgics. Concerning it see ZACCAGNINI, *Le fonti della Nautica* in *Giornale St. d. Lett. Ital.*, vol. XL., p. 366, and PROVASI, *Contributo allo studio della Nautica di B.B.* (Fano, 1903). The *Egloghe Miste* were dedicated to Ranuccio Farnese in 1590, and consist of nineteen poems in various metres in a Theocritan vein. Cf. RUBERTO, *Le Egloghe edite e inedite di B.B.* in *Propugnatore* (1882), and for *Epigrammi*, RUBERTO, *op cit. An. cit.* His youthful erotic poems were published under the title *Lauro* (Pavia, 1600), and, not to speak of other volumes, the *Sonetti Romani* appeared in *Versi e Prose* (Venice, Franceschi, 1590). His works in prose were very numerous. I note here *La Descrizione del Palazzo Ducale d'Urbino* (*circa* 1587), and the *Vite* of Federigo and Guidobaldo I. of Urbino, the first published in Rome in 1820 and a bad edition of the second in Milan, 1821. He wrote also a *Cronaca* (Urbino, 1707), a life of Federigo Comandino, the *Encomio della Patria*, cf. ZACCAGNINI, *Uno scritto inedito di B.B.* in *Le Marche* (Fano), vol. I., p. 4; and the *Lettere Familiari*, cf. POLIDORI, *Lettere di Baldi* (Firenze, 1854), RONCHINI, *Lettere di B.* (Parma, 1873) and SAVIOTTI, *Lettere di B.* (Pesaro, 1887).

Of these a number were translations, chiefly from Arabic and other Oriental tongues. It is evident that his own preference lay towards his compositions in verse, a judgment which wants confirmation if continued popularity be the test. Yet several of his fugitive poems, and especially some sonnets on the ruins of Rome, possess much lyric beauty; and, though his epic on the Deluge is but a wretched attempt at novelty in versification, that on the Art of Navigation is a work of merit for the age which produced it. Hallam, after classing it with Bernardo Tasso's *Amadigi*, as two of the most remarkable productions of that sort then written in Italy, pronounces the *Nautica* "a didactic poem in blank verse, too minute sometimes, and prosaic in detail, like most of its class, but neither low, turgid, or obscure, as many others have been. The descriptions, though never very animated, are sometimes poetical and pleasing. Baldi is diffuse, and this conspires with the triteness of his matter to render the poem somewhat uninteresting. He by no means wants power to adorn his subject, but does not always trouble himself to exert it, and is tame where he might be spirited. Few poems bear more evident marks that their substance had been previously written down in prose." But what he wanted in genius—for therein lay his great deficiency—he in some degree supplied by wonderful versatility. Whichever of his many subjects he took up seemed that in which he was born to excel. Of his painstaking diligence we have said much, but we may add the pertinent remark of Grossi, "that so extensive was his reading as apparently to leave no time for writing, and yet that he wrote about as much as it seemed possible for any one to read." To this Tiraboschi adds the more flattering testimony that "his praises would be appropriate to almost each chapter of this history, for there was scarcely any department of literature and science in which he did not apply himself and attain excellence."

By an author so prolific, redundancy and diffuseness, the blemishes of his age, were inevitable. But in his lives of the two Montefeltrian dukes, these are conjoined with a tendency to elaborate his details into microscopic minuteness, which weary and distract the reader, and which, though valuable adjuncts to the testimony of an eye-witness, engender more suspicion than credit in a narrative compiled, after a long interval, from less specific authorities. Being, however, a shrewd observer and diligent narrator, anxious to do full justice to his subject, these works, although deficient in personal interest, and relieved by no enlarged views or general application, fulfil the task prescribed by his patron, the last Duke della Rovere; and, were his life of Francesco Maria I. to be published,[1] Baldi would be our standard historiographer of the duchy. In him are, indeed, wanting the qualities of a philosophic historian,—elevation of sentiment, variety of matter, selection of incident; but they belonged not to his age, and were scarcely compatible with his position. The fate of Scarpi and Varchi gave timely warning to the literary world, that historic verity might have its martyrs, as well as metaphysical speculation of religious truth. His life of Duke Federigo, written in 1603, was printed in 1824; that of Guidobaldo I., completed in 1615, saw the light in 1821. The substance of these narratives had, however, been appropriated and published by Reposati, omitting imaginary conversations and supposititious harangues. Of the degree of impartiality with which they were compiled, an idea may be formed from the following extracts of letters addressed to their author by his sovereign, proving that his judgment was not by any means left unfettered:—"It has given me satisfaction to hear all that you have written me in regard to the life of Duke Federigo of happy memory, and I fail not to acknowledge with pleasure your devotion and diligence. In mentioning my house, I ap-

[1] Vat. Urb. MSS., No. 906.

prove of your naming it of Montefeltro rather than Feltrian, but as to seeking out its source and foundation, I do not recollect telling you to pass these over in silence. On the contrary, I deem it necessary to discuss this, yet not in the way I saw it treated at Urbino, attributing to it a mere bourgeois and private origin, much humbler than its deserts. It will, therefore, be well to keep this in view, observing in your eulogies, and generally throughout the work, a becoming consideration and regard for it, such as, without further hint, I look for from your sound discretion."—"As to the Life of Duke Federigo, only a few days have passed since I have done looking through it; but we must talk it over together more than once, ere anything can be decided on."[1]

Had Baldi lived among our fathers, he would have dwelt in Grub Street, and become, by his powers of application and memory, a successful book-maker; among ourselves, he would have proved valuable as a penny-per-line scribe. In Italy, his renown was, for a time, more brilliant, but it has now passed into comparative, and not unmerited, neglect. Yet his is a name of which his native city may justly be proud, and may cherish with respectful approbation this epitaph, once proposed for his tomb:—

"Ah! happy he who spent a lengthened span,
Not in the vulgar dreams of grovelling man,
But passed his days in living truly well;
Urbino's honour! Passenger, farewell."

Among the literary labourers of this age GIROLAMO MUZIO *[2] is entitled to a prominent place, more from the variety and volume of his writings than from their actual worth. The epithet Giustinopolite, usually applied to him,

[1] Oliveriana MSS. In 1602 the Duke instructed his resident at Venice to procure for Gian Battista Leoni access to its archives for the life of Francesco Maria I. he had commissioned him to write, which was published three years later.

*[2] On Muzio, see GIAXICH, *Vita di Girolamo Muzio* (Trieste, 1847); MORPURGO, *Girolamo Muzio* (Trieste, 1893), NOMI, in *Miscellanea Stor. della Valdelsa*, No. 24; NOTTOLA, *Appunti sul Muzio poeta* (Aosta, 1895).

is latinised from Capo d'Istria, the adopted home of his family, who were originally emigrants from Udine, and spelt their name Nuzio. He, however, was born at Padua, in 1496, and, after receiving a good education, finding himself dependent upon his own exertions, was fain to sell his services of sword or pen to the highest bidder. The same rule of self-interest that actuated Italian condottieri was too often followed by literary adventurers in that country, conscience and glory being generally made subservient by both to a livelihood. Girolamo had a double chance, in his twofold capacity of soldier and author, and tells us "that it was ever his fate to earn his bread by serving in the armies and courts of popes, emperors, kings, or petty princes; sometimes with one Italian commander, sometimes with another; now in France, then in Upper, again in Lower Germany." Through these vicissitudes it were needless to follow him. For a time he was rival or successor of Bernardo Tasso in the promiscuous affections of Tullia d'Aragona, a lettered courtezan, and, without her sanction, published, in 1547, her Dialogue on the Infinitude of Love. In the preface he avowed a connection which occasioned him neither compunction nor shame, and which, in days when love was a science as well as a passion, was openly shared by Varchi, Speroni, Strozzi, and Molza. Four years later a dangerous illness taught him reflection on his past ways, and brought him to a devotional frame of mind. It was about the same time that he became an inmate of the court of Urbino, receiving from Duke Guidobaldo the ample pension of 400 scudi, with permission to "attend to his studies, appearing only when he chose." The Duchess Vittoria countenanced him much, and he spent a good deal of time in her society, probably in consequence of his appointment as governor to her eldest son, and of his marrying a lady of her suite. From thence he went to reside at Rome, about 1567, and died in Tuscany, in 1576.

Tiraboschi declines the task of compiling the long catalogue of his various writings, in poetry, sacred and profane history, moral essays, and familiar letters,*[1] nor need we undertake it. A large portion of his works were directed against protestant doctrines, and, having reformed the habits of his somewhat stormy youth, he lent willing and efficient aid in strangling the progress of Calvinism in Italy, after a protracted struggle, upon which the investigations of Dr. M'Crie have thrown much valuable light. Muzio is alleged to have exhibited in this contest more of martial dexterity than theological acumen; but his controversial effusions, being published in Italian, and clothed in a homely slashing style, were probably supposed quite as efficacious against the progress of heretical opinions among his countrymen, as the disquisitions of more profound theologians. It was not, however, for the dogmas of faith alone that Muzio wielded his pen. The soldier of fortune was quite as happy, and more at home, on topics belonging to the chivalry of his profession. His treatises on Duels and the Point of Honour were suited to the spirit of the age, and had in consequence a considerable run of popularity, now of course long ago past. The like fate has befallen his didactic poem on the Art of Poetry in the literature of his own country. What most concerns us are his Lives of Dukes of Urbino. That of Federigo is dedicated to Guidobaldo II., and the original is deposited in the Vatican Library. Having been compiled with considerable care, it continues our best narrative of his reign, and has been greatly drawn upon by Baldi and Riposati. The edition printed at Venice in 1605 is but an abridgment, containing less than half the original matter. His Life of Francesco Maria I. was left unfinished, and remains unedited in the Vatican.[2]

*[1] The fullest collection of his letters seems to be that of GIOLITI, 1551. Cf. also ZENATTI, *Lettere inedite* (Capodistria, 1896).

[2] Vat. Urb. MSS. No. 1011, and No. 1023f. 50.

We shall mention but one more prose writer of Urbino. FEDERIGO BONAVENTURA was born in 1555, and owed to Cardinal Giulio della Rovere a fashionable education at Rome. On his return home, the marked favour of Francesco Maria II. was attracted by his good sense and winning manners; but finding his courtly accomplishments unequal to the profound pursuits of that young prince, he laboured assiduously to supply his own deficiencies. By close application, his progress in Greek, mathematics, and natural philosophy was amazingly rapid; but these studies were happily blended with the business of life, and, directing his powerful judgment to political affairs, he established his reputation by a work on public polity, which, for the first time in Italy, methodised the principles of government. These talents his sovereign turned to account by sending him on various diplomatic missions. Conforming in many respects to the maxims inculcated by the Cortegiano, he filled in the Duke's court somewhat the same place which Castiglione had done in that of Guidobaldo I., and died in 1602.

CHAPTER L

Italian versification—Ariosto—Pietro Aretino—Vittoria Colonna—Laura Battiferri—Dionigi Atanagi—Antonio Galli—Marco Montano—Bernardo Tasso.

THE liquid vocables of the Italian language flow in melody with a facility perilous to genius, fatal to mediocrity: its stream is equally apt to dilute Castalian inspiration, or to quench poetic fire. Hence the poets of Italy are far outnumbered by its versifiers; and hence among the laureates of Urbino we find but few historic names. But, in absence of native bards, the dukes of the second dynasty attracted to their court several of those most conspicuous on the Ausonian Parnassus, under whose influence a great change came over the manner and spirit of national poetry. Hitherto their predecessors had before them two models, whose excellence is still universally admitted. Dante, in founding an epic literature, chose the grandest and most difficult theme ever dared by man, and his success, by immeasurably distancing his few competitors, has deterred competition. Petrarch addressed himself to passions and sympathies essentially earthly, and constructed a lyrical versification demanding no sustained exertion; whose trammels sufficed, in his melodious and pliant idiom, to stimulate ingenuity without imposing labour; whose perfection depended rather upon elaborate polish than upon originality or vigour. Thus, while Dante continued a model, Petrarch became a snare; and hence, a "multitude of imitators, satisfied with copying the latter in his defects; who could easily follow him in the choice of his subject, but not in the beauty of his style, the variety of his knowledge, and the elegance of his imagery." Sonnets are indeed the most peculiarly Italian form of poetry, but they are avowedly ill-suited to the naïve expression of pure and artless feelings. Their laboured strain and studied melody are adapted to an artificial cast of sentiment; they encourage exaggeration and tend to mannerism and common-place. Singly they are charming, but "when taken collectively we become indifferent to their unity, felicity, and grace, and accuse them of what under other circumstances we might possibly commend, their recurring metaphors, their uniform structure, and the unfailing sweetness of their versification."[1] Yet in their complex form, a prolonged repetition of the same rhyme tends, like the return to a simple air amid difficult variations, touchingly to renew the feeling originally and pleasingly evoked; and thus is it that sonnets often possess a charm of which, in their ambitious attempts, their authors were probably quite unconscious.[2]

It is not now our object to analyze the varied metrical arrangements to which the fertile language of Italy willingly lent itself, and which its minstrels,

"A mob of gentlemen who wrote with ease,"

delighted to mingle and multiply. Enough, in addition to the polished sonnet, to name noble canzoni, sublime odes, and tender elegies. But the absence of ballad poetry, with its wide-circling echoes of long antecedent events and feelings, is remarkable, and has been imputed to an early addiction of the nation to prosaic habits of trade. This solution is, however, little satisfactory in itself, and is equally at variance with the genius and the language of the people. Perhaps it would be more just to assign

[1] British and Foreign Quarterly Review, xi. 376.
[2] See above, Vol. II., cap. xxv.

a diametrically opposite cause, and to seek in their vivid imaginations, and in the exuberant facility of their melodious tongue, that universality of versification which tended to depreciate its quality, or, at all events, to diminish the estimation bestowed even on their most popular compositions. It is accordingly in nations among whom poetry is a rare gift, and whose idiom can embody it in terse and simple diction, that we find those lyrics which, possessing a traditional popularity, are at once the germ and index of national sentiment.*[1] We seek in vain for such among the recognised literature of Italy; and though the dulcet chants of the Venetian gondolier, and the monotonous lazzaroni ditties of Naples, may be deemed of that class, their infinite and ever-changing variety appears to divest them of the historic charm that attaches to the chivalric redondillas of Spain, and to the pensive minstrelsy of our fatherland.

In poetry alone did the age of the della Rovere excel that of the Montefeltri, and among the great names whom it was their pride to shelter were Ariosto and Tasso, the only ones worthy to rival those of the bards of Hell and of Love.

LUDOVICO ARIOSTO*[2] was born of noble parentage at Reggio, in 1474, and, after a precocious struggle against the uncongenial legal career for which he was intended, was left by his father to follow the bent of his genius in

*[1] How could Italy have a ballad poetry full of national sentiment before she became a nation? Her living poetry then and for centuries before, as now, is the *Rispetto*. Cf., for the *Poesie Popolari* generally, D'ANCONA, *La Poesia Popolare Italiana* (Livorno, 1906); for the Marche especially GIANANDREA, *Canti Popolari Marchigiani* (Torino, Loescher, 1875).

*[2] I shall not attempt to give a bibliography, however scanty, of Ariosto. He has really nothing to do with Urbino, and the work done concerning him would fill a library. The best life after those of Baretti, Campori, and Baruffaldi is that of Cappelli prefacing the *Lettere* (Hoepli, Milano, 1887). The best edition of his poems is that of PAPINI (Firenze, Sansoni, 1903). For *Bibliographia Ariostesca*, see FERRAZZI (Bassano, Pozzato, 1881). For the controversy, Ariosto-Tasso, see VIVALDI, *La Più Grande polemica del Cinquecento* (Catanzaro, Caliò, 1895). Consult also EDMUND GARDNER, *Dukes and Poets at Ferrara* (Constable, 1904), a charming and a learned book.

SUPPOSED PORTRAIT OF ARIOSTO
After the picture by Titian in the National Gallery

favour of general literature.*[1] From an early age he had composed dramas on Thisbe and similar themes, and had secretly drilled his brothers and sisters to perform them; but when about seventeen, his youthful inclination was gratified by accompanying Duke Ercole I. to Pavia and Milan, for diversion, and to enact certain comedies. These boyish efforts have not been preserved, but the Cassaria and Suppositi, composed in 1494, engraft upon classic models the licentious speech of his age. Though well-born, he had the double misfortune to require a patron, and to find an ungrateful one in Cardinal Ippolito d' Este, whose ferocious character and lax morals exceeded even the ordinary licence then permitted to members of the Sacred College, and whose taste for literature, or perhaps emulation of a prevailing fashion, led him to favour men of genius. The services of Ariosto were invoked, as a soldier and diplomatist, when Ferrara was exposed to imminent danger in the wars following the League of Cambray. As ambassador to Julius II. in 1512, he braved perils greater perhaps than those of the field; but his fine temper and knowledge of the world ensured his safety, and bespoke the regard even of that domineering Pontiff, whose threats mellowed into favours before his conciliatory bearing.

The time at which he first visited Urbino is uncertain; but in 1515, when the designs of Leo X. upon that duchy and Ferrara, the only Romagnese principalities which still withstood the grasping policy of the papacy, had given rise to anxieties in the families of d'Este and della Rovere, the Cardinal repaired to Francesco Maria I., in order to concert measures for their common safety. Ariosto accompanied him on this journey, and, having been detained at the Furlo pass by an attack of fever, which in his eighth Capitulo he mentions as dangerous, he repaired

*[1] Ariosto has told us in great part his own life in his *Satire;* best edition that of Tambara (Livorno, 1903).

to recruit his health at Urbino, whilst Ippolito proceeded to Rome. The greeting which met our poet at that lettered court partook of the discriminating hospitality which genius could ever there command; and though his own poetical reputation was as yet but dawning, his intimacy with Guido Posthumo of Pesaro was probably a claim in his behalf to special distinction, which the publication of his *Orlando Furioso*, before the end of that year, firmly established. On proceeding to Rome, the favour bestowed upon him at the Vatican was not such as either to satisfy his just anticipations, or to do credit to the Pontiff's discernment. In his third and seventh Satires, Ariosto comments upon the long and intimate friendship of their former years, when the Cardinal de' Medici had proffered him a fraternal partiality, and vows that never again will he rely on other men's promises, postponed from ides to calends, and from calends to ides. The reception he at first met with might well give confidence to his hopes; for on his presentation Leo stooped forward to press his hand, saluting him on both cheeks. But, as the Venetian envoy caustically observed, his Holiness promised largely, but performed not. All that followed this flattering accolade was a privilege of copyright, not even gratuitously issued; and as those substantial benefits, which his merits deserved and his position required, were vainly expected, the poet quitted Rome "with humbled crest," a disappointed man. Yet he was of too kind a nature to harbour malice, as well as of a temper too easy for courtly struggles. He returned to the quiet of his native state, content to seek some respectable employment, and avowing his indifference to scenes of wider or more varied ambition.

> "Let him who golden spur or scarlet hat affects
> Serve king, or duke, or cardinal, or pope;
> This suits not me, who care for neither gaud."[1]

[1] Part of this third Satire will be found translated in ROSCOE's *Leo X.*, ch. xvi., where the demands of nepotism upon his Holiness are playfully exposed.

Whether his patron's proverbially slighting reception of a dedication of the first fruits of his epic muse proceeded from obtuseness, or, as Tiraboschi suggests, was a poor jest, it could not but be mortifying to a man of delicacy and conscious genius. Ere long a breach occurred between them, on Ludovico declining to attend the Cardinal in a distant and fatiguing embassy to Hungary.*[1] This occurred in 1517; but he was soon after admitted into the Duke of Ferrara's service with a monthly salary of seven crowns, and allowances for three servants and two horses. His first employment in this new sphere was a mission, in 1519, to condole with Lorenzo de' Medici, the usurping Duke of Urbino, on the loss of his consort Madeleine of France; but ere he reached Florence, Lorenzo's own death had supervened. It was on this occasion he composed his first Capitulo, where, and in his Stanze, he speaks of that prince in the usual fulsome style of courtly bards, alluding to his uncles Leo and Giuliano as

> "Twin suckers from that long descended laurel stem,
> Which in its verdure decked a golden age."

How little the duty thus imposed upon him consisted with his own tastes may, however, be gathered from an incident characteristic of the age. The venal conduct of Duke Francesco Maria's Spanish followers having brought to a sudden close his attempt to regain his patrimonial states, in the manner detailed in our thirty-sixth chapter, one of their number resented an imputation to that effect, cast upon his comrades by some gentlemen of Ferrara. A challenge was the result, each party selecting a bravo to maintain their cause. This duel by deputy took place on the Neapolitan territory, and, of the combatants, who fought naked with swords, the Spaniard was left dead on

*[1] Cf. Satire II., vv. 1–24, 85–93, 97–114, 217–231, 238–265, and III., 1–81.

the field. The victor returned to be fêted in the capital of the d' Este; and Ariosto composed his thirty-fifth sonnet upon "Ferrara's true paladin, of truth, genius, worth, and valour, who has cleared up the Spaniard's slippery trick upon the good Duke of Urbino, and testified to Italian bravery." We may well suppose the satisfaction with which the minstrel saw this "good Duke" restored to his station in 1521, and may conjecture that he paid him homage in his mountain capital. A room in the ducal palace there, decorated with his portrait, went by his name, and he was enrolled among the *Assorditi* academicians.[1] In 1532, a few months previous to his death, Prince Guidobaldo wrote to ask of him an unacted comedy, for representation at Pesaro, to which he replied, regretting his inability to comply with the request, as he had long ceased to write such things.

Ariosto's life presents few remarkable incidents, considering the space which his name justly occupies in the literary annals of Italy. Though honoured and complimented by the Dukes of Urbino and Ferrara, and by Leo X., he seems to have incurred few solid obligations from these Maecenases of his age. The only promotion awarded to him was the administration of Garfagna, a mountain-holding under the d' Este family, chiefly peopled by banditti, which he obtained in 1522, but resigned after three years' sad experience of the turbulent charge. His coronation by Charles V. is apocryphal, although he is understood to have received from that Emperor a diploma as his poet laureate. He died on the 6th of June, 1533, in his home at Ferrara, and was buried in the old church of S. Benedetto. In 1573 his body was transported to the new church, and in 1801 to the Public Library of Ferrara.

It would be foreign to the object proposed in these pages to enter fully into the merits of works so universally known, and so little connected with our immediate subject,

[1] See above, pp. 255-6.

as the heroic poems of Ariosto. But we have ample evidence of the popularity enjoyed by his *Orlando Furioso*, during the first half-century after its publication, in the testimony of one not likely to be partial to a successful rival: "And if the aim which a good poet ought to keep in view be that of imparting pleasure and enjoyment, it is obvious that this was accomplished by Ariosto; for there is neither artisan, nor man of learning, nor boy, nor girl, nor old person, who is satisfied with a second perusal of him. Are not his stanzas a solace to the jaded pilgrim, who sings them to alleviate the irksomeness of his hot and weary way? Do you not hear them chanted all day long in the highways and the fields? I believe that there have not been printed as many copies of Homer or Virgil as of the *Furioso*, during the time that has elapsed since that most accomplished gentleman published his poem; and if so, as cannot be doubted, is not this a clear proof of its beauty and excellence?"[1] We set aside the minor faults which have been found in the execution, and most gladly escape from all critical discussion of the vexed question, as to its due observance of unity and sustained action. The absence of perfections so questionable is by many accounted a charm. Nowhere has imagination been more freely indulged, nowhere the poetic vein left to play such fantastic tricks; but in its sallies, effort and restraint are alike unknown. As the figures in a magic-lantern, or the endless changes of the kaleidoscope, its phantasmagoria appear and pass by, without our being aware of the machinery which called them up; yet, from time to time, there occur images of life so veracious, traits of nature so touching, that we are again summoned to the realities of existence and the sympathies of humanity, with a startling

[1] Bernardo Tasso, Lettere, II., No. 165. In a privilege of copyright granted in very complimentary terms by Leo X., the *Orlando* is pedantically described by Bembo as "a work in vernacular verse regarding the feats of those called knights-errant, composed in a ludicrous style, but with long study, and the laborious application of many years."—Bembo, *Epistolæ nomine Leonis X.*, Lib. X., No. 40.

effect scarcely less marvellous than the wild creations which precede and follow these charming episodes. Even extravagance thus ceases to be a blemish, whilst facility and freshness are ever multiplying new beauties. Episodes and incidents, serious or grotesque, capriciously introduced into the poem, give it a motley and heterogeneous aspect; variety of matter and diversity of style are its familiar characteristics; and its unequal execution is, perhaps, less pardonable than the desultory character of its plan. Nor is it only by its novelty that this freedom of action sustains the interest of the work. The introduction of real personages and recent events relieves the tedium of long continued allegory, and stamps nature and individuality on adventures in themselves extravagant and apocryphal.

In estimating the rank of this poet, critical judgment has too often been diverted from the quality of his verses to the fittingness of his style; and in comparing him with Tasso, the argument resolves itself into a contrast between romantic and classic poetry. Upon such a discussion we purpose not to enter. Ariosto found his countrymen under the charm of old legendary histories, perpetuated by tradition from the days of Charlemagne and his paladins, and more recently popularised in Pulci's burlesque epic of the *Morgante Maggiore*, and by Boiardo's unfettered fancy in the *Orlando Innamorato*. He was content to sail with the stream, spreading his canvas to the prevailing breeze, rather than to strike out another course, and steer in search of newer attractions. This decision necessarily limited the scope of a highly original genius to varying the details and episodes of inventions already familiarised to his readers by other less inspired pens; and it were difficult to account for his thus contentedly following their track, except from the conviction that none else was so certain a guide to success. Domenichi and Berni, aware that Boiardo had unworthily handled his theme, were content to employ themselves in recasting it into more attractive shape, and Le Sage's French translation is a mere paraphrase. But Ariosto chose the higher aim of taking up the story where Boiardo had left it incomplete, and working it out in forms less exaggerated and fanciful, but far more nobly conceived, and executed with infinitely greater polish and poetic beauty.

Pietro Aretino*[1] has been designated by Ariosto[2] "the scourge of princes," a description somewhat more just than the epithet of "divine," which is added possibly in irony; for few men, it is hoped, have been so destitute of those high aspirations which form the link between human and divine nature. He has been aptly compared to an ill-conditioned cur, ever ready to yelp and snap at all who do not feed or fondle him, but to such as do, the most fawning of his species. He was born at Arezzo in 1492, and was natural son of one Luigi Bacci. After serving his apprenticeship to a bookbinder at Perugia, he went to push his fortunes in Rome, where his first remarkable productions were verses illustrating a set of engravings by Marcantonio, after designs by Giulio Romano,—a work so scandalously offensive to decency that scarcely any copies have escaped destruction.*[3] After the death of Giovanni

*[1] A good edition of the *Lettere* of Aretino was published under the care of Vanzolini and Bacci della Lega, in four volumes, in Bologna, 1873–75. The best edition, now very rare, of *I Ragionamenti* is that of Florence, 1892. See also Fabi, *Opere da P.A.*, Milano, 1881. For his life, consult Luzio, *P.A. nei primi suoi anni a Venezia e la corte dei Gonzago* (Torino, 1888); Gauthiez, *L'Aretin, 1492–1556* (Paris, 1895); and Sinigaglia, *Saggio di uno studio su P.A. con scritti e documenti inediti* (Roma, 1892). It was, I think, Mr. Claude Phillips who wittily called Aretino not the scourge but "the screw of princes." Nevertheless, those who knew Aretino best will appreciate him most. Titian was wise enough to have him for a friend, and, indeed, he was capable of many very human and even beautiful actions, as when he would daily throw wide his doors at nightfall and take the lost and the beggars into his house. After all, those he blackmailed were blackmailers themselves. He made even the Pope fear him.

[2] *Orlando Furioso*, XLVI., st. 14.

*[3] These designs have lately been found and photographed and published in Paris. They are impossible, but extremely vigorous and lovely. The verses are even more terrible than the drawings, but splendid too, with a sort of fullness of joy.

de' Medici *delle bande nere*, his earliest patron, he went to Venice, and subsequently visited most of the Italian courts. His foul scurrilities and loathsome adulation were dealt out with equal readiness, as best served his insatiable avarice and undisguised selfishness. These base qualities, tempered by tact and great readiness, gained for him a success equally unaccountable and undeserved; he became rich, caressed, applauded, dreaded, and is said to have earned not less than 70,000 scudi during his career. The popularity which his writings enjoyed among all ranks seems an infatuation,*[1] considering their very moderate merit, and must be viewed as symptomatic of a generally depraved taste, though no doubt his own ineffable conceit and insolence contributed to the delusion. "There truly never was a man who combined such haughty presumption with equal ignorance of literature, meanness of spirit, and debauchery of morals. His style possesses no elegance or grace; indeed he seems to me one of the first to introduce those ludicrous hyperboles and extravagant metaphors that came so generally into use during the next century. Never assuredly have I met with books so empty and useless as those of this impostor, whose baseness equalled his profound ignorance, and the sole object of whose writings was self-interest and lucre. As to his manners, they are amply testified by his works, wherein, besides a prodigal sprinkling of obscenity, there are mentioned the women with whom he intrigued, and the children these bore him; they in fact prove him destitute of moral or religious principle; and if ever he makes a show of compunction or amendment, it is but to relapse speedily into his wonted profanity. Truly such a fellow, who ought hardly to have ventured to show himself in public, stands unequalled in presumptuous arrogance. But the most

*[1] His writings have much of the undoubted fascination of the daily paper, but are on the whole less vulgar and probably less harmful and enervating.

Alinari

PIETRO ARETINO

After the picture by Titian in the Pitti Gallery, Florence

surprising thing is to see a majority of European princes, and not a few learned Italians, humbling themselves before him without a blush, and rendering him a degrading tribute of gifts and eulogies. Chains of gold, considerable sums of money, pensions, and handsome presents of every sort, came in so constantly from various quarters, that he confesses to receiving from different princes 25,000 scudi within eighteen years. The most amusing part of it is that these rich donations were made because he assumed the proud epithet of *scourge of princes*, on the plan, as it would seem, of threatening them with his indignation, and with attacks upon their actions in his writings; yet never was there a more sordid adulator of the great, and no work of his contains a single word against any sovereign." It would be difficult to select words more graphic or more just than this description by Tiraboschi, which we have preferred adopting, to the task of reviewing so filthy a character.*1 We shall elsewhere allude to him in connection with Michael Angelo and Titian, and other notices might be selected of his intercourse with Duke Guidobaldo II. The self-assumed privilege of his position did not however always protect him from the merited consequences of his meanness and malevolence. Boccalini (an author scarcely less mordent than himself, who is said to have expiated his satiric vein by being beaten to death) calls him "a magnet of fisty-cuffs and cudgels, whose enemies' hands, rivalling the promptitude of his own pen, had scarred him all over with as many lines as a navigator's chart." Among those who met him with his own weapons was Antonio Francesco Doni, a literary adventurer of Florence, whose arrival about 1552 at the court of Guidobaldo II. inspired Aretino with jealousy which exploded in an impertinent letter. The intruder, however, maintained

*1 This is sheer hypocrisy. Aretino's intercourse with Urbino was so slight as to be easily ignored, and Dennistoun, as a fact, says next to nothing of it.

his ground till 1558, the year after his opponent's characteristic death, and retaliated in a volume published in 1556, entitled *Doni's Earthquake, overthrowing the great beastly colossal Antichrist of our Age; a Work composed in Honour of God and the Holy Church, and in Defence of good Christians*, and dedicated "to the infamous and rascally source and fountain of all malice, Pietro Aretino, the putrid limb of public imposture, and true Antichrist of our time."

Still more pungent was the epigrammatic epitaph proposed for him by Francesconi:

"Arezzo's hoary libeller here is laid,
Whose bitter slanders all save CHRIST essayed:
He for such slip this reason good can show,—
'How could I mock one whom I do not know?'"

Aretino, returning a Roland for his Oliver, rejoined:

"Francescon, wretched rhymer, here is laid,
Who of all things save asses evil said:
His plea in favour of the long-eared race,
A cousinship that none could fail to trace."[1]

But enough of such ribaldry. The writings of Aretino and his biography are in one respect useful to the historian of his time. The degrading views of human nature afforded by both form a contrast to the bright luminaries which yet lingered above the horizon, whilst by their shadows they complete the verity of the picture. Favoured by fortune far beyond his deserts during life, his memory is equally indebted to art. The encomium of Ariosto has already been quoted, and the pencil of his friend Titian has preserved his person in several portraits; one of them,

[1] "Qui giace l' Aretino, poeta Tosco,
Che d' ognun disse male fuorchè di Christo,
Scusandosi col dir—'Non lo conosco."'

"Qui giace Francescon, poeta pessimo,
Che disse mal d' ognun fuorchè del asino,
Scusandosi col dir—che egli era prossimo."

which, though unfinished, is perhaps the noblest commemorated on Vecellio's canvass, adorns the Pitti Gallery, and almost persuades us that Aretino was a gentleman.

From an age too prolific in parasitical literature and in shameless morals, there has descended to us a name radiant with genius, and unsullied in reputation. The historian of Urbino may contribute a leaf to the garland which fame has hung upon the brows of VITTORIA COLONNA,*[1] for her mother was a princess of Montefeltro, and to her maternal ancestry she seems indebted for her heritage of talent. She was daughter of Fabrizio Colonna, by Agnesina daughter of Duke Federigo of Urbino, and was born in 1490. When but four years old she was betrothed, in conformity with the usage of her times, to a mere infant. Yet her marriage may be deemed fortunate, for her husband, Ferdinando Francesco Marquis of Pescara, was not only a cadet of the very ancient house of Avalos, which had accompanied Alfonzo of Aragon from Spain to Naples, and had married the heiress of Aquino and Pescara in the Abruzzi, but, among the warriors of an era still fertile in heroes, none was more early distinguished or promoted. He died prematurely at thirty-three, while in command of the imperial troops. His consort, imitating her grandmother Battista Sforza, had learned to console the childless solitude of his prolonged absences by habits of study, and in them found resource amid the bereavements of a widowhood which no offer of marriage could tempt her to infringe. But though

*[1] For the life of Vittoria Colonna, see CAMPORI, *Vittoria Colonna* in *Atti e Mem. della Dep. di St. Pat. dell' Emilia*, N.S., vol. III., (Modena, 1878). LUZIO, *V.C.*, in *Rivista St. Mantovana* (1885), vol. I., p. 1 *et seq.* On her mother, Agnese di Montefeltro, cf. CASINI-TORDI, in *Giornale Vittoria Colonna*, vol. I., No. 10. On her poems, cf. MAZZONE, *V.C. e il suo Conzoniere* (1900). She was born at Marino in 1492. She was married 27th December, 1509, in Ischia, to Ferrante d'Avalos Marchese di Pescara. Miss MAUD JERROLD has published recently (Dent, 1907) a work in English on Vittoria Colonna which should be excellent.

she sought not the world or its incense, her high rank, wealth, and personal graces, gained many an admirer, whilst the elevated beauty of her poetry, the charms of her conversation and correspondence, attracted to her the respectful adoration of the learned. She cherished her husband's memory with rare constancy, modifying grief by spiritual solace. In her piety there was neither blind superstition nor cold formality. Devotional exercises and religious intercourse shared her hours with poetry and literature tinged by their influence, and among her most welcome visitors were some of those Italian divines who favoured the Reformation. On this account she has been claimed as a convert to protestantism, but upon insufficient grounds. She adhered apparently to the faith of her fathers, and was spared by a timely death, in 1547, from witnessing the persecutions undergone by her friends of the new creed.*[1] Among those to whom the sympathies of genius and piety united her was Michael Angelo, who testified his respect by a visit to her death-bed, and his regret by a touching sonnet to her memory.*[2] Not less gratifying was the tribute to her worth which Ariosto has embalmed in seven stanzas of the Furioso, canto xxxvii.:—

"One will choose, and such will choose, that she
All envy shall so well have overthrown,
No other woman can offended be,
If, passing others, her I praise alone;
No joys this one but immortality,
Through her sweet style, and better know I none."

Of her writings few remain, and these but fugitive pieces.*[3] We are happy in being able to make our readers

*[1] See, on this subject, RODOCANACCHI, *V.C. et la Réforme en Italie* (Versailles, 1892), and TACCHI-VENTURI, *V.C. fautrice della riforma cattolica* (Roma, 1901).

*[2] For her relations with Michelangelo, see RACZYNSKI, *Les Arts en Portugal* (Paris, 1846, pp. 1–78).

*[3] For her writings, see FERRERO e MULLER, *Il Carteggio di Vittoria Colonna* (Torino, 1889), with the supplement (1892) of TORDI, who has also published (Pistoia, 1900) *Il codice delle rime di V.C. app. a Margh. d'Angoulême*, and some unpublished *Sonetti* (Roma, 1891).

acquainted with them through the graceful translations of the late Mr. Glassford, selecting three sonnets in which she tenderly alludes to the blight of her widowhood, mildly inculcates the cloisters' quiet, and clothes in glowing language orisons of holiest fervour.

I.

"Methinks the sun his wonted beam denies,
Nor lends such radiance to his sister's car;
Methinks each planet mild, and lovely star,
Has left its sweet course in the spangled skies.
Fallen is the heart of noble enterprise,
True glory perished and the pride of war;
All grace and every virtue perished are,
The leaf is withered and the floweret dies.
Unmoved I am, though heaven and earth invite,
Warmed by no ray nor fanned if zephyr blow;
All offices of nature are deranged:
Since the bright sun that cheered me vanished so,
The courses of the world have quite been changed;
Ah no! but sorrow veils them from my sight.

II.

"If those delights which from the living well
Above are dropped into the heart contrite
Were also visible, and others might
Know what great peace with love divine can dwell,
Perhaps it would be then less hard to tell
Why fame and fortune have been counted light,
And how the wisest men transported quite
Would take their cross and seek the mountain cell,
Finding that death-sweet life; and not alone
In prospect, but now also while the blind
And erring world from the shadows will not cease.
When the awakened soul to God has flown
With humble will to what He wills inclined,
Then outward war to such is inward peace.

III.

"Thanks to thy sovereign grace, O God! if I
Am graff'd in that true vine a living shoot,
Whose arms embrace the world, and in whose root,
Planted by faith, our life must hidden lie.

But thou beholdest how I fade and dry,
Choked with a waste of leaf, and void of fruit,
Unless thy spring perennial shall recruit
My sapless branch, still wanting fresh supply.
O cleanse me then, and make me to abide
Wholly in thee, to drink thy heavenly dew,
And watered daily with my tears to grow.
Thou art the truth, thy promise is my guide;
Prepare me when thou comest, Lord, to show
Fruits answering to the stock on which I grew."

In Italy the Muses have ever had numerous priestesses, welcomed with an enthusiasm measured rather by the gallantry of their admirers than by their real deserts. Among these was LAURA BATTIFERRI, born at Urbino in 1522–3, whose genius has inspired the pens of Caro, Varchi, Mazzuchelli, and others; and whom by a questionable, and, as regarded her morals, a most unmerited compliment, Pietro Vettori compared to Sappho. Following a very different model, she, like Vittoria Colonna, composed many devotional pieces, often versifying the sadder portions of sacred writ, two volumes of which were published at Florence. Rarer perhaps, and more creditable than her poetic celebrity, was the reputation for moral worth transmitted to us in connection with her name, which she happily exchanged by her union with Bartolomeo Ammanati, notwithstanding frowns from a high quarter. The Duchess Vittoria, proud of her talents, laid upon her an injunction not to marry out of her native state. This restriction had the usual result; her husband was a Florentine sculptor, and it required all the influence of Cardinal Alessandro Farnese with his sister to obtain pardon for such flagrant disobedience.

"In 1558, there were at the court of Urbino—of old the resort of talented persons—many great and famous poets, such as Messer Bernardo Capello, Messer Bernardo Tasso, Messer Girolamo Muzio, and Messer Antonio Gallo, whose whole occupation it was, like white gentle swans, emulously to sing, and celebrate in verse, the eminent beauty, and far more eminent virtues, of the illustrious Duchess." With these names might be coupled Dionigi Atanagi, the writer of this euphuism, and also Annibale Caro, Antonio Allegretti, Marco Montano, and Cornelio Lanci. Of Tasso and Muzio we elsewhere speak. Caro and Capello were connected with the ducal family only by one or two complimentary effusions, in return for occasional hospitality. Allegretti indited an epithalamium on the marriage of Duchess Vittoria, in which, alluding to the heraldic bearings then united, he celebrated the prudent hand of the wise shepherd (Paul III.), who transplanted that virgin Lily into good soil under the shadow of the mighty Oak; in conclusion, he summoned the attendants to scatter acorns and *fleurs-de-lis* before the bridal pair. Lanci's comedies no longer "fret and strut their hour upon the stage," but they are said to deserve the praise of comparative purity in an age when decency was no necessary ingredient of scenic merit. Three names remain for consideration, who, as natives of the duchy, may claim a brief notice.

DIONIGI ATANAGI was born at Cagli, and, after twenty-five years spent at the Roman court, returned, in 1557, to recruit his constitution in his native air. He was invited to Pesaro by his sovereign, at the suggestion of Bernardo Tasso, who wished him to revise the *Amadigi*; but there he found his health still further impaired by mental fatigue. Several of his sonnets are addressed to members of the ducal family and court; one of them, inscribed to Guidobaldo II., lauds him as "a prince and captain of invincible valour, of wisdom superhuman, of bounty and benignity past belief, of ineffable eloquence, of incomparable liberality and magnificence, a paragon of religion, the lofty stay of Italian honour and renown. Being the natural sovereign as well as special patron and singular benefactor of the author, whose every hope rests in him next to God, it is his desire, in the full knowledge how much is due to his Excellency's infinite merits, to fill with heroic praises of him whatever work he may undertake; but overwhelmed by the grandeur of the theme, his silence is broken only by excuses for his deficiency." This fulsome trash is no unfair specimen of such compositions. The following invitation to Urbino, as an asylum of the Muses, is in a somewhat happier vein, which we have endeavoured to render:—

"Anime belle, e di virtute amiche,
Cui fero sdegno di fortuna offende,
Sì che ven gite povere e mendiche,
Come e lei piace, che pietà contende;
Se di por fine alle miserie antiche
Caldo desio l' afflitto cor v' incende,
Ratte correte alla gran QUERCIA d' oro,
Ond' avrete alimento ombra e ristoro.

"Qui regna un Signor placido e benigno,
Ch' altro ch' altrui giovar unqua non pensa,
Cortese, e d' ogni real laude degno;
Che ciascun pasce a sua ricca mensa,
E 'n buon revolge ogni destin maligno,
Mentre le grazie sue largo dispensa
GUIDOBALDO, di principi fenici,
Che può col guardo sol far l'uom felice.

"Qui le buone arti ed i nobili costumi,
Senno, fede e valor, fido albergo hanno;
Qui fioriscon gl' ingegni, e chiari lumi
Via più ch' il sol spargendo intorno vanno:
Qui mel le piante, qui dan latte i fiumi;
Qui pace è queta senza alcuno affanno;
Qui 'l vizio è morto, e virtù bella è viva
Beato chi ci nasce e chi ci arriva."

I.

Ah! beauteous souls, to virtue ever prone,
Whom evil Fortune's cruel grudge offends,
Bereft of every stay, and left to groan
By her caprice, while heavy grief impends;

If in your aching hearts that grief evoke
  A wish such lengthened miseries to close,
Speed 'neath the umbrage of the golden OAK
  To share its genial shelter and repose.

2.

A gentle and benignant Prince there reigns,
  On other's weal exclusively intent,
Courteous, and worth all praise in royal strains,
  From whose well plenished table none are sent.
Each evil destiny by him disarmed,
  His gracious boons are scattered widely round;
E'en by his winning glance is each one charmed,
  Phœnix of princes, GUIDOBALDO crowned.

3.

Ennobling arts and noble manners here,
  With wit, and faith, and courage have their home,
While genius' meteor gleams more bright appear
  Than Phœbus flickering in the skiey dome.
Here honey-laden meads and milky streams
  To painless peace attract, and gentle rest;
Here vice is dead, while worth resplendent seems:
  Happy such duchy's native, or its guest!

Among the men of letters whom it was the pride of Guidobaldo II. to attract round him, was ANTONIO GALLI, of Urbino. His uncle, the Cavalier Angelo, had preceded him, both in the cultivation of the muses, and in the good graces of the Dukes, having been employed on various political missions by Guidantonio, Oddantonio, and Federigo; during his leisure hours he had composed sonnets and canzonets in imitation of Petrarch, then the popular model for minor poets. For Antonio has been claimed the questionable honour of introducing pastoral dramas, which long exercised a debilitating influence on the literature of Italy, and spread from there the vitiating style to other lands. He, too, held diplomatic appointments at the courts of Rome and Spain, and to the republic of Venice; and having acquired the reputation of a man, not less of business than of letters, the Duke entrusted him with the superintendence of Prince Francesco Maria, until his death in 1551. His contemporary and friend MARCO MONTANO enjoyed his sovereign's favour without sharing any public employments. In youth he had been secretary of Cardinal Carlo Borromeo, and afterwards addicted himself to Latin and Italian verse, with a success sufficient to gain him applause from Baldi, and from Tasso the compliment of being ranked next to Guarini among the living bards of Italy. The suffrage of these partial friends has not been confirmed by posterity; for Montano's poetry lies forgotten, and his name is cherished only in connection with the literary history of his native state.

Among the names which shed a lustre upon Urbino, in return for hospitalities received at that court, was that of BERNARDO TASSO,*[1] whose splendour would have been more conspicuous in the galaxy of Italian poets, had he not given birth to a son of yet brighter genius. The house of Tasso was of ancient descent in the Bergamasque territory; but Bernardo drew his first breath at Venice, the home of his mother, a lady of the Cornari. Of his youth we know nothing, except that he enjoyed the advantage of a liberal education, and that his morals were no exception to the lax habits of the age. An avowed lover of the matronly Ginevra Malatesta, he sang her beauty in strains complaining of her continence; and at Rome he dangled in poverty after Tullia d' Aragona, one of those splendid examples of wasted powers and successful vice over which the philosopher puzzles while the historian sighs, whose talents were given to the Muses, whose graces were devoted to Venus.

Finding himself past thirty without either an independence or a career, he commenced the life of a literary courtier, for which the social condition of Italy under her

*[1] Cf. PASOLINI, *I Genitori di T. Tasso* (Roma, 1895).

BERNARDO TASSO

From a picture once in the possession of James Dennistoun

many principalities held out considerable inducements. His first essay was as private secretary to Count Guido Rangone, a warrior chief of some distinction; and during the Lombard campaign in 1526 Bernardo was sent by him on missions of importance to the Doge of Genoa and to the Pope.*[1] He remained with the latter on Bourbon's approach, and was commissioned by his Holiness to seek out Lannoy at Siena, and urge him to repair to Rome, take command of the imperial troops, and put an end to their outrages. In this journey the speed of his Turkish charger enabled him to escape from an assault which proved fatal to one of his attendants. Though unsuccessful in the negotiation, his dexterity recommended him as papal envoy to the court of France, in order to arrange the advance of Lautrec, whom he accompanied into Italy. After the destruction of the French army before Naples, we find him for a time secretary to Laura Duchess of Ferrara, and he accompanied the Marquis of Vasto on the Turkish campaign in Hungary.

It was in 1531 that he entered the service of Ferdinando or Ferrante Sanseverino, Prince of Salerno, whom he attended to Africa in the expedition of Charles V. against Tunis. His patron was a prince of ample means, and of corresponding generosity to persons of literary merit; and Tasso, having distinguished himself by several published collections of verses, as well as by the able performance of his more immediate duties, was rewarded by offices and pensions yielding him about 1000 scudi a year. Finding himself thus independent at forty-six, he married Porzia de' Rossi, the beautiful, accomplished, and well-dowried daughter of a noble family in Pistoia, and settled himself at Sorrento, where he spent the best and happiest years of his life, and, with occasional interruptions of business and calls to the camp, pursued his poetical studies.*[2]

*[1] He went in 1528 to Paris on behalf of Conte Guido.

*[2] Cf. CAPASSO, *Il Tasso e la sua famiglia a Sorrento* (Napoli, 1866).

On that plain which matures a tropical luxuriance of vegetation, and where nature lavishes the brightest of her varying tints, his inspiration was developed, and the more brilliant genius of his son imbibed its earliest impressions. The casino in which Torquato first saw the light[1] commanded a view of unparalleled beauty;—the bright bay and its far-off islands of picturesque outline,—Naples, with its endless line of white suburbs glittering along the shore, —Vesuvius, the marvellous workshop of volcanic wonders, —golden sunsets of unclouded glow, and mellowed combinations of mountain and marine scenery awaiting the pencil of Salvator Rosa. Nor were these the only charms which the poet found in this spot. He has celebrated in his correspondence its balmy and healthful climate, and the courteous hospitality of its inhabitants. These qualities still attract strangers to the Piano di Sorrento, and the villa which sheltered Torquato on his escape from Ferrara is now a comfortable hotel, inviting them to gaze from its beetling cliff on the scenes of his youthful inspiration.

The *Amadigi* was commenced in that genial spot, and the Prince of Salerno complacently anticipated the extended reputation which it promised to his protegé. But the storm, meanwhile, gathered, which was to sweep patron and poet from their palmy state. The Prince, by entanglements which we need not trace, found himself compromised with the Viceroy, Don Pedro Toledo, and, from mingled alarm and pique, sacrificed his vast hereditary stake, by passing over to the French service. This happened in 1552,*[2] and Tasso followed his fortunes without being involved in his treason. After accompanying him to France, he came, in 1554, to Rome, where he took up his abode, in the hope of soon being joined by his wife and family, and of establishing himself there. But she was

[1] On the 11th of March, 1544; Bernardo was born the 11th November, 1493.

*[2] 1547.

detained at Naples, for the purpose of recovering part of her husband's property, or at all events her own fortune, which had been escheated on his flight. Her difficulties were increased by the selfish conduct of her own relations, and at length, in the spring of 1556, she died suddenly, not without suspicion of poison. "I have lost," writes her husband, "a woman whose virtues and estimable qualities rendered her beloved and endeared to me as life itself, who was worthy of general admiration, and in whose bosom I had hoped peacefully to pass the closing years of my old age!" But other cares were falling thickly around him. Though joined by his son Torquato, he could never rescue his only other child Cornelia from her maternal relations, and suffered intense anxiety for her welfare. Still nominally in the Prince of Salerno's service, and actually employed as his confidential agent, he found himself estranged from his regard, his correspondence interrupted, and his salary irregularly paid. Bitterly experiencing the not unfrequent guerdon of fidelity to fallen dignitaries, he thus addressed his patron in February, 1556:—

"Your Excellency has now to learn the influence of unstable and malignant fortune upon this your unhappy servant. You know how often you have quoted me as an instance of happiness, saying that I had a beautiful and virtuous wife, by whom I was beloved, and on whom I doated; that I had the finest children, ample means, an excellent house well decorated, as well as comfortably furnished; and that I enjoyed the respect and good opinion of the world, as well as that most important advantage of all, your favour. Now you may see in how brief an interval I have fallen from that height of happiness into the depths of misery. I have lost my means, earned, as all know, most honourably, and with no small fatigue and peril. I have lost my independence; and, in a word, my every comfort. I have been deprived of my dearest wife, and with her have occasioned to my unhappy children the sacrifice of their mother's dowry, and of all my remaining prospect of maintaining them, and conducting them to that position which every respectable and affectionate parent would desire. But, worst of all, I perceive from obvious symptoms, that I have forfeited your favour without having given you the slightest cause. The reason of my sinking into these misfortunes, being obvious to the whole world, should not be concealed from you. I am so situated, that any one refusing to compassionate me must be devoid of pity and all good feeling; and if you still retain the smallest share of that magnanimity, generosity, or gratitude which you were wont so honourably to manifest to your servants, you will yet have pity on me, and will endeavour to raise me from that abyss of wretchedness into which I have fallen in your service."

This sad appeal meeting with no response, he retired from the Prince's service with a nominal pension of 300 scudi, which seems never to have been paid him. Writing to a friend, he says, "I have thrown out into this sea of troubles many anchors of reason, to save my tempest-tost mind from shipwreck. But I fear that, in the long run, if not conducted into port by a favouring breeze from some benignant prince, I may be swamped, from the cable of my constancy parting; for it is hard from prosperity and happiness to fall into misery, and struggle with famine." Scared away from Rome by the din of coming war, in the renewed strife between France and Spain for the domination of the Peninsula, and

"Eating the bitter bread of banishment,"

he had reached Ravenna, when an invitation arrived from Guidobaldo II., Duke of Urbino, a cousin of his late patron, whose court offered to genius just such a haven as he had hoped for. In October, 1556, he reached Pesaro, where the Duke assigned as a residence for the poet his casino called the Barchetto, a house which still stands within the walls of Pesaro, surrounded by a smiling garden. Its very limited accommodation, now used by the gardener, cannot have afforded a commodious dwelling, but such as it was, it appears to have satisfied Bernardo, who after a few weeks was encouraged by the Duke's courtesy to send for his son, with a view to establishing himself in that capital. His residence there somewhat exceeded two years, during which we gather from his correspondence few incidents beyond his literary occupations. Though avowing himself in the service of Guidobaldo, he does not seem to have had from him either employment or a fixed maintenance, but was probably supported by his hospitality. He now put the finishing touches to his *Amadigi*, begun fourteen years before, and repaid the favours bestowed upon him with the usual homage of a courtly poet. Anxiously clinging to the hope of making his peace with Spain, in order to recover his own and his wife's property which had been confiscated at Naples, he obtained the mediation of several courts in his favour, and even had recourse to the good offices of Cardinal Pole with Philip II., then husband of the English Queen Mary. In this object Guidobaldo particularly interested himself, and it was at his suggestion that Bernardo dedicated his poem to that monarch, whose praises, with those of his consort, had been already sung in its eleventh canto. But his pearls were lavished unavailingly on one incapable of appreciating either the gift or the donor, and a long apologetic letter from Girolamo Ruscelli, which accompanied the peace-offering, remained unacknowledged.

In these times literary advertisements were unknown, but the reputation of a forthcoming work was heralded by a scarcely less effectual expedient. Passages of it were handed about in manuscript among literary circles, and criticisms were requested from the author's more intimate friends. Thus was it with the *Amadigi;* and Bernardo has not shrunk from giving to the world the letters by which he sought for or replied to such suggestions. Dionigi Atanagi was summoned from Cagli by the Duke, for the purpose of making those verbal corrections which were rendered irksome to the poet by weak sight. Sperone Speroni writes to the author that, in two revisions, he had removed the vulgarisms, roughnesses, and redundancies, cancelling above two hundred stanzas, and that, in a third reading, he would probably delete as many more. The first conception was that of a regular epic; but the cold reception which it met with from his friends induced Bernardo to adopt a manner more conformable to the romantic and less fettered taste of the age. In the summer of 1557 he read a canto each night, at Urbino, to the Duchess Vittoria and a select audience. Having thus raised public anticipation, the poet was anxious to reap the fruits of his labours in honour and emolument; but he found a double difficulty in obtaining the 500 scudi required for the expense of an edition, and in procuring the papal licence without having the work submitted regularly to the censure. At length, in 1560, it issued, by the aid of Guidobaldo, from the press of Giolito, at Venice, in which town Tasso had chiefly resided for eighteen months, and where he, for a short time, acted as secretary to a literary academy, established in 1558, before which he read his Essay on Poetry. His remaining years produced few incidents. After an ineffectual overture to take service at the court of Savoy, he became chief secretary to the Duke of Mantua, who made him governor of Ostiglia. There he died on the 4th of September, 1569; and the epitaph penned by his son, but never placed over his ashes, runs thus:—

Erected by his son Torquato to
BERNARDO TASSO,
Distinguished for the fertility and eminence of his genius, in the relaxation of poetry and in the affairs of princes, in both of which he has left memorials of his industry, as well as for the fickleness and inconstancy of his fortunes.
He lived LXXVI. years, and died IV Sept. MDLXIX.

His bereavement was thus intimated by Torquato to the Duke of Urbino: "On the 4th of September it pleased the Lord God to call to himself the blessed soul of my father, whose death, although in all respects mature, is nevertheless felt by me as most untimely, and, I am persuaded, will be very unacceptable to your Excellency, who by so many proofs of regard considered him among your most esteemed servants, and towards whom I know his especial reverence. Of this respect, and of the infinite obligations under which he lay to your Excellency, I am most willingly the representative; and if that favour which your Excellency ever extended for his protection, and that of his interests, be devolved upon me, I shall deem it an ample patrimony that he has left me. And herewith praying a happy issue to all your honoured desires, I humbly kiss your hands. From Ferrara, the 28th September, 1569."

An amiable disposition and agreeable manners procured for Bernardo Tasso, in all the fluctuations of his career, troops of friends, including the brightest names of his age. In the many situations of trust which he filled, his prudence and address, his fidelity and sincerity, acquired for him general estimation. Although his literary reputation now hangs, in a great degree, upon that of his son, his contemporaries, who knew not what the latter had in store for them, regarded him as the first epic poet of his age, comparing him even with Ariosto, whom he freely and avowedly imitated. To draw out some fifty-seven thousand verses on a borrowed and almost barren theme, in a style anticipated by several preceding minstrels, was an effort repugnant to fine genius, and susceptible of no marked success. Its necessary failing is diffuseness, varying from inflation to languor; its redeeming merit an acknowledged facility, sustained at times by fertile images, and by delicately beautiful descriptions. It is generally flowing, though, at times, feeble; yet is considered by Panizzi "unquestionably the best romantic narrative from amongst those not founded on the traditions respecting Charlemagne." Indeed, his poetry, while sharing with coeval productions the blemishes of exuberant ornament and quaint conceits, is seldom surpassed in pathos, and his dulcet numbers reconcile us to his faults of manner. What, to its author, was probably its most important quality, is now, perhaps, its greatest defect,—the profuse flattery of which it was made the medium. "To eat the bread of others" was the often hard, usually degrading, tenure self-imposed on court poets; and to such, a subject admitting of endless episodes, and the frequent introduction of existing personages, in their real characters or under transparent allegories, was a harvest of princely favour and of wealth. This, however, was an error of the age, which ought not to be charged on any single poet, least of all on one who had given his best and worthiest efforts to a barren soil. The fugitive poetry of Tasso partakes largely of this adulatory colouring. But, for him is claimed such praise as the invention of the Ode deserves; and this was deemed creditable service to a literature which has often invested trifles with undue importance.

Bernardo was a secretary ere he became a poet, and his reputation rests more surely upon his correspondence than on his verses. That rhetoric which Bembo inculcated by precept and practice had become a fashion among men of literary pretension; their letters were composed as models of style, and manuscript or printed collections of them were in very general circulation. Such compositions, when thus written for the public, wanted the freshness and simplicity which constitute their best charm; but they gained attractions of another sort, and came to be read more for their manner than their matter. To this class belong the letters of the elder Tasso: nitid in style, but cold in feeling, they exhibit the niceties of Italian idiom, rather than the familiarities of Italian life. A very favourable specimen, but too long for insertion here, is that in which he proposes to his wife the principles which ought to guide her in bringing up their children, and in the formation of their manners and character. Though sometimes smoothed down to common-place, it breathes a fine spirit of paternal affection, and combines religious observance with a becoming knowledge of the world.

CHAPTER LI

Torquato Tasso—His insanity—Theories of Dr. Verga and Mr. Wilde—His connection with Urbino—His intercourse with the Princess of Este—His portraits—His letter to the Duke of Urbino—His confinement—His death—His poetry—Battista Guarini.

OUR passing notice of Italian song would be incomplete without the name of Italy's favourite bard, even had TASSO *[1] found no hospitality at Urbino, no sympathy from its Duchess Lucrezia. Yet what shall we say of one whose loves and woes have filled many volumes,—whose life, character, and motives, after baffling biographers, and puzzling moralists, are still matter rather of controversy than of history, of speculation than of fact. That he was imbued with true genius, with its failings as well as its powers, is fixed by the unanimous verdict of posterity. That his misfortunes have tended greatly to enhance the sympathising veneration which hangs around his name, may be quoted in proof of the eternal justice of Providence, The rolls of Parnassus may exhibit names more gifted, the annals of human suffering are inscribed with greater calamities and deeper griefs, but in no other case, perhaps, have talents and trials been more mingled together on an equally prominent stage. His supposed persecutor was elevated enough to command the world's gaze, and upon

*[1] For the life of Torquato Tasso, see SOLERTI, in three volumes (Torino, 1895). The first contains the *Vita;* the second, *Lettere inedite e disperse di T.T. e di diversi;* the third, *Documenti e appendici.* See D'ANCONA'S review in *Rass. Bibl. Lett. Ital.*, vol. IV., p. 7 *et seq.* The most complete modern edition of his works is ROSINI'S, in 33 vols., 8 vo. (Pisa), and of the *Rime*, that of SOLERTI, in 3 vols. (Bologna, 1898–99).

TORQUARTO TASSO
From a picture once in the possession of James Dennistoun

him there accordingly has been heaped the blame of a wretchedness in a great measure self-imposed, and inseparable from a morbid and diseased temperament. The complaints of the poet have been embodied in notes alternately of wailing and of fire, by a poet of a nation whom he would have deemed barbarous.[1] The charge which history has recorded against Tasso is to this purpose. That, whilst a retainer of Alfonso II. of Ferrara, his heart was enslaved by that Duke's sister, Princess Leonora d' Este, and that his passion was ill-concealed in the verses it inspired. That Alfonso having suspected the audacious fault, harshly visited it with a series of persecutions, and finally shut him up for seven years in bedlam as a lunatic.

From infancy he manifested decided symptoms of "a genius to madness near allied." Indifferent to toys, he seemed exempt from the emotions and the tastes of childhood. Precocious in all mental powers, he spoke intelligibly at six months, knew Greek and wrote verses at seven years, and at eighteen published the *Rinaldo*, a sustained and applauded epic.*[2] The reverses of his early days on which we have already dwelt in our notice of his father, the premature loss of his mother, the injudicious liberty of thought and action allowed him by Bernardo, and the rough criticisms to which his writings were subjected ere his character and knowledge of mankind were developed—all these tinged deeper the gloom of his constitutional sadness, and formed a training the most fatal to one of innately morbid sensibilities. The results were obvious. Bald before his time, his digestion enervated, subject to faintings and fevers intermittent or delirious, his health at thirty was ruined, his nerves and brain shattered. The natural consequence of his precocity was an overweening pride in his accomplishments, which

[1] BYRON'S *Lament of Tasso*.

*[2] See on the *Rinaldo*, PROTO, *Sul Rinaldo di T. T.* (Napoli, 1895).

rendered him jealous, touchy, and quarrelsome; and though destined from youth to wander in search of given bread, nature had neither granted him the humble resignation required for such a lot, nor imbued him with a daring spirit to rise above it. Men who live in courts must be prepared to encounter intrigues; those who publish poetry should lay their account with unsparing strictures; and the smaller the court, or the more prominent their poetic merits, so much the greater need have they of forbearance and philosophy. But Tasso possessed neither; and the jealousies of Pigna and Guarini, the malice of the della Crusca critics, stung him to the quick.*[1] A slight or fancied affront, which he met with from one of the courtiers of Ferrara, though avenged by a duel, brought his symptoms to a head.*[2] From that moment, when in his thirty-third year, we find him a victim to the restlessness, suspicions, fears, sad forebodings, and hopeless misery, which afflict lipemaniacs.

Under such sinister influences the crisis speedily arrived. Whilst seated in the Duchess of Urbino's apartment, in her mother's palace, he rushed with his dagger on an attendant who chanced to enter. This, whether a premeditated assault, or an idle hallucination, seems to have been the ground on which he was, by order of Alfonso, placed under restraint; but when the paroxysm was passed, he was reconducted to the Duke's presence with ample assurances of pardon. The iron had, however, entered into his soul, and the idea that he was in disgrace, owing to the malicious backbiting of foes real or imaginary, could not be driven from his mind. He retired from their

*[1] Cf. D'OVIDIO, *Di una antica testimonianza circa la controversia della Crusca con Tasso* (Napoli, 1894) and VIVALDI, *La più grande polemica del Cinquecento* (Catanzaro Caliò, 1895). SOLERTI reviewed this last in *Giornale Stor. d. Lett. Ital.*, vol. XXVII., p. 426.

*[2] It was in September, 1576. Tasso had in July thought himself insulted by Ercole Fucci and his brother Maddalò; he boxed Ercole's ears. Then, in September, they met him and assaulted him. There was no duel. Only Solerti has found out the truth.

supposed persecutions to a Franciscan convent,*[1] but, finding in its quiet no peace for his troubled spirit, he fled in disguise from these illusions, and, led perhaps by the bright memory of his early days, arrived on the sunny shores of Sorrento, where he sought a refuge with his married sister. But alas! the charms of that radiant land shed no gladsome influence on his soul. Ere a few months passed, he returned to Ferrara, in hopes of proving to the Duke that the crimes and the frenzy, of which he believed himself accused, were equally calumnies. In the festive and kindly reception with which he was greeted, the wayward poet found new grounds for jealousy, imagining a plot to be formed against his literary fame, by plunging him in a round of dissipation, whilst "others" (meaning his patron) should reap the glory and profits due to his creative genius. That conduct so provoking should have brought upon him real slights, in addition to his imagined wrongs, can scarcely be doubted; and, wounded at heart, he again had recourse to flight, wandering aimlessly by Mantua, Padua, and Venice, to Pesaro, the refuge of his happier youth. We shall elsewhere introduce the letter which he there addressed to the Duke of Urbino; though it obtained him a compassionate welcome, his new host naturally counselled his return to the home of his adoption, as the place where he was most certain to be cared for. But in a fresh access of disease, he escaped from such suggestions, and obeyed them not until after he had visited Turin, disguised by poverty and filth.

If these views of Tasso's malady*[2] are as conformable to truth as they appear to be with the representations of his biographers, the time seems to have been now

*[1] He was placed under restraint in S. Francesco, in Ferrara, in fact.

*[2] On the whole subject of Tasso's madness, see CORRADI, *Le Infermità di T.T.* in *Memorie dell' Istit. Lombardo* (1880), vol. XIV.; RONCORONI, *Genio e Pazzia in T.T.* (Torino, 1896); and GAUDENZI, *Studio Psicopatol. sopra T.T.* (Vercelli, 1898); and SOLERTI, *op. cit., supra.*

fully arrived for his seclusion, as a measure of justice to himself and of security to others. It is quite another question how far the treatment he met with at Sant' Anna was that best suited to his symptoms. Had he lived in times when the pathology of mind was more fully understood, and more ably managed, his genius might, by timely care, have been saved from a miserable wreck; but his brain surely then required such aid as medical science could afford. If this be granted, the defence of Duke Alfonso is complete, whatever might have been the discipline resorted to in the hospital. Yet it may be well to remember, from the testimony of the poor maniac, as well as of others, that the delusions which for years had haunted him, regarding wrongs supposed to have been received from that sovereign and his courtiers, had given bitterness to his words, and pungency to his pen, little in accordance with the fulsome language of his age, or the haughty temper of his patron; that if the poet was a victim of imaginary affronts, the Duke had met at his hands with real insults. But even were Alfonso's motives not those of unmixed kindness, the necessity of seclusion for Tasso cannot be affected by any such consideration, nor by the consequent aggravation of his malady from defective skill.

An admission of Tasso's mental alienation was made by his intimate friend Manso, and has been repeated by various writers; yet other biographers, anxious to relieve their hero from the reproach of madness, have essayed to screen him by charges of cruelty against the Duke of Ferrara. Whilst Verga's theory appears to place the poet's malady upon its proper footing, and, by implication, to absolve his patron, that author goes a step further, and maintains that the oldest and best informed authorities bear out a belief in the uniform and considerate kindness of Alfonso towards his wayward laureate, and prove that the allegations of Torquato's insanity having been but

Neurdein Frères

LAURA DE' DIANTI AND ALFONSO OF FERRARA
After the picture by Titian in the Louvre

the pretext of a stern tyrant, bent on punishing the presumption of an unworthy aspirant to his sister's love, were piquant additions of after writers. We shall presently have a few words to add in regard to this entanglement; meanwhile, let us see the conclusion drawn by Dr. Verga, from his able argument. "We may, therefore, infer that the Duke shut up Tasso in Sant' Anna, neither as a punishment for ambitious love, or unguarded and offensive expressions, nor as an obstacle to his conferring the illustration of his genius on rival courts, but simply because he saw that the poet's melancholy rendered him beside himself, dependent upon skilful treatment, and perhaps dangerous to others. I repeat, in the name of common sense, that his madness was the sole cause of his seclusion, not the effect of it, as some would persuade us."

Although we have passed rapidly over those circumstances that impart to Tasso's life its romantic and mysterious interest, we must detail somewhat more fully the various links connecting the thread of his chequered existence with the ducal house of Urbino. The arrival of his father, Bernardo, at the court of Pesaro, in 1556, has been already mentioned[1]; and six months later he was joined by Torquato, then completing his thirteenth year, who was permitted to share the education of the hereditary Prince, and to mingle occasionally with the accomplished circle at the Imperiale, until Bernardo carried him to Venice, in 1559. On a mind of such premature powers these opportunities were not wasted, and the remembrance of them cheered many an after hour of despondency. The homeless position and unsettled habits of his father, whose wanderings he generally accompanied, interfered somewhat with his education, which was then directed to the law, as his future profession. But whilst supposed to

[1] At p. 303 above.

be engrossed by canonists and civilians, the youth was secretly devoting his hours of study to the muses. Fearing to avow these derelictions to his father, he imparted his boyish efforts to Duke Guidobaldo, who showed them to Bernardo in 1562, when the latter came to offer him a printed copy of his *Amadigi*. It was not, however, for two years more that the paternal sanction was obtained for publishing the *Rinaldo*, a dedication of which is said to have been declined by the Duke, perhaps from a fastidiousness which ere long he had to regret. Encouraged by the unlooked-for success of this poem, written by him in ten months at the university of Padua, Torquato began his great epic, of which he had already selected the theme. Whilst pursuing his studies at Bologna, in 1563, he is believed to have transcribed the first sketch of it, under the title of "*Il Gierusalem*," which is now No. 413 of the Urbino Library at the Vatican. It is preceded by a short notice of the subject, and consists of a hundred and sixteen stanzas, eventually incorporated into the three opening cantos of the poem; but its variations from the printed version are so extensive, that it has been given entire in the collected works, published at Venice, in twelve vols. 4to, 1735. The dedication was this time accepted by Guidobaldo.

At twenty-one, he first saw the court of Ferrara,*[1] which, in honour of his marriage with the Archduchess Barbara, the magnificent Alfonso was then rendering

"The revel of the earth, the masque of Italy."

It was in these festive scenes that the bard made acquaintance with the Princess Lucrezia. Among the portraits in the Palace of Courtesy, whither *Rinaldo* was conducted, and which, by an ingenious turn of flattery, are made to

*[1] On the Court of Ferrara, cf. CAMPORI e SOLERTI, *Luigi*, *Lucrezia e Leonora d'Este* (Torino, 1888), and SOLERTI, *Ferrara e la Corte estense nella secunda meta del sec. XVI.* (Città di Castello, 1899).

represent those personages whom Tasso was most disposed to conciliate, were those of Duke Guidobaldo and his son, with their respective consorts. The passage may be thus literally rendered :—

"He of expression stern and brow severe,
His mien ennobled by a royal state,
The great Francesco Maria's son, is here,
In peace superior, in the field his mate ;
Beneath whose prudent sway, no peril ere
Urbino's favoured duchy shall await,
While o'er her happy vales, and golden plains,
A joyous and enduring summer reigns.

"Such is the sire to whom our planet owes
Yon youthful gallant, with expression bright,
Second to none, a terror to his foes,
A wary leader though a dauntless knight :
On him the weight of thousand wars repose,
A thousand armies guiding to the fight.
Whoe'er is doomed to immortality
Shrined in men's hearts and mouths, HE may not die.

"Turn your admiring gaze to yonder side
On all that heaven of loveliness can yield,
Elsewhere unmatched within Sol's circuit wide,
From whose bright beams no beauty lies concealed ;
The ducal crown and robe can scarcely hide
The regal bearing on that brow revealed :
Vittoria she, from great Farnese traced,
Courteous and gentle, generous and chaste.

"Lucrezia d' Este is yon other fair,
Whose dazzling tresses seem a treasure given
For guileless love therewith to weave a snare
And toils, purveyed by Him who rules in heaven.
Say, do Minerva and the Muses share
Praise and disparagement in portions even,—
Praise, since she them to imitate is fain ;
Blame, that their rivalry with her is vain ?

"These dames, in charms and chastity compeers,
And proudly rich in every virtue rare"—

Such compliments from a poet of promising fame could not be indifferent to one taught to prize genius as almost the equal of rank; nor were they the less acceptable to a lady of thirty-one, that their author had barely attained manhood. She received him with her sweetest smile, and presented him to her father the Duke, and to her sister Leonora, in terms which secured him a most flattering reception. Love and chivalry were fashions of the day, cultivated in common by all who strove to shine in the brilliant atmosphere of Ferrara, and the genius of Torquato lent itself gracefully to both. In many phases of Italian literature, it has been difficult for posterity to decide whether the fervour of amorous poetry was kindled by successful passion, or fanned by affected sentiment. The like mystery overhangs the love-notes which Tasso warbled in these palace-bowers. That his aspirations were not free from pedantry is proved by their, on one occasion, selecting the form of a public disputation, after the most approved scholastic models, wherein, during three days, he maintained against all comers, a series of abstract propositions regarding love and its developments. And though such singular exhibitions may sometimes have been suggested by deeper feelings, or accepted as the incense of the heart, they were doubtless in other cases but tournaments of gallantry, in which the name of some fair lady was adopted, to inspire the combatants to a victory extending not beyond the lists. Equally platonic might have been such love-tissued lyrics as our minstrel ever and anon dedicated to the sister Princesses, without any scandal, and probably without compromise of their purity. One of these, in supposed allusion to the favoured sister, having been specially excepted from the sentence of posthumous destruction pronounced upon many of his fugitive pieces by the poet when about to take a journey, must have ranked high in his estimation, and is thus translated by Glassford:—

"Now that my charmer breathes another air
In woods and fields, how barbarous to remain
In this deserted place, where grief, and pain,
And darkness dwell, a region of despair!
Nothing is joyful here, and nothing fair:
Love grows a boor, and with the rustic train
Now feeds his flock, and now in sultry plain
Handles the scythe, or guides the pondrous share.

O, happy wood! O smiling banks and gay,
Where every beast, and every plant and stone,
Have learned the use of generous customs mild.
What shall not yield to her whose eyes alone
Can, as they lend or take their light away,
Polish the groves, and make the town a wild."

During the four years which glided by in this charmed existence, the youthful bard appears to have remained faithful to his first friend Lucrezia; and it was not until her marriage to the Prince of Urbino in 1571, that the superior charms of her younger and more sedate sister effected for her that alleged conquest of his heart, which long-continued assertions have almost established as a truth.

It would be interesting could we fix the comparative encouragement which the bard enjoyed from the sisters, and ascertain the amount of favour severally vouchsafed him; on this much contested but conjectural ground we shall not, however, enter.*[1] Love-making, which is frequently a science rather than a passion, becomes almost invariably so where its flame is habitually fed by poetry or pedantry, and such were naturally the loves of Tasso in the atmosphere of a court whose polish was heightened by these accomplishments. The siren-notes of Italian song draw their melody from epithets calculated to soothe the ear even when they reach not the heart, and seldom afford

*[1] Cf. D'OVIDIO, *Il carattere, gli amori e le sventure di T.T.* in *Studi Critici* (Napoli, 1879); see also CAMPORI e SOLERTI, *op. cit., supra*, p. 229, note *1.

evidence as to which of these organs they are meant to fascinate. This uncertainty gives life to a tribe of commentators, and has originated volumes of idle speculation as to the material existence of Laura and Beatrice, the platonic or passionate intercourse of Torquato with the Princesses of Este. The language of sonnets and *canzoni* is equally suited to express or to feign, to indicate or to veil, heartfelt homage; and those of Tasso thus are capable of whatever interpretation best accords with the temperament or the theory of his critics. Such, for example, are the tributes of his muse on the marriage of Lucrezia, wherein, however, a suspicion of somewhat undue tenderness might attach to such lines as—

> "Sad as a mourning convoy seems to me
> Your merry dances, and your Hymen's torch
> Will to my funeral pile a flame supply." [1]

In a *canzone* of the same date, he makes that god descend from Parnassus to preside at her nuptials [2]; but the deity seems to have turned a deaf ear to this tuneful invocation, and we have elsewhere seen that no favour of his crowned the inauspicious union.

On his return from France in 1572, Tasso was, by intercession of the Princesses, received at Ferrara as a salaried courtier; and in the following spring, his pastoral drama, the *Aminta*,*[3] was performed at the palace. Anxious to witness a representation elsewhere so universally applauded, the Princess of Urbino invited him to Pesaro, where he recited his poem in presence of the old Duke, who hailed in him the honoured son of his former protegé. From thence he accompanied Francesco Maria and his consort to their *villeggiatura* at Castel Durante, and it was

[1] "Liete danze vegg' io, che per me sono
Funebri pompe ed un istessa face
Nell' altrui nozze, e nel mio rogo è accesa."

[2] "Lascia Imeneo Parnasso, e qui descende."

*[3] Cf. Mazzoni, preface to his edition of *Rinaldo e l'Aminta* (Firenze, Sansoni, 1884).

then, perhaps, that their domestic peace was most endangered by the poet. The field-sports and manly exercises which attracted the Prince to that secluded spot had no charm for Lucrezia, long accustomed to a life of artificial splendour; and whilst he passed his days in the far-spreading forests, she was exposed to the temptations of ennui, added to the perils of opportunity. It is, therefore, not surprising that a warmer tone pervades the *componimenti* addressed to the Princess in this retirement. Two sonnets, in particular, sing, in cadences of sweetest harmony, her hand imparting perfume to the scented glove, that enviously veiled, from her minstrel's greedy eyes, a whiteness before which the snow would blush, and her bosom, the garden of love, the paradise of the poet, its ripened charms surpassing the budding beauties of early spring.[1]

To write amatory verses on a lady of appearance as matronly as her years, required singular tact; but Tasso boldly met the difficulties of his theme. In another sonnet, excelled by nothing in the whole range of passionate song, after seeking for a parallel to her "unripe" youth in the opening rosebud, or in the unearthly beauty of the early dawn, that gilds the mountains and scatters pearls along the plain, he avows the flower to be most attractive when its leaves have unfolded their odours, just as the mid-day sun outshines its morning lustre. The same delicacy of allusion was needful in regard to both the princesses, of whom Leonora appears to have had the advantage in looks more than in age, for she was but a year younger than her married sister. We again avail ourselves of Mr. Glassford's paraphrase, in order to present it to such readers as are not acquainted with the charming original.

"We saw thee in thy yet unripened green,
Like folded rose, whose damask leaf unspread
To the warm sun, still in its virgin bed
Retires and blushes in the bud unseen.

---

1 "La man ch' avolta in odorate spoglie:" and—
"Non, non, si vaghi i fiori onde la natura."

Or rather—for such earthly type is mean—
Like to Aurora, who with earthly red
Pearls the plain and gilds the mountain head,
Kindling with smiles the dewy sky serene.
Nor is thy riper year in aught less fair;
No youthful beauty in her choice attire
Can so engage, or equal charms display.
Thus sweetest is the flower when to the air
Unbosomed; thus the sun's meridian fire
Exceeds the lustre of its morning ray."

But these seductions did not divert Torquato from the loftier theme which engaged his muse. Far from the gaieties and the squabbles of Ferrara, he drew a fresher inspiration from glorious nature, and among the delightful descriptions suggested by the scenery around Castel Durante are generally numbered those of the gardens of Armida. Whatever may have been the true footing on which the poet's devotion was received by the Princess, and whatever the secret cause of her domestic misunderstandings, her husband never showed, on this or any future occasion, jealousy of his early playmate; and in 1574 Tasso returned to Ferrara, laden with compliments and presents from the august circle at Pesaro, including a jewel of price from the Princess, which his necessities afterwards obliged him to dispose of.

Lucrezia had become Duchess of Urbino in 1574, and her separation from the Duke took place three years later, in circumstances of which we have elsewhere spoken.[1] Released from ties in which affection had never any part, she sought in her brother's palace distractions more suited to her lively temperament, and renewed her intimacy with its silver-tongued laureate. Among the reasons which incline us to believe that this connection was chiefly sought upon her side, is the desire which Tasso about this time manifested of exchanging the protection of the d' Este for a residence at Rome. His intention was not

[1] At pp. 153, 154 above.

realised, for his visit to the Eternal City did not extend beyond a month, and before the close of 1575 he was at Florence.

On returning to Ferrara in January, 1576, a new tie was created to the reigning family, by his appointment as its historiographer, on the death of Pigna. This was the turning point of his existence, whence the symptoms of mental disease gradually and fatally advanced until June, 1577, when, after that outbreak of insanity in presence of the Duchess of Urbino, to which we have already alluded, he was interdicted by Alfonso from corresponding with her. This command she observed, but Leonora occasionally consoled him by letters during his flight to Naples, of which we have spoken in tracing the progress of his lipemania. It was in the autumn of 1578 that he arrived at Pesaro, after his second flight; and, in this melodious but unfinished *canzone*, bespoke shelter under the mighty oak [della Rovere] watered by the Metauro:—

"To the River Metauro.

"O thou illustrious child
Of mighty Apennine, humble though you lie,
In story brighter than thy silver tide;
O stranger fleet and wild,
To this thy friendly and protecting side,
Well pleased, for safety and repose I fly.
The lofty Oak, with mantling branches wide,
Bathed by thy stream, and from thy cisterns fed,
Shadowing the mountains and the seas between,—
Embower me with its screen!
Inviolate screen, and hospitably spread,
Thy cool recesses undisturbed and sweet
Shroud me in deepest covert, thick entwined,
So hid from blind and cruel fortune; blind,
But not for me, whom still she sees to meet,
Though far by hill or valley I should stray,
Or in the lonely way
Have passed at midnight, and with noiseless feet;
And by this bleeding side well understood,
Her aim unerring, as her shaft is good.

"Since first I breathed this air,
Ah me! since first I met the glorious light,
Which never to these eyes unclouded shone,
I was her fatal care,
Chosen to be her mark and her despite;
Nor yet those early hurts by time outgrown.
Well to that spirit pure my words are known,
Beside whose sainted tomb my cradle stood.
Might they have laid me in the peaceful ground
When I received the wound!
Me from my mother's bosom fortune rude
Tore while a child: O yet I feel those last
Kisses and burning tears upon my cheek,
With sighs remembered; still I hear that weak
And ardent prayer, caught by the rising blast,
Then parted ever; no more face to face
Folded in strict embrace
And held by close and loving arms so fast,
Ah! but like Ilus or Camilla hied,
With steps unequal, by my father's side.

"In banishment I grew
And rigid want, instructed by our strange
Disastrous flight to shed untimely tears,
Nor childhood's pleasure knew;
But bitterness to me of chance and change
Brought immature the bitterness of years.
Despoiled and bare, his feeble age appears
Before me still. Alas! and is my store
Of griefs become so scanty, that my own
Are not enough to moan?
That others than myself I must deplore?
But seldom, though I bid, will come the sigh,
Or from these wells the gushing water spring,
In measure suited to my suffering.
Dear father; now my witness from the sky,
Whom sick thou knowest how I moaned, and dead
Poured on thy grave and bed
My ardent heart; thee, in thy mansions high
All bliss beseems, and unalloyed with pain;
Only for me the sighs and tears remain."[1]

[1] GLASSFORD, p. 203.

The morbid feeling and heart-stricken melancholy which, in the language of Gibbon, "disordered his reason without clouding his genius, and which thus exaggerated the trials of his early life, gave way to another train of thought in the following letter, addressed by him, about the same time, to Duke Francesco Maria, which we insert as the most satisfactory record left us of the friendship and protection bestowed on him by that Prince.

"TASSO TO THE DUKE OF URBINO.

"If any action of mine has tended to confirm the rumour of my insanity, it surely was my directing my steps after my flight otherwise than to the court of your Excellency. For certainly I could not have repaired elsewhere without some degree of danger, or at all events some indignity and inconvenience; nor could I hope to find in any other quarter more acquaintance with my real position, nor greater courtesy, knowing no prince more generous, more efficiently compassionate to my misfortunes, or more prompt in the protection of my innocence. Hence, to pass by an asylum near and secure, as well as suitable and honourable, in order to make my way, without comfort, or, at all events, with little credit, to a distant and less safe place, was, if not a sign of folly, at least a proof of impudence and stupidity. Notwithstanding all this, unlike other men who blush and repent when made aware of a blunder, I derive from my ill advised step pleasure and comfort rather than shame and regret, because, being conducted, not where I desired, but whither I ought to go, and having there found the haven which I had supposed far off, across the high seas, I clearly perceive that my steps have been guided by wisdom from on high. And it must be much more pleasing to me to have been brought hither by divine Providence than by human prudence, seeing how much the more infallible guide is the latter to the best appointed end. And although, had I come here in reliance on being received under your Excellency's protection, it would have afforded me much satisfaction to find my hopes realised, and your courtesy equal to my anticipations; yet my gratification is certainly, and beyond comparison, greater, seeing that you have not only anticipated, but overmatched, my desires, and that you have at once equalled and exceeded my expectations. I say exceeded them, because upon the obliging demonstrations of affection and pity which you have shown me, and on your promise to undertake my protection, I found rather an assurance than a hope of safety, peace, and honour. Enough, indeed more than enough, for me, is that which you have promised. Were I to doubt as to the rest, or look forward with such every-day hope as one is apt to entertain regarding uncertain prospects, I should discredit your Excellency's affection, judgment, authority, and power, and I should prove myself unworthy, not only of what you are about to perform, but of what you have already done in my favour. Thus, be assured that I live not only securely, but happily, under your protection. On this account my regrets are less at being so fiercely and iniquitously buffeted and beaten down by fortune, than is my satisfaction at being raised again by the arm of your Excellency; and were there no other way to lead me to you, and to place me in the shadow of your favour, but this most hard and rugged one, with its toils and persecutions, still I should delight to arrive by it; and I account as not only endurable, but as joyful and well-timed, those pangs which brought me to be yours, as it was ever my wish to be, even in my days of less adversity. It is for this reason I dare to appropriate these famous words of Themistocles, 'I were undone, did I not rush upon my ruin.'

"I shall now pass by the long and melancholy tale of my wrongs as indeed superfluous, since the little that your Excellency has heard of my mishaps has sufficed to move your magnanimous heart to extend me aid. Nor shall I try to awaken in your soul any compassion beyond what it voluntarily fostered, without artifice of mine; for I rejoice that in this noble and courteous act my exertions have no part, all being your own, and springing from the greatness and compassion of your individual mind. Most gladly should I thank your Excellency for what you have done, and will do, in my behalf, could I invent words and terms fit for such thanks; but what can I, or what should I say to you? To you I neither can nor ought to use such phrases as servants employ to their masters, benefited to their benefactors, favoured to those who confer obligations, because, as my misery was incomparable and unprecedented, so it would become me to invent expressions signifying how much I owe to your Excellency who rescues me from it. I shall, therefore, say, that since, thanks to you, I emerge from a condition so low, so disgraced, so wretched, and so reduced in reputation and in the opinion of mankind, who looked upon me as virtually dead, I seem to have received a new health from you, by reason whereof I acknowledge your Excellency, not only as a prince and benefactor to whom I owe much, but it may almost be permitted me to add, as a creator, and I seem to say but little in avowing myself your most obliged and highly favoured servant, if I add not *creature*.[1] Such, accordingly, I shall formally avow myself, and in that light I pray you for the future to regard me, and to contrive that I am regarded by others, taking entire possession of me and of my free will, which I fully submit to your sway. And this I should do with all my affairs, were it in my power; but some of them are not at my own disposal, or they should be placed at that of him to whom I have surrendered myself.

[1] The letter is taken from an old transcript, No. 430, of the Oliveriana MSS., p. 210, but it has been printed at vol. IX., p. 104, of the Venetian edition of Tasso's works.

And herewith humbly I kiss your hands, assuring you that these words have been engraven by me on my heart, ere they were traced upon this sheet."

The expectations which dictated this touching letter were amply realised. After a reception of singular kindness, the good Duke recommended medical advice for Tasso's now obvious malady; and an issue prescribed for his arm was dressed by the Princess Lavinia della Rovere, whose sedulous care was rewarded in a madrigal. By such solace his restlessness, however, prevented him from long profiting. After reaching Ferrara some months later, his mania broke out in more threatening symptoms, and, on the 21st February, 1579, he was consigned to the hospital of Sant' Anna.

From the sadder scenes and secrets of his life it were useless to raise the veil. Even the year after he entered it, Montaigne, a shrewd and unbiased witness, whose testimony may countervail much hearsay and conjecture, found him in "most pitiable state, surviving himself, neglectful of his person and works." Seven years had worn away in pitiable isolation, when a violent fever nearly closed his darkened existence, after which, whether from an abatement of his phrenetic symptoms, or in the hope of contributing to his physical restoration, Alfonso sanctioned his liberation, at the request of Prince Vincenzo of Mantua, the supposed assassin of our Admirable Crichton, who undertook the watchful care which his case required. Princess Leonora died in 1581, and, on various subsequent occasions, Duchess Lucrezia interfered with little success in his behalf, but, from the time of his leaving the hospital, his intercourse with her family was at an end. He had written from thence several letters to the Duke of Urbino, and, after his convalescence, addressed to him a rambling discourse on his real and imaginary grievances, which shows a mind still shaken, if not unhinged. But, though the kind feelings of his early playmate underwent no change, Tasso returned not to Urbino during many after wanderings, fearing perhaps to revisit, in circumstances so altered, the scenes of his brighter days.[1] The nine remaining years of his life were, on the whole, less afflicted; for, though ever restless in body, and often haunted by imaginary evils and visions, he enjoyed intervals of comparative serenity, especially in his beloved Bay of Naples, and at the house of his kind friend and biographer Manso, of which, half a century later, John Milton was the honoured guest.

His death partook of the melancholy shade that had overhung his career. Declining a new invitation from Duke Francesco Maria, in 1594, he brought to Rome all that mental and bodily sufferings had left him of broken health and blighted genius, to receive the honours of a laurel crown; and, in the monastery of S. Onofrio, he awaited the issue of arrangements which the warning voice of exhausted nature told him were made in vain. From thence he addressed to his friend Constantini*[2] the following touching farewell:—"What shall my Antonio say, when he hears the death of his Tasso? Nor, in my opinion, will the news be long delayed; for I feel my end to be at hand, having found no remedy for this troublesome malady, which, added to my many habitual ailments, is evidently sweeping me away like an impetuous and irresistible torrent. To say nothing of the world's ingratitude, which would prove its triumph by consigning me in penury to the tomb, the time is now past for speaking of my inveterate fortune; yet, when I think of the glory which this age will derive from my writings, in despite of all opposition, I cannot be left entirely unrequited. I have had myself brought to this convent of S. Onofrio, not only

[1] With that constitutional coldness we have seen in his life, the Duke spares but one line of his Diary to notice Torquato's death.

*[2] Cf. D'Ancona, *T. T. ed Ant. Costantini* in *Varietà Storiche e Letter.* (Milano, 1883), vol. I., p. 75 *et seq.*

because the air is commended by the faculty more than that of any other part of Rome, but also, to begin as it were from this elevated spot, and in the conversation of these holy fathers, my celestial intercourse. Pray to God in my behalf, and rest assured that, as I have ever loved and respected you in this life, I shall do the like towards you in a better, as is the part of true and unfeigned affection; and to the Divine grace I commend you and myself. From Rome, at S. Onofrio."

Tasso's mind was habitually under devotional influences, which grew upon him as he experienced the delusive results of his early ambition, the emptiness of success, and the bitterness of failure. Religion was in him a deeply rooted sentiment; it soothed long hours of suffering, cheered the decline of life, and brightened those hopes for which the laurel crown had lost its charm Gazing from the convent garden over a scene of all others the most inspiring to the poet, the most solemn to the moralist, he caught the seeds of malaria fever. His springs of life were already dried up by twenty long years of suffering, and, after a few days of peaceful and resigned preparation for a change that to him had no terrors, his spirit was released from its shattered tenement. He died on the 25th April, 1595, wept by many warmly attached and pitying friends, and lamented by the citizens, who lost in his death the spectacle of his coronation, to which they had long looked forward with an anxiety unusual even among the fête-loving populace of Rome.

Tasso's was a life of painful contrasts and of blighted hopes. The prospects of his childhood, bright as the sky which witnessed his birth, were quickly shadowed by a storm of tropical violence. The courtly favour that met his manhood proved baneful as a siren's smiles. The greenest garland that Italy could offer to her favourite minstrel was reserved until his brow was clammy with the dews of death. The honours lavished on his funeral have been grudged to his tomb. His resplendent genius was linked to the saddest and most humbling of human afflictions. The fame for which he felt more than a poet's thirst, and which he challenged as his due, was withheld by envy until no trumpet-note could reach his dull cold ear. But time, the avenger, has rendered him tardy justice, and Torquato is the popular bard of Italy, whilst the cumbrous pedantry of his della Crusca impugners is consigned to contemptuous oblivion.

Of works so universally known as those of Tasso it would be presumptuous to offer new analyses, and superfluous to encumber our pages with trite criticism. The edition of them by Rosini extends to thirty quarto volumes, a startling testimony to the copiousness of his commentators, as well as to his own wonderful fertility. His pen ranged over a wide field both in prose and verse,—the former including essays—moral, literary, and political,—dialogues, and letters; the latter touching upon themes sacred, heroic, romantic, sylvan, pastoral, and lyric. It is, however, as an epic poet that he has gained a niche in Parnassus, and the admiration of posterity. No rivalry could arise with Dante, in whose Vision the things of time are strangely interwoven with revelations of eternity; and his muse is of a nobler caste, though less touching character, than that of the bard of Arqua. But it is otherwise with the fourth great name of Italian minstrelsy, and no one discusses the merits of Tasso without keeping those of Ariosto in view. This, however, arises from habit rather than necessity. The latter name was dragged forward by the della Crusca Academicians as a stalking-horse to mask the malice of their attacks upon the later of Ferrara's two laureates, whose successive appearance on that stage alone induced a contrast for which their respective works were by no means adapted. The comparison thus forced upon the world has been declined by Tiraboschi, who, in the exercise of a sounder criticism, has assigned to each his peculiar excellence. Bearing in mind that the Orlando is intrinsically a romantic poem, whilst the Jerusalem is composed upon the epic model, there can be but little technical analogy between them, and the beauties of the one would become blemishes in the other. The striking and unlooked-for episodes of the former, running ever into extravagance and burlesque, must have outraged the grave unities required in the latter, and have proved more serious faults than any which the jaundiced optics of the academicians were able to discover. But perhaps Tasso's greatest triumph over his jealous detractors has been the continued preference of his earlier and greater work to his continuation of the same theme, in which he studied to profit by their criticisms. Many Italians, among whom the romantic school took its origin and maintained its influence, have preferred Ariosto, whilst transalpine critics have more generally given their suffrages to the poem of Tasso, as more regular in its plan, and better preserving the elevation and the unities observed by the best classic models.

It has been the boast of some minstrels to mould the temper of the age to the tone of their poetry. Tasso chose a less hazardous aim, and, seizing in his great epic upon a theme at once the most fertile and the most popular, gained the sympathies of all. The Crescent, once more in the ascendant, had swept the Mediterranean, overrun Greece, and threatened Vienna. The spirit of the crusades revived. The often-mooted movement of all Christendom in the holy cause was at length carried into effect, and victory crowned the Cross at the great naval conflict of Lepanto. But alas! his was the last great name in Italian poetry; *[1] and thenceforward genius fled

*[1] This, of course, is nonsense. Leopardi, at any rate, was yet to come, and in our own day we have heard the eager and noble voice of Carducci in verse that, it might seem, is not less great than Tasso's and far more in touch with life.

from the land of song, or bowed unresisting before an all-prevailing mediocrity. Morbid repetition, redundant verbiage, far-fetched figures,—all those faults for which its liquid language afforded such fatal facilities, sprang up in rank deformity, and smothered generous inspiration. The academies sent out their many songsters, who poured forth notes artfully sweet, but rarely thrilling; and already

> "Their once-loved minstrels scarce may claim
> The transient mention of a dubious name."

Nor did they merit a better fate; for their conceptions were extravagant, their imagery redundant, their execution alternately glaring and languid. Unnatural contrasts, startling conceits, ill compensated in them for vigorous diction and the stamp of genius. Yet the lyric muse was not utterly extinct, and from time to time its warblings may yet be heard in the orange groves and laurel bosquets of that bright land.

Guarini's is another name shared between Ferrara and Urbino.*[1] He was born at the former city in 1537, of a family already possessing claims upon literary distinction during three generations, his great-grandfather having been Guarini of Verona. In conformity with the custom of employing men of learning upon diplomatic missions, he served Duke Alfonso II. at various courts, until, in 1575, he undeservedly lost his favour by the failure of a quixotic negotiation, having for its object to place the crown of Poland upon his brows. During the seclusion which followed, he wrote the *Pastor Fido*, a pastoral drama of more complex incident than had been hitherto produced, and whose refined polish and seductive strains, though misapplied upon a factitious style, long retained their popularity. It was composed in avowed emulation

*[1] For Guarini, consult ROSSI, *B. Guarini ed il Pastor Fido* (Torino, 1886). See also CAMPORI, in *Giorn. St. d. Lett. Ital.*, vol. VIII., p. 425, etc.

of Tasso's *Aminta*, and he carried the rivalry into ducal saloons, and even ladies' boudoirs, with the results naturally to be looked for among the peppery tribe of poets. But when Torquato's hour of darkness arrived, Guarini proved himself a generous opponent, and, in the edition of 1581, he did his utmost to rescue the cantos of *Gerusalemme* from the adulteration of unfriendly pens. When his country's subjugation had followed upon his patron's death, he was fain to seek other service with the Medici; and soon thereafter the Duke of Urbino wrote to Abbé Brunetti, his envoy at Venice, in the following terms: We shall with much pleasure look over the pastoral which the Cavaliere Guarino has reprinted with notes and engravings, for we greatly esteem his meritorious works, and are aware how much we are indebted to his affection and courtesy. You will therefore thank him in our name for his remembrance of us."[1] This presentation copy procured the author a substantial reward in the following letter to Brunetti, dated some weeks later.

"Most magnificent and most reverend,

"In consequence of deaths and other circumstances, we find ourselves so ill provided with persons of such quality as was Albergato, that we must find some one as soon as may be. And recollecting the Cavaliere Guarino, who was known and entertained by us many years ago, we should be well pleased could we have him, provided his health be equal to his duties, not indeed for long journeys, but for attending upon our person, and accompanying us both in the carriage and on horseback, advising and conversing with us in all times and occasions. And we believe, if due means be adopted, this affair might be arranged to our mutual satisfaction, as we remember that,

[1] Oliveriana MSS. 375, vol. XV. 104. The poem was his *Pastor Fido*, of which the twentieth edition, with the author's note, appeared at Venice in 1602.

when lately quitting Tuscany, he seemed, from what he wrote to us, not averse to the idea of betaking himself hither, and in our answer we in no way discouraged the plan. We have, however, chosen to impart the matter to you, that you may manage it in whatever way you consider most proper for appearances; and should you think it well, we have no objection to your even going in person to Padua, on some other pretext. As to terms, we believe that the Cavaliere's modesty, and our partiality towards him, would readily bring everything to an issue; but you will give it all due consideration, answering separately this our letter, with whatever occurs to you on the subject. And so health to you. From Castel Durante, the 10th of June, 1602. Yours,

"FRAN^co^. M^a^. DUCA D'URB."

The following letter, from Guarini to his sister, proves that the arrangement was completed to the satisfaction of both parties; and an entry in the Duke's Diary shows that, notwithstanding a desire to return home, his departure from that court did not take place until July, 1604.

"My Sister,

"I should like to get home, for I have great need and wish to be there, but am so well treated here, and have so many honours paid me, and so many caresses, that I cannot. I must tell you that all my expenses and those of my servants are paid, so that I have not a farthing in the world to spend for anything I want, and orders given to let me have all I ask; besides which, they give me 300 scudi of yearly pension, which, with the expense of furnished house and maintenance, amounts to above 600 scudi a year. See, then, if I can leave this. Our Lord God give you every happiness. From Pesaro, the 23rd of February, 1603.

"Your most loving brother,
"BATTISTA GUARINI."

A letter from him condoling with the Duchess of Urbino on the death of her sister Leonora has been printed in Black's *Life of Tasso*, II., 451, but this brief notice may suffice to close the literary annals of our mountain principality.

CHAPTER LII

The decline of Italian art: its causes and results—Artists of Urbino—Girolamo della Genga, and his son Bartolomeo—Other architects and engineers.

THE zenith of Italian art, especially of Italian painting, was attained between 1490 and 1520. That brief span, scarcely a generation of human life, not only embraced the entire artistic life of Raffaele and witnessed the finest efforts of Leonardo, Luini, Bellini, Giorgione, Francia, Ghirlandaio, Fra Bartolomeo, Sodoma, Perugino, Pinturicchio, Spagna, and Salerno; it also ripened the earlier and better fruits of Buonarotti's genius, of del Sarto's too quickly degenerate palette, and of Titian's

"Pencil pregnant with celestial hues."

It saw the metropolitan St. Peter's commenced, the Stanze and Logge well advanced; it assembled in the Vatican halls the noblest band of painters ever united by one scholarship. That bright spot, the Pausilippo of our pictorial journey, has been passed. Our onward way lies through dreary days of progressive degeneracy, often fitfully illuminated by its reflected lights, but more rarely gladdened by gleams of original genius, or efforts of self-forgetting zeal.

In reviewing the history of painting, its stages of progress will be readily distinguished. The Byzantine period may be regarded as its starting point of stationary conventionalism.*[1] This was followed by an age of sentiment, when earnest thought gradually ameliorated penury of invention, and supplied intensity to expression. To it succeeded an epoch of effort, the hand failing to realise the aims of mind,*[2] the eye awaking to truths of nature, but bewildered by their hidden meanings. Next came the age of mastery;*[3] one of difficulties surmounted and doubts made clear. But the summit when attained was speedily quitted; the period of facility was too soon one of decline. In the words of Fuseli, painters then "uniformly agreed to lose the subject in the medium." Mechanism became the great object, copiousness a prized merit, until mediocrity sought refuge in a multitude of figures, or fell back upon theatrical artifice. The close of the fifteenth century was indeed a cycle of rapid progression, opening many new channels for the efforts of mind, and it was in Italy that this expansion was primarily felt. The ultra-

*[1] I do not understand what this means. The "Byzantine period" was not the starting point of anything, but rather a decadence; and how can anything be the starting point of something "stationary"? Christian art comes to us in the first centuries as absolutely dependent on Roman pagan work. It did not contrive a new force of expression, but very happily used the old. For the history of art is continuous, and in Byzantine work we see merely a decadence, not something new. The Renaissance in painting is based on Roman art of pagan times in the work of the Cosmati and the Cavallini, from whom in all probability Giotto learned all he could learn. It is the same with sculpture. Niccolò Pisano is a pupil of the ancients, a native of Apulia. The northern influence came later.

*[2] Yes? In Duccio's work, for instance. But the hand of man cannot achieve anything finer than the work of these early men—than the Annunciation of Simone Martini, for instance. That they preferred a decorative convention to a realistic does not accuse them of incompetence. Dennistoun would have said that the Japanese could not draw. It was not that "the hand failed to realise the aims of the mind," but that the mind saw things from a standpoint different from ours. It is easy to talk of the "truths of nature." What are the truths of nature? It is a question of appearance, of a manner of seeing, of an attitude of mind, of soul, toward nature and toward itself. Simone Martini was as great an artist, in the true sense of the word, as Raphael, in his own convention. Raphael's convention is still ours, but we are already passing out of it. Is it not so?

*[3] Yes; an age of realism. It is as though one preferred a Roman work of the best period to a Greek work of the fifth century B.C. What came was the tyranny of the body, without the old excuse, for we no longer believed in the body; we no longer believed in anything but unreality. It is not that the earlier men were "right" and the later "wrong," but that both

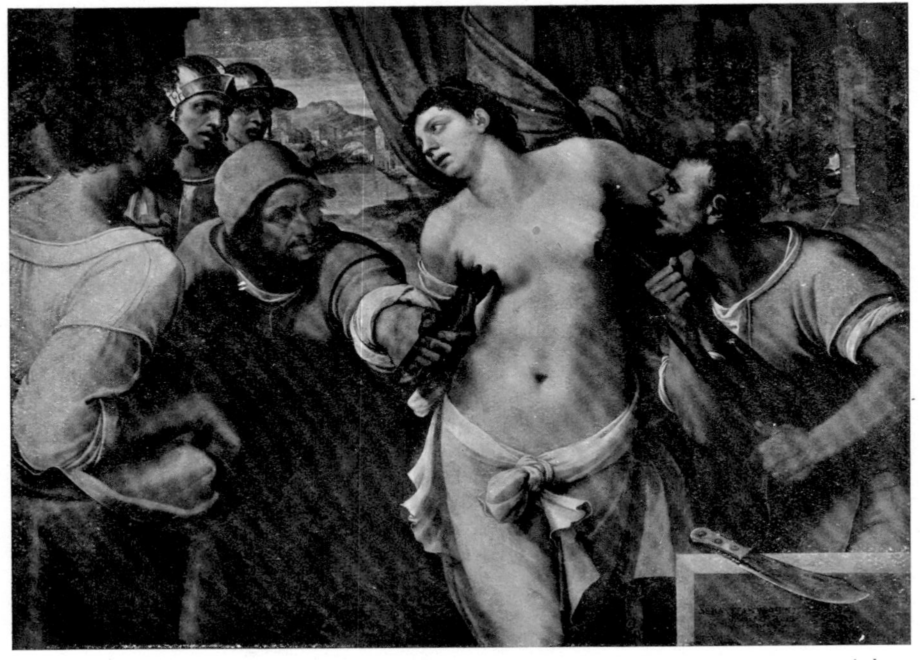

Anderson

MARTYRDOM OF S. AGATA

After a picture by Seb. dal. Piombo, once in the Ducal Collection at Urbino, now in the Pitti Gallery, Florence

montane invention of printing was then eagerly adopted; the cultivation of revived philosophy, and the convulsions consequent upon foreign inroads, introduced elements of change into the Peninsular mind as well as its politics. In nothing was this movement more felt than in the fine arts. During early times, the ideas of artists exceeded their means of expression.*[1] Yet their works, even when trammelled by fetters, partly of limited skill, but more of traditionary mannerism, are often fit exponents of simple thoughts, while the coincidence between the conception and style renders solecisms of execution less startling. The forms may be timid or stiff, but they are always careful and earnest. But now a further range has been given to individual fancy. The choice and conception of the theme, its character and composition, were alike freed from conventional trammels, and became subjective (in the German sense) rather than objective. Religion and its ritual remained the same, the hero-worship of saints continued among its prominent features, art still furnished aids to devotion. But, as books became abundant and readers multiplied, pictures were no longer the written language of holy things for the multitude. The high mission of Christian art had been fulfilled; its limners, less impressed with their themes, thought more of themselves; they appealed rather to the judgment than to the feelings. They aimed at imitating nature to the life more than at embodying transcendental abstractions.*[2] We

are equally right and wrong where right and wrong do not count since only beauty may decide. Dennistoun speaks as he does because he could not possibly have spoken otherwise. He is wrong not so much in what he asserts as in what he denies.

*[1] Here, again, I do not understand. How can an artist's ideas exceed his means of expression?—I do not say his power of expression. What means of expression did Dante lack that Milton enjoyed, or Sophocles? In what was Donatello poorer than Michelangelo or Niccolò Pisano than either? Giotto had the same means of expression as Apelles or Leonardo, for the work he undertook, and before a new means of expression was invented, he could not have conceived the use of it.

*[2] Their aim was perhaps rather the realistic imitation of life than the expression of it.

have already seen how the devotional inspirations of early painting, which Beato Angelico's pencil had mellowed into loveliness, attained, under the guidance of Raffaele, to consummate beauty of form. But the impulse that had forced pictorial art to its culminating point allowed it no rest, and the descending path was too quickly entered. The speculative minds of its creators and its admirers craved for novelty, for fresh themes and further powers. Elevation of sentiment or purity of design no longer sufficed,*[1] and with the competition which ensued for the guidance of public taste, there sprang up many solecisms to degrade it. Much that was in itself valuable was exaggerated into deformity. The knowledge of anatomy which enabled Michael Angelo to embody the terrible, that element of invention which he was the first fully to develop, also tempted him to combinations outraging nature and harmony;*[2] and his style has transmitted to our own day an influence dangerous to genius,*[3] fatal to mediocrity. Less permanent, because less healthful,*[4] was the opposite quality, introduced by Correggio, whose grace, founded upon artifice, degenerated under Parmegianino and Baroccio into meretricious affectation. A third ingredient, not so perilous and more pleasing, was brought to perfection in Venice, where alone can be appreciated the golden tints of Titian*[5] and the silvery harmony of Veronese. It is indeed remarkable that all the schools most celebrated for colouring have arisen in maritime localities, and been deficient in accurate design.

In a preceding portion of this work we have alluded to the innovations of naturalism in painting, by men who in-

*[1] They never sufficed.

*[2] Too strong. Michelangelo was always master of the weapons he used, however destructive they may have been to his disciples.

*[3] Nothing is dangerous to genius, not even mediocrity.

*[4] This term applies to the science of medicine, not to æsthetic.

*[5] Titian can be seen to advantage only in Madrid, Paris, Vienna, or London. In Venice he is almost absent.

troduced perspective, created chiaroscuro, cultivated design, and mastered nude action. Through their example, it not only extended a predominating influence over pictorial treatment, but quickly obtained that place as a canon of artistic criticism which it has since continued commonly to hold. It may seem rash to impugn a principle so universally adopted; and if perfection in art really depends upon an accurate imitation of nature, it would be folly to gainsay it. But the principle may be carried too far; and if we are to allow to art a nobler mission,—if we recognise in painting and sculpture a language wherein gifted men can embody, develop, and elaborately adorn the conceptions of beauty and sublimity, or it may be the sallies of humour and the scintillations of wit that flit across the fancy—a key whereby they can impart to their fellows, and transmit to all ages and nations, their emanations of genius, their poetic flashes, their benevolent sympathies, their devotional aspirations,—then surely a higher standard should be applied to what are often ranked as merely imitative arts, and are tested by their supposed fidelity as transcripts of external objects.*[1]

Such views will to many seem visionary and strange heresies. Yet they are truths by which painting reached its golden era, and which, even in its decline, have been largely drawn upon. Under Louis XIV., a vile epoch of a faulty school,*[2] allegory triumphed over reality, and the best feelings of humanity were forced into masquerade. But what shall we think of the taste which admits such solecisms against nature, whilst objecting to the conventionalities practised by the early Christian masters, and adopted by the purists of our own day? What, indeed, is art but a tissue of conventionalities, even when the imitation of external objects is its aim? Upon what laws of

*[1] After all, Dennistoun is on the side of the angels—though a little unctuously.

*[2] One of the sad days. Cf. vol. II., p. 95, note *1.

nature are regulated the gradations of aerial perspective, or the receding or flattened surfaces of basso-relievo? Does not the landscape painter, in modifying the tones of his colouring, remember that his mimic scenes are to be enclosed in gilt frames, an appendage for which Providence has made no provision in the real ones? But to such imitations art neither is nor ought to be confined. As the language of genius, it expresses loftier themes, and none but kindred spirits can fitly judge of its style, or set bounds to its range. The rustic who spells through Burns or Bloomfield would pause upon Paradise Lost, and throw down Hamlet in despair; whilst, to the presbyterian who ornaments his walls with Knox's portrait, or the Battle of Bothwell-brig, the Last Judgment would seem unintelligible, the Transfiguration blasphemous, the Judgment of Paris a flagrant indecency. In like manner, those who have neither imbibed the spirit of the Roman ritual, nor studied the forms of Christian art, may fully appreciate the dishevelled goddesses of Rubens, or the golden sunsets of Claude,—the glowing tints of Titian, or the transparent finish of Teniers; but let them understand ere they sneer at those sacred paintings which for successive ages have confirmed the faith of the unlettered, elevated their hopes, and inspired their prayerful ejaculations.

When the Christian mythology, which had supplied art with subjects derived from inspired writ or venerated tradition, was supplanted by an idolatry of nature content to feed spiritual longings with common forms copied without due selection from daily life, men no longer painted what religion taught them to believe, but what their senses offered for imitation, modified by their own unrestrained fancies. Painting thus became an accessory of luxurious life, and its productions were regarded somewhat as furniture, indicating the taste rather than the devotion of patrons and artists. These accordingly followed a wider latitude of topics and treatment. In proportion as devo-

Alinari

HOLY FAMILY

After the picture by Sustermans, once in the Ducal Collection of Urbino, now in the Pitti Gallery, Florence

tional subjects fell out of use, a demand arose for mythological fable and allegory. Profane history, individual adventure or portraiture, supplied matter pleasing to vanity, profitable to adulation. But while the objects of painting became less elevated, its mechanism gained importance; it became ostentatious in sentiment, ambitious in execution. The aim of professors, the standard of connoisseurs, declined from the ideal to the palpable. A fresh field for exertion was thus opened up. Schools attained celebrity from their successful treatment of technical difficulties. Michael Angelo attracted pupils by his power in design; Titian by his mastery in colour; Correggio by his management of light; while the eclectic masters of Bologna vainly aspired to perfection by nicely adjusting their borrowed plumes; and the *tenebristi* of Naples sought, by impenetrable shadows, to startle rather than to please. A demand for domestic decoration led to further exercise of ingenuity. Landscapes, first improved by the Venetian masters as accessories, became a new province of art; and transcripts from nature in her scenes of beauty were succeeded by the clang of battles, the inanities of still life, the orgies or crimes of worthless men.*[1] In architecture and in sculpture, the departure was scarcely less remarkable from the pure style and simple forms of the fifteenth century: a free introduction of costly materials and elaborate decoration deteriorated taste, without compensating for the absence of ideal beauty. The masters of this, which we may distinguish as the "newest" manner, must accordingly be tried by a new standard. Those of the silver and golden ages, Angelico and Raffaele, sought a simple or vigorous development of deep feeling; the Giordani and Caravaggii, men of brass

*[1] An undue sense of right seems to have led Dennistoun to the brink of an absurd precipice. Why should not the orgy or crime of a worthless man, make as good a picture as the orgy or crime [or the good deeds either, for that matter] of the worthy man? Poetry surely would seem to confound him here.

and iron, whose technical capacity outstripped their ideas' aspired not beyond effect. Effect is, therefore, the self-chosen test to which artists of the decline should be subjected, though it may detect in them false taste and vulgar deformity. Under their guidance, energy was substituted for grandeur, bustle for dramatic action; while flickering lights and fluttering draperies ill replaced the solidity and stateliness of earlier men. Art thus, like literature, became copious rather than captivating. Ambitious attempts were not wanting, but the effort to produce them was ever palpable. Ingenuity over-taxed gave birth to bewildering allegories, affected postures, startling contrasts, exaggerated colouring, meretricious graces. Nature was invoked to stand godmother to the progeny, but she disavowed them as spurious.

The rapid decline of art when imitation of nature became more strictly its object, has led to scepticism in some quarters as to the expediency of adopting such a guide. Until human ingenuity shall attain the means of embodying and preserving perfect copies of external objects, it would be presumptuous to decide how far such copies realise that standard of beauty which high art demands. The daguerreotype and kalotype, which give the nearest known approach to such a result, are far from solving the question in accordance with naturalist views; for, on their metallic plates and porous paper, a beautiful woman is, in general, coarsely caricatured; whilst a bust of her, or a bas-relief, always retains the grace of the sculptured original, and a chalk drawing is exquisitely reproduced. Were it enough to depict with perfect precision the forms and incidents reflected on the retina, a painter would be little more than a mechanic, in whom original genius might be almost dispensed with. But, though he will treasure in his portfolios a judicious selection of such impressions as he can daily gather from actual life, these, however nearly they may approach to nature and truth, are only materials of future creations. For high art,—and of such alone would we speak whilst Italy is our theme,—something more than mere nature was undoubtedly required; *[1] yet her guidance became indispensable after the revolution in taste and feeling which dismissed mediæval traditions and types. So various, however, are the freaks of individual fancy, so fantastic the vagaries of reason uncontrolled by authority, that the new path was beset by new pitfalls. The mediocrity of early masters found a refuge in mean but inoffensive common-place; that of their successors, mistaking freedom and novelty for original genius, revelled in extravagant creations. The acute agonies, physical and moral, which sadly consummated the Atonement for man, were figured by the former in limbs wasted as by prolonged disease, stiffened as by a lingering death: the deep affliction of the Madonna Addolorata over the Saviour's body assumed in their hands an expression of such grief as knew not the relief of tears. But the artists of the "new manner" gave to crucifixions anatomical accuracy developed in spasmodic writhings, and bespoke sympathy for the mother of Christ by convulsive weepings, with perchance the accessory of a pocket-handkerchief! In pictures of this class, corporeal sufferings were rendered with horrible truth, muscular energy was substituted for mental woe. Living in times which needed fresh subjects as well as added powers, these painters laid aside such themes as treated of the mysteries of faith, the legends of primitive times, but especially such as, demanding spiritualised feelings in the author and the spectators, were uncongenial to both. To a contemplative religion, untroubled by sectarian movements, had succeeded a church militant, armed by bigotry, and struggling for existence. The revived catholicism of Caraffa and Ghislieri required art of a character as gloomy as itself, and commissioned

*[1] Art does not desire more than nature, but more than an imitation of nature. The artist should create life, not imitate it.

works wherein the terrors of the Inquisition replaced the promises of the Gospel, earthly martyrdoms supplanted celestial hopes, and pure faith was clouded by priestcraft. Henceforward, religious representations were reserved chiefly for church decorations, and even there they assumed an historical character, as in the miracles of our Lord, or the acts of his apostles. Alexander VI. had decorated the pontifical palace with incidents from the Gospel; but those which Paul III. and his successors selected for the Sala Regia commemorate the triumphs of an aggressive church in the Massacre of St. Bartholomew, and the naval action of Lepanto. Michael Angelo, in depicting the Last Judgment, the chief glory of that pontificate, introduced Charon as a prominent personage; and, with inconsistency, if possible, more glaring, Poussin has painted Moses, the type of Christ, watched in infancy by a river-god, in classical allusion to his preservation from the perils of the Nile.

Whilst we have thus had to consider the prevalent imitation of external objects as an element tending to the corruption of purist feeling, it unquestionably enlarged the scope and stimulated the mechanism of painting. Such was the naturalism by which Raffaele, Michael Angelo, and Titian developed the comparatively feeble and stunted efforts of their predecessors into forms ennobling nature, and redolent of intelligence. But, in studying these palpable qualities, the more subtle ingredients of spirit and feeling were often overlooked; indeed, most of the creators of the new style outlived it, and saw it supplanted by a yet newer and far more degrading naturalism, which, with few bright intervals, has continued to cramp and pervert the manner of their successors. Such were and are those painters who, on the strength of their sketches from the life, and their studies of landscape and architecture, or with the plea of occasionally introducing portraits into sacred or historical compositions, proclaim

Anderson

THE KNIGHT OF MALTA

From the picture by Giorgione, once in the Ducal Collection at Urbino, now in the Uffizi Gallery, Florence

themselves followers of nature, whilst their works outrage or caricature her. There may be great anatomical accuracy, and much truth in the separate heads, combined with inventions the most unreal, movements the most constrained, mannered attitudes, draperies meagre or overloaded, and a general substitution of mean conceptions for pleasing realities. The elaborate finish invariably found in the early masters was either bestowed upon accessories in themselves trifling, but stamping an extraordinary verity upon their works, or, as in the Sienese or Venetian schools, it was lavished upon gorgeous costumes illustrative of national manners. But similar details in later pictures are justly considered to remove them in some degree from the category of artistic performances to that of mere decoration, and are despised by those who, aiming at breadth of effect, sometimes adopt the most hopeless of all affectations, that of slovenly superficiality. Whence then this difference? and why should jewels and embroidery, that seem beautiful in Crivelli's saints or Dello's pageants, be vulgar gewgaws on recent canvasses? Merely because, in the former, *all* is minutely worked, but all is subsidiary to the general sentiment, whilst, in the latter, the absence of a simply pervading expression leaves each individual detail crudely prominent; because the ancient masters made everything subservient to that one overruling feeling of the picture, which, in most modern works, is totally wanting.

The Dukes della Rovere of Urbino had hereditary duties as patrons of art. Popes Sixtus IV. and Julius II., the founders of their family, had munificently encouraged it; the antecedent princes of Montefeltro had been its generous and discriminating friends. If the later dynasty fell short of these examples, they were not without excuse. Though the divine Raffaele parted his mantle among many pupils, no shred of it fell to his native duchy.

Francesco Maria I., on succeeding to that state, found in it no lack of churches, palaces, or pictures, and little native genius meriting support; so he was content to call Titian from Venice to portray himself and his Duchess.*[1] His two successors were less devoted to arms, and more liberal to arts. They numbered among their subjects Baroccio and the Zuccari, who once more gave a pictorial name to Urbino, and they judiciously divided their commissions between these natives and foreign painters.

In a former portion of this work it was our endeavour to interweave the artistic notices which we had to offer in connection with Urbino, into a rapid sketch of Christian painting in Umbria. Resuming the subject, it will no longer be possible thus to generalise our views, for the time had arrived when each aspirant selected his own course to the temple of Fame; and in glancing at the various paths which chance or fancy suggested to them, our readers must be prepared for occasional repetitions. The ground, in itself less interesting, is more beaten; and though none of the competitors approximated the elevation gained by Raffaele, their numbers may be considered as some compensation for their comparative mediocrity. Lazzari, in his *Dictionary of Artists* belonging to his native duchy, has enumerated, under the Feltrian dukes, five painters, one sculptor, one architect, and one military engineer; while under the Princes della Rovere, these numbers are increased to twenty painters, eight architects, and sixteen military engineers. Of sculptors, during the latter period, there is no account; but along with eighteen followers of mechanical arts connected with the higher

*[1] Francesco Maria may have called, but Titian did not come to Urbino. The first commission he had from the Duke was in 1532, when he was asked to paint as good a portrait of Hannibal as he could and a picture of the Nativity. They were delivered in 1534. The Duke wanted then a portrait of the Duchess, and asked Titian to paint it on his way to Naples. This journey, however, never took place. If Titian had any sittings, it was at Murano during the Duke and Duchess's sojourn there in the autumn of 1537.

Alinari

JUDITH WITH THE HEAD OF HOLOFERNES

After the picture by Palma il Vecchio, once in the Ducal Collection at Urbino

branches, we find workers in bronze, stucco, wood-carving, engravers, and makers of watches and mathematical instruments, besides two potters and three painters of majolica. It would be not less irksome than useless to follow all this catalogue, but we shall endeavour to throw together whatever is generally interesting of art in Urbino, during the sixteenth century, whether by native painters, or foreigners employed by the dukes; concluding with a chapter on minor arts, especially that of *majolica*, or earthenware, for which the duchy was long celebrated.

Our catalogue of artists under the della Rovere dynasty may be fittingly commenced with a name not unknown to their predecessors, the Feltrian dukes. GIROLAMO DELLA GENGA was born at Urbino, in 1476, of respectable parents, who destined him for the woollen trade, by which the wealth of Florence had, in a great measure, been gained. But the bent of his youthful mind was decidedly towards design, and his pencil so interfered with his proper business, that, after much vain opposition, his friends yielded, and sent him, at fifteen, to the studio of Luca Signorelli. It was the mission of this able painter to engraft upon the devotional traditions of Umbrian art, imbibed from Pietro della Francesca, a novel energy of thought and pencil; and Girolamo had the advantage of aiding him upon those wonderful compositions in the duomo of Orvieto, which Michael Angelo scrupled not to imitate in his Last Judgment, as well as warmly to commend. After attending his master during the execution of other commissions, he passed into the school of Perugino, where he found his precocious countryman, the young Raffaele. There he remained for three years, devoting himself chiefly to perspective, and thence repaired to Florence to complete his education. At Siena he was largely employed, along with Signorelli, by Pandolfo Petrucci; returning from whence to Urbino, he formed an enduring intimacy with Timoteo della Vite. They wrought together upon a chapel in the cathedral, which no longer exists; but the works there assigned to Genga were chiefly scenic and decorative, from his acknowledged superiority in architectural perspective; and for these, the various festive amusements then in fashion, such as pastoral dramas, triumphal processions, cavalry trappings, and temporary arches, occasioned in that gay capital a perpetual demand, during the latter days of Guidobaldo I., and the first years of his successor. His invention was especially called into play to welcome Duchess Leonora to her states, and to supply scenery for the representation of Bibbiena's *La Calandra* in 1513. These apparently mechanical performances were not, however, irreconcileable with excellence and fame in the higher branches of art; and it was whilst thus engaged that, during a short visit to Rome, he painted, for the oratory of Sta. Caterina of Siena in the Via Giulia, an altar-piece of the Resurrection, justly considered his chef-d'œuvre.*[1] The figure of Christ, soaring upwards amid sprawling angels, somewhat anticipates Raffaele's Transfiguration, but with a copious infusion of Michael Angelesque feeling. The latter influence predominates in the violent attitudes and excited action of the guards, four of whom, suddenly aroused by the supernatural event, are rushing about without aim or self-possession; yet, the movement of one who awakens a still slumbering comrade is extremely natural. The Marys, approaching from the other side of the picture, recall Timoteo's manner. The colour, concealed however under an accumulation of dirt, is of a solid quality, and the chiaroscuri are skilfully managed, while the inscription, *Girolamo Genga Urbinas facieb.*, satisfactorily secures its authenticity.

In 1497, Guidobaldo had granted to the Counts della Genga an exemption from taxes, for which Girolamo

*[1] I know nothing of this oratory, and cannot find it.

Alinari

HEAD OF CHRIST

After the picture by Titian, once in the Ducal Collection, now in the Pitti Gallery, Florence

showed his gratitude by sharing the exile of Francesco Maria, when deprived by the tyrannical usurpation of Leo X. He retired with his family to Cesena, where, as at Forlì and other places in Romagna, he executed various church pictures of merit; of these, the Baptism of Christ, the Conversion of St. Augustine, and one representing the Almighty, with the Madonna, and the Doctors of the Church, have found their way to the Brera, at Milan. On the Duke's restoration, he was appointed his architect and engineer, and thereafter discontinued painting, devoting himself almost entirely to his new duties. Among the churches which he built, were those of the Zoccolantines at Urbino and Sinigaglia, but it was chiefly on the ducal palaces that he was employed. Of these, the first committed to him was the Imperiale villa, already mentioned.[1] Vasari describes it as a "very beautiful and well-contrived fabric, full of chambers, colonnades, courts, balconies, fountains, and delightful gardens, which every prince passing that way goes to see; and which Paul III. visited, with his court, when on his way to Bologna, and was quite pleased with all he saw." It would seem from his account that the most important ameliorations made by Genga upon that long-neglected residence, were the tower and internal decorations. The former remains, of handsome proportions; but its chief merit is said, by the Tuscan biographer, to have consisted in the management of a concealed wooden stair, reaching the summit in thirteen flights of steps, one hundred and twenty feet in all. In 1543, Bembo wrote to Leonora,—"I have visited your Excellency's Imperiale with much pleasure, both because I greatly wished to see it, and because it seems to me constructed with more intelligence and true artistic science, as well as with more antique fashions and finely contrived conceits, than any modern building I have seen. I heartily

[1] See p. 49.

congratulate your Ladyship upon it, for certainly my gossip Genga is a great and gifted architect, far surpassing all my anticipations." The frescoes, illustrating his employer's life, were distributed by him to several foreign artificers, the duchy not boasting any painter of talent since the recent death of his friend Timoteo Vite. Among these was his pupil Francesco Minzocchi of Forlì, who, living on the limits of the old manner and the new, succeeded in uniting many excellences of both; yet, his works at Padua, Venice, Forlì, and Loreto, though highly creditable, scarcely merit the exaggerated praise bestowed on some of them by Vasari. That biographer's oversight, and his own modesty, have, on the other hand, done scimp justice to Raffaele del Colle, whose attractive pencil is scarcely appreciated, notwithstanding Lanzi's eulogy. A pupil of the incomparable Sanzio, and of Giulio Romano, he preserved a healthy style amid prevailing deterioration; and many of his pictures still adorn the churches of Central Italy.[1] Contemporary with these was Angelo Bronzino, who maintained at Florence, during an age of general feebleness, the reputation transmitted by Andrea del Sarto and Pontormo. The grace of a Cupid, which he painted upon a corbel at the Imperiale, gained for him the patronage of Prince Guidobaldo, who employed him in small productions more congenial to his genius, including his portrait, and a harpsichord cover, both of them greatly admired, but now lost. The landscape ornaments in the villa were entrusted to the brothers Dossi, of Ferrara, or rather perhaps to Giovanbattista, the younger, and less able of them; but so total was their failure, that they were

[1] He left some valuable works in the upper valley of the Metauro, now almost destroyed. Such are his Prophets and Sybils in ten lunettes round the Corpus Domini at Urbania, with two Nativities in the same church, one in fresco, the other on canvas. An altar-piece, in the church of the Servites at S. Angelo in Vado, is very inferior to his Madonna and Saints in S. Francesco of Cagli. Some frescoes at Gubbio, lauded by Lanzi, and dated 1546, are among his best works.

immediately thrown down, and replaced by others from Genga's designs. More successful in that light style were the portions committed to Camillo of Mantua, whose rural decorations are praised by Vasari and Lanzi.

We have thus far chiefly followed Vasari's authority, reconciling, as best we might, inconsistencies and errors, the result of his imperfect acquaintance with the locality. The paintings he describes at the Imperiale were probably part of Duchess Leonora's labour of love, to welcome her lord's return from his long campaigns. But the condition to which they are reduced, by time and unworthy degradation of the building, renders it impossible now to form an opinion of the various hands that have wrought upon them, or to discover their respective merits and subjects. The roofs of two saloons are occupied by small historical compositions, from the actions of Francesco Maria ; but these are irrecoverably defaced. Two of them, ascribed to Bronzino, are said to have represented the Duke haranguing the band of adventurers whom he collected in Lombardy, for the invasion of his duchy in 1517; and his reception by the Venetian senate in 1523, as their captain-general. The ornaments of the remaining rooms are merely decorative.

Additions were made by Francesco Maria to his other residences at Urbino, Pesaro, and Castel Durante; on all of which, and Gradara, Genga seems to have been employed. Him also he entrusted to build a casino, within the walls of Pesaro, called the Barchetto, in which a ruin was imitated, with a spiral stair commended by Vasari: this house was subsequently assigned by Duke Guidobaldo to Bernardo Tasso, as a home to himself and his son Torquato; and part of it is now occupied by a gardener. Another work of Girolamo was the reparation of the fortress at Pesaro, which, however, he undertook merely in obedience to his sovereign, military architecture being little to his taste. In acknowledgment of these services, he had, in 1528, a grant of Castel d' Elce, with its feudal immunities, afterwards confirmed by Guidobaldo II. Some years later, he remodelled the episcopal palace at Mantua, and began an imposing church to St. John the Baptist at Pesaro, which was completed by his son. Among his minor efforts in the immediate service of the ducal family may be mentioned funeral decorations for Francesco Maria, and a monument to him, erected by Bartolomeo Ammanati of Florence, in Sta. Chiara of Urbino, but long ago removed. Enriched and honoured, he spent his declining years in leisure, and died in 1551. Vasari thus testifies to his exemplary character:—"Girolamo was an excellent and honest man, of whom no evil was ever heard. He was not only a painter, sculptor, and architect, but also a good musician, an excellent and most amusing talker, and was full of courtesy and affection to his relations and friends." Among his numerous pupils, Baldassare Lancia, of Urbino, was distinguished as a military engineer, whilst Bartolomeo his second son, Bellucci of San Marino his son-in-law, and Federigo Baroccio his nephew, all ably maintained his artistic reputation. In the person of Leo XII., one of his family has recently attained the highest station offered to the ambition of the Roman Catholic world.

BARTOLOMEO DELLA GENGA was born at Cesena in 1518, during his father Girolamo's emigration, and was sent to Florence at eighteen to study design in its various branches, under Vasari and Ammanati. At twenty-one he returned to his father, who, seeing his talent lie towards architecture, advised him to acquaint himself at Rome with the best models. His first commission on returning home was to prepare festive arches for Duchess Vittoria's reception after her marriage. He then accompanied Guidobaldo to Lombardy, as his military engineer, and, by examining the celebrated fortresses in that country,

Alinari

THE RESURRECTION

After the banner painted by Titian for the Compagnia di Corpus Domini, now in the Pinacoteca, Urbino

added greatly to his professional experience. He at this time refused very eligible appointments from the King of Bohemia, and subsequently from Genoa, wishing to dedicate his services to his own sovereign. Accordingly, on his father's death, he became ducal architect, and built large additions to the palaces of Urbino and Pesaro, especially the wing of the former, facing S. Domenico. He also erected a number of churches in the duchy, and prepared plans for a harbour at Pesaro, which were not carried into effect. Having attended the Duke to Rome in 1553, he gave some hints to Julius III. for the new fortifications of Borgo S. Spirito.

His reputation being thus established, the Order of Malta selected him to superintend the new defences proposed for their island, and in 1557 sent two knights on a mission to obtain the Duke of Urbino's sanction of Genga's engagement. During two months Guidobaldo resisted all importunities, and they at length succeeded only through a Capuchin friar, who, possessing his ear, represented the work as one in which all Christendom was interested. On Bartolomeo's arrival, he had but time to prepare a series of plans for civil and military architecture, when he was cut off by fever consequent upon exposure in the burning heat, having scarcely completed his fortieth year. Of this family also was SIMONE GENGA, who, after fortifying many Tuscan strongholds, carried his engineering talents to Gratz, in Austria. From Stephen, King of Poland, he had, in 1587, a monthly salary of 76 dollars, besides allowances for four servants and as many horses, whilst completing the defences of Varadino. Other architects of Urbino are mentioned by the Marchese Ricci as leaving structures in La Marca, such as LATTANZIO VENTURI, who, in 1581, built the communal palace at Macerata, with an allowance of 30 scudi for his plan, and 40 more for overseeing its execution. Six years later, he completed the façade of Loreto church, in the charge of which he was succeeded by his son Venturo. His countryman, LUDOVICO CARDUCCI, having accompanied him to Macerata, was employed on various ecclesiastical edifices there, his designs for which were submitted for approval to the Duke of Urbino. From Venturo Venturi the superintendence of Loreto devolved, about 1614, upon GIOVANNI BRANCA, of S. Angelo in Vado, who died there in 1645, aged seventy-four. His *Manual of Architecture* had passed through six editions previous to the present century.

CHAPTER LIII

Taddeo Zuccaro—Federigo Zuccaro—Their pupils—Federigo Baroccio and his pupils—Claudio Ridolfi—Painters of Gubbio.

IT was just after the fatal sack of Rome had dispersed the goodly company of painters, who, reared by Raffaele, and linked together by the recollection of his genius and his winning qualities, gave promise of long maintaining in the Christian capital that manner which he had brought to perfection,—that there was born to Ottaviano Zuccaro, or Zucchero, an indifferent artist of S. Angelo in Vado, a son destined to revive the pictorial reputation of Urbino. TADDEO ZUCCARO saw the light in 1529, and, while yet a boy, perceiving little hope of excellence under such instruction as Umbria could then afford, or of remedying the poverty of his paternal fireside, he boldly sought a wider field of improvement and enterprise, and at fourteen found his way to Rome. The hardships which he there underwent are touchingly described by Vasari. Aided by no friendly hand, his education was neglected, and he was driven to menial labour for the support of a precarious existence. Wandering from one studio to another, he earned a crust of bread by colour-grinding; and, unable to afford light for his evening studies, he spent the moonlight nights in drawing, till sleep surprised him beneath some portico. Under this hard life his health gave way, whilst his spirit remained indomitable, and he sought rest and renewed vigour in his native mountain air. But his thirst for improvement was not stayed by these sufferings. On his return to Rome with recruited energies, he was received into the studio of Jacopone Bertucci of Faenza, a follower of Raffaele, whose few independent works entitle him to more honourable mention than has been afforded him by Vasari or Lanzi, and who united the tasteful design of that master with somewhat of Lombard feeling. Taddeo subsequently aided one Daniello di Por, who carried to Rome much of the Parmese manner, imitating Correggio and Parmegianino. At eighteen he executed on his own account, on the exterior of the Mattei Palace, a series of nine events in the life of Camillus, which attracted general admiration, and established his popularity as a historical painter. These, and several other works in fresco done soon after, have been destroyed.

His rising reputation having reached Urbino, Guidobaldo II. summoned him there, when about fifteen, to undertake the exterior decorations of a chapel in the cathedral, which had been painted by Battista Franco, and soon after carried him on his tour of inspection of the Venetian terra-firma fortresses. On his return, he was established in the palace at Pesaro, where he painted the Duke's portrait and some other cabinet pictures. Two years thus passed away without his being able to commence the chapel, although the designs for it were well advanced; and being dissatisfied with this loss of time, he availed himself of his sovereign's absence at Rome to follow him thither. Orders now crowded upon him, for no contemporary painter was better qualified to supply those slight and rapidly executed works then in fashion for the external and internal decoration of Roman palaces and villas. Most of these have perished; but somewhat superior in character were the incidents in the Passion, painted in 1556, in the Church of Consolation under the Capitol. They are still in good preservation, but though cleverly conceived and carefully executed, these merits scarcely compensate for the exaggerated mannerism of

Alinari

THE LAST SUPPER

After the picture by Baroccio in the Duomo of Urbino

their sprawling attitudes and solid draperies, whilst their violent emotions are anything but devotional. From this time his brother Federigo was associated in most of his labours, and the speed with which their commissions were finished brought them easy gains, and gave satisfaction in an age when taste had sadly degenerated. An arrangement, whereby Taddeo agreed to accompany the Duke of Guise to France, with a salary of 600 scudi, was interrupted by the Duke's death; but soon after our artist had a more important commission, from Cardinal Alessandro Farnese, to paint in his palace of Caprarola, near Viterbo, the heroic actions of his family. This was precisely the class of subject for which the manner and ideas of the Zuccari were most adapted, and the results were highly satisfactory. Accordingly, these paintings, engraved by Prenner in 1748, remain a standard of that style of palatial decoration. Taddeo's allowance was 200 scudi a year, for which he undertook to prepare all the cartoons, and to superintend their execution by his brother and other young artists. Among those whom he was thus enabled to bring forward, several, including Baroccio, were his seniors, a natural consequence of the good fortune which brought him early into repute as a clever head-master of the contract work then in vogue. His mural paintings in the Sala Regia of the Vatican, and his sacred subjects in the chapel of S. Marcello there, were also undertakings of considerable extent, sharing his attention with Caprarola during the latter years of his life. His last work was the Assumption of the Madonna in the Trinita del Monte, upon which death surprised him in 1566, and his dust reposes in the Pantheon, near that of his more illustrious countryman Raffaele, like whom, he died on the day his thirty-seventh year was completed.

His brother FEDERIGO, fourteen years his junior, was brought to Rome in 1550, and committed to his charge. The advantage of an associate on whom he could rely was immense to one whose works were, even from youth, in a great measure, executed by others; and fraternal affection, cemented by a similarity of tastes and pursuits, grew up into an identity of character and habits which extended to their respective works, and enabled the younger Zuccaro satisfactorily to terminate the commissions which Taddeo left unfinished. Precocity was a characteristic of both; and the only interruption to their harmony arose from the latter having retouched some frescoes done by Federigo, when but eighteen years old, outside of a house in Rome. The quarrel having become serious, a compromise was effected by mutual friends, on an understanding that the designs, but not the finished works of the youth, should be submitted to his brother's correction. During his residence in Rome, Federigo was, however, chiefly employed on those mural paintings which we have already mentioned as undertaken by Taddeo; and when about twenty-two, he spent a considerable time in Venice, painting, on his own account, in the Grimani Palace, whilst his contemporaries were still busy with their preliminary studies. There was even a proposal to assign to him the façade of the great council hall, but jealousy among the native artists prevented this taking effect. He was, however, consoled by the friendship of Palladio, who engaged him to decorate a large temporary theatre, and whom he subsequently accompanied on a tour through Friuli and Lombardy. Thence he visited Florence, in time to take part in the festive decorations which welcomed Joanna of Austria to her new capital, and, after a visit to his family, arrived at Rome early in 1566. It was about this time he painted for Duke Guidobaldo the Liberation of St. Peter from prison, now in the Pitti Gallery, a picture of no great intrinsic merit, though dexterous in effect; and now, too, Verdizotti of Venice complimented his early promise in this elegant sonnet, wherein the "tree of Jove" means the oak, the badge of Urbino and its dukes.

"Ecco! del glorioso arbor di Giove
Un giovinetto ramo uscir sì altero,
Ch' a speme di bei frutti ogni pensiero
Desta al fiorir de le sue frondi nove.
"In lui tai gratie il ciel benigno piove,
Che simili in altrui poch' altre spero;
Gratie, per cui virtù gli apre il sentiero
Ad ogni honor, che meraviglia move.
"E già le cime dei più culti allori
L' inchinan' grate, e lieto augurio danno
D' eterno pregio ai suoi giorni migliori.
"Alhor l' amate ghiande illustri andranno
Di sì fin or, ch' al par de' suoi splendori
Gli alti raggi del sole ombre saranno."

His brother's premature death made him heir of his fame and fortune: the latter he speedily increased, but the former he was scarcely adequate to sustain. Yet the dexterity by which he mastered, and the rapidity wherewith, by numerous assistants, he completed works of great extent, not only obtained him the commissions which Taddeo left imperfect, but secured him a preference for all undertakings of that description in Rome. It was upon this principle that he was called to Florence, to terminate the cupola of the cathedral; yet for the abortive effect of this vast composition, which has more than once narrowly escaped whitewash, Federigo is scarcely to be held responsible. The irretrievably hopeless attempt of filling suitably so immense an expanse with a figure composition, had been begun by a better artist than himself, and the blame of so gross a blunder must lie with Vasari. Don Vincenzo Borghini suggested the theme—Paradise allegorically treated in eight compartments, in seven of which are set forth the seven mysteries of our Lord's passion, while the eighth celebrates the triumph of the Romish church. The chief interest of this colossal performance lies in its monstrous compass; containing, it is said, three hundred figures, some of them thirty feet high. Returned to Rome, he was employed by Gregory XIII. on the roof of the Pauline chapel, whose walls had been decorated by Michael Angelo. The favours which fortune thus showered upon him soothed not the petulance of an irritable temper; and the bitter satire wherewith he caricatured some supposed enemies in a picture of Calumny, obliged him precipitately to quit the Holy City. This was a congenial subject, which he often treated. Once it was done for the Orsini of Bracciano; another of large size is noted in Pelli's catalogue of the Urbino pictures; and there is a small one in the gallery of the Uffizii. There are some curious particulars in Gaye's *Carteggio* of the annoyance to which this sally subjected him.[1] In 1581, he was held to bail for 500 scudi, to answer a charge of slander which it was hoped might be founded upon the testimony of his three assistants, who were imprisoned until they should supply a key to the suspected personalities. On this emergency he sought protection from the influence of his sovereign, and of the Grand Duke Francesco I. of Florence, by whose mediation he made his peace, and returned to Rome at Easter 1583. The Duke of Urbino's application was not disinterested, being anxious to secure Federigo's services for a chapel he was then building at Loreto, dedicated to the Madonna dell' Annunziata, regarding his frescoes in which we shall presently have some observations to offer. It is unnecessary to follow his several journeys to foreign courts and distant countries, whence he returned honoured and enriched. In 1574, after his flight from Rome, he passed through Paris, Flanders, and Holland, to England, where he probably remained for some time, painting portraits; but his works there do not seem to have been ascertained, or examined with much criticism. Several are loosely mentioned by Walpole, and his annotator Dalloway, one of which, representing Queen Elizabeth's gigantic porter, is said by Stirling to bear date

[1] Vol. III., p. 444.

1580. His chalk drawings of her and Leicester, engraved by Rogers, can scarcely be the same mentioned by Borghini as executed in 1575.

On his return to Rome, Olivarez, ambassador from Philip II., whose overtures to Paul Veronese had been unsuccessful, proposed that he should proceed to Madrid. There he arrived in January, 1586, and, after being received with great splendour, was immediately named king's painter, with 2000 dollars of pension, and an apartment in the Escurial. From that palace he, on the 29th of May, wrote a letter descriptive of his first works, which merits notice as showing his opinion, and that of the age, on the fitting tone and treatment to be followed in high religious art. "My apartment contains excellent rooms, besides saloon and study, where his Majesty frequently deigns to come and see me work, loading me with favours. I observe you desire now to hear something as to what I have done or am about. There are four large pictures, for two altars of the relics, opening and closing like organ-doors, to be painted on both sides. They are dedicated to the Annunciation and to St. Jerome; and I have treated them thus:—On opening the former is seen our Lady, somewhat startled and confused by the angel's entrance, while on the outer side I have made her assenting to the salutation in the words, 'Behold the handmaid of the Lord.' The exterior of St. Jerome is penitent; not as he is usually made, simply repenting, but having that faith and hope in God without which neither abstinence nor remorse can avail, together with the love, charity, and filial awe, that ought ever to connect us with God and our neighbour. And these I fancy as grouped together in idea before the saint; so I have set in front of him a cross, with Christ in the last agony, in order to inspire him with increased contrition, and at the foot thereof the three theological virtues among clouds. On the interior of the two doors, I have depicted

St. Jerome, as a doctor of the church, writing: and as companion to the idealised penitence without, I thought fit to introduce the means and aims of study, so that the saint, though writing, is in a contemplative ecstasy, attended by three angels. Two of them, typifying perseverance and love of study (without which no science can be learned, no fruit obtained), hold his book and inkhorn; the third stands at his ear, suggesting thoughts and sentences, and pointing out, on the other door, the entire subject he is writing about: I intended this one for the guardian angel, or for that intelligence and thought, whereby all is contrived and composed; and I endeavoured to represent him as incorporeal, transparent, and spiritual, a style little used on account of its difficulty. On that other door, I embodied the whole theme which St. Jerome, the most holy divine and doctor, is inditing, as to the Saviour's passion and man's redemption, dwelling specially on the considerations that induced the Father Almighty to send his only begotten Son into the world, to redeem mankind by his great sufferings. I imagine Charity as appearing in his vision, and saying 'It was I who moved God, and made Christ descend on earth'; to express which symbolically, a saint-like matron presses one hand on her breast, and indicates with the other a dead Christ borne by angels through the air. But what most pleases his Majesty and all beholders, being of peculiar mystic meaning and charming effect, is the three little Cupids who, at the feet of Charity, disport themselves with St. Jerome's lion, which comes forward most opportunely, his ferocity so tamed by these children, that he lets them pat, handle, and ride upon him, licking and fondling them the while, a clear proof that our God is not a God of anger and vengeance, but of love, peace, charity, and grace. During this winter I made all the designs and cartoons for these subjects, and have already coloured and entirely completed the first Annunciation, and the

St. Jerome writing; at present I have in hand the Charity; and all, thank God, is to his Majesty's taste. This done, his Majesty wishes me to commence the *retavola* of the high altar [for the Escurial], where there will be eight great pictures in oil, those others being on panel." [1]

In this second commission our painter was less fortunate. The eight pieces represented St. Laurence's Martyrdom, five events in the life of Christ, the Descent of Tongues, and the Assumption. As they rapidly advanced, aided by several youths who had accompanied Federigo from Italy, he observed with anxiety the courtiers' cold or contemptuous silence; and, desiring to test his patron's feelings, he presented the Nativity to Philip with the arrogant exclamation, "Here, Sire, is all that painting can accomplish, a picture that may be viewed closely or from a distance." After long gazing on the canvas, his Majesty asked if those things in the basket were meant for eggs. So paltry a criticism says little for the monarch's connoisseurship, and the mortified artist was consoled by seeing his work placed on its destined altar. Mr. Stirling informs us that, upon this failure, he was set to paint six frescoes in the Escurial cloister, which gave as little satisfaction. In order to test his complaints of his assistants, he was then desired to execute the Conception without their aid, but with no better result. After his departure, several portions of his *retavola* were dismissed from the high altar, and most of his frescoes were defaced; but notwithstanding these repeated disgusts, and the moderate success of two other altar-pieces mentioned by Conca, Zuccaro remained for nearly three years in Spain, and was finally dismissed with gifts and pensions exceeding the remuneration stipulated for his services. The solution of his disappointment is simple. The artistic

[1] Vat. Urb. MSS. No. 816, f. 64–72.

genius of Italy was greatly exhausted: that of Spain was a virgin soil promising many golden harvests.[1]

Some letters of Federigo Zuccaro in the Oliveriana Library further illustrate the turn of thought which influenced religious art in the end of the sixteenth century. He had been employed in 1583 by Francesco Maria II. to decorate a chapel in the church of Loreto; it was dedicated to the Madonna, and the theme prescribed for his frescoes was her life. The altar-picture by Baroccio represented the Annunciation; and the scenes selected for mural paintings were her marriage, visitation, death, assumption, and coronation. Of these the first three belonged to a class of dramatic compositions adapted to the prevailing taste, while the others partook of the Umbrian influence which still lingered around that shrine. The subsidiary ornaments being of course under the direction of Zuccaro, he felt puzzled how to fill up certain spaces offered by the architectural arrangement, and wrote to the Duke. After consulting the chief theological authorities among the hierarchy of Loreto what would best develop the "humble and mystic" sentiment which it was his object to sustain, the artist suggested that figures emblematic of glory and perpetuity should support the Coronation of the Madonna, as expressing the inherent attributes of that subject. In like manner he proposed to accompany her Death with Faith, Hope, and the Fear of God, the best supports of a death-bed; whilst the Assumption was to have Charity on one hand, Perseverance on the other, and above Joy, the fruit of these virtues and the foretaste of glory. As accompaniments for the Annunciation, he submitted that there should be two prophets or sibyls, the instruments through whom the incarnation of the Word was predicted. Giotto or Fra

[1] In referring to the *Annals of the Artists of Spain*, it is a sincere pleasure to bear my feeble testimony to the merits of that excellent work. It is replete with information new to the English reader, and is enriched by apt and copious illustrations selected from a wide range of literature and æsthetics.

Angelico would have chosen the prophets of the Old Testament; Michael Angelo would have preferred pagan sibyls; Perugino or Raffaele might have invoked them both; Zuccaro, painting at Loreto, thought either equally appropriate appendages to his allegorical creations.[1] Yet Federigo was not altogether blinded to the barbarous tendency of the taste around him. In writing of Milan, he says that the painters there had in his day "wofully diverged from the beautiful simplicity and arrangement of those living early in the century; and that the Proccaccini, especially Giulio Cesare, introduced a set of scoffing heads, and certain angels so debauched looking, and devoid of all reverence in the presence of God and the Madonna, that I know not how they are tolerated, unless it be that they are excused for the sake of many other commendable parts."[2]

Of the large number of important works he executed in Venice, Milan, Pavia, Turin, and other towns of Upper Italy, we shall not attempt a catalogue, nor of his many frescoes in the Roman palaces and churches. We cannot, however, pass by an altar-picture still in the Church of Sta. Caterina in his native town, which was carried to Paris by the French plunderers. It represents Peter, Francis, and other saints, presenting to the Madonna the Zuccaro family, consisting of two men, a woman, and seven children—probably Taddeo, himself, his wife and offspring; and it is inscribed "Federigo Zuccaro dedicates this monument of his affection to the intercessors of his family and birthplace, 1603." Besides the interest attaching to the portraits, it is a satisfactory specimen of his usual manner. A work of his brother, connected with the

[1] In reference to appropriate lights, Baroccio entirely condemns the use of stained glass, as darkening the interior, and injuring, by coloured rays, the effect of paintings. Zuccaro, however, recommends the introduction of a tinted armorial bearing, surrounded by a wreath of fruits and flowers, as likely to mellow without obscuring the chapel.

[2] *Lettere Pittoriche*, vii., p. 513.

history of the duchy, has been described in a previous volume.[1]

Academical instruction is considered as favourable only to mediocrity by many who maintain that genius must be cramped by the fetters of uncongenial routine, or by the prescribed duties of a conventional curriculum. The Academy of St. Luke was, however, founded under Gregory XIII., and Federigo Zuccaro was, in 1593, elected its first president, an honour appreciated far beyond the favour of princes or the decoration of knighthood. After inauguration, he was conducted by a crowd of artists to the palace he had built for himself on the Pincian Hill, at that corner otherwise consecrated by the residences of Claude, Salvator Rosa, and Nicolò Poussin. Here he afterwards held meetings of the Academy, where he read his discourses; and by will he left to it that house, failing of his natural heirs. His death occurred in 1608, at Ancona, at the age of sixty-six; but the clause of remainder in favour of the Academy has never become effectual, the palace in the Via Sistina being still possessed by his descendants. It is well known as the Casa Bertoldy, and may be regarded as the cradle of the modern German school of painting. The frescoes on which Overbeck, Cornelius, Schnorr, and Veit first essayed that elevated and pure style which has regenerated European taste, there attract many an admirer, little aware that the basement rooms, abandoned to menial uses, contain some of the latest efforts of cinque-cento decoration that have fair pretensions to merit. The richest of them has its vaulted roof studded with allegorical delineations of the arts, sciences, and virtues, painting being justly pre-eminent in a painter's house. The lunettes of another are crowded by portraits of the Zuccari, extending over four generations, and numbering twenty-one heads, true to nature. The third, which was Federigo's nuptial chamber, exhibits

[1] Vol. II.

the ceremony of his marriage, around which are figures of Chastity, Continence, Concord, and Felicity, in the fashion of an age when genius had been replaced by ingenuity, grandeur by dexterous execution.

The infirmity of Federigo's temper, to which we have already alluded, may account for his unworthy treatment of Vasari. In the marginal notes upon his copy of the Vite de' Pittori, now in the Royal Library at Paris, as well as in an original work which we are about to mention, he takes every opportunity of sneering ungenerously at one whose biography of his brother, and whose allusions to himself are conceived in kind and flattering terms. Although his *Idea de' Pittori, Scultori, ed Architetti*, printed in the year of his death, is supposed to be but a compend of his lectures at St. Luke's, he is believed to have intended it as a triumph over Vasari's justly popular writings. In this, however, he signally failed; it has the mysticism of philosophy without its spirit, while its pedantic subtleties are puerile rather than profound. This, and his *Lamento della Pittura*, are books of great rarity, but in no way merit a reprint. A mannerist with pen and pencil, the conceits of the former equal the allegories of the latter; nature and feeling are alien to both.

Although the Zuccari were little identified by their works with their native state, and obtained less of the ducal patronage than their contemporary Baroccio, their names have reflected much lustre upon Urbino. Yet the space which they occupied in the public view was owing to the smiles of propitious fortune,—to a happy facility of executing without exertion whatever commissions were offered,—to a certain magnificence and liberality in their manner of life,—and, in the case of Federigo, to an overweening vanity, rather than to any positive artistic excellence. Their reputation has accordingly waned, as the remembrance of such incidental qualities waxed faint, and as a distant posterity applied to them that only sure test, the merit of their works. Nor were these the only advantages of their position. An analogy has been deduced between Taddeo and the immortal Raffaele, not from any supposed resemblance of their pencils or genius, but because both were natives of the same state, both painted extensively in fresco at Rome, both died when "exactly thirty-seven," and both were buried in the same corner of the Pantheon. Federigo, on the other hand, was, like Titian, invited to courts, decorated and enriched by monarchs; like Raffaele and Michael Angelo, he was an architect and a sculptor as well as a painter; like Vasari, he aimed at a literary reputation. The works of the brothers display a marked similarity, a natural result of their long painting together; yet deterioration became perceptible as their distance from the golden age increased, and the younger may be distinguished by a pervading inferiority of taste and design, but especially by a growing mannerism and laxity in his conceptions, and by the overcrowding of his subjects. To balance these deficiencies, his person was attractive, his general attainments were far more comprehensive, and a longer life was granted for the enjoyment of his fortune and the extension of his fame, than fell to the lot of Taddeo. The failing mainly attributable to both was absence of style. Their inventions were often flimsy, and their compositions, deficient in unity and dignity, are often little more than figure groups.

A necessary consequence of the low style of art which the Zuccari adopted was that, notwithstanding the number of assistants whom they constantly employed, their school neither attained to considerable repute among their contemporaries, nor put forth many pupils of note; offering in this respect a marked contrast to that of their countryman Baroccio, whose pleasing manner attracted a host of admirers and imitators. Two natives of Pesaro, however, possess a certain reputation in the semi-mechanical church decorations then largely produced. They were Nicolò Trometta, generally called NICOLÒ DA PESARO, and GIAN GIACOMO PANDOLFI, the latter of whom was the earliest instructor of Simon Cantarini da Pesaro. The various works which these and other Zuccaristi have left in the duchy are quite unworthy of special description, and we may dismiss them with the mention of CAVALIERE DOMENICO CRESTI DA PASSIGNANO, whose chief title to fame is reflected from that of his pupils TIARINI and LUDOVICO CARACCI. Among the painters less known to fame were BIAGIO and GIROLAMO D' URBINO, both of whom were employed in the Escurial; the former left Spain along with Federigo Zuccaro, in 1588; the latter wrought under Pelegrino Tibaldi. Ottovevenius, after spending seven years with Federigo, carried his influence beyond the Alps, and eventually numbered Rubens among his scholars.

Among the artists who repaired to Urbino at the summons of Duke Federigo, for the construction of his palace, was Ambrogio Barocci, or Baroccio, a Milanese sculptor, who established himself there, and, after long labouring on its plastic decorations, founded a family singularly distinguished in the higher branches of mechanical and pictorial art. His two daughters were married to Girolamo and Nicolò della Genga, and his great-grandson Federigo, upon whose biography we must dwell at some length, had an elder brother Simone, who after studying the exact sciences under Federigo Comandino, became the best mathematical instrument maker that had hitherto been seen. His cousins, the Cavaliere Giovanni Battista and Giovanni Maria, were not less famous in watchmaking, an art successfully patronised by the Dukes delle Rovere, which we shall mention in our fifty-fifth chapter. FEDERIGO BAROCCIO was born in 1528, and initiated into the rudiments of design by his father, who practised engraving and modelling. His early efforts having been approved by his grand-uncle Giralomo Genga, he was placed under the tuition of Battista Franco of Venice, an indifferent painter, much employed in the majolica shops at Urbino, whose taste for designing from antique sculpture directed his pupil's attention to those effects of chiaroscuro which distinguished his matured style. After assiduous labours in this way, he repaired to Pesaro, then his sovereigns' residence, where were placed their accumulated treasures of art. There he observed the works of Raffaele and Titian, under the guidance of Genga, who carefully advanced his artistic education, especially in perspective. At twenty he went to Rome, anxious to see the triumphs of his great countryman, which he forthwith set himself to study. Several anecdotes are told of his modesty, which kept him in the background until chance obtained for his drawings a passing compliment from Michael Angelo, and the warm sympathy and encouragement of Giovanni da Udine, delighted to find in the youth a countryman as well as an admirer of his former master. After imbibing inspiration from these healthful fountains, he returned home, and executed some church paintings. But the casual arrival of one who brought some cartoons and crayon drawings from Parma gave a new turn to his ideas. Forgetting the grandeur of Buonarrotti and the pure beauty of Raffaele, he aimed at those meretricious graces which have borrowed from the dexterity of Parmegianino, and the luscious pencil of Correggio, a fascination unsupported by their intrinsic merits, and pregnant with mischief to art. To him, however, belongs the credit of introducing into Lower Italy a harmonious application of light and shade, to which his early lamp studies from sculpture may have conduced.

Returning to Rome in 1560, he found Federigo Zuccaro in the ascendant, and from him received a hint as to the tendency of this manner, which it would have been well that he had adopted. Having, at the request of Federigo, painted two children on a frieze, with a fusion of colour very rarely effected in fresco, the latter, considering this to be overdone, retraced the outlines with a brush, imparting to them that force which was wanting to the work. Baroccio took the reproof in good part, but profited not by it. During his first visit he had become known to Cardinal Giulio della Rovere, by whose influence, probably, he procured employment at the Vatican and Belvidere, in company with Zuccaro. With the decline of their art, the good feeling of the painters' fraternity waned, and the kindly sympathies of that glorious band, whom Raffaele had imbued with a portion of his amiable nature, no longer animated their successors. Those who saw in Baroccio one who would have raised the standard of taste from the abandonment which immediately succeeded the dispersion of that noble school, instead of seconding his efforts poisoned him at a banquet. He survived the potion, but four years of pain and feeble health elapsed ere he could return to his labours. When his system had in some degree resumed its vigour among his mountain breezes, he was called to Perugia to paint for its cathedral the Deposition from the Cross, a work which, far from exhibiting any prostration of power, greatly surpassed his previous efforts. No scriptural theme offers greater technical difficulties, or demands a larger share of those grand and energetic qualities in which Baroccio was usually deficient. It is, therefore, one of his most remarkable efforts, as regards its own qualities, and the circumstances under which it was produced. It occupied him during three years, and was followed by the Absolution of St. Francis, for the Franciscans of Urbino, on which he laboured in their convent for above twice that period. In consideration of their poverty, he charged but a hundred golden scudi for the work, to which they gratefully added as many florins.

It is not our intention to give a catalogue of even his

more important productions, although a large proportion of them were executed for the decoration of his native state, which his patriotism induced him to prefer to the splendid offers made him by foreign monarchs. Among those commissioned by his sovereign was the Calling of St. Andrew, finished in 1584, and presented to Philip II., that saint being patron of the Spanish order of the Golden Fleece. It was about the same time that Duke Francesco Maria dedicated to the Madonna del Annunziata, a chapel in the church of Loreto, which we have already mentioned as decorated in fresco by Federigo Zuccaro. Its altar-picture was committed to Baroccio, the subject naturally being the Annunciation. This was in all respects a labour of love, the theme being in perfect unison with his dulcet manner, and it was accordingly considered by himself his chef-d'œuvre, a merit which, in the opinion of many, is shared by his Deposition, and, in that of Simon da Pesaro, by his Santa Michelina. Modern connoisseurs may decide between the first and last of those three great works, as they hang side by side in the Vatican Gallery, the former of them, and the Deposition, having been returned from Paris. The Annunciation is certainly a very favourable and pleasing specimen of the Baroccesque manner, but an eye versed in the criticism of sacred art must demur to the judgment of Bellori, who found maiden humility in the Virgin, a celestial air in the angel, and spiritual character in the tinting. The principal figure is the portrait of a young lady of the Compagnoni of Macerata, whose features are equally devoid of purity and of noble expression; the colouring, though delicately beautiful in itself, is meretricious in effect, transmuting flesh into roses; and the whole sentiment of the picture is anything but devotional. On the other hand, it is distinguished above a majority of his important works by unity of composition, although, like most productions of his age, the action is exaggerated

Anderson

NOLI ME TANGERE

After the picture by Baroccio, once in the Ducal Collection at Urbino, now in the Uffizi Gallery, Florence

and the details mannered. A copy in mosaic was sent to replace this favourite effort, which was often reproduced by the master and his pupils. A repetition of it was presented by Francesco Maria to the court of Spain, and another, left unfinished, remains at Gubbio. The Santa Michelina, protectress of Pesaro, was painted for the church of S. Francesco there, and exhibits a striking deviation from this artist's wonted style. A single figure kneeling on Mount Calvary in ecstatic contemplation, amid the war of convulsed elements, admitted of no paltry prettiness, and could scarcely fail to attain grandeur. There is, accordingly, in the breadth of composition, and in the prevalent low neutral tone, an approach to severe art, inducing us to overlook the fluttering draperies and girlish forms that belong to the master.

Rome possesses by a better title three other pictures deserving the notice of those who desire to appreciate Baroccio. The Presentation of the Madonna (1594), and the Visitation, adorn the Chiesa Nuova, where the latter is said to have often inspired S. Filippo Neri's devotions; the Institution of the Sacrament according to the Romish rite, in the church of the Minerva, was a present from the Duke of Urbino to Clement VIII., who conferred upon the painter a gold chain. It is related that, in the original sketch, Satan was introduced, whispering treason into the ear of Judas, but was afterwards omitted, in deference to his Holiness's opinion, that the Devil ought not to be represented as "so much at ease in the Saviour's presence." On occasion of the same Pontiff's visit to Urbino, in 1598, he received from his host a golden vase for holy water, beautifully chased, with a painting by Baroccio at the bottom, wherein the infant Christ, seated on the clouds, gives the benediction with one hand, and supports the globe with the other. This charming miniature so delighted the Pope, that he had it removed from the benitier, and affixed to his daily office book.

The Cathedral of Urbino contains the latest of his great church pictures, representing the Last Supper, as well as the St. Sebastian, one of his early works, and it is interesting to contrast their respective styles. The St. Sebastian was commissioned for 100 florins in 1557, whilst the inspirations of Rome still hovered over his palette, and imparted vigour to his already Correggesque manner. This hackneyed and generally harrowing subject is treated with pleasing novelty, the group consisting of the saint, a graceful figure bound to a fig-tree, an imperious judge who has condemned him, and a brawny archer who carries the sentence into effect, whilst the Madonna and Child appear on high to support the martyr's faith and hope. In the Cenacolo, the fair promise of that able production is sadly abandoned: all those great qualities of his predecessors, which he began by happily imitating, are there replaced by extravagance, and even harmony is absent from his multifarious tints. Of his innumerable minor works we cannot pause to take note, and he scarcely ever painted in fresco. It is remarkable that, although his manner was, even in its defects, well suited to the voluptuous character of mythological fable, and to many a scene of mundane grandeur, he limited himself to sacred representations, almost the only exception being portraits. Of the latter, his most successful is Duke Francesco Maria, in rich armour, as he returned from the fight of Lepanto; it has been deservedly honoured with a place in the Tribune at Florence, and an equally beautiful repetition adorns the Camuccini collection at Rome.

The amount of his labours is inconceivable, considering the constant sufferings which he is represented to have undergone, from an almost total destruction of digestion, and habitual sleeplessness, consequent upon having been poisoned at thirty-two years of age. The large pictures we have mentioned are but few of those which he produced, yet no artist was more painstaking. Bellori assures us that he always prepared two cartoons and two coloured sketches, drawing exclusively from the life, and made many studies of drapery, separately perfecting his chiaroscuros from figures repeatedly modelled by his own hands, ere he transferred them to his paper. Such conscientious diligence could scarcely have been looked for in an artist whose works owe little to their outline, and may appear unnecessary to those who imitate his fusion only as a trick to mask defective design. This peculiar quality of his colouring was likewise matter of unwearied application, and he endeavoured to facilitate its results by an artificial scale, corresponding to notes in music, as a test for the gradation of his "tuneful" tints.

The merits of Baroccio consist in much variety and novelty of conception, in skilful management of his lights, and in the dexterous blending of strongly contrasted tints into a harmonious whole. The Correggesque tone of his pictures admirably conformed to the soft and gentle turn of his character; but whilst his design is more exact, and his foreshortenings are more true, he wants the breadth of Correggio; though his lights are more silvery and superficially lucent, his chiaroscuro neither attains to the force nor the depth of his prototype. The peculiar beauty at which he constantly aimed degenerates into a deformity; the almost cloying sweetness of his faces produces in the spectator a surfeit, inducing a desire for simpler fare. His figures are often deficient in self-possession, his colouring in verity, his compositions in solidity and repose. In a word, Baroccio shared the usual fate of eclectic painters, who, distrusting their own resources, seek to make up a manner from the combined excellences of their predecessors. Striving to engraft the grace of the Parmese upon the design of the Roman school, he fell into a flimsy mannerism, which, in straining after meretricious charms, departs from dignity and devotional feeling.

The days were nearly over when genius loved to master

several branches of art; and it would have been better had our painter limited his labours to the palette, and to spirited etchings from his own compositions. At the command, however, of his sovereign, he, in 1603, undertook to supply designs for a long-contemplated statue of Duke Federigo; and Gaye gives us several of his letters regarding the difficulties of this commission, which baffled him for six months. His great aim was to retain the peculiar character of the head, without rendering prominent the unseemly defect in the eye and nose,—an object hitherto effected by portraying the old warrior only in profile. He worked chiefly from the bas-relief over the library door in the palace, and that at the church of S. Giovanni.[1] The execution of his design was committed to Girolamo Campagna at Venice, a sculptor of note, who cannot justly be held accountable for this poor and awkward performance. It was placed, in 1606, on the palace stairs at Urbino, where it remains.

But for the misfortune of his broken health, Baroccio would have been as happy as his estimable character deserved. He was fortunate in his temper, in his extended reputation, in his easy circumstances, in his multiplied orders, and in his many scholars. His infirmities prevented him from accepting flattering invitations to the courts of Austria, Spain, and Tuscany, but the friendship of his own sovereign never failed him. Having fitted up in his house at Urbino a sort of exhibition room for his works, it was repeatedly visited by Francesco Maria, whose Diary not only mentions this, but notes his death and that of his brother Simone, "an excellent maker of compasses." On the 1st of October, 1612, is this entry: "Federigo Baroccio of Urbino died, aged seventy-seven, an excellent painter, whose eye and hand served him as well as in his youth."

[1] Carteggio, III., pp. 529–35. This medallion is now removed from the library door to the first landing-place of the great stair. It may have been by the medallist, Clemente of Urbino, mentioned in vol. II.

His real age seems to have been eighty-four, and there can be no doubt that he retained his faculties, painting without spectacles, until struck at the last by apoplexy, a remarkable triumph of mind over protracted bodily infirmities. Yet the deterioration of his later works, which may still be seen at Urbino and Pesaro, sadly belies the Duke's tribute to his green old age. A list of many of those which he executed for that kind patron will be found in the last number of our Appendix. At his funeral in S. Francesco, a church standard, painted by himself, with a Crucifixion, was placed at the foot of his bier: the tablet inscribed to his memory has been excluded in rebuilding the nave, but remains in the adjoining corridor.

The popularity of Baroccio, both personally and as a painter, recruited to his studio many young artists, eager to enter the path which he had successfully trodden. But the faults of his style were of a sort which imitation was sure to exaggerate, and the absence of solid qualities in the master prevented the felicitous development of such talent as nature had granted to his pupils. We accordingly search in vain among his many scholars for a single name of eminence; and we might pass over the *Baroccisti* without further notice, but that a considerable proportion of them claim a passing word as natives of the duchy. ANTONIO VIVIANI, son of a baker at Urbino, was a favourite of his master, though probably not his nephew, as supposed by Lanzi. In early life, his productions imitated those of Baroccio with great success, as may be seen at Fano and in various parts of the duchy, but on proceeding to Rome his style rapidly deteriorated. Emulating the flimsy and faulty manner of the Cavaliere d' Arpino, by which high art was then fatally degraded, he painted against time in the Vatican and Lateran palaces, as well as on many altar commissions. These, when compared with other contemporary trash, obtained a degree of applause which sounder criticism is compelled to withhold from il Sordo, the nickname by which their author was generally known. But he sacrificed his art without improving his fortune; and an old age, passed in poverty, was closed in disappointment and want. His brother Ludovico, "wicked, graceless, and disobedient, unworthy the name of son," had from his father's will five farthings in lieu of his patrimony, and his career maintained the prestige of this sad outset, both in his character and works.

ALESSANDRO VITALE, born at Urbino in 1580, so completely caught the amenity of his instructor's manner, as to be employed during his advanced years to copy many of his works, which, with a few finishing touches, passed as originals. ANTONIO CIMATORIO, *alias il Visacci* or the Ugly, was chiefly employed on festive and scenic decorations, aided by GIULIO CESARE BEGNI of Pesaro: the latter went afterwards to Venice, and, devoting himself to better things, left not a few good pictures in the March of Treviso. GIORGIO PINCHI of Castel Durante, and ANDREA LILLIO of Ancona, both approached the Baroccesque manner with considerable success, and shared the labours of il Sordo on the pontifical frescoes in Rome. Among those who carried the same style to a distance, may be named ANTONIO ANTONIANO of Urbino, who, after aiding Baroccio with his great picture of the Crucifixion, was sent by him with it to Genoa, and there settled. GIOVANNI and FRANCESCO, two brothers of Urbino, and probably offsets of this school, emigrated to Spain, and painted in the Escurial, under the patronage of Philip II. FILIPPO BELLINI, a native of the same city, though a pupil of Baroccio, adopted a more vigorous manner, but his works are scarcely met with out of Umbria. To this catalogue it is enough to add the names of Francesco Baldelli, Lorenzo Vagnarelli, Ventura Marza, Cesare Maggieri, Bertuzzi, and Porino, all born in the duchy;

and those of Bandiera and the Pellegrini of Perugia, the Malpiedi of La Marca, and the Cavaliere Francesco Vanni of Siena, the latter of whom, though not among his scholars, so thoroughly adopted the peculiarities of Baroccio, as to be perhaps the happiest of his imitators. TERENZIO TERENZI of Urbino, known by the soubriquet of Rondinello, earned a dishonourable reputation by his successful imitations of the older masters, which he passed off as originals; and having fallen into merited disgrace with his kind patron, the Cardinal of Montalto, in consequence of pawning upon him one of his forgeries as a Raffaele, he died of vexation in the first years of the seventeenth century, aged thirty-five.

CLAUDIO RIDOLFI, though born in Verona in 1560, may be considered a subject of Urbino. His family was noble, but not rich, so adopting painting as a profession, he studied its principles under Paul Veronese, at Venice. But the temptations to idleness which beset him at home so interfered with success that he resolved to escape from them. On his way to Rome he stayed some time at Urbino with Baroccio, in whose glittering style he lost somewhat of the better manner of his early master. But his journey to the "mother of arts and arms" was interrupted by more powerful fascinations; for he married a noble lady of Urbino, and settled at Corinaldo, some miles above Sinigaglia, attracted by the beauty of its site, and fain to enjoy, in provincial retirement, exemption from the jealousies and struggles which often beset artists in a city life, where tact or fortune are apt to confer a success denied to merit. Though he returned for a time to his native city, and painted many excellent works in it, and in the principal towns of the Venetian state, the charms of Corinaldo and his wife's influence induced him to spend there the greater part of a long life. He died in 1644, aged, according to his namesake Carlo Ridolfi, eighty-four, or to Ticozzi, seventy years. To the glowing tints of the Lombard school he eventually added the merit of more accurate design; but his principal excellences were a chastened composition, and a close attention to the proprieties of costume, as contributing to a proper intelligence of the subject. A vast number of his productions are scattered over Umbria and La Marca, and there issued from his studio not a few pupils of provincial eminence, most of whom tended considerably towards the Baroccesque manner. Of those belonging to Urbino the most conspicuous was BENEDETTO MARINI, who, though scarcely known at home, produced many important works in Lombardy, and excelled in the management of crowded compositions, such as his immense Miracle of the Loaves and Fishes, painted at Piacenza in 1625. Patanazzi and Urbinelli belong to a less distinguished category, and though Girolamo Cialderi is ranked with them by Lanzi, he seems referable to a subsequent period.

Gubbio continued in the sixteenth century to maintain a school which, though acquiring little more than a provincial reputation, was not without merit. BENEDETTO NUCCI was born there about 1520, and, imbibing from Raffaelino del Colle certain inspirations of the golden age, left in his native town many respectable church pictures. He died in 1587, having seen his son Virgilio escape from his studio to place himself under Daniel di Volterra at Rome. Among his pupils, but of ever progressive mediocrity, were FELICE DAMIANO and CESARE DI GUISEPPE ANDREOLI, the latter an offset of a family whose eminence in the art of majolica will be mentioned in our fifty-fifth chapter.

CHAPTER LIV

Foreign artists patronised by the dukes Della Rovere—The tomb of Julius II. by Michael Angelo—Character and influence of his genius—Titian's works for Urbino—Palma Giovane—IL. Semolei—Sculptors at Urbino.

IT would occupy a full chapter were we to trace the history of what Julius II. meant to have been his tomb, from the chisel of Michael Angelo Buonarroti; yet the subject is too illustrative of that Pontiff's grandiose spirit, and of the artist's unfulfilled aspirations, as well as too intimately connected with the ducal house of Urbino, to be overlooked. The work was commissioned by Julius himself, who, early in his pontificate, called Buonarroti from Florence to execute a resting-place for his ashes, which, in the words of Vasari, should "surpass in beauty and grandeur, in imposing ornament and elaborate sculpture, all antique and imperial sepulchres." The vast size and colossal proportions of the first design were worthy of artist and patron, and cannot be at all estimated from the curtailed and aimless substitute which now challenges our criticism. Yet there was exaggeration in the ideas as well as the forms; the allegories were far-fetched, the adulation fulsome, and the intention obscure. Such at least is the impression left by the descriptions of Vasari and Condivi. Without attempting to reconcile these with the sketch engraved in the Milanese edition of the former author [1811], it is enough to say that the original plan was an isolated parallelogram, with about ten statues and seven caryatides on each façade, and a sarcophagus aloft for the

Pope's body, the estimate for all which seems to have been 10,000 ducats, augmented by his executors to 16,000. Its destined site was St. Peter's, and its utter disproportion in style and extent to that time-worn basilicon appears to have suggested to the indomitable Pontiff the vast idea of reconstructing the metropolitan church of Christendom. This more engrossing undertaking absorbed much of the enterprise and materials destined for the tomb, so the latter remained unfinished at the death of Julius, who barely survived the completion of those Sistine frescoes to which he had transferred the sculptor's reluctant labours. A new and reduced contract having been made by his executors for its completion, Buonarroti resumed it with the preference due to a favourite work; but he sought in vain for leisure to proceed with it on the accession of Leo X., who, by a strange misapplication of his powers, sent him to work the marble quarries of Pietra Santa. Indeed, the executors failed to obtain implement of his undertaking under either of the Medicean popes, alienated as these were from the della Rovere, and intent upon otherwise employing the genius of their gifted countryman.

At length Francesco Maria I. took up the forgotten memorial of his uncle, whose over-ambition of monumental honours had meanwhile led to a total oversight of his place of sepulture. As early as 1525, we find the Duke addressing complaints and threats to Buonarroti, whom he charged with idleness, after receiving prepayment of his stipulated price, unaware apparently that he had been overborne by higher authority, and thus compelled to employ himself on commissions less germane to his feelings and tastes. A misunderstanding in regard to the sums so advanced further complicated this unfortunate affair, which was throughout fraught with disappointment and annoyance to Michael Angelo. It slept on till 1532, when a further modification was made of the plan

Alinari

THE COMMUNION OF THE APOSTLES

By Giusto di Gand, in the Palazzo Ducale Urbino. (From the Ducal Collection)

to a single façade whereon six statues were to be placed; but amid competing calls upon his "fearless and furious" chisel or pencil, little progress was made in the next ten years. Irritated by continual exercise of the papal control, such as his independent spirit could ill brook, fretting at the uncongenial labours often thrust upon him, and galled by repeated allegations against his gratitude and his integrity, Buonarroti turned his eyes to Urbino, as a home where his genius would be appreciated without sacrificing his freedom of action, and took steps to retire thither and redeem his pledge to the Duke. But in Paul III. he had a yet more exacting task-master, from whom there was no escape, and in November, 1541, Cardinal Ascanio Parisani wrote to Duke Guidobaldo that the Pope having commissioned the sculptor to paint the Last Judgment, which would occupy his undivided attention during several years, to the exclusion of the monument, he had to propose, at the instance of his Holiness, a new arrangement, whereby the statues for its reduced design, so far as not already finished by Michael Angelo, were committed to other artists, working upon his models and under his eye. Yielding gracefully to the necessity of the case, the Duke wrote the following letter.[1]

"Most excellent Messer Michelangiolo,

"His Holiness having deigned to [inform] me of his urgent desire to avail himself for some time of your labours, in painting and decorating the new chapel he is making in the Apostolic Palace, and I, esteeming and gratefully acknowledging all service and satisfaction given to his holiness as bestowed on myself, in order that you

[1] There is a copy of it in the Magliabechiana Library, class viii., No. 1392, to which Gaye has from other sources supplied the date of 6th March, 1542. Carteggio, II., 289-309. From him, Ciampi, Vasari, and Condivi, we have condensed the very confused details respecting the monument of Julius which have come down to us.

may more freely give your mind to that matter, am perfectly content that you place on the tomb of my uncle of blessed memory, Pope Julius, those three statues already terminated entirely by your hand, the Moses included. And in order, as nearly as possible, to perfect the whole in terms of our last stipulations, which, as I am informed, you are anxious and ready to do, [I consent] that you commit the execution of the other three statues to some good and esteemed master, but after your own designs and under your superintendence; relying confidently, from your good-will to his sacred memory and to my house, that you will bring the work to a satisfactory issue, and so contrive that it shall be deemed most laudable, and in all respects worthy of you. Such a result will fully satisfy me; and I again beseech you to see to this, as conferring on me a special obligation; offering myself at all times [ready] for all your commands and pleasure."

Under this final alteration of his contract, Michael Angelo forthwith assigned to Raffaele da Montelupo the execution of his designs for a Madonna with a Child in her arms, and for a prophet and a sibyl seated, at the price of 400 scudi; employing at the same time two decorative stonecutters upon the ornamental details of the façade, at a cost of 800 more. The statues from his own hand were to be Moses, and two caryatides holding captives, who had been introduced into the first plan, as allegorical of the cities in Romagna subdued by Julius. But, finding these too large for the reduced design, he proposed to substitute for them two other figures from his chisel, already far advanced, and which he would entrust to be finished by others at a cost of 200 scudi, his Moses being destined to stand between them. All this is stated by him in a petition to the Pope of 20th July, 1542. The two substituted statues were finished by Buonarroti, and, in the documents printed by Gaye, are named by him Active and Contemplative Life. This, however, is a free interpretation of the allegory, the figures being, according to Visari, Leah and Rachel. The recumbent Pope was the wretched work of one Maso di Bosco or Boscoli; and the prophet and sibyl by Montelupo are said to have greatly dissatisfied Michael Angelo. The two rejected caryatide prisoners found their way to Paris in the time of Francis I., and remain in the Louvre; another similar is in the great hall of the Palazzo Vecchio, at Florence; and some grandiose, half-blocked ideas, still to be seen here and there, whose rough power identifies them with Michael Angelo, may have belonged to his original plan. About the beginning of 1545, forty years after it had been undertaken, the work was placed in the Church of S. Pietro in Vincoli, of which Julius had been Cardinal-presbyter. Though meant as his tomb, it is but his monument; for the bones of that imperious high priest have found a fitter resting-place in the grandest of Christian fanes, his own creation, and best memorial. Few works of art have occasioned greater variety of opinion. In his Lectures, Fuseli has exposed several of his defects, and the impression it most frequently leaves upon the spectator is thus aptly expressed by him in an Italian letter to the translator of Webb on the Beautiful:—

"In the Moses, Michael Angelo has sacrificed beauty to anatomical science, and to his favourite passion for the terrible and the gigantic. If it be true that he looked at the arm of the famous Ludovisi satyr, he probably, also, studied the head, in order to transfer its character to the Moses, since both of them resemble that of an old he-goat. There is, notwithstanding, in the figure a quality of monstrous grandeur which cannot be denied to Buonarroti, and which, like a thunder-storm, presaged the bright days of Raffaele."

This monument must ever be regarded as but the

epitome of a grand design, curtailed without scale or measurement, deformed by colossal portions from the original in combination with dwarfish details of its pigmy substitute, marred by incomplete allegories, and eked out by supposititious figures. Yet few will leave the spot without another glance at the tremendous Moses, nor will any connoisseur avert his gaze until the awful majesty of that one statue has eclipsed the petty incongruities of its location. It is among those rare creations of man's mind which, rising above the standard of human forms and human sympathies, demand a loftier test. The pervading sentiment alone challenges our intellectual regard, and bespeaks our verdict; yet with playful prodigality, the artist has lavished an ivory finish upon its details, without detracting from the sublime character of the irate lawgiver.[1]

Although this work is the only link directly connecting Michael Angelo with the ducal house of Urbino, we may be allowed a passing tribute to that genius which has hammered huge rocks into colossal compositions, and embodied themes the most difficult in forms the most daring. Of the simple element of beauty we, indeed, find in him few traces. Gentleness and pathos had no place either in his wayward spirit or in his works.*[2] Discarding the

[1] A favourite workman of Buonarroti, often met with under the patronymic Urbino, was Francesco Amadori di Colonello, of Castel Durante, who lived with him from 1530 to 1536. See GUALANDI, *Nuovo Raccolta di Lettere sulla Pittura*, I., 48–52.

*[2] No? Consider then the Pietà of S. Pietro in Vaticano, the unfinished Pietà of S. Maria del Fiore. All that Dennistoun says of Michelangelo is full of misunderstanding. For instance, he never "startles" though he may terrify one. It would be ridiculous to defend him. His work is beautiful, with the beauty of the mountains in which he alone has found the spirit of man. His figures, half unveiled from the living rock, are like some terrible indictment of the world he lived in: an indictment of himself too, perhaps, of his contempt for things as they are; it is in a sort of rage at its uselessness that he leaves them unfinished. In him the spirit of man has stammered the syllables of eternity, and in its agony of longing or sorrow has failed to speak only the word love. All things particular to the individual, all that is small or of little account, that endures but for a moment, he has purged

Anderson

GIOVANNI AND FEDERICO, ELECTORS OF SAXONY

After the portraits by Cranach, once in the Ducal Collection at Urbino, now in the Uffizi Gallery, Florence

beau-ideal aimed at in antique sculpture, where movement was restrained by the observance of form, and passion modified to the measure of fair proportion, he either startled by impossible postures, gnarled limbs, and sturdy deformity, or, in the words of Fuseli, "perplexed the limbs of grandeur with the minute ramifications of anatomy." Hence, when tried by the rules of art, many of his creations are found wanting; when submitted to the standard of pure taste, their faults become glaring. In straining to shake off the trammels of manner, he often fell into mannerism the most infelicitous; and the impression too commonly left on the spectator is that of energy wasted and talent misapplied. But his mind was of that lofty cast which, soaring above common themes, and spurning conventional restrictions, substituted power for beauty, and challenged our wonder rather than our approbation. Awed by the sublimity of his ideas, we overlook their inadequate development, until, descending to details, we impugn the unfinished sketch, and half-chiselled marble, painfully reminded that superhuman gifts are often marred by very ordinary weaknesses.

No one, perhaps, fully aware of Michael Angelo's celebrity, ever looked for the first time upon one of his principal works without a shade of disappointment. Inventions appealing to the intellect without sympathy from the feelings,—attitudes struggling with difficulty rather than aiming at elegance,—muscular masses, rugged as the blocks from which they are rudely hewn; such things surpass the comprehension of superficial observers, and disenchant common minds. Yet there is a spell around all of them which arrests the most careless, and recalls the most disappointed, and the longer they are examined, especially by persons of cultivated understanding, the more

away, so that life itself may make, as it were, an immortal gesticulation almost monstrous in its passionate intensity—a shadow seen on the mountains, a mirage on the snow.

certain will be the final tribute to their transcendent qualities, the more unreserved the avowal that their author stands out among the foremost geniuses whom the world has seen. Feebleness or insipidity had no place in his conceptions, and no individual ever left the impress of his vigorous mind upon so many various arts. He was a poet of no mean pretensions. His architecture is as successful as bold. It is difficult to say whether his frescoes or his sculptures are the more admirable. Even his oil paintings are worthy of more notice than they have met with; and, the few ascertained specimens display a mastery of finish little to be looked for from their wayward and impetuous author, and develop in their execution, as well as in their design, an extraordinary pictorial science. The trite assertion that he never painted but three easel pictures seems fully negatived by the mechanical perfection which, notwithstanding a certain languor of colouring and flatness of surface, these exhibit, and which must have been gained by extensive practice. In his house, even a miniature on parchment is shown as his work; and not a few tiny productions in bronze and ivory bear the stamp of his invention, if not of his hand. These were probably labours of those early days when, with equal verity and shrewdness the Gonfaloniere Soderini recommended him to the Roman court as "a fine young man, unequalled in his art throughout Italy, or perhaps the world. He will do anything for good words and caresses; indeed, he must be treated with affection and favour, in which case he will perform things to astonish all beholders."[1] In the sacristy of S. Lorenzo, at Florence, these anticipations were amply realised on the monuments of two of the Medici, with whom an earlier portion of these pages has made us acquainted. These works were, however, no labour of love to the sculptor, whose sympathies had been alien to that race from the

[1] See Gaye, *Carteggio*, II., 83–109, sub anno 1506.

days when Pietro ceased to walk in the ways of his fathers. Accordingly, their greatest fault is, that the artist absorbs our interest almost to the exclusion of the personages commemorated, to whom the allegorical compositions appear to have no reference. It is, indeed, only their portraits that recall the purpose of the monuments. That of the elegant and gentle Giuliano awakens no association that might not be suggested by the statue of some nameless warrior of the classic age. More appropriate is the bearing of Lorenzo, the usurper of Urbino. The stern gloom that broods over his casque, and shadows his repulsive features, scowling upon the world from whose sympathies he seems a voluntary alien, is an enduring index of his unamiable character. But it is in the Sistine chapel that Buonarroti sits pre-eminent. Who that stands beneath its grand frescoes can doubt the daring, the originality, and grasp of his genius, who triumphantly called into existence forms and movements before which ordinary minds shrink into pigmy dimensions? Yet, who that observes the rapid decline of the Michael-Angelesque school into mannered contortion and extravagant caricature, can question its mischievous influence, or the danger of opening up such fields to uninspired labourers? On both sides of the Alps, its followers or imitators, mistaking extravagance for energy, manner for power, and servilely substituting exceptional attitudes for the sublimity of nature and the dignity of repose, have copied his design without imbibing his spirit, and have embodied feeble conceptions in preposterous forms.

Freely have we spoken of a name to whom all honour is due, whose failings may be noted as a warning, without diminishing our respect for his manifold attainments. Our readers may appreciate his success as a poet through Mr. Glassford's felicitous version of a sonnet worthy the noblest of art's disciples. *[1]

*[1] Cf. J. A. SYMONDS, *The Sonnets of Michelangelo.*

"Now my fair bark through life's tempestuous flood
Is steered, and full in view that port is seen,
Where all must answer what their course has been,
And every work be tried, if bad or good.

"Now do those lofty dreams, my fancy's brood,
Which made of ART an idol and a queen,
Melt into air ; and now I feel, how keen !
That what I needed most I most withstood.
Ye fabled joys, ye tales of empty love,
What are ye now, if twofold death be nigh ?
The first is certain, and the last I dread.
Ah ! what does Sculpture, what does Painting prove,
When we have seen the Cross, and fixed our eye
On Him whose arms of love were there outspread !"

The home patronage of the della Rovere dukes was, however by no means limited to their subjects, and TITIAN*[1] enjoyed high favour from the first two sovereigns of that dynasty. The coronation of Charles V., in 1532, having attracted to Bologna a concourse of distinguished persons, Titian, then in his fifty-fifth year, was honoured by an imperial invitation to join the throng. The monarch, himself reputed no mean craftsman, delighted to pass what time he could snatch from business, in conversing with the painter, and observing his progress, till one day, having picked up a fallen pencil, he returned it, saying, "Titian deserves to be waited on by an Emperor." The Duke of Urbino, who may have known the Venetian in his native city, was among the sovereigns and cardinals whose commissions on that occasion contended for preference, and but a short time, probably, elapsed ere his own and his consort's portraits were produced,*[2] although Vasari and

*[1] For Titian, consult GRONAU, *Titian* (Duckworth, 1904). By far the best handbook on the painter.

*[2] As before stated, the first works that Titian painted for Francesco Maria were a portrait of Hannibal, a Nativity, a figure of our Lord. The Duke writes him concerning them in 1533 as follows (cf. GRONAU, *op cit.*, p. 91):—

"Dearest Friend,—
"You know through our envoy how much we wish for pictures . . .

Anderson

LA BELLA
After the picture by Titian in the Pitti Gallery, Florence.
Supposed portrait of Duchess Leonora

Ridolfi have erroneously fixed their date in 1543, five years after Francesco Maria's death.

Few of Titian's likenesses have been more lauded than the Duke's, both as regards truth and execution; but we shall quote only the testimony of Aretino, who knew well the painter and his subject. "In gazing upon it, I called

and the longer we have to wait the more eager we are to have them . . . and so we beg you to satisfy us as soon as possible. Finish at least one of the pictures, that we may rejoice in something by your hand."

The portraits were begun in 1536, in which year (October) Aretino wrote a sonnet on that of the Duke. They were finished early in 1538. Of the earlier pictures, the figure of Christ is probably that in the Pitti Gallery (228); the others apparently have perished.

In 1536 the Duke wrote again asking for a *Resurrection* for the Duchess, and begging Titian to finish the "picture of a woman in a blue dress as beautifully as possible." This latter is probably the *Bella* of the Pitti Gallery (18), which some have thought to be Eleonora Gonzaga, Francesco Maria's wife. She was then forty-three years old, and her portrait was painted at this time by the same master (Uffizi, 599) as a companion for that of the Duke (Uffizi, 605).

Duke Guidobaldo, while yet but Duke of Camerino, had sat to Titian, and had bought from him the picture of a "Nude Woman" (GRONAU, *op cit.*, p. 95). In March, 1538, he sent a messenger to Venice, who was instructed not to leave the city without them. He got one, but the other had not been delivered in May of that year. The Duke wrote to him to beware lest it passed elsewhere, "for I am resolved to mortgage a part of my property if I cannot obtain it in any other way." This picture was probably the *Venus* of the Tribune (Uffizi, 1117) who is so like the *Bella*. Now if we are right in supposing the pictures alluded to in the letters—the lady in the blue dress and the nude woman—are the pictures we know (which came from Urbino), it seems obvious that they cannot have been portraits of the Duchess. And, again, we have the Duchess's portrait painted at this time, in which we see a woman of forty-three, which was in truth her age.

In June, 1539, Guidobaldo, Duke of Urbino now, received three portraits, of the Emperor, the King of France, and the Turkish Sultan, from Titian. Vasari speaks of them, but they have been lost. In 1542–44 he painted a banner for the Brotherhood of Corpus Domini at Urbino—the Resurrection and the Last Supper. The pictures were shortly afterwards framed, and are now in the Urbino Gallery (10). Then in November, 1546, Duchess Giulia Varana of Urbino writes impatiently to Titian, sending at the same time some sleeves he had asked for, and hoping that he will not delay longer to finish "our portraits" (GRONAU, *op cit.*, p. 99). And letters of Aretino in 1545 confirm the fact that Titian was painting portraits of the Duke and Duchess. Then in February, 1547, one of the courtiers of Urbino sent Titian a dress of the Duchess, adding that "a handsomer one would have been sent if he had not wished for one of crimson or pink velvet"; a damask one was sent of the desired colour. The portrait by Titian in the State Apartments of the Pitti Palace, discovered only a few years ago, is said to be of Catherine de' Medici, by Tintoretto. It is, however, certainly Titian's (GRONAU, *op. cit.*, p. 100), and is probably the missing portrait of the Duchess Giulia.

Nature to witness, making her confess that Art was positively metamorphosed into herself; and to this, each wrinkle, each hair, each spot bears testimony, whilst the colouring not only exhibits vigour of person, but displays manliness of mind. The vermilion hue of that velvet drapery behind him is reflected in the lustrous armour he wears. How fine the effect of his casquet-plumes, reproduced on the burnished cuirass of the mighty general! Even his batons of command are perfect nature, chiefly that of his own adventure, thus budding on the faith of his renown, which began to shed its glories in the war which humbled his private foe. Who would assert that the truncheons confided to him by the Church, Venice, and Florence, were not of silver?"[1] In Aretino's letter were enclosed two sonnets on the portrait and its companion; they will be found in the Appendix, No. XI., together with one in which Bernardo Tasso appeals to Titian for a like-

It is unfinished, and the dress is of rose colour. It is one of his finest portraits.

There were two portraits at least of Guidobaldo by Titian, one of 1538 and one of 1545; one of these is said to have been in Florence in the seventeenth century. Gronau suggests that the "Young Englishman" of the Pitti Gallery (92), the finest portrait even Titian ever painted, may be one of them. But I cannot persuade myself that that figure is other than English. Yet if it be, it might well companion the Bella.

In 1545 Titian, on his way to Rome, travelled by Ferrara and Pesaro, where Guidobaldo, who had accompanied him, entertained him and made him many presents, sending a company of horse with him to Rome. There follows an interval of twenty years, in which their friendship seems not altogether to have been forgotten. Then between 1564 and 1567 Titian painted several pictures for Guidobaldo, among them a "Christ" and a "Madonna"; in 1573 he apparently had another commission. It is impossible to say what these pictures may have been.

[1] The style of Aretino was often rugged, wayward, and unintelligible, like his character. He seems to imagine that, of the three batons placed behind the Duke, one, bearing acorns and oak leaves, alludes to his successful campaigns on his own account, for recovery of his states. *Lettere Pittoriche*, I., App. No. 29. The force of colour peculiar to this, above all Titian's works, cannot be fully given by the burin, especially not by the *mezza macchia* style in which it has been engraved for this volume. Our frontispiece, though accurate as a likeness, is accordingly among the least effective illustrations in our work. No other original portrait of the Duke has fallen under my observation; and if the slight youthful figure introduced by Raffaele into the Disputa and School of Athens really was meant for him, no resemblance can be traced in it.

Anderson

THE VENUS OF URBINO

Supposed portrait of the Duchess Leonora, after the picture by Titian in the Uffizi Gallery, Florence
Once in the Ducal Collection

ness of his lady-love. Aretino's lines regarding the Duke may be thus literally rendered :—

> "Fear on the crowd from either eyebrow falls;
> Fire in his glance, and pride upon his front,
> The spacious seat of honour and resolve.
> Beneath that bust of steel, with arm prepared,
> Burns valour, prompt all peril to repel,
> From sacred Italy, that on his worth relies."

The other sonnet, descriptive of Leonora's likeness, alludes to the master's harmonious tints as figuring varied charms met in her character, such as humility of disposition, decorum in dress and manners, sustained by a dignified expression. In her features, beauty united with modesty, a rare combination; and grace was enthroned on her eyebrows. Prudence presided over her becoming silence, and other excellent qualities marvellously adorned her forehead. Nor are these praises exaggerated. Those who attentively observe this portrait in the Uffizi Gallery will readily acknowledge that, although, perhaps, more elaborated in its details than any other from the master's hand, his pencil never attained greater breadth, nor embodied high art in more severe character.[1]

The connection thus formed by Titian with the house of Urbino was maintained after the accession of Duke Guidobaldo, through whom Paul III. invited him to Bologna in 1543, where he painted that Pontiff with his wonted success. About the same time the Duke commissioned from him a likeness of himself, which was finished two years later. The misfortune sustained by its disappearance may be appreciated from the words of Aretino, who, writing to Guidobaldo, says, "For he has so embodied in his colours the very air you breathe, that in the same

[1] The *zebelino* on the Duchess's knee was the fashionable bag or reticule of that day, made of an entire sable-skin, the animal's head, richly jewelled, forming its clasp. Giulia della Rovere d' Este commissioned such a one from a jeweller at Bologna in 1555, and paid him forty-six dollars to account.

attitude as you at this instant appear to others at Vicenza, we now behold you in Venice, where we circle, bow, and pay court to you, just as do your suite who are in waiting upon you there." Vecellio lived among men whose talents, and fame, and forms, and dress deserved commemoration; and to such he did justice, for painter and sitters were worthy of each other, conferring a mutual and enduring illustration. His pencil, and those of his followers, were singularly happy in preserving individual character, although wanting in ideality and intense expression. But their great excellence displayed itself in the representation of voluptuous scenes, adapted alike to their glowing tints and the taste of their countrymen.

In 1545, Titian repaired to Rome, at the request of Cardinal Alessandro Farnese, visiting Urbino*[1] on the way, and receiving several commissions which he could not stay to execute. Setting forward on his journey, he was conducted by Guidobaldo in person to Pesaro, and thence by an escort to Rome. The impression left upon the painter in this passage is thus described to the Duke, by his friend Aretino:—"Titian writes me, 'Worship the Lord Guidobaldo, gossip!—worship him, I say, gossip! for no princely bounty can compare with his.' And these exclamations are his grateful acknowledgment of the mounted escort of seven attendants which your Excellency provided for him, with good company, and all paid; over and above the ease wherewith, amid caresses, honours, and gifts, you made him feel quite at home. I was, indeed, melted by the account he gave me of your marvellous efforts to benefit, honour, and welcome him." We have, to the like purpose, the less exceptionable testimony of Bembo, who, on the 10th of October, wrote to Girolamo Querini: "I must add that your old friend Maestro Tiziano is here, who represents himself as much beholden to you.

*[1] Apparently he only went to Pesaro. Cf. note *2, p. 390.

Anderson

SLEEPING VENUS

After the picture by Giorgione in the Dresden Gallery, after which the Venus of Urbino was painted

. . . The Lord Duke of Urbino has treated him with exceeding kindness, retaining him about his person, and bringing him as far as Pesaro, and thence forwarding him thither, well mounted and attended, for all which he acknowledges himself under great obligations."

Vasari mentions, as executed by Titian for the court of Urbino, portraits of Popes Sixtus IV., Julius II., and Paul III.; of Charles V., Francis I., Sultan Solyman, and the Cardinal of Lorraine. I have not succeeded in tracing any of these with certainty, but two half-lengths of beautiful women, added to the list by Ticozzi, may probably be the Flora*[1] now in the Uffizi Gallery, and the Bella in the Pitti Palace: their features exhibit considerable analogy with each other, and with the former of two pictures we are now to describe. In the last number of the Appendix we shall rectify various errors regarding Titian's two celebrated Venuses in the Tribune at Florence. One of them, painted for Guidobaldo II., has no proper right to that title, being correctly called in the old Urbino inventories, "a naked woman lying." She is stretched at full length along a bed, on which is a linen sheet, with a green curtain above. A tiny spaniel crouches at her feet, and two waiting-maids are searching in a chest near an open balcony, for garments wherewith to veil her all-exposed charms. The languor of her eye, the listless attitudes into which her limbs have dropped, personify voluptuousness, and express a mind quietly gloating over the past. A certain harmony and warmth of tone, fused throughout the vast surface of delicate flesh-tints and snowy linen, over which broad daylight streams without shadow, are worthy of our highest admiration; and the relief given to the figure, with little aid from the chiaroscuro, is probably unrivalled. The companion picture,

*[1] It seems unlikely that the *Flora* was ever in Urbino. At any rate, in the seventeenth century it was in the collection of the Spanish ambassador at Amsterdam (cf. GRONAU, *op cit.*, p. 289).

which was not, however, executed for Urbino, represents an equally nude figure on a couch of purple damask, near a balcony opening upon a distant landscape. The boy of love, archly toying upon her bosom, decides the subject to be Venus; and her glowing eye-ball expresses the ardour that thrills through her veins. The full aud solid flesh is true to those developed forms which, still characterising the women about Treviso, formed the standard of female perfection in Titian's studio; and although the skill with which they undulate, softened by chiaroscuro, demands all praise, there may yet be some who, dissenting from such an ideal of beauty, wish this mortal mould had been refined into the symmetry of that "perfect goddess-ship" which close by "loves in stone." Having thus noticed these nudities, it may be well to add, that the shameless Aretino, while boasting of his own unrestrained debaucheries, bears testimony to the purity of Titian's morals, and the habitual control under which his passions were maintained.

As an antidote, perhaps, to so sensual a production, Titian sent to Urbino, with his Venus, a picture offering the utmost contrast in sentiment and artistic treatment. It was the first of those Magdalens,*[1] frequently repeated by him with slight variations, of whom not a few school copies may be seen passing for originals. Ridolfi tells us that he caught the idea from an antique sculpture, transforming it into a penitent daughter of sin. Yet he has treated it according to those ideas of female beauty which it was the peculiar province of the Venetian school to develop, and which in Italy have passed into the proverbial phrase of *un bel pezzo di carne*, meaning a buxom dame. To borrow the words of Ticozzi, "he has represented a noble lady, who, while yet in her prime, had

*[1] Pitti Gallery, No. 67. We know nothing of this picture save that it must have been painted about 1530–35, and that Vasari saw it in the Guardaroba of the Palace of Urbino.

PORTRAIT OF HIS WIFE, BY LUCAS CRANACH

From the picture in the Roscoe Collection, Liverpool. Possibly modelled on the Venus of Urbino

abandoned the delights and delicacies of her station. With due regard to her past position, he has lavished upon her the beauties of form and complexion; her repentance he has characterised with the most devoted expression of which art is capable." The ascetic sentiment prevailing in this work is well adapted to the sympathies of the Roman Church, among whose followers it has ever been more a favourite than with Protestant amateurs.

Our notice of Titian in connection with the court of Urbino, may be closed by a letter, which, in the servile phrase of this century, ventures thus to dun Guidobaldo for payment of a picture sent him five months before:—

"To the most illustrious and most excellent Lord, the Lord Duke of Urbino.

"Most illustrious and most excellent Lord,

"Very many days have now passed since your most illustrious Excellency desired that I should be advised how your [servant] Agatone ought to have remunerated me for the picture which I sent to your most illustrious Excellency. Which he not having done, although six months are nearly elapsed since the 10th of March, but having only put me off with words, I have chosen to take the step of informing your illustrious Excellency by these lines, that your boundless liberality may aid my necessity, though I admit that I may thereby appear wanting in modesty. I know that your illustrious Excellency, occupied by important affairs, cannot have your mind distracted by such trifles, yet I consider it my duty respectfully to let you know my difficulty; and beseeching you to retain me in your wonted favour, I humbly kiss your most distinguished hands. From Venice, the 27th of October, 1567. Your most illustrious Excellency's most humble servant,

"TITIANO VECELLIO."

In one of his visits to Venice, about 1559, Guidobaldo, chancing to enter a church of the Crociferi, where a youth was engaged in copying the St. Laurence of Titian, he entered into conversation with him, and subsequently returned more than once to observe his progress. On one of these occasions, while the Duke was hearing mass at a neighbouring altar, the young artist seized the opportunity to sketch his likeness, which was shown him by an attendant. Pleased with its success, and with the painter's manners, he invited him to enter his service. The object of this casual patronage proved not unworthy of it. He was JACOPO PALMA the younger, a name already known to art; for his grandfather, who bore it, had distinguished himself among the scholars of Giorgione and Titian; and his aunt, Violante, was mistress and favourite model of the latter. Palma Giovane, then in his sixteenth year, accompanied the Duke to Pesaro, where he employed his pencil in copying works of Raffaele and Titian. The only anecdote preserved of his residence in the court of Urbino proves that he continued to enjoy his patron's favour; for, in a dispute with the house-steward as to his luncheon, the latter was ordered to treat the youth with more consideration. In order to obtain for him every advantage, the Duke sent him to the charge of his brother, Cardinal della Rovere, at Rome. After there diligently studying antique marbles, with the works of Michael Angelo and those of Polidoro di Caravaggio, Palma, at twenty-four, returned to Venice. On his way, he paid a visit of thanks to Guidobaldo, and by his works removed certain unfavourable impressions made by unfriendly detractors in his absence. Of those which he may have executed for this court, no account has reached us, beyond a notice that Francesco Maria II. paid him, at Venice, 1591, 86 scudi for a Madonna and a St. Francis, which do not, however, appear in the wardrobe inventories. He painted for the metropolitan cathedral at Urbino the Discovery of the Holy

Cross, a picture praised by Lanzi beyond its merits; and for Pesaro, a S. Ubaldo, and the Annunciation.

Another Venetian, patronised by Guidobaldo, was GIAN-BATTISTA FRANCO, surnamed *il Semolei*, who was brought to Urbino on a recommendation of Girolamo Genga, in order to paint the choir of the cathedral. He there treated the favourite Umbrian theme of the Coronation of the Madonna in a manner utterly at variance with the old feeling, taking as his prototype the Judgment of Michael Angelo, of whom he was a devoted and assiduous imitator. This work having been destroyed by the fall of the roof in 1789, we shall content ourselves with the description of Vasari, who had seen it, and whose leaning must have been favourable to a work produced under such influence. "And so, in imitation of Buonarroti's Judgment, he represented in the sky the glorification of the saints, scattered on clouds over the roof, with a whole choir of angels around our Lady, in the act of ascending to heaven, where Christ waited to crown her, whilst a number of patriarchs, prophets, sibyls, apostles, martyrs, confessors, and maidens, in varied groups and attitudes, manifested their joy at the arrival of the glorious Virgin. This subject might have afforded to Battista an excellent opportunity of proving his ability, had he adopted a better plan, not only in the practical management of his fresco, but in conducting his entire theme with more judicious arrangement. But in this work he fell into his usual system, constantly repeating the same faces, figures, draperies, and extremities. The colouring was likewise utterly destitute of beauty, and everything was strained and puny. Hence the work, when finished, greatly disappointed the Duke, Genga, and every one, much having been expected from his known capacity for design." Several easel pictures of his, in the sacristy of the Duomo, are weak in composition and poor in colour; but one of St. Peter and St. Paul, before the Madonna and Child, is an exceedingly grandiose production, in the Buonarroti style. We shall have further occasion to speak of this artist in our next chapter. He was born about 1498, and lived to the age of sixty-three; but aware of his deficiencies as a painter, he betook himself in a great measure to engraving, for which his accuracy as a draftsman well qualified him.

In absence of native sculptors of eminence, the plastic art never was much cherished in our duchy, and few commissions were given, except for decorative or monumental purposes. The festive arches on Duchess Vittoria's marriage were probably designed by Tiziano Aspetti, a bronzist of Upper Italy. Her husband having acquired a Leda by Bartolomeo Ammanati of Florence, he was called to Urbino, to construct a memorial for Francesco Maria I. It does not, however, appear to have been successful, and being quite disproportioned to the little octangular church of Sta. Chiara, of which it occupied the centre, it was removed after the Devolution, and probably destroyed. SEBASTIANO BECIVENNI of Mercatello, was celebrated as a decorative sculptor, and his dexterity is attested by two pulpits in the duomo at Arezzo, dated 1563. In 1581, Francesco Maria II. commissioned two small statues from John of Bologna, and in the following year his minister at Rome wrote, proposing to send him a miniature painter from thence, at a monthly salary of ten golden scudi, besides board and travelling expenses. Late in life, he had his own and his father's portraits executed in mosaic by Luigi Gaetano at Venice. The statue of Duke Federigo, which we have already mentioned as modelled by Baroccio, was executed for this Duke by Girolamo Campagna of Venice, and one of his grandfather, attired as a Roman warrior, leaning on his baton of command, and resting upon a stump, was the work of Giovanni Bandini of Florence, an eminent scholar of Bandinelli. After his sovereignty had virtually passed from the bereaved Duke, he disposed of this memorial of its brighter days in a touching letter to the Doge of Venice, which finely illustrates the resignation beautifully exemplified in all the correspondence of his latter years:—

"Most serene Prince,

"My grandfather, the Lord Duke Francesco Maria, was during life honoured by your serene state with such high authority and dignities, that, even after his decease, its esteem and favour have ever been specially exhibited towards his posterity and race; in these, now about to close in my person, your Highness will lose a line of supporters whose services are well known to you. Yet, being unwilling that these good offices should pass entirely from memory, I have resolved to present to the serene Republic and your Highness, the statue which I erected in testimony of dutiful respect to my said grandfather; for nowhere can it be more fittingly placed than in your renowned city. I therefore herewith send it to you, and with the more pleasure from knowing that your state will gladly receive the portrait of one who so faithfully served it, and who, though no longer able to do so directly, will, virtually and by example, demonstrate how your Republic ought to be served. It will, at all events, afford irrefragable evidence of his attachment to that cause for which he would have desired longer life, and will prove a sure token of my unbounded devotion to your Highness, which, indeed, I cannot more fittingly demonstrate: beseeching, however, that your Highness will regard this act as a solemn testimony of the old and continued love of my house for your distinguished state, which God preserve as long as my unbounded wishes; and so I kiss your Highness's hands with devoted affection.

"Your Highness's most devoted son and servant,

"FRANCESCO MARIA DELLA ROVERE, DUKE.[1]

"From Castel Durante, this . . ., 1625."

[1] *Carteggio d' Artisti*, vol. III., 540.

The statue now stands in the court of the Doge's ducal palace, thus inscribed: "To Francesco Maria I., Duke of Urbino, leader of the armies of this Republic; erected at Pesaro, and recommended to the affectionate care of Venice by Francesco Maria II., when bereaved of progeny." The original inscription ran thus: "To Francesco Maria an eminent general, leader of the armies of the holy Romish Church, the Florentine republic, the Venetian state, and the princes of the League against the Turks, and of his own troops; the conqueror, subduer, and sustainer of potentates at home and abroad; his grandson, Duke Francesco Maria II. had this erected."

CHAPTER LV

Of the manufacture of majolica in the Duchy of Urbino.

THE influence of beauty upon arts usually considered as mechanical, and the exercise of creative talent upon substances of a common or trifling character, are equally proofs of a pervading refinement. It was accordingly a striking feature of Italy in her golden days, that nearly every sort of handiwork felt that influence, and in its turn served to maintain public taste at an elevated standard. To uncultivated or unobservant minds it may seem ridiculous to appreciate the state of high art in a country from the forms of culinary utensils, the colouring of plates, or the carving of a peach-stone; yet the elegance of Etruscan civilisation is nowhere more manifest than in household bronzes; the majolica of Urbino has preserved the designs and the feeling of Raffaele; the genius of Cellini did not spurn the most homely materials. The architects of the Revival were often sculptors; its engineers constructed clocks; while painters then exercised the crafts of jewellery and wood-gilding, or lent their pencils to beautify the potter's handiwork. Our undertaking would accordingly be incomplete without some notice of majolica, or decorative pottery, which under the patronage of her princes brought fame and wealth to the duchy of Urbino.[1]

[1] We have had frequent occasion to notice the encouragement given at Urbino to the exact sciences, and the consequent success of those arts most depending upon them. Thus the Barocio family were celebrated for the

The earliest work on the ceramic art is that of Giambattista Passeri of Pesaro, who was born about a hundred and fifty years since, and whose inquiries into geology and antiquities attracted him to a subject cognate to them both. While studying the fossils of Central Italy, the transition was not difficult to their fictile products; and after vainly endeavouring to methodise the pottery of Etruria and Magna Grecia, he tried the same good office with better success upon the majolica of his native province.[1] Nor is his theme of so narrow an interest as might on a superficial view be supposed. The existence of pottery has frequently proved a valuable aid to historical research; and even now our surest test of Etruscan refinement is supplied by the painted vases ex-

accuracy of their mathematical instruments and timepieces, while watchmaking attracted great attention from all the della Rovere dukes. Their family portraits very generally exhibit a table-clock of some eccentric form, and their gifts to princes and royal personages were often chronometers made in their state. One of these, sent to Pius V., exhibited the planetary movements and other complex revolutions of the solar system; another, worn by his Holiness in a ring, marked the hours by gently pricking his finger. In 1535, Francesco Maria I. presented to Charles V., at Naples, a ring wherein a watch struck the hours; and many similar notices occur in the correspondence of his grandson, the last Duke. Guidobaldo II. was especially fond of such mechanical curiosities. Having received from one Giovan Giorgio Capobianco of Vicenza, the Praxiteles of tiny chiselling, a ring which held a watch, whereupon were engraved the signs of the zodiac, with a figure that pointed to and struck the hours—he interfered to save the artist's life, when condemned to death for an assassination at Venice. In gratitude for this favour, the latter made for the Duchess a silver chessboard contained in a cherry-stone; nor should we omit to add that he displayed the same ingenuity on a wider field as an architect and engineer. So, too, Filippo Santacroce, of Urbino, and his sons, are celebrated by Count Cicognara for their minute carvings on gems, ivory, and nuts.

[1] The subject has since met with more attention, but no other work has been expressly dedicated to it. We may refer to VASARI, LANZI, and GAYE, *passim;* RICCI, *Notizie delle Belle Arti in Gubbio; Kunstblatt*, No. 51; MONTANARI, *Lettera interno ad alcune Majoliche dipinte nella collezione Massa* in *Giornale Arcadico di Roma*, XXXVII., 333; BRONGNIART, *Traité des Arts Ceramiques;* MARRYAT, *History of Pottery and Porcelain.* It is both an advantage and a pleasure to refer readers unacquainted with this interesting art, to the charming and accurate representations of azulejo, Robbian ware, and majolica, given in the last of these works. It is greatly to be desired that Mr. Marryat may, in continuation of his subject, and with access to English collections unknown to me, supply much information which this slight sketch cannot include.

MAIOLICA

A plate of Urbino ware of about 1540 in the British Museum

humed from the sepulchres of an almost forgotten race.[1] It is not, however, important merely as affording landmarks useful in tracing the civilisation of nations; for, by combining taste with ingenuity, it gives to materials the most ordinary and almost fabulous value, thereby constituting one of the notable triumphs of mind over matter, and largely promoting the advance of intellectual culture. Even in early stages of national improvement, the plastic art, after contributing to the necessities of life, has often been the first to inspire elegance or embody true principles of form and afterwards of colour. Dealing with a substance readily found and easily manipulated, wherein nature might be imitated or fancy developed, it was the precursor of sculpture, the patron of painting, and the handmaid of architecture.

The earthenware made in Central Italy was usually called *majolica*, in our spelling maiolica. The derivation of its etymology, from the island of Majorca, seems no mere superficial inference from similarity of sounds. Its peculiarity was a glaze, which, besides giving a vehicle for colour, remedied the permeable quality of ancient pottery. Such a glazed surface had long been known to the Saracens, and was imported by the Moors into Spain and the Balearic Isles, in the shape of gaily-tinted tiles, arranged in bands or diaper on their buildings. To these succeeded *azulejos*, generally of blue in various shades, which were mosaicked into church walls in various histori-

[1] We enter not upon the contested question of the origin of these productions; wherever made, they prove the taste of those who owned and appreciated them. Besides, the ruder varieties were certainly indigenous to Central Italy from an early period. Neither need we trace the analogy between majolica and enamel. The latter was not unknown to the ancients, though brought by them to no ornamental perfection. During the dark ages, it was used as an accessory of metal sculpture for many purposes of religious art, and was even introduced into large works, such as bronze doors. The splendid reliquary at Orvieto, enamelled on silver at Siena by Ugolino Vieri in 1338, as well as the *paliotti* of Florence and Pistoja executed in that and the following centuries, show to what perfection this art had attained, ere the painting of porcelain was practised in Italy.

cal compositions, from designs which Mr. Stirling ascribes to Murillo's pencil. The conquests or commerce of the Pisans imported this fashion, at first by incorporating concave coloured tiles among brickwork, afterwards, at Pesaro, by the use of encaustic flooring. Nor can we exclude from view that the earliest Italian ware has decorations either in geometrical patterns, or with shamrock-shaped foliations, of a character rather Saracenic than indigenous, and more indicative of moresque extraction than were the apocryphal armorial bearings of Spain and Majorca, at a period when such insignia were often borrowed as mere ornaments, in ignorance of their origin and meaning. The fabric thus introduced spread over most of Central Italy, and between 1450 and 1700 was largely practised at the towns of Arezzo, Perugia, Spello, Nocera, Città di Castello, Florence, Bologna, Ferrara, Ravenna, Rimini, Forlì, and Faenza (whence its French name *fayence*), Pesaro, Urbino, Fermignano, Castel Durante, and Gubbio, as well as at various places in the Abruzzi.

There is, however, another quarter to which vitrified or encaustic ware may be ascribed, in so far at least as regards improved methods and more important results. Luca della Robbia*[1] was born at Florence in 1399, and from being a jeweller, took to modelling statues and bas-reliefs in clay. Annoyed by the fragile nature of these, and perhaps by the doubtful success of *terra cotta*, he discovered a mode of glazing the surface of his beautiful works, with, it is said, a mixture of tin, *terra ghetta* (from the lake of Thrasimene), antimony, and other mineral substances. The secret of this varnish was transmitted in the inventor's family until about 1550: it ended in a female, with whose husband, Andrea Benedetto Buglione, it died. Recent attempts to revive the art at Florence have proved but partially successful, and wholly unre-

*[1] For all that concerns the Della Robbia, cf. MAUD CRUTTWELL, *Luca and Andrea della Robbia and their School* (Dent, 1904).

munerative; indeed, the mechanical difficulties exceed those of sculpture, including the separation of the work into sections before drying and burning it, and its eventual reunion into one piece. Although neither mild nor equal, the climate at Florence does not seem to influence the Robbian fabrics in the open air, but they have suffered from the frosts and snows of our duchy, where several are broken or blistered, such as the lunette of S. Domenico at Urbino. By much the finest specimen I know there remains [1843] in the desecrated oratory of the Sforzan palace [of 1484] at Gradara; it may be by Andrea della Robbia, and represents an enthroned Madonna and Child, nearly life-size, with attendant saints, the predella complete, and the whole a fine monument of Christian art. Originally, the plastic surface of Robbian ware was of a uniform glistening white, which, though cold in effect, is very favourable to the pure religious sentiment at which it generally aimed. The eyes were then blackened, in order to aid expression. Next, the pallid figures were relieved against a deep cerulean ground. The followers of Luca added fruits and flowers, wreathed in their proper colours. Agincourt justly regrets that these men were led into such innovations by a desire for mastering difficulties, and the ambition of adding to sculpture the beauties of painting; for when colour is given to draperies, the eye is ill-reconciled to an addition which seems to transfer such productions from the category of high art to the level of waxwork. By a further modification, the flesh parts were left unglazed, bringing the warm tone of terra cotta to harmonize with the coloured costumes, architecture and backgrounds being still usually white or deep blue. Passeri, however, asserts for this coloured glaze an earlier discovery in his own province, where pottery was certainly made in the fourteenth century. But it is generally admitted that the art of combining with it lively colours was greatly improved after Pesaro had passed under the Sforza. In 1462,

Ventura di Maestro Simone dei Piccolomini of Siena established himself there, along with Matteo di Raniere, of a noble family at Cagli, in order to manufacture earthenware, and may have directed attention to the productions of della Robbia, who had already been employed at Rimini by its tyrant, Sigismondo Pandolfo Malatesta.

An account of majolica*[1] ought to contain the various places noted for its manufacture, the peculiar qualities distinguishing their respective productions, the methods by which these qualities were given, and the artists most successful in producing them. But on most of these points we are left in great ignorance, which my limited observation has not enabled me to dispel. All I can offer is a list of the manufactories and artists, classed to the best of my power, and preceded by a few very general notices of the process.

The Chevalier Cipriano Picolpasso, of Castel Durante, doctor in medicine and majolica-painter under Duke Guidobaldo II., left a MS. professing to record the secrets of his art; but Passeri, after examination, pronounces his revelations trite, and his historical notices barren. It is, however, agreed that Pesaro was the first site within the duchy of Urbino where the fabric attained celebrity, and that its earliest efforts were called *mezza* or "half" majolica. This is distinguished by a coarse gritty fracture, of dirty grey colour, and a glaze which does not take much lustre or transparency. It is generally in the form of plates, many of them huge, all clumsily thick, and frequently of a dingy, ill-vitrified yellow on the back. The lustre on the front is rather pearly than metallic; but prismatic, or even golden, iridescence is met with. These productions are assigned, by Passeri and others, to the fifteenth century; but the arms of Leo X. appear on one

*[1] The finest collection of Italian majolica in the world is probably that in Pesaro in the possession of the Municipality.

MAIOLICA
A plate of Cartel Durante ware of about 1524
"The divine and beautiful Lucia"

in the mediæval exhibition of 1850 (No. 543, belonging to Mr. S. Isaacs), and on another in the Hotel Cluny, at Paris; while, in the museum of the Commendatore Kestner, Hanoverian minister at Rome, is a third, designed after Marc Antonio. The "fine" majolica attained its greatest perfection at Urbino between 1530 and 1560, and it was prized chiefly for the perfect vitrification and transparency of its varnish, the comparative thinness and whiteness of the texture, the brilliant colouring, and masterly design. Gubbian pottery combined in some degree the qualities of half and fine ware, but excelled all others in metallic and prismatic glaze.

We shall not encumber our pages with conjectural or vague hints as to the processes of these interesting fabrics. Iridescent lustre obliquely reflected, and a white glaze of dazzling transparency, were the objects respectively aimed at. The former was attained by preparations of lead, copper, silver, and gold; the latter was imparted by dipping the half-baked pottery into a white varnish, over which, while moist, the subject was rapidly painted, correction or retouching being incompatible with the immediate absorption of its colours, which, apart from accidental fusion of tints, and flaws in the furnace, abundantly accounts for the frequent inaccuracy of design. The metallic lustre depended a good deal on lead, the whiteness on a free use of tin.

Those early plates of Pesaro were very rarely signed by their artists; but one in the Hague Museum bears a cipher resembling C. H. O. N., whilst another, quoted by Pungileoni, has a mark composed of G. A. T. interlaced. In 1478, Sixtus IV. wrote his acknowledgments to Costanzo Sforza for a present of "*Vasa fictilia*, most elegantly wrought, which, for the donor's sake, are prized as if of gold or silver rather than of earthenware."[1] In a similar letter, Lorenzo the Magnificent thanked

[1] Archiv. Dipl. Urbinate at Florence [1845].

[Roberto] Malatesta, observing that "they please me entirely by their perfections and rarity, being quite novelties in these parts, and are valued more than if of silver," the donor's arms serving daily to recall their origin.[1] Passeri gives a curious proclamation by the Lord of Pesaro, in 1486, narrating that, for good favour to the citizens, and considering a fabric of earthen vases to have been of old practised in that city, superior, by general admission, to all others produced in Italy, and that there were now more workshops than ever,—importation of any species thereof from foreign parts was prohibited, on pain of confiscation and fine, half to the informer, oil and water jars only excepted; and further that, within eight days, all foreign vases should be sent out of the state. In 1510, majolica was numbered among the trades of Pesaro, and in 1532, Duke Francesco Maria confirmed the protection for it which we have just cited. I have not met with the patent for "application of gold to Italian faience," quoted by Mr. H. Rogers as granted, in 1509, to Giacomo Lanfranco of Pesaro, by Duke Guidobaldo, who, by the way, was then dead.

It may have been soon after this date that "fine" superseded "half" ware in the potteries of Pesaro, where the art obtained a new stimulus on transference hither of the court by Duke Guidobaldo II. Thereafter it is impossible to distinguish earthenware issuing from these establishments from that of Urbino, their quality being similar, and the artists in many cases identical; but by that Prince's patronage it unquestionably attained its greatest perfection. A petition by certain makers of Pesaro for protection, is given in X. of the Appendix, as illustrating then received principles of trade, as well as of this fabric. It bears date in 1552; and in 1569, the Duke

[1] GAYE, *Carteggio*, I., p. 304. He was probably Roberto Malatesta, who served the Florentines in 1479, and died 1482; so Gaye's date of 1490 seems erroneous.

granted to Giacomo Lanfranco, of that city, a patent for twenty-five years, guarded by 500 scudi of penalty, for his inventions in applying gold to vases, and in constructing them of great size (exceeding the capacity of two *some*), of antique forms, and wrought in relievo. As a further encouragement, he and his father Girolamo were exempted from every impost or tax, and from mill-dues on grinding ten *some* of grain annually. Proud of the reputation of his native pottery, Guidobaldo was in the habit of presenting services of majolica to foreign princes and personages, who again often sent commissions to be executed in the duchy, bearing their arms. A double service was, according to Vasari, given by him to Charles V.; and another to Philip II., painted by Orazio Fontana from Taddeo Zuccaro's designs; while Passeri mentions a set presented to Fra Andrea of Volterra, each piece inscribed *G. V. V. D.* [*Guid Vbaldonis Urbini Ducis*] *Munus, F. Andreæ Volaterano.* I found in the Oliveriana MSS. a letter addressed to his brother the Cardinal of Urbino, describing a *buffet* for Monsignor Farnese, with its inventory, which will be found at XI. of the Appendix. The most important, however, of the ducal commissions was a very numerous set of jars, of many sizes and shapes, for the use of his laboratory [*spezeria*], a fashion imitated by other dilettanti. Blue, yellow, and green are their prevailing hues; they are always labelled with the name of some drug or mixture, and occasionally have a portrait or other subject. The original set was gifted by Francesco Maria II. to the treasury of Loreto, where about three hundred and eighty of them still serve their original purpose, many duplicates being met with in collections. Specimens will be found engraved by Bartoli, and in Mr. Marryat's beautiful volume; the offers of various crowned heads to replace them by others of gold and silver, are well-known travellers' tales, but in truth they are far from choice specimens.

Like other branches of fine art, majolica-painting showed an early preference for sacred themes; but the primitive plates of Pesaro bear effigies of saints much more frequently than scripture histories, or doctrinal representations. Then came in a fashion for portraits of living or historical persons, including warriors, high-born dames, and classical heroes, inscribed with their names. These paintings are all flat and lifeless, with scarcely an attempt at relief, or graduated tints; the ornaments are rude, inclining to Moorish, and totally different from what is called arabesque. From the della Robbian influence were probably borrowed plates brimming with coloured fruits in relievo, a variety of little interest, but reminding us of similar French productions in a later period. In the sixteenth century, the mania of classicism, elsewhere discussed,[1] much affected majolica; and in its designs, although events of the Old Testament were not abandoned, saintly legends gave place to scenes from Ovid and Virgil. For behoof of the unlettered curious, the incident was shortly, often clumsily, described in blue letters on the back, with a reference to the text. In a few cases (perhaps of *amatorii* or nuptial gifts), I have found the very finest productions degraded by grossly indecent designs; in more numerous ones groups of nude figures disport themselves in the manner of Giulio Romano. Those in which Raffaelesque arabesques prevail, belong chiefly to the latter portion of Guidobaldo's reign. From that time the fabric decayed rapidly, owing partly to a general decline of æsthetic taste, partly to the impaired state of that Duke's finances, and the indifference of his successor. Even after historical compositions were neglected, considerable dexterity was displayed in painting trophies, arms, musical instruments, utensils, marine monsters, children, grotesques, birds, trees, flowers, fruits, and landscapes, designs of that class being easily repeated

[1] See vol. II.

MAIOLICA

A plate of Urbino ware about 1535. (The arms are Cardinal Pucci's)

and their inaccuracies passing for studied extravagance. But the drawing got worse, the colouring more feeble, as good artists dropped off, carrying with them their sketches, and superseded by engravings from Sadeler and other Flemings, whose vile taste contributed to lower the standard of better times.[1] Public favour, ever capricious, was successfully wooed by the oriental porcelain, which now found its way among the higher ranks, while the augmented supply of silver encouraged a more extended use of plate. Thus discredited, the manufacture progressively deteriorated, until, in 1722, the stoneware of Urbania was of the most ordinary description, the efforts of Cardinal Legate Stoppani to reinstate a better fabric having totally failed; and thus neglected, the most beautiful productions of its happier time were dispersed, or passed to the meanest uses, from which another whim of fashion, as much as the revival of a better taste, has suddenly rescued them.

Much of what has been said of the fine majolica of Pesaro is applicable to that ascribed to Urbino, most of which appears to have been made in the neighbouring towns of Fermignano, Gaifa, and Castel Durante (now Urbania), the alluvial washings of the Metauro being peculiarly adapted for the purest white glaze. Yet Pungileoni has wormed out of some old notorial protocols the names of M°. Giovanni di Donnino in 1477, and of M°. Francesco in 1501, both designed of Gardutia, potters *(figuli)* at Urbino. He also establishes that coloured figures were executed there in vases in 1521. Passeri denies that those ruby and gold colours for which we shall find Gubbio celebrated, and which certainly were known in the workshops of Pesaro, ever came into use at Urbino,— a conclusion which we shall have occasion to correct.

[1] In 1845, the Canon Staccoli at Urbino showed me a plate equally feeble in design and colour, signed *F. M. Doiz Fiamengo fecit*, a proof that it was no despised production of the time.

Indeed, this secret of metallic iridescence is said to have been known at Florence, and I have seen a plate of golden lustre bearing the emblem of the woolstaplers' guild [*arte della lana*]; but if such manufactory existed, I have found no notice of it, and the still flourishing one of Ginori in the Val d' Arno pretends to no such antiquity. I was shown at Florence a tile, on which Annibale Caracci's Galatea was represented with great accuracy of design, but poor and hard in colour, signed "*Ferdinand Campani*, *Siena*, 1736." In the latter town there is said to have been a fabric known by the name of *Terchi;* the analogous one, near Fermo, in the Abruzzi, called *Grue*, sent forth, I believe, most of those tiles, small plates, or cups and saucers,—ornamented with landscapes of tolerable design, but tinted in sickly yellow or blue, and totally devoid of style,—which abound in Lower Italy.

The prismatic glaze, especially of gold and ruby colour, was unequalled in those plates painted at Gubbio by Maestro Giorgio Andreoli, who appears to have come hither from Pavia with his brothers Salimbeni and Giovanni. His name was there enrolled among the nobility in 1498, but the dates affixed to his plates extend from 1518 to about 1537. He had previously executed several plastic works of the nature of della Robbia's figures, the principal of which was a Madonna del Rosario altar-piece for the Domenican church, which has been enthusiastically described in No. 928 of the London *Athenæum*. It was torn down by the French in their wonted course of rapine, and, to the disgrace of the local authorities of Gubbio, lay neglected for several years after the peace, until purchased for the Steidl Institut at Frankfort. The only other of his productions remaining at Gubbio is a life-sized statue of St. Anthony in the same church, quite inferior as regards design and religious feeling to those of the Tuscan sculptors, and which, though coloured, has no metallic lustre. He is said by Passeri to have lived until

1552; and of his family, who long occupied an honourable station in their native city, only a son, Cencio, followed his father's profession. I have seen a plate of this school at Mr. Forrest's, 54 Strand [1850], rudely signed with G; others have R, perhaps il Rovigese, whom I shall presently mention. M°. Prestino da Gubbio wrought about 1557, but the latest date I have seen with metallic lustre and the Gubbian mark is 1549, on which the iridescence was extremely feeble.

Passeri's assertion, that the Gubbian glaze was borrowed from the half-majolica of Pesaro, may be correct; but we might, perhaps, maintain for it a date as early as 1474, on the authority of a beautiful small plate possessing its peculiarities, and exhibiting Duke Federigo's name and profile in relief, within a coloured border of oak-leaves also in relief, made, possibly, on occasion of his alliance with the della Rovere, by marriage of the Lord Prefect with his daughter in that year. This interesting memorial is No. 2286 of the Mediæval Gallery at the Louvre. In Mr. Marryat's choice cabinet is a half-ware plate, bearing on the back a monogram, which that gentleman supposes of Maestro Giorgio's early period, before he had discovered the mode of obtaining iridescent varnishes. It displays a group of nude figures in pale greyish tints, without any approach to brilliant colouring. His usual signature was dashed off with a metalliferous brush on the back, *M°. G°. da Vgubio*, with the date, as at No. 11 of the same facsimiles, from a plate in my possession. Such pieces are rare, and highly prized; their subjects are usually saints, classical groups, or grotesques, vases being very seldom met with. A branch of this fabric is said to have been seated at Nocera; and several, with bright red and blue tracery on a gold metallic ground, dated 1537–8, in the choice cabinet of Signor Serafino Tordelli at Spoleto [1845], are supposed by him of that fabric. Among other exquisite specimens, he has one by Maestro Giorgio, 1529, rivalling the finest miniature, and representing Archimedes measuring a globe, in front of the Communal Palace at Gubbio.

Thus much regarding the various manufactories of majolica connected with Urbino. The forms and purposes to which it was turned were very various. The first plates of Pesaro, chiefly of great size [*bacili*], were probably for table use, but a variety of them, called *amatorii*, were either tender souvenirs or marriage gifts. These usually had the lady's portrait, with the complimentary epithet of Bella, as in this example now in my possession; at other times united hands and a transfixed heart, with a motto of affection, moralising, or banter. Several such have been described by Passeri, Marryat, and others, but I shall add a few which have come under my observation. 1. At Florence: *Francesca bella a paragon di tutti*, "Frances, of beauty comparable to any one." 2. At Rome: *Nemo sua sorte contentus erat*, "Each has something to grumble about." 3. Sir Thomas B. Hepburn; a lady holding a gigantic pink: *Non è si vago el fiore che non imbiacca o casca*, "There is no flower so lovely but fades or droops." 4. Rome; a dame of rueful countenance: *Sola miseria caret invidia*, "Only the miserable escape envy." 5. Pesaro, Massa collection: *Per dormire non si acquista*, "The indolent get nothing." 6. Florence: *Chi bien guida sua barcha sempre emporto*, "Who steers well his bark, always makes the harbour." 7. Pesaro:—

S' il dono è picolo e di pocho valore,
Basta la fedel povere se redore.

"If small the gift and scant of merit
A poor slave's faith,—enough, you share it."[1]

[1] The rules of syntax are in these often overstepped, and conjecture left to eke out the sense. My reading is literal, of *basta la fe del povere sevedore*, which is intelligible, and rhymes, as is not the case with *basta la fede, e' l povere se vedo*, the version of Passeri. This author tells us of a certain coy or mischievous Philomela who pierced her lover's present with holes and

MAIOLICA

Plate of Cartel Durante ware about 1540, with a portrait medallion within a border of oak leaves. This pattern was called "Cerquata" or "al Urbinata," the oak being the badge of the Rovere house

8, 9. Florence, and evidently nuptial presents: *Per fin che vivo, io sempre t' amero*, "While I live, you I love"; the other, a bridegroom and bride exchanging a hearty kiss. Most of these portrait-plates were deep, and are said not to have been delivered empty. Brides received them brimming with jewels; for dancing partners they were filled with fruits and confections; to a lady in child-bed was presented a salver containing the sort of chamber service called in French a *déjeûner de marié*, appropriately decorated with infant legends of gods and heroes; at children's balls, were given tiny plates of sugar-plums, whereon a dancing Cupid sounding his cymbal was often painted. 10. Massa collection,—this has a sadder import: *Un bel morire tutta la vita onora*, "A beautiful death confers illustration on a lifetime," was, no doubt, in memory of some venerated friend, and might have been used to serve her funeral meats.[1]

made of it a mouse-trap! Also of an exquisite Gubbian plate, portraying the *Daniella Diva*, who displays a wounded heart with the legend *Oime!* "Ah me." A drug-bottle in Mr. Marryat's collection, and engraved in his work, has the portrait of a lady whose squint is given to the life.

[1] In order to finish our notice of mottoes, a few others may be here added. 11. Massa collection; a female portrait, on whose breast are the arms of Montefeltro: *Viva, Viva il Duca di Urbino.* 12. Rome, Kestner Museum; another female portrait: *Ibit ad geminos lucida fama pollo* (?). 13. Kestner Museum and that at the Hague; St. Thomas probing the Saviour's wound: *Beati qui non viderunt et crediderunt*, "Blessed are they that have not seen, and yet have believed." 14. Spoleto, Tordelli collection; a beautiful female resisting a crowd of armed soldiery: 1540. *Italia mesta sottosopra volta, como pei venti in mare letorbid' onde, ch' or da una parte et hor da l' altra volta.* "1540. Dejected Italy, tossed like the wind-lashed waves, turning now hither now thither." 15. Rome,—satire on the sack of Rome; a warrior in antique armour strikes with a two-handed sword at a naked woman stretched in a lascivious posture, behind whom five others tremblingly await their fate: it is inscribed behind. 1534. *Roma lasciva dal buon Carlo quinto partita a mezza. Fra Xanto a. da Rovigo, Urbino.* "Rome, the wanton, cut up by the good Charles V.; by Brother Xante of Rovigo, at Urbino." This plate, glowing with iridescence, contradicts Passeri's opinion (already quoted) that stanniferous glaze was never practised in the Urbino workshops, as does the tile introduced three pages below. 16. Rome; a grandly draped female, sitting in desolation over a dead child: *Fiorenzo mesta i morti figlii piange*, "Disconsolate Florence weeps for her lifeless offspring," in the plague visitation of 1538. Though with the most brilliant ruby and gold lustre I ever saw, it has in blue the cipher X, probably also of Xante in Urbino.

But to return to the uses of this pottery. Those who have observed the rich effect of the majolica sparingly displayed in the late Mediæval Exhibition at the Adelphi [1850] may readily admit that, on a buffet lit up by Italian suns, its glowing tints and attractive forms were no mean substitute for the as yet scarce precious metals. Ingenuity was taxed to invent designs and adaptations of an art in which fashion ran riot:—Tiles for floors or panelling; vases of mere ornament; beakers; epergnes; wine-coolers; perfume-sprinklers; fountains, whence there flowed alternately, as if by magic, water or wine of nine varieties at the bidding of the bewildered guests; wine-cups clustered with grapes, through an orifice in which the liquor was sucked, anticipating the American device for discussing sherry-cobbler. Of drug-bottles and pots we have spoken. Sauce-boats, salt-cellars, and ink-stands gave rise to endless caprices, in the guise "of beasts, and of fowl and fishes"; and to these may be added figure-groups of saints, grotesque characters and animals, fruits, trees, and pilgrims' bottles.

In the decorations there was generally a consistency, too often lost sight of by modern artificers. Thus, toilet-basins were painted with marine deities, water-nymphs, or aquatic allegories; fruit-stands with fruit and vintages; wine-cups with vine-festoons. Among the oddities may be mentioned tiny tea-cups, into the paste for which was mingled a portion of dust carefully gathered in sweeping out the holy house at Loreto, their sanctity being vouched by the inscription, *Con pol. di S. C.*, "With dust from the Santa Casa." The effigy of the Madonna of Loreto is often affixed, in colour and design on a par with the superstition. A pair of these was shown at the Mediæval Exhibition of 1850, No. 562 of the catalogue, belonging to a Mrs. Palliser.

Having thus considered the various sites and sorts of

Urbino majolica, its processes and purposes, we shall mention some of the artists employed upon it. Of these there were two classes, the potter who mixed and manipulated, modelled and moulded clay-clod into an article of convenience or luxury, and the painter whose pencil rendered it an object of the fine arts; latterly, however, these branches were combined, and were carried on by a class of artificers caller *vasaii* or *vasari*, and *boccalini*, according as vases or bottles prevailed in their workshops. The little that has come to our knowledge regarding those by whom the early Pesarese and Gubbian ware was fashioned and decorated will be found in a former page. The latter makers of Pesaro and Urbino have more frequently left us the means of identifying their performances in monograms or signatures, usually inscribed in blue characters on the back of plates. But before considering these, we may dispose of the vulgar error which has given Raffaele's name to Italian porcelain. Superficial or romancing writers have often seriously repeated, with purely fictitious additions, Malvasia's petulant sneer, which he was fain quickly to retract, that the great Sanzio was a painter of plates; others have, without better grounds, made him assistant to his father, a potter. There is however nothing connecting him with the ceramic art beyond a loose notice by Don V. Vittorio, in his *Osservazioni Sopra Felsina Pittrice* (pp. 44, 112–14), of a letter from Raffaele referring to designs supplied by him to the Duchess for majolica. That he did supply such drawings is possible, though discredited by Pungileoni, and, if true, it in no way compromises his status, at a period when high art lent a willing hand to decorate and elevate the adjuncts and appliances of domestic life. This much is certain, that compositions emanating from Sanzio and his school were employed in ornamenting porcelain during the sixteenth century, but they were doubtless obtained from his pupils, or from the engravings of Marc Antonio. Such is the title here introduced from the original in my possession (8½ inches by 7), which is one of the most Raffaelesque I have met with, and which, though not signed, displays the colouring practised by Fra Xanto, the blue and green being deep and well marked, the orange and yellow of the clouds and curtain in metallic iridescence.

In this, as in most instances, the design is somewhat marred by the colours having run when laid on, or during vitrification. The mistake as to Sanzio has been partly occasioned by confusion with Raffaele del Colle, who painted at the Imperiale, and is said by tradition to have contributed sketches for the Pesarese workshops, and also with another Raffaele Ciarla, who seems to have been a potter, about 1530–60. Battles, sieges, and mythological figures resembling the vigorous inventions of Guilio Romano, are not unfrequent; and in the Kestner Museum, I have observed several plates of choice design and Raffaelesque character, especially the Fall and Expulsion of our first Parents, and the Gathering of Manna. But these are satisfactorily accounted for by Paseri's statement, that, with a view to improve a native manufacture which brought to his state both estimation and wealth, Duke Guidobaldo II. took infinite pains in collecting a better class of drawings and prints from celebrated masters, on the dispersion of which, in consequence of their being sought for by collectors, the pictorial excellence of majolica rapidly declined. The first symptom of decay was the substitution of monotonous arabesques, weak in colour and repeated from the type introduced by Raffaele, in place and figure groups and other subjects requiring composition and design.

Premising that we cannot now distinguish exactly between potters and the painters, where these cognate occupations chanced to be divided, and that the same persons occasionally wrought at various places in the duchy, we shall supply a notice of the names we have met with in connection with the workshops of Pesaro, Urbino, and Castel Durante, during the sixteenth century.

Terenzio Terenzi painted vases and plates at Pesaro, one of which he signed "Terenzio fecit, 1550," but his usual mark was T. Another is inscribed, "Questo piatto fu fatto in la Bottega de Mastro Baldassare, Vasaro da Pesaro e fatto per mano de Ferenzio fiolo di Mastro Matteo Boccalaro." He was doubtless the person who, under the surname of Rondolino, became notorious at Rome for his clever pictorial forgeries of the great master's works, although said by Ticozzi to have been born at Pesaro in 1570. The signature "Mastro Gironimo, Vasaro in Pesaro, J. P." occurs from 1542 to 1560, and to him Mr. Marryat ascribes, on what authority I know not, the mark A. O. connected by a cross, which Passeri quotes as of another artist in 1582; the letters I. P. that gentleman reads *in Pesaro.* This Girolamo Lanfranco was a native of Gabicce, near Pesaro, and died in 1599, leaving sons Girolamo and Ludovico. In his favour, and that of his son, were granted the privileges already referred to, as dated 1552 and 1569.

In connection with the workshops of Urbino, we have these names. Giovanni and Francesco di Donnino had a commission for a set of vases for Cardinal Capaccio. *Fra Xanto. a. da Rovigo in Urbino* signed platters of great size and beautiful design, about 1532-4, some of which show a very fine metallic and prismatic lustre. The mark X, occurring on pieces of that quality, does not, however, always refer to him. A splendid plate in Mr. Marryat's rich collection, commemorative of the taking of Goletta, in Africa, by Charles V., is inscribed *In Urbino nella botteg di Francesco de Silvano, X.* MDXXXXI.; and a Judith of great beauty, in the Tordelli cabinet, signed F. X. 1535, is, no doubt of that master. Contemporary and very analogous are plates with an iridescence rivalling that of Maestro Giorgio, signed *Mastro Rovigo di Urbino*, or *Da Rovigiese:* of this artist, probably the countryman of Xanto, we know nothing, but he may be the same who signs Gubbian plates with R. Equally little can we say as to Giulio of Urbino, who is mentioned as working for the Duke of Ferrara, about 1530; or of Cesare da Faenza, then employed in the shop of Guido Merlini, of Urbino. Much more noted are the Fontana family, originally of Castel Durante. From thence Guido, son of Nicolò, emigrated to the capital, where his son Orazio painted many of the finest productions of the reign of Guidobaldo II., including the best vases of his laboratory, his usual mark being this, meaning *Orazio Fontana Urbinate fece.* Among the treasures and trash of Strawberry Hill was a very large vase, with serpent handles, and designs ascribed to Giulio Romano, inscribed *Fate in botega di Orazio Fontana.*[1] A plate described by Passeri, has the story of Horatius Cocles, with the motto *Orazio solo contra Toscana tutta, fatto in Pesaro* 1541, which appears to be a *jeu de mots* intended by Fontana as a challenge to the rival fabrics of Tuscany.[2] For him has been claimed the invention of Gubbian glaze; while others say his discovery was a mode of preventing the mixture of colours during vitrification. He died in 1571, his labours having been shared by a brother Camillo, who carried the art to Ferrara, and a nephew Flaminio, who settled in Florence.

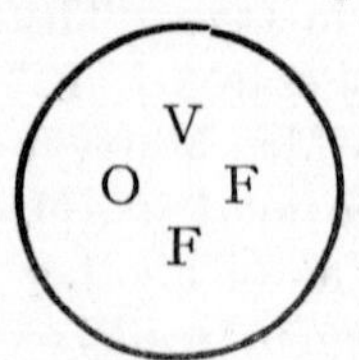

Among the pupils of Orazio was Raffaele Ciarla, whose name we have noticed as confused with that of Raffaele Sanzio, and who painted a buffet of porcelain, after designs

[1] A magnificent pair of triangular fonts in the same collection brought at the sale 168*l*.

[2] The ancestors of Giorgio Vasari were surnamed from their occupation of vase-makers (*vasari*), at Arezzo. The Ginori establishment near Florence is comparatively modern.

by Taddeo Zuccaro, which his sovereign presented to Philip II. of Spain. He wrought between 1530 and 1560. Gianbattista Franco, a Venetian painter of whom we have lately spoken, was invited by Duke Guidobaldo II., about 1540, to supply designs for majolica, in consequence of his reputation for clever drawings in the dangerous style of Michael Angelo. The loss of his cupola for the cathedral at Urbino is not to be regretted; but in a humbler sphere he acquitted himself better, and some of the vases in the laboratory bear his signature, B. F. V. F., *Battista Franco Urbinas fecit.* Among the latest artists was Alfonso Patanazzi, who was born at Urbino of a noble family, and died in 1694; but his productions (signed in full, or with his initials) have no artistic merit whatever.

It remains to mention those who wrought chiefly at Castel Durante, or, as it was named after the Devolution to the Holy See, Urbania. The Chevalier Cipriano Picolpasso, from being a professor of the healing art, took to pottery about 1550, and left a MS. account of some of the secrets of that fabric and of its glazes, which was used by Passeri for his work. Mr. Marryat considers that he was peculiarly successful in painting trophies. Guido di Savino is said to have carried the art from Castel Durante to Antwerp; and he or Guido Fontana may be author of a plate, in the Soane Museum, of the Fates, signed *In botega di M°. Guido Durantino in Urbino.* To either of them I am disposed to assign the monogram, No. 12, of our 18th plate of facsimiles, which Mr. Marryat reads as Castel Durante, but which seems to me a G. D., for Guido Durantino. Alessandro Gatti, of that place, had three brothers, Giovanni, Tiseo, and Luzio, whom Picolpasso mentions as having emigrated to Corfu, and there established the same fabric. Cardinal Stoppani, Legate of Pesaro, in last century, made some ineffectual attempts to restore the manufacture at Urbania, and the only pottery now produced in the duchy is of the most ordinary white stoneware. It would be interesting to know the scale of remuneration for mere artistic varieties of majolica, but the prices given by Passeri, from Picolpasso's MS., refer only to the more ordinary and mechanical designs, such as grotesques with monsters, arabesques, trophies with armour, fruit, flowers, and foliage; of these the first was the most costly, the last the cheapest, varying from two Roman scudi to about two and a half pauls per hundred. Supposing money in 1560 to have been six times its present value in Italy, these sums may be considered equal to fifty shillings and six shillings respectively.[1]

In Italy, the collection of majolica made by the Chevalier Massa, at Pesaro, is specially worthy of notice, and contains specimens of most varieties made in the duchy. It was chiefly got together between 1825 and 1835 when these were still abundant and little sought after; but the district was nearly cleared of them about twelve years since, by an agent of Parisian dealers. The Chevalier, who was in extreme old age in 1845, had bequeathed his majolica—consisting of about five hundred pieces, with a few indifferent pictures—to his native town, unless he could, during life, sell the whole for about 1000*l.*, destined by him to charitable purposes. Another numerous collection is that of Signor Mavorelli, at La Fratta, near Perugia. The small but choice cabinet of Signor Serafino Tordelli, at Spoleto, has already been mentioned. Specimens may still be picked up in Rome, Florence, Paris, and London; but perhaps the most specimens are in the hands of English amateurs.

[1] Pungileoni quotes a demand made in 1683 of 50 scudi (about 11*l.*) for a plate reputed to have been painted by Raffaele; this, at thrice the present money value, would give 32*l.* as its price.

APPENDICES

APPENDIX I

(Page 21)

CORRESPONDENCE OF CLEMENT VII. WITH DUKE FRANCESCO MARIA BEFORE THE SACK OF ROME, 1527

THERE are several brieves preserved in the Archivio Diplomatico at Florence, affording evidence of the Pope's feeble and inconsistent policy. His missive, announcing to the Duke the truce with Lanoy, was dated the 16th of March, and was followed by one of the 20th of April, which we shall here translate:—

To our beloved Son, the noble Francesco Maria, Duke of Urbino, Captain-general of the Venetians.

Beloved Son, health and apostolic benediction!

We have written but once to your nobility since coming to this armistice with the enemy, for, matters not being yet fully settled, we had nothing certain to apprise you of. But we understood that, by the letters of our dear son and lieutenant, Francesco Guicciardini, you were already made aware of all we could have asked of you, and had by your own good conduct anticipated it, which is to us most pleasing and acceptable, and daily more realises our hopes of you. As to this suspension of arms, we stooped to it more readily from being destitute of means or assistance, and from measuring the inclinations of others by our own pacific dispositions. But now that our enemies' conduct seems rather to abuse our clemency and moderation than to approach any equitable course, we do not well see how we can safely come to any terms with them. Thus, induced by necessity, and by your worth and good will, as well as cheered by the entire justice of our cause, we desire to make your nobility aware that we have utterly dismissed from our mind all truce with adversaries so perfidious, and are willing and ready rather to hazard any peril of war than submit to such unworthy and iniquitous conditions; yet, believing victory much more imminent than danger, we trust that their obstinacy and insolence will be easily put down, provided your forces can timeously coalesce with our own, and you exercise all zeal and caution in effecting this. We therefore not only exhort your nobility to this, but we fully rely on your doing it, as matter at once of duty and propriety, and from your disposition in favour of the Italian liberties and the dignity of ourselves and this Holy See. We, on our part, shall maintain towards our beloved sons, the Venetian government, that firm attitude which shall satisfy all of our constancy, things being now come to such a pitch that we must either sink dishonoured on failure of your aid and support, or by your help shall emerge with credit. As regards our paternal and affectionate concern for your personal dignity and interests, we can add nothing to the promises already made you by letters and envoys, which we shall amply carry out. Let your nobility, therefore, go on as you have so well begun, nor relax until we and you and all Italy be rid of all these barbarian excesses. After perusing these brieves, your nobility will forward them to the Doge and Signory of Venice, for, news of the enemy's obstinacy and faithlessness reaching us by express at midnight, we had to write to your nobility before we could communicate anything to their ambassador.

Given at St. Peter's, Rome, under the fisher's signet, the 20th April, 1527, in the fourth year of our pontificate.

Blosius.

On the 22nd and 30th the Pope wrote again, but in general terms, and referring for details to the accredited bearer and to former despatches. He exhorted the Duke, in formal and measured phrase, to do his utmost towards fulfilling the expectations reposed on him and the Venetians, upon whom were based all the Pontiff's hopes; but neither in letter nor spirit do these brieves indicate any perception of the extreme hazards of his position.

APPENDIX II

(Page 21)

THE SACK OF ROME

I. *Letter from the Bishop of Modula to the Generals of the League.*[1]

Most illustrious Lords of the League,

Let your most illustrious Lordships speed on quickly without loss of time, seeing by these presents that the enemy have carried the Borgo, though our Lord and all Rome were well fortified. Monsignor de Bourbon is dead of an arquebus-shot below the abdomen, and a man has just come in who happened to aid in carrying off his body. More than three thousand of the enemy have fallen. Let your Lordships, then, press on, for the enemy are in the utmost disorder; quickly, quickly, without loss of time. Your servant,

GUIDO, BISHOP OF MODULA.

From Viterbo, the 7th of May, 1527, 3 P.M.

To the most illustrious Lords, the Duke of Urbino and the Marquis of Saluzzo, Captains of the League.

II. *Letter from Scipione . . . to Alessandro Moresino, alias Venezianello, Master of the Chamber of the Prince Guidobaldo, dated at Urbino,* 20*th of May,* 1527, *narrating the destruction of Rome.*

Most dear as an honoured brother,

I wish I were fitter than at present, and more easy in mind, to write you of the strange, horrible, and atrocious event befallen the wretched, miserable, and ill-fated city of Rome. Although

[1] Sanuto Diarii MSS. Bib. Marciana, xlv. f. 132.

I feel assured that, from different advices, you will have had partial, if not full accounts, nevertheless, that I may not fail in duty, I have thought it best to inform you of all I have yet heard, notwithstanding that I tell it with aching heart and tearful eye.

I therefore inform you that eight days ago last Monday, being the 18th inst., about 22 o'clock [half-past 5 P.M.], the Spanish imperial army presented itself at the bastion of the gate. Their object was to make trial, and see how and by whom it was guarded, not having courage to attack; but after consulting together, and deciding to assault, and even to make their way into the city, they took some food, and then suddenly and all in a mass attempted with furious impetuosity to force the bastion, which is said to have been ill guarded, there being but four thousand regular infantry in Rome. In this attack, both sides behaved with great bravery, and were supposed to have lost about one thousand men, including the flower of the Spaniards. Bourbon, observing the slaughter and immense confusion, rushed on with all the lansquenets. The castle maintained a fire of artillery as they best could; but the air being obscured by a dense fog, they could not see the effect of it, and battered down a piece of wall.[1] Through it, and by storming the bastion, the Imperialists entered, and there Bourbon met his death from an arquebus-shot, which passed quite through his belly. The papal troops, unable to offer more resistance, fled towards the castle, into which most of them were admitted, especially those who arrived first. It is rumoured, but not confirmed, that the Lord Stefano Colonna, who commanded the guard at that bastion, capitulated. Next day, being Tuesday, the enemy, though within the town, made no aggressions, but proceeded cautiously, dreading some ambush. Having, however, assured themselves that there was no cause for mistrust, they began to spread over the city, and to plunder the monasteries, nunneries, and hospitals, with great slaughter of those found therein. The hospital of San Spirito was destroyed, and the patients were

[1] This letter, though inaccurate in several details, the author writing at a distance from the events, affords curious evidence of the consternation generally occasioned by the sack of Rome.

thrown into the Tiber, after which they commenced attacking the palaces of cardinals and gentlemen, with much bloodshed and cruelty; and I have been told this morning by Francesco, son of Battista Riceco, that one Maestro Jacomo, the first perfumer in Rome, is come to his house, having escaped with four other chance companions, whom, being a very old friend, he has thought it necessary to receive kindly in his house; and he learned from him as certain, having been witness to it, that the lansquenets, that inhuman and villainous race of Lutheran infidels, slew without mercy those of all ages, sexes, and conditions whom they found in the streets; also, that they attacked Cardinal Cesarini's palace, wherein were many Roman gentlemen, guarded by two hundred infantry; and having stormed it, put them all to the sword, it being uncertain if the Cardinal himself were there. Thence they proceeded to the Spanish Archbishop of Cosenza's palace, wherein were some five hundred of his countrymen, men of credit inhabiting Rome, who had retired thither as to a place of safety; but all, without exception, were cut to pieces. They next went to the house of Messer Domenico de' Massimi, a Roman gentleman, who had there his wife and two children, with many noble persons of the city of all ages, every individual of whom were slain—men, women, children, servants, maids; and it was the same in many others, whose names I do not remember, so that the dead bodies lie in heaps in the houses and palaces of the nobility, each day getting worse. Fancy the affliction of the poor ladies, seeing husbands, brothers, children massacred before their eyes, without the power of aiding them, and worse still, they were themselves killed next moment. It is not believed that had the Turk come on such an enterprise, his barbarity would have equalled that daily, continuously, and perseveringly practised by these ruffians. I cannot imagine a greater purgatory or hell than to hear the weeping and lamentation there must be in that afflicted city.

But I forgot that he told me they were barricading the Marchioness of Mantua's palace, as he left Rome, in which were her Excellency, with many Roman ladies, who had fled there as to an asylum, but the result was not known. He also said that the *Bande nere* of the late Lord Giovanni de' Medici were to have from the Pope double pay for their services, which his Holiness refusing, a part of them remained in Rome, and the rest went off in disgust and joined the Spaniards in plundering, being the foremost to assault that bastion which was defended by their comrades, and having, in fact, secured the Imperialists their victory, as without them neither the lansquenets nor Spaniards had ever got into the city.

The Pope is in the castle, with many cardinals and other persons of station: they are said to have a year's provisions, with ample ammunition and artillery. This Maestro Giacomo says he heard that the Imperialists, dubious of succours, thought of fortifying the bridges, with the intention of holding their ground against any who might annoy them. As yet the lansquenets have made no prisoners, but the Spaniards have pillaged immensely, and taken vast numbers of men, women priests, and people of all sorts, so that there is, from Rome to Naples, an uninterrupted stream of baggage and prisoners sent by them. He also mentions that the chief of Colonna most courageously charged the lansquenets, crying Colonna! Colonna! but after a great fray, he was beaten and his followers killed, whereupon Pompeo Colonna, thinking to elevate himself and put down his enemies, fled away, and neither he nor any of his house have been since heard of. It was reported that four soldiers were killed in entering the castle, but this is since contradicted. Cardinal del Monte and many more cardinals are missing. and it is not known if they got in there, or are dead, or taken, or escaped. It is suspected that these anti-Christian dogs will put all Rome to flames; and we may anticipate that after suffering all this rapine, pillage, slaughter, and captivity, it will soon have to endure a grievous pestilence, from the number of dead bodies left in the palaces and houses, which no one removes for burial, and which are putrefying in masses, so that no one can enter, on account of the stench, without inhaling infection. It is also said that, a day or two ago one of the Pope's chamberlains was secretly sent by his Holiness from the castle in the night to our Duke [of Urbino], to inform him of the state of matters, and to exhort him and the other captains of the League to push on with the army to his aid; and that all these other leaders having repaired to consult with his Lordship, they unanimously resolved to press forward. We hear that his Excellency is to-day at Orvieto, and will reach Viterbo to-morrow; also that he will make a general levy, and give bounty to all who will enlist. His Excellency has written the Governor a very affectionate letter, praying him to exhort all those here who have been soldiers to go in search of honourable service, with money and all they may require. The Governor has circulated copies of this letter throughout the state, and has made proclamation, so that they are embodying many men to join his Excellency. On Saturday, Vincenzo Ubaldino and Pier-Matteo di Thomasello will start from this with a fine and good detachment. I am sorry not to be able to send you a copy of this letter, which it would really have done your heart good to read. You could hardly believe how much vexation this misfortune to Rome has caused here; and when people of station discuss it, as they often do, I assure you I have seen them weep as freely as if it were their own. All that I have related I tell you just as I heard it from others. I would I were speaking untruths, and that it were all false; but I shall say no more. The Lady Madonna Emilia sends you hearty commendations, and reminds you not to give yourself such airs as to forget her. From Urbino, the 20th May, 1527. Entirely your brother,

Scipione Arris. . . . .

III. *Letter from Mercurino da Gattinara, Commissary of the Imperial Army during the sack of Rome, wherein he informs the Emperor of the entrance into that city, of the slaughter and havock inflicted, and of the arrangement made through him with Clement VII., and how during four successive days he repaired to the Castle of St. Angelo to negotiate with the Pope and thirteen cardinals there inclosed.*[1]

Most sacred Cæsar,

I have this written in Italian by another hand, being unable to do so with my own in consequence of meeting with an accident, as I shall presently explain. I have to inform your Majesty that Monsieur di Borbone, being near Florence and Siena with his

[1] Vat. Ottob. MSS. No. 2607.

army, and understanding that the former of these cities was well fortified, and contained the forces of the League ready to defend it, rendering a siege impossible, or at all events so protracted as to endanger your Majesty's troops from want of provisions and other stores, whilst the lack of pay risked their disbanding and losing all;—aware, on the other hand, that Rome had been disarmed, and that to seize and bring it and the Pontiff to great straits was to gain everything, or at all events would prove a measure so useful and advantageous as to content your Majesty; —it appeared to him better to abandon his designs upon Florence, and, advancing by forced marches, to beleaguer Rome, thereby anticipating the army of the League, and preventing them from succouring it, for which purpose he determined to leave his artillery in Siena. Accordingly, when this was decided, the confederates being in Florence, and we thirty miles on this side of it, we advanced with the utmost diligence, doing twenty or four-and-twenty miles a day, which was something quite new for the army, so numerous, so distressed by past fatigues, and by recent and actual hunger.[1] Thus, on Saturday the 4th instant, it was quartered at Isola, seven miles from Rome. M. di Borbone and his officers were astonished that the Pope and cardinals should await the army and the threatened danger, whilst Rome was incapable of defence, without submitting some proposal by envoy or letter, or even answering a despatch sent to his Holiness by M. di Borbone and the Viceroy as to the terms of agreement. Some of your Majesty's good servants suggested that were the army under the walls it was doubtful if they could carry them, from want of artillery, in which event their own destruction would follow; on the other hand, that in case of taking the

[1] As a specimen of the very loose diction even of public despatches in this age, and of the obstacles which a translator has to encounter. we shall render literally the next sentence, or rather half page, sentences not being divided in the original. "And so the fourth day of the present month of May, which was Saturday, the foresaid army made his lodgment at seven miles from Rome, in a place which is called the Isle; Monsieur di Borbone and all the principal persons were filled with much wonder that the Pope and so many cardinals and all Rome, being disarmed, should wait for such an army and great danger, without sending to the said Monsieur di Borbone an ambassador to make some parley, nor letters, or answer to his letters which the said M. di Borbone had formerly written, and the Viceroy, to his Holiness about the affair of the agreement."

city it would be sacked, which could be no good service to your Majesty, as its plunder would occasion the army to disperse, the Spaniards and Italians straggling towards Naples, or, should they not break up, they might demand immense arrears of pay, which not being discharged from want of means, everything would fall into confusion. For these reasons they recommended Borbone so to dispose his forces as to keep matters open for arrangement with the Pope. Of this advice he openly approved, desirous of any plan which should provide pay for the army. He, however, declared that he would not abstain from annoying the enemy, nor allow them time to provide for their interests, alleging that the Admiral [Bonnivet] of France, from not having taken Rome when he could, in order to save it from a sack, was unable afterwards to do so, it being defended by the Lord Prospero Colonna: also that, on another occasion, when Monsieur di Chaumont beleaguered Bologna, Fabrizio Colonna threw in succours whilst the French general was treating with Julius II., who thereupon broke off the parley: finally, that it became a pontiff rather to seek a capitulation than to wait until it was demanded of him.

Monsieur di Borbone accordingly decided on approaching the walls, and on Sunday morning the 5th we made a lodgment within [beyond?] St. Peter's palace, hard by the monastery of S. Pancrazio. Yet he did not neglect addressing a letter to the Pontiff on that morning, exhorting him to make a favourable capitulation rather than abide the unpleasant alternative. It was at the same time suggested whether it might not be well for him to repair to his Holiness; but considering that he could not go for want of a safe-conduct, it seemed better for him to remain; he, however, sent the letter by a trumpet, whom the enemy did not allow to pass, the missive remaining in their hands, and we know not whether it reached the Pope; at all events, no answer ever came, which was demanded before half-past seven P.M. of that day, after which it would be no longer possible to restrain the army. For these reasons, as evening approached, it was resolved to get the ladders all prepared for an assault the following morning on the Borgo towards the furnaces, where the wall was considered very weak. And so the assault was given on Monday morning the 6th of May in this year 1527, when by an unlucky chance the Lord di Borbone was hit in the abdomen towards the right thigh, of which wound he presently died. Yet notwithstanding this accident, which was not at once known to the army, the undertaking was carried through, and the Borgo was plundered that morning. The Pope, with most of the cardinals and court, were in the castle, but on hearing what had occurred they hastily retired to the castle of S. Angelo. Meanwhile our soldiery sacked the whole Borgo, and slew most of the people whom they found, taking a few prisoners. The enemy's forces then in the city are supposed not to have exceeded three thousand, unused to arms, so that it was scarcely defended; the dense fog which prevailed during that day was likewise inopportune, preventing them seeing each other; and the struggle did not last in all above two hours. We afterwards learned that the Pope and the citizens, relying upon the assurances of Renzo da Ceri, considered both Rome and the Borgo to be impregnable without artillery, and looked for support from the confederate army.

The Pontiff being thus within the castle, and such of the citizens as were armed having joined their handful of troops for defence of the bridges and of the Transtevere quarter, the Borgo was occupied by a large portion of our army, and its leaders were assembled in council, when there arrived the Portuguese ambassador to say that some Romans, his neighbours, had, with the Pope's sanction, urged him to make terms. The answer given him was that the council would be ready to treat, so soon as the Pope had placed in their hands the Ponte Molle and Transtevere, to which proposal no reply was returned during that day. A brigade of our troops having carried the Transtevere, and possessed themselves of the Ponte Sisto and Sta. Maria, the whole army passed into the city early on that evening of the 6th. As the inhabitants in general relied on its being defended, none of them had fled or removed their property, so that no one of whatever nation, rank, condition, age, or sex escaped becoming prisoners—not even women in the convents. They were treated without distinction according to the caprice of the soldiery; and after being plundered of all their effects most of them were compelled by torture or otherwise to pay ransom. Cardinals Cesarini, della Valle, and di Siena, being imperialists, considered themselves safe, and remained in their houses, whither also there retired Cardinal . . . , Fra Giacobatio, and many friends with their women and valuables; but finding no sanctuary there, they had to compound with certain captains and soldiers for security of their persons and property; notwithstanding which, these houses were completely pillaged three or four days afterwards, and they had enough to do to save their lives. Some women who had carried all their earthly possessions to Cardinal Colonna's residence were left with but a single cloak and shift. Cardinals S. Sisto and della Minerva, who stayed at home, are still in the soldiers' power, being too poor to pay their ransom. All the church ornaments are stolen, the sacred utensils thrown about, the relics gone to destruction—for the troops in abstracting their precious receptacles heeded these no more than as many bits of wood: even the shrine of the *sancta sanctorum* was sacked, although regarded with peculiar reverence. St. Peter's church and the papal palace from top to bottom have been made into stables. I feel confident that your Majesty as a Catholic and most Christian emperor will feel displeasure at these gross outrages and insults to the Catholic religion, the Apostolic See, and the city of Rome. In truth, every one is convinced that all this has happened as a judgment from God on the great tyranny and disorders of the papal court; but however this may be, there has been vast destruction, for which no redress can be had but from your Majesty's arm and authority. This army has no head, no divisions, no discipline, no organisation, but every one behaves according to his own fancy. The Lord Prince of Orange and Giovanni di Urbino, with the other leaders, do what they can, but to little purpose; for in entering Rome the lansquenets have conducted themselves like true Lutherans, and the rest like actual . . . Most of the troops are enriched by the enormous booty, amounting to many millions of gold. A majority of the Spaniards will, it is supposed, retire to Naples with their spoil.

But to resume our narrative. On the morning after our entry, being Tuesday the 7th, the Pope wrote a letter to our leaders, praying them to send me to his Holiness to hear certain proposals. By their order I went into S. Angelo, where I found thirteen cardinals in great affliction, as was natural in the circumstances. His Holiness in their presence told me, that since fortune, on which he too much relied, had brought him to this pass, he would not think of any resistance, but was content to place his own person and that of the cardinals, and his state, in your Majesty's hands, and that he desired me to mediate with the captains for some favourable arrangement. I did my best to comfort his Holiness and the cardinals, showing them how satisfied they must be that your Majesty never intended to injure either his Holiness or the Apostolic See; but that great blame attached to them, seeing they might, on certain fair conditions and by a sum of money, have prevented our army from approaching so near, which would have averted the destruction of Rome; since, however, God had so willed it, that his plan seemed to me good, of placing himself in the hands of your Majesty, as there was no remedy or redress to be looked for but from that quarter. Taking upon me the charge imposed by my office as mediator, I passed several times between the council of war and the Pontiff, and succeeded in the course of four days in concluding a capitulation, which is generally considered reasonable and advantageous to your Majesty's service, as to which I shall only say that your Majesty will judge, after seeing its terms and learning its progress. There arose on our side an obstacle to prevent the execution of this agreement, which was the bad discipline of the Germans, who took a fancy not to quit Rome, nor confirm any truce, until they had received all arrears of pay, amounting, according to their calculation, to 300,000 scudi. But as the Pope could put down but 100,000 scudi, even after selling everything within the castle, of his own valuables and those of the cardinals and prelates, and the church ornaments, the affair could not be brought to a happy issue, so much so that I greatly feared the brutality of these Germans and the blunders of others would have lost all the fruits of our enterprise, especially as the army of the League is supposed not to be more than twenty or twenty-five miles distant, and as some of their detachments have already tried to carry off his Holiness by night. After several days had passed in disputing with the lansquenets, the expedient was adopted of handing them over all the cash produced by the Pontiff—the Prince of Orange and other captains undertaking that they should be paid [the balance] out of the first moneys raised, and Parma and Piacenza being consigned in security. I was obliged to concede to them these conditions, in order to carry through the capitulation, and so secure the benefit of our enterprise, as well as to elude their anxiety to get the Pope and cardinals into their clutches, upon which they were greatly set. And this arrangement is really of such importance that most of your Majesty's servants are willing to undertake any obligation towards these lansquenets, in order to ensure the Pope's and cardinals' safety. There is still some hitch about raising the 100,000 scudi, but we trust means will be found; meanwhile, it has been resolved to throw three hundred infantry into the castle to-morrow, under some leader, to secure it and all in it; and we shall see gradually to get the rest brought about.

In return for my toils, anxieties, and services, I was wounded from an arquebus in S. Angelo on the fourth day, whilst approaching the castle to treat with the Pope. The ball passed through my right arm, which prevents me from writing, but I hope in time to get over it. And notwithstanding this accident befallen me, from no fault of his Holiness, whilst on your Majesty's service and in so righteous a work, I shall endure it all patiently, in the hope that your Majesty will consider my exertions, and the losses sustained by me in limb and estate, and out of your clemency and compassion will not omit some fitting recompence.

After writing the above on the 19th inst., I returned to the castle to conclude the arrangements with the Pope and cardinals, and complete the convention; and in consequence of certain articles being added regarding the entry of our people into S. Angelo, I sought to remodel the treaty. The Lord Vespasiano Colonna, and the Abbot of Nigera accompanied me; and after protracted discussion with the Pontiff regarding the difficulty of raising the 100,000 scudi, we had recourse to certain merchants who, on a guarantee from his Holiness and the cardinals, promised to make up a balance of 20,000 wanted to complete that sum. This point being settled, I insisted on reforming the treaty, and that your Majesty's troops might on that very day take possession of the fortress, as had been agreed on. But his Holiness endeavoured all day to postpone this on various pretexts, and at length, when pressed by us to decide, as we would wait no longer, he replied, "I shall speak frankly; having advices that the confederate army is at hand to relieve me, I desire, meanwhile, that you give me a limited time to await their succours, on the expiry of which I shall perform all the stipulations of the capitulation. Nor is this any unreasonable request, as I shall be satisfied with six days, and as similar conditions are never refused to any fortress about to surrender." I replied to the Pontiff and the cardinals, that your Majesty's army had little apprehension of any such succours, being always victorious; but that his Holiness would do well to consider how your Majesty's captains, on receiving such an answer, would conclude him and the cardinals to have been merely trifling with them to gain time: indeed, I was satisfied that they would consider it a positive rupture, and would suddenly assault the castle, and storm it so furiously that these, or even better terms, would no longer be listened to, leaving no opportunity for repentance or remedy short of the final destruction of the Holy See. On hearing these views, the Pope and cardinals were greatly bewildered, apprehending that they would be realised should they wait for relief, and in this dilemma remained gazing on each other, but asked a quarter of an hour for consultation. Eventually there arose a wrangle among the cardinals, those of the French faction wishing to await succours at all hazards; so the Pontiff excused himself from settling the matter according to his own wish, ever urging a delay of six days. I believe the authors of this opposition to have been Alberto da Carpi, the Datary Orazio Baglione, Gregorio Casale the English ambassador, and such like.

Having retired from the castle with Lord Vespasian and the Abbot, we related everything to our leaders, whereupon it was decided to open that very night a trench round the fortress, the whole army turning out under arms. It was found no easy matter to muster them, all being idle and intent on pillage; nor would they quit the houses, especially the lansquenets, who at first thought it a mere trick to get them out. At length, after great exertions, the enemy being ascertained but seven miles off, all ran to arms, and your Majesty's army was well disposed for battle: indeed, I suspect the enemy found their calculation disappointed, that most of our soldiery having become rich, would no longer flock to their standards. Some Spanish and German troops are expected; but I know not if they will arrive in time, as the trench is already made, so that neither Pope nor any one else shall escape.

Such is the present state of your Majesty's affairs, and I trust they will ever have successful issue. Yet it is true that, after the death of M. di Borbone, great confusion occurred in the army, as no one knew whom to acknowledge as its chief. I think that had he lived, Rome would, perhaps, not have been sacked, and matters might have taken a better course and result for your Majesty's interests. Yet God so willed it, and we need not talk of what cannot now be helped. But my affectionate duty to your Majesty requires me to report certain things requiring from your Majesty the oversight of a captain-general; of the individual I say nothing, not wishing presumptuously to name any one. On M. di Borbone's death, the day we entered Rome, the captains and counsellors in the army discussed giving its command to the Viceroy of Naples, then at Siena. The Prince of Orange remarked that he had acknowledged the authority of di Borbone, but would not submit to the Viceroy. It being suggested by some that the Duke of Ferrara was coming as your Majesty's captain-general, the Prince replied, that on his arrival, he would acknowledge him, but that meanwhile, no one being commissioned by your Majesty, he neither would set himself up as captain, nor at all permit others to be so without your Majesty's command. These words he addressed to Giovanni d'Urbino, who then, and on subsequent occasions, modestly remarked that he was content to acknowledge the Prince, with other complimentary phrases. Now the Prince has taken the notion of being himself captain-general, and thus affairs are conducted in his name, not, however, with that title, but as the first person in the army, being much liked by the Germans. Your Majesty will do as seems best.

One thing requires your Majesty's careful consideration,

namely, how this city of Rome is to be governed, and whether or not anything of the Apostolic See is to be retained. I shall not conceal the opinion of some that it should not be entirely abolished; for if that See were transported elsewhere, it seems certain that it will be utterly ruined, seeing that, in that case, the King of France will set up a patriarch in his realm, refusing obedience to the Apostolic See, the English and Spanish Sovereigns doing the like. But this should be seen to without delay, otherwise the professional men and notaries will all be gone, and Rome will be quite reduced, as they will lose both their appointments and their practice. The Pope and those cardinals with him, told me that your Majesty should make provision for this, otherwise all would be lost. Your Majesty will act in this for the best.

There are three other points to which it is necessary that your Majesty should attend by anticipation. One is, what would your Majesty wish done, should his Holiness and those cardinals go to Naples as has been proposed; ought they to be taken to Spain or not? Another is, what if the Pope should escape from the castle by aid of the enemy? In the third place, should it come to an assault and the Pontiff unluckily fall? It is my belief, however, that, on expiry of the six days which he has demanded, and which are already running, he, on finding no efficient succour, will again come to parley and propose a capitulation. Yet I have my misgivings lest your Majesty's interests should be crossed by the fury of the lansquenets, who declare they must get hold of him. But your Majesty's faithful servants will not cease to consider how these interests can be promoted; and now that the Lord Marquis del Vasto, the Lord Don Ugo, with Marcone, are coming, perhaps their advice will put things into better train.

I have resolved to discharge my duty by informing your Majesty of these occurrences, but would to God I could have despatched a courier to your Majesty daily as they proceeded. Four days ago the Cardinal and others of the Colonna were not in the neighbourhood, but he is since arrived, with Lords Vespasiano and Ascanio, who do their best in your Majesty's behalf.

The above I have retained until the 24th of May, and as no courier is gone, I shall here note what has since happened. Your Majesty must know that on the Pope declining to accept the capitulation which I have mentioned above, your Majesty's captains and counsellors began diligently to surround the castle with trenches, &c., &c.

APPENDIX III

(Page 22.)

THE DUKE OF URBINO'S JUSTIFICATION, 1527.[1]

WE print this document with hesitation, and solely from its being the Duke's own and formal defence against very serious charges; which, however, it leaves untouched. It is a futile attempt to evade these by feeble and puling recrimination; to distract attention from their true merits by circumlocutions and reiterations, which our version has somewhat condensed. The original is one unbroken sentence, rudely constructed, apparently of purpose to mystify the reader.

Letter of the Lord Duke of Urbino, Captain-general to the Signory of Venice, dated under Monteleone, 9th July, 1527.

By your Sublimity's letters to the most illustrious lord Provveditore Pisani, and from my ambassador accredited to you, I have learnt, to my infinite dissatisfaction and surprise, the suspicions entertained by you lest the illustrious lady Duchess, my consort, and my son should secretly leave Venice, and the doubts of my good faith which you by implication exhibit in denying them permission to quit the city; regarding which it seems necessary first to recapitulate to your Signory what I had formerly charged my resident to explain to you, to this effect. Since, from the very outset of this war, it has generally happened to me not to accomplish my intentions for your service and my own honour, and to be blamed for failures resulting from the occurrence of impossibilities, or from the blunders of others, whilst with mind and

[1] Sanuto Diarii, xlv. 352.

body I was exclusively occupied on what might prove advantageous and creditable,—I determined, for these and other considerations which, out of modesty, I omit, seeing the bad success with which I had, on this occasion, borne arms, to yield to my evil fortune on the expiry of my engagement; which I considered to be clearly ended at the close of three years; nor again to expose my honour to question, from no fault of mine. And, on this account, I have all along and often said I would not continue, which may be attested by all the commissioners employed by your Serenity in this war, to whom, as to many others you are accustomed to credit, I repeatedly stated this. Passing over for the present the good reasons, already well known to your Sublimity, which induced me to forget all this, and treat of a re-engagement, with the disposition to remain on,—as well as those considerations which, renewing the first impressions, made me again deliberately fall back upon my project, yet with the full intention not to abandon the cause of your Sublimity, unless the expected succours should arrive, or until I had placed it in safety, even should this necessitate my staying long after the conclusion of my service; thinking also that, I having no opposite interest, the enemy ought to let me rest in my intention, and in a firm resolution neither to take up arms, nor otherwise act against your Sublimity and your interests; nevertheless, considering that, were I to quit you at the close of three years, from all these and numerous other reasons, which might probably occasion me annoyance, I might be exposed to the surmise of having acted, not from such motives, but that, on observing the success of the other side, I wished, by attaching myself to a prosperous cause, to evade adversity; and my chief object ever being to preserve my honour intact, not only from stain, but even from suspicion; —on these accounts, and from the difficulty that arose as to finding myself at freedom in regard to the two years of *beneplacito*,[1] I decided to serve, in order not to expose my honour to any reflection. Yet, in addition to all that passed in private between the Proveditore and myself, when I told him I would and should serve your Sublimity without further demands, and that he might

[1] A *condotto*, or military engagement, was usually for so many years certain, and one or two more at the option or *beneplacito* of parties.

freely dispose of me, I, even in the public council, stated my views as to maintaining these bands, and constituting them the mainspring of the war. For the whole of which considerations, I declared that I would serve your Sublimity, without regard to life or anything else, as I have uniformly done, in order more fully to satisfy all the Lords of Council that what I proposed I was, and more than ever am, anxious to do, in conjunction with them. And if the dates of letters be examined, it will be distinctly seen that each of these circumstances occurred much before I had heard, or could have heard, a word as to any doubt or distrust of me being exhibited, which, in my opinion, ought not to be, even were I to take my leave. Thus I had no apprehension; yet, as my intention of so acting was founded on what might fairly be done, I did not suppose that by your Sublimity it would have been not only opposed, but even gainsaid, in restoring to me my son when I should ask him of you, as I meant to do. In such case you might well consider that, even had I any intention to fail you,—a thing you could not and ought not to suppose from my former life,—you would have known how to adopt, and would have adopted, measures suitable to such intentions, and not so frequently have said and reiterated, chiefly to the agents of your Sublimity, that you wished me to be gone; and this after I had voluntarily given into your hands my lady consort and my son, when there was, and could be, no obligation to do so beyond the suggestions of my thorough sincerity. And, with a view to establish this, I lately offered you three proposals, —first, my person, which is here at your Sublimity's disposal in your service; second, my son, who is now in your hands; third, my state, with its fortresses, which I willingly would offer your Sublimity, to be kept, along with myself, in your service and disposal, as full guarantee and security; although I know not what better satisfaction you can require besides my free action, whereby I so long and often have manifested my disposition. And most clear, in my opinion, are the many reasons which freely induced me; all of which, and more too, were they not already so known, I am prepared to maintain in case of need. Hence my modesty, serene Prince, will not, in these circumstances, let me stop to say how great a wrong I suffer; yet to no one, not even to your Sublimity, have I given cause or occasion to depreciate my good faith, which was, is, and ever shall be, most sincere. And, although it be considered impossible that you can do anything without that wisdom which becomes your dignity, I nevertheless have grounds for complaint, and am exceedingly vexed that my ill luck has been so in the ascendant as,—after all the efforts and perils of my life, and the loss of so many followers in your service, for which I have heeded no calamities,—instead of the gratitude which I might reasonably have promised myself from you, to occasion such marked dishonour; so that, ever since my birth, I may say that my life has been passed in ceaseless travails and difficulties. And, if you have thought fit to believe any malicious and spiteful fellow, I ought not to be the victim, though he be an astute and wily foe, who, well aware that I maintained myself to be at liberty, and very often declared myself unwilling to remain, has spread some rumours against me, reckoning that, if in nothing else, he would, at all events, have the satisfaction of circulating that distrust of me which is already apparent, although I ought not on that account to be slandered. I do, therefore, with the greatest possible urgency, beseech you to investigate the truth; and, if I be blameable, to visit me with such punishment as I merit; or, if found innocent, to liberate me, by a suitable public acknowledgment, from the stigma under which I lie. And, commending myself to your favour, I remind you that all these past thoughts of mine arose from no private interest of my own, but from despair at being unable, by no fault of mine, to do what your service and my honour demanded, and at being prevented, by past circumstances, from effecting what I had previously hoped to accomplish, although no exertions of mind or body were wanting on my part. From beneath Monteleone, the 9th of July, 1527.

APPENDIX IV

(Page 27.)

SKETCH OF THE NEGOTIATIONS OF CASTIGLIONE AT THE COURT OF MADRID, 1525 TO 1529, COMPILED FROM THE ABBÉ SERASSI'S PREFACE TO VOL. II. OF CASTIGLIONE'S LETTERS, AND CORRECTED FROM AUTHENTIC SOURCES.

ON his arrival at Madrid, in March, 1525, Castiglione found the Emperor and his ministers much disposed for peace; but matters soon assumed a totally different aspect, on news of the victory of Pavia, which, by annihilating the army of Francis, and leaving him a prisoner, established the supremacy of Charles, and placed him in a position to dictate terms. This event modified the policy of the Italian princes, and especially that of the Pope, who, naturally irresolute, knew not what part to take, unwilling to abandon his avowed neutrality, yet seeing no security in standing aloof from a power so dominant as that of the Emperor. On the whole, he thought it safest to come to a provisional arrangement with Don Carlos de Lanoy, Viceroy of Naples, giving him 100,000 ducats for payment of his troops, as the price of his aid in recovering for the Church Reggio and Rubbiera, which the Duke of Ferrara had seized on the death of Adrian VI. He at the same named as his legate to the leading powers of Christendom, for the purpose of concluding a general peace, Cardinal Giovanni Salviati, who proceeded to Madrid to attend the conferences for the liberation of Francis and the security of Italy. In consort with Castiglione, the Legate urged that an envoy should be forthwith despatched to Rome and

Venice, in order to remove those suspicions of the Emperor's design to make himself master of the entire Peninsula, which had arisen in consequence of the Marquis of Pescara taking possession of the chief fortresses of the Milanese, and besieging Francesco Sforza in his capital, on a pretext of his plotting with the other princes to drive the Spaniards out of Lombardy, and to deprive them of Naples; it being obvious that once established in these provinces, Charles would be paramount in Italy. As to the liberation of Francis, they could get nothing beyond professions of the utmost moderation, that matter being secretly negotiated by the Viceroy.

The Pontiff, getting no satisfaction on these points, began to lend an ear to a proposed league of France, England, and Venice; but, when on the point of subscribing it, he, to the infinite disgust of his colleagues, postponed his signature on a rumour that the Commendatore Herrera was at Genoa, on his way to offer very acceptable proposals; at length, however, finding that these reports were but opiates to set him asleep, he was induced to join the confederation, notwithstanding entreaties and promises of the imperial ambassador. This league filled Charles with indignation, as he fully understood it to be directed against himself, though masked by a condition sanctioning his adherence to it. But his rage was immoderate on receiving, through Castiglione, a papal brief, which justified the confederacy as necessary for the safety of Italy and the Holy See, and complained generally of the measures of his ministers, specifying various instances wherein they had ill responded to the pacific and affectionate dispositions entertained by his Holiness towards their master. Stung to the quick by a despatch which laid bare the secret tricks of their paltry intrigues, they persuaded the Emperor to return a sharp answer, appealing to a general council whatever steps Clement might have recourse to against him, which they represented as likely to endanger his possession of Naples, and even his tenure of the imperial crown. Castiglione, who enjoyed high personal favour, was able by dexterous representations to extract from Charles himself the hope of a milder reply, and meanwhile had from him authority to assure the Pontiff of his friendly intentions, and of his resolution to comport himself as a humble and liege son; and these favourable dispositions were the more readily effected, as he had received from the wavering Pontiff a revocation of the offensive brief the very day after it had been delivered. It was, therefore, with dismay that, when shown the secretary's answer, he found it in the utmost degree bitter and spiteful; and hurrying to the Emperor, he complained of the disrespect thus shown to his Majesty's wishes in an affair of such moment, protesting that he neither could write to his master what his Majesty had already instructed him, without belying the whole negotiation, nor could he, after such treatment, rely upon or report those favourable dispositions which his Majesty had hitherto professed. Charles replied that his real iutentions were conformable to his previous professions, although he had been advised by his ministers to write in such terms as might justify and secure himself, in the face of such groundless imputations as had been made in the objectionable brief; adding the most solemn abjurations, that, if his Holiness comported himself peaceably towards all, he should ever continue a good and obedient son. In an autograph letter to the Nuncio, he reiterated this explanation of his answer, with a hope that the Pope would not take offence at its contents, and an assurance that Castiglione would never be belied by him. The document which the diplomatist had the tact thus to obtain, is relied upon by his biographers as a satisfactory negative to the suspicions of Varchi, that he betrayed the Pontiff and the Church, during his vexatious relations with the Spanish court.

Meanwhile, Francis having been released, on terms which he was unable as well as unwilling to execute, and his sons consequently remaining as hostages, the new League proceeded with hostilities against the Imperialists in Lombardy, and took Lodi, whilst their ambassadors still negotiated at Madrid for the Emperor's adherence to their confederation, and for release of the French princes. This farce of armed protocolising was further complicated by various by-plots, and by endless jealousies and misunderstandings among these diplomatists, so that the Spanish ministry found no difficulty in protracting it by a succession of petty cavils, in the hope of some favourable news from the seat of war. Such was the state of matters when the first sack of Rome by Don Ugo da Moncada and the Colonna, in September 1526, reached the imperial court, and along with it the hurried truce imposed upon Clement. Charles, affecting great indignation, immediately sent to the Pope Cesare Fieramosca, his master of horse, to disown the proceedings of Moncada, and to lavish professions for the peace and welfare of Italy, the only effect of which was to lull the facile and nerveless Pontiff into a fatal security, rudely dispelled by the assault of Bourbon on the heights of the Vatican.

APPENDIX V

(Page 140)

ACCOUNT OF THE ARMADA OF THE MOST SERENE DON JOHN OF AUSTRIA, DRAWN UP AT MESSINA THE LAST OF JULY, 1571.[1]

1. Spanish Infantry, including those at Corfu.

Don Gabriel Hig^{r} of the third of Naples	3000
Of Sicily	1900
Mechil Moncada	1560
Pietro Ciaida	300
Don Giovanni Figarola	280
D. Lopez Figarola	130
Alonzo Ruiz di Carion	144
Francesco Aldana	290
Total	7604

2. Italian Infantry.

The Count of Soriano	1650
Tiberio Brancatio	2000
Paolo Sforza	1800
Pietro Villa and Giorgio Moncada	3000
Paolo Golfario	280
Fra Matteo Belhuomo	200
Vincenzo di Bologna	500
Total	9430

[1] Vat. Urb. MSS. 816, fol. 144–5.

3. Private Individuals.

The Lord Prince of Parma	350
The Lord Paolo Giordano	400
The Marquis of Trevico	100
The Marquis of Briense	750
Giulio Gesuoldo	40
Antonio Doria	30
D. Giovanni di Gueriaza	40
Count di Landriano	80
D. Giovanni di Avalos	20
Count di Vicari	40
Cecco da Lofredo	30
The Prior of Hungary	25
Total	1905

Also of knights from Germany and Burgundy on their own costs	150
The captains of adventure, of very fine appearance and very well armed, may amount to above two thousand; say in all	2150
German infantry (no successor to the Count Lodron yet appointed)	4361

[Abstract.]

Italian infantry	9950
Spanish ,,	7604
Private men-at-arms	1905
Captains of adventure	2150
Germans	4361
Total	25,970

Naval Force.

33 ships, each carrying from 1500 to 4500, or from 6400 to 7000 souls.

Those carrying 700 remain for the westward.

9 large barks, part of them left for the westward, and partly taken for his Highness' effects and for artificial fireworks.

The division of the great galleys to be taken on or left behind is not yet made, not knowing the amount of duty required, nor the eighty paid by the court.

ARTILLERY.

13 canons of 50 lb. fully supplied.
1 ,, of 60 ,,
5 ,, of 35 ,,
3 ,, of 25 ,,
2 ,, for stones.
2 colobrines of 16 lb.
14 sagri of 7 ,,
10 falconets for the great barks.
12 pieces of seven mouths sent by the Grand Duke of Tuscany.

—

62 in all.

AMMUNITION.

7050 iron balls of 50 lb.
3450 ,, ,, of 35 ,,
3250 ,, ,, of 25 ,,
1200 ,, ,, for the colobrines.
3644 iron balls for the sagri.
767 stone balls.

—

19,361 in all.

—

1360 cantars of powder, Neapolitan weight, 100 to each cannon.
1980 cantars of rope for the arquebuses.
1800 cantars of lead.

PROVISIONS.

7000 cantars of biscuit already carried on to Corfu, whereof 1000 lent to the Venetians, and 2000 to the Pope's galleys, leaving 4000 for those of the Marquis Sta. Croce.

26,000 cantars more are returned as in the kingdom of Naples (including the 3000 for the Venetians and his Holiness) under charge of the Marquis of Terranuova, who is to ship 19,000 for the supply of the armament during four months.

3500 pipes [*botte*] of wine in the ships at Corfu.

2500 ,, to be shipped for the Levant by the Marquis of Terranuova.

7400 cantars of salt-meat in the ships at Corfu will be divided at Messina.
1050 cantars for the westward squadron.
8000 ,, of Sardinian cheese at Corfu.
5000 barrels of pickled tunny and anchovies at Corfu for the armament.
1500 cantars of rice } for both armaments.
150 quarters of vetches }
1025 ,, ,, ditto remain in Messina.
600 casks of vinegar.
3570 baskets of oil, Neapolitan measure.

His Highness has resolved that Doria shall accompany his galleys to the Levant, and assist in the transport of stores, under orders to return speedily with twelve galleys; and has made him Proveditore of the western squadron, consisting of forty galleys and other vessels.

APPENDIX VI

(Page 167)

INDULGENCE CONCEDED TO THE CORONA OF THE GRAND DUKE OF TUSCANY BY POPE PIUS V., AND CONFIRMED BY THEIR HOLINESSES URBAN VIII. AND ALEXANDER VII. 1666.

"THIS Corona is called the Corona of the bowels of our Lord Jesus Christ, and consists of ten Ave Marias and one Pater Noster. Every person possessing this Corona shall obtain the remission of all his sins and plenary indulgence.

"Each time that he shall take it up in full faith, and look upon it, saying, 'Lord Jesus Christ, I pray thee by the merit of thy most holy Passion, have mercy on my soul and my weighty sins,' he shall obtain remission thereof; and whoever daily looks upon it and kisses it, for the merit of the most holy Passion, shall receive as above.

"Further, each time that he shall say this, he shall liberate a soul from purgatory, and saying it a thousand times, a thousand souls shall be liberated through the privilege of this Corona; and whoever shall look upon it by the merits of our Lord's Passion, or shall touch it in full faith, shall obtain plenary indulgence and remission as above.

"And further, any ecclesiastic wearing it whilst he says the holy mass shall have the like plenary indulgence and remission, and those hearing the mass shall gain forty days' indulgence.

"Power is given to the Grand Duke to dispense seven Coronas to as many persons, from time to time for ever, warning them that they must ask them in the name of God and through the merits of His most sacred Passion; and these should be delivered gratis."

[From a contemporary copy in Bibl. Cassinatensis, x. iv. 39, p. 369.]

APPENDIX VII

(Pages 210)

MONUMENTAL INSCRIPTIONS OF THE DUCAL FAMILY OF URBINO.

WE have here collected the various inscriptions in memory of the sovereigns of Urbino and their consorts, so far as these have come to our knowledge. Several are taken from Giunta, Abozzamento della Città di Urbino, a MS. in the Albani Library at Rome; or from Lazzari, *Dizionario dei Pittori di Urbino*, where not unfrequent errors occur: others from the originals.

I. Count Guidantonio.

On a pavement tombstone in the old church of S. Donato, close to the Zoccolantine Monastery near Urbino, is a sculptured effigy in the Franciscan habit, with the following doggerel, in some parts illegible:—

"Ploret in Hesperia tellus ! plorate Latini !
  Guido Comes, moriens hoc requiescit humo.
Non fuit a cœlo princeps clementior alter ;
  Prævalidas urbes rexit et ipse potens.
Non fuit in terris unquam qui sanctior heros
  Cappam Francisci posset habere sacri ;
Quem dabit eternis probitas venerabilis ævo
  Mors animam cœlo reddidit alma suo.
Vos igitur superi socio gaudete superno,
  Et Divum servet curia sacra Ducem :
Mille quadringentis domini currentibus annis
  Quadraginta tribus, Februarii vigesima prima."

II. Duke Oddantonio.

Quoted by Lazzari from a broken statue in the palace, which had been inscribed during his life:—

"Serenissimo Oddantonio, principi præclaro, Urbini Duci primo, qui vetusti generis splendore propriâque virtute insignis, ducali diademate a santissimo Eugenio IV. recto fuit judicio decoratus."

III. Duke Federigo.

On his statue in the palace by Girolamo Campagna of Verona.

"Federigo Urbini Duci optimo, S.R. ecclesiæ Vexillifero, fœderatorum principum ac aliorum exercitum imperatori, expugnatori, præliorum omnium victori, propagatæ ditionis ædificiis, et militaris virtutis literis exornatori, populis insigni prudentia, pietate, pace, justitiaque servatis, de Italia benemerenti, Franciscus Maria Dux, abnepos, faciendum curavit."

IV.

On his monument in the Zoccolantine Church of S. Bernardino, near Urbino:—

"D.O.M. Federigo Montefeltrio Urbini Duci II., Sanctæ Romanæ Ecclesiæ vexillifero, Italici fœderis aliorumque exercituum imperatori, præliorum passim victori nunquam victo, ditionis et bonarum artium propugnatori, celebris bibliothecæ et insignium ædificiorum, tum ad magnificentiam tum ad pietatem structori, quem licet aliis preferas, nescias tamen belli an pacis gloria seipsum superavit. Obiit ann. dom. MCCCCLXXXII. suo. LXV."

V. Duke Guidobaldo I.

On his monument in the same church:—

"Guidobaldo Federici filio, Urbini Duci III., qui adhuc impubes, paternam gloriam emulans, imperia viriliter fœliciterque gessit, juvenis de adversâ triumphans fortunâ, sed vi morbi corpore debilior animo vegetior, pro armis literas, pro militibus viros selectissimos, pro re bellica rem aulicam ita coluit, fovit, auxit, ut ejus aula ceteris præclarissimum extet exemplar. Obiit an. Dom. MDVIII., suo XXXVI. Et Elizabethæ Gonzagæ, miræ pudicitiæ feminæ, ipsi jugali amore et egregia virtute conjunctissima."

VI. DUKE FRANCESCO MARIA I.

From a mural slab in Sta. Chiara at Urbino; written by Bembo.

"Francesco Mariæ Duci, amplissime belli pacisque muneribus perfuncto, dum paternas urbes, per vim ter ablatas, ter per virtutem recipit, et receptis æquissime moderatur; dum a pontificibus, a Florentinis, a Venetis exercitibus præficitur; deinceps et gerendi in Turcas belli, dum princeps et administrator assumitur, sed ante diem sublato, Leonora uxor fidissima et optima merittissimo posuit, et sibi."

VII. DUKE GUIDOBALDO II.

From the same church:—

"D. O. M. Guidus Ubaldus Monfeltrius de Ruvere, Urbini Dux quintus, sanctæ Romanæ ecclesiæ, Philippi Hispaniarum Regis, Venetæque reipublicæ exercituum præfectus et imperator summus, magnanimitate et liberalitate adeo excelluit ut eum regia cum majestate aliis potius profuisse quam præfuisse dixeris. Obit humanum diem sexagenarius, anno Dñi MDLXXIII."

VIII. DUCHESS VITTORIA.

From the same church:—

"Victoria Farnesia Guidi Ubaldi Urbini Ducis V. conjux, maximorum principum filia, soror, amita, parens: annis quidem plena, sed præter, mulierum captum virtutibus plenior, migravit e vita anno Dñi, MDCII."

IX.

On the centre slab of the pavement of S. Ubaldo, at Pesaro, where the two last-mentioned sovereigns were interred.

"Guid. Ub. II. Urb. Ducis V. et Victoriæ uxoris ossa."

X. Cardinal Giulio della Rovere.

From a mural slab in Sta. Chiara, at Urbino.

"Julio Montefeltrio e Ruvere, sanctæ Romanæ ecclesiæ cardinali; Umbriæ bis legatione magna cum laude perfuncto; Urbini, Ravennæ, aliarumque ecclesiarum antistiti; Lauretanæ domûs ac Sancti Francisci ordinum patrono; justitiâ, pietate, beneficentiâ, Principi celeberrimo; mortalitatem explevit nonas Septembris, anno Domini MDLXXVIII., ætatis vero XLIV."

XI. Prince Federigo.

Over his tomb in the pavement of the crypt in the cathedral at Urbino.

"D. O. M. In hoc quod Franciscus Maria II., postremus Urbini Dux, sibi paraverat sepulchro, quiescunt ossa Friderici ejus filii immatura morte prærepti, III. Kal. Julii, MDCXXIII., et suæ æt. ann. XVIII."

XII.

From a mural slab in Sta. Chiara, at Urbino.

"Federicum Urbini Principem, in quem Roborea domus recumbebat, dies fugiens incolumem, cunctisque fortunæ muneribus vidit præfulgentem, eundemque primam intra juventam inopinatâ morte extinctum, dies veniens aspexit, III. Kal. Julii, MDCXXIII. Abi hospes, ac disce felicitatem vere vitream tunc præcipue frangi, cum maxime splendet."

XIII. Duke Francesco Maria II.

From the Church of the Crucifixion, near Urbania.

"Inclina Domine aurem tuam ad preces nostras, quibus misericordiam tuam supplices deprecamur, ut animam famuli tui Francisci Mariæ, Urbini Ducis, quam de hoc seculo migrare jussisti in pacis et lucis regione, constituas, et sanctorum tuorum jubeas, esse consortem."

XIV. PRINCESS LAVINIA DELLA ROVERE.

"Laviniæ Feltriæ de Ruvere, Guidobaldi V. Ducis Urb. V. fiilæ, Alfonsi de Avalos, Vasti March., Hispani Magnatis conjugi, regiis virtutibus et forma spectabili, Italorum principum Romani Pontificis et Catholici Regis conciliatrici; qui inclyto orbata viro, virginibus claustra, pauperibus bona, Christo seipsum dicavit; demum avitâ major gloriâ victrix, ad eternam evocata pacem, eam sanctimoniæ famam reliquit, ut divinitus datum noscas ultimum Roboris in materno solo arvisque ramum, qui primus gloriosiorque vigebat. Obiit A.D. MDCXXXII., suo LXXV."

APPENDIX VIII

(Page 246)

STATISTICS OF URBINO

IT would be interesting could we, in concluding this work, offer some details as to the statistics of Urbino under its native princes. But although, under the genial sun and favouring circumstances of Italy, man has in various ages advanced beyond his fellows in mental culture and social development, the science of maturing the capabilities of his position, and of marking their progression, is of modern growth. The duties of rulers and subjects consisted until lately in defence of the common weal against obvious dangers: the promotion of its general prosperity, and the registration of its gradual ameliorations, were no part either of scientific government, or of individual study. Accordingly, the lights thrown upon statistics, by historians and general writers in the best days of Italian splendour, are too few and flickering to guide us to important facts; and, though we may familiarise ourselves with the Athenian court of Duke Guidobaldo I., its manners and its gossip,—though we may recall from the ample description of many authors the stately decorations of its palaces, the pageantry of its processions, the brilliancy of its revels,—we are left in total ignorance of the internal state of the country, of its resources and industry, of the numbers and the condition of its inhabitants, of the financial position of its government. It is not till late in the sixteenth century that we meet with some materials, which,—though meagre and inaccurate, and too often bearing the double impress of carelessness and contradiction,—enable us to form some tangible estimate as to these points.[1] Here, as in most

[1] From a league between Count Antonio, of Urbino, and Barnabo Visconti, of Milan, in 1376 (MSS. Oliveriana, No. 374, vol. I., p. 1), we

cases, recording the impartial evidence of watchful observers, the Venetian Relazione are of considerable value. Those of Mocenigo and Zane, ambassadors at Urbino in 1570–74, have been already drawn upon in this work, but it is chiefly from the latter that we have gathered the following notices.

About the middle of the sixteenth century the revenues of the duchy did not exceed 40,000 scudi, and by the terms of its investiture the imposts could not be raised without papal sanction. This restriction having been removed upon the marriage of Duke Guidobaldo II.'s daughter to the nephew of Pius IV., that prince promptly availed himself of his new prerogative, augmenting them gradually to about double that amount. The reductions consequent upon the Urbino insurrection brought down the state revenues to about 60,000 scudi, and in 1570 Mocenigo estimates the whole income, including the allodial estates, at 100,000 scudi, adding an opinion that it was capable of being much increased. Of the 60,000 scudi, one-sixth part was derived from the salt, and two-sixths from licences granted for the export of corn [*tratte*], the remaining half being drawn from small taxes upon tne townships, to which the rural population do not appear to have directly contributed. The corn-trade was carried on coastwise from Sinigaglia, amounting in ordinary years to about 150,000 *staji* or bushels of wheat, partly smuggled from the papal territory, which chiefly went to supply Venice and its dependencies. The palpable inadequacy of these resources was eked out by pay and allowances drawn by the last dukes from the Venetian Republic, the Church, or the King of Spain. The *cense* or annual payment to the Camera Apostolica under the investiture is variously stated at from 2190 to 2907 scudi, falling due on St. Peter's day.

With these Venetian Relazioni, a document of much apparent interest has been printed in the *Archivio Storico*, under the title of "Balance of income and expenditure in the state of Urbino."[2] On nearer inspection, however, its value falls far short of its

gather an isolated notice. Free import from the territory of Urbino into Florence was stipulated for all sorts of grain, fruit, and vegetables, the customary duties being paid upon wheat, oats, and barley.

[2] Series II., vol. II., p. 337, from a MS. in the Siena Library, K. iii. 58: it is dated 1579, but contains posterior entries.

promise, for the entries are so confused, and the arithmetical summations so incorrect, as to destroy nearly all confidence either in the details or the general results. Still it seems to have established a few facts throwing light upon the resources of the duchy in the last years of the sixteenth century.

The revenues may be thus classified:—1. Those of twelve towns, five smaller places, and the province of Montefeltro, derived from various taxes,[1] duties on butcher-meat, salt, wine, straw, weighhouse duties on grain and other provisions, and on merchandise, passenger toll at Pesaro, rents of houses and inns, tax on the Jews (producing 953 scudi), and a variety of minor imposts varying in different places. The customs of Pesaro yielded 1226 sc.; those of Sinigaglia 160, besides 436 for pot dues, and 6000 for grain and vegetables shipped for exportation. 2. Income from manufactures[2] in various towns, stated at 5712 sc. 3. The salt duties, or perhaps monopoly, 5407 sc. 4. Revenue from mills, payable in wheat (*grano*) at 4 sc. a *soma*, 5832 sc. 5. Value of barley and oats (*spelta*) contributed by various communities, 1020 sc. 6. Mountain rents, 610 sc. 7. Donatives paid in wine, wood, and straw, to the value of 630 sc. 8. Produce of allodial lands, in wheat, oats, barley, beans, lupinse, peas, vetches, buckwheat, flour, hay, straw, hemp, lint, wine, walnuts, wool, cheese, pigeons, and waterfowl, to the gross amount of 7321 sc. The return of expenditure is too vague and confused to be of any use, but it contains provisions to the Duchess, amounting to about 7000 sc. From these returns the Venetian estimates would appear to be understated, and a contemporary writer, whose anonymous Reports upon the Italian principalities issued from the Elzivir press, sets down its revenues in 1610 at above 200,000 scudi, of which 8000 were paid as cess to the Camera Apostolica. The imposts were considered light, for the soil was in many parts productive, and grain was exported largely from it and the adjoining Marca, at the port of Sinigaglia. The Duke's treasure in S. Leo is reckoned at 2,000,000 of scudi, a palpable error for 200,000. In 1024, the *Mercurius Gallicus* estimates the revenues of the duchy at 300,000 scudi, besides allodial lands, and estates in Naples amounting to 50,000 more.

[1] The word used is *colte*, which might mean crops.
[2] *Fabbriche* might mean only shops.

In regard to population, the estimate of Zane is 150,000, the majority of whom devoted themselves to agriculture and arms, commercial industry being almost unknown. He calculates the military force at 10,000 men, half of them being trained, and about three-fourths ready for foreign service; and he dwells upon the benefit which his Republic might derive from conciliating a state whence such a force could on any exigency be quickly obtained, without the necessity of seeking free passage from any other power. The report of 1610, which evidently verges upon exaggeration, gives the fighting men at 20,000, nearly all infantry. In 1591, as we learn from an original MS.,[1] the military force of the duchy amounted to 13,313 men, of whom 8300 carried arquebuses, and 3783 wore morions. From the same authority is taken the following tabular view of the whole population, classed under townships, and amounting in 1598 to 115,121 souls.

List of mouths in all the places of the state, drawn from the Rasegne de' Grani, &c., in 1598[2]:—

Urbino	18,335
Pesaro	16,409
Gubbio	18,510
Fossombrone	1,882
Cagli	6,811
Montefeltro	15,090
Sinigaglia	8,535
Massa	9,845
Mondavio	3,738
Pergola	3,254
Mondolfo	1,820
Sta. Costanza	1,504
Orciano	1,234
Barchio	1,479
La Fratta	1,449
Montesecco	1,711
Montebello	395
Castelvecchio	225
Poggio di Berni	507
Fenigli	434
La Tomba	1,953
	115,121

[1] Vat. Urb. MSS., No. 935. [2] *Ibid.*

A report upon Urbino, drawn up for Urban VIII. during the last Duke's life, and preserved in the Albani Library, estimates the men trained to arms at from 8000 to 10,000, but badly officered, and ill-armed or accoutred. Since the Devolution, population had increased, and the last census of the legation, nearly corresponding with the duchy, gave 220,000 souls within an area of 180 square leagues, the city of Urbino containing 7500, besides 4500 in the adjacent district.

In 1574, few or none of the nobility drew from their estates a rental exceeding 3000 scudi, but there were many burgesses owning from 300 to 400 a year. The few merchants were chiefly foreigners. Most of the small towns had been dismantled of their fortifications, only some fifty having them kept in repair, of which about twenty belonged to as many petty feudatories.

A writer soon after the Devolution states the Duke's revenues at 100,000 to 120,000 scudi, including 20,000 of Spanish subsidy, as much of allodial income, and 30,000 from escheats, penalties, and the port duties of Sinigaglia, whence a great grain trade was carried on by the Venetians out of the Marca.[1] Some years after the duchy had lost its independence, although this export was then prohibited by Urban VIII., and notwithstanding the loss of the allodial estates, the Camera drew above 100,000 scudi from direct and fiscal taxation. The militia at that time numbered 8000 infantry and 500 cavalry, besides the garrison of Sinigaglia. The *fattorie*, or allodial farms, yielded to the Duke 14,000 scudi when leased, but afterwards, when administered on his account, they produced 18,000: the income from mills was about 6000; that of S. Leo 10,000, of which above 6000 were spent in maintaining the place.

Some idea may be formed of the provisions for administering justice from a narrative compiled after the Devolution, but which expressly states the arrangements for this purpose to be the same as adopted by the Dukes.[2] The judges were entitled vicars or captains, podestàs, commissaries, and lieutenants, and were removable at pleasure. The vicars or captains resided in certain small towns, and were notaries, who acted as judges and clerks

[1] Vat. Ottob. MSS., No. 3135, f. 279.
[2] *Ibid.*, f. 277, 321.

within their assigned bounds. Their jurisdiction extended to all cases of injury or quarrel, which they were bound to decide according to the respective municipal statutes, or, in absence of such, according to those of Urbino. In civil causes they were limited to a certain amount; above which, recourse was had to the judge of the chief district town. They had no proper criminal jurisdiction, but were bound to report all accidents to the sovereign, who frequently remitted to them to examine into slight delicts; those inferring corporal punishment being sent to a doctor, under whom the vicar acted as clerk. The podestàs were judges-ordinary in all civil and criminal cases within their bounds: and where there was no resident commissary or lieutenant, the public administration and police were intrusted to them; to each of them there was assigned one clerk for criminal cases, called *maleficj*, and named by the Duke, and two for civil causes chosen by the community. The system of appeal from one of these courts to another, being founded upon local reasons, was complicated, and need not be detailed. The court of final resort in civil matters was the Collegiate Rota of Urbino, over which thirteen judges presided, five of whom were necessarily ecclesiastics. They held office for life, and vacancies were filled up by the sovereign from a leet of three voted by the remaining number. They sat twice a week, five being a quorum; and they had also the review of ecclesiastical causes, in which, however, the lay members had only a consultive voice. In certain suits their decision might be brought under review of the sovereign.

There were likewise three auditors, who had no ordinary jurisdiction, but sat daily in presence of the sovereign as an executive council, to whom all criminal matters were reported by the magistracy. Their salaries after the Devolution were 400 scudi a year. They were also bound to take cognisance of all fiscal affairs, and of all complaints brought before them, and they were charged with the interests of widows and orphans, and generally with all matters voluntarily brought before them by consent of parties. After the Devolution, their salaries were 400 scudi a year; that of the fiscal advocate, 384; and of the secretary of justice, 320. The income of the judges, whom we have already mentioned as located in the towns and villages, varied from half a scudo yearly to 240 scudi, the latter being the pay of the Captain of Urbino. The lower class of these officers were all notaries, but, after allowing for professional gains and fees, such remuneration was disgracefully small, especially as it was paid in the ducal money, which had become depreciated to two-thirds of the currency value in the papal states. The pay of the legate was 1400 scudi, that of the vice-legate 600, besides about 1200 of fees.

APPENDIX IX

(Page 391 note *[1])

TWO SONNETS BY PIETRO ARETINO ON TITIAN'S PORTRAITS OF DUKE FRANCESCO MARIA I. AND HIS DUCHESS LEONORA

I.

ON DUKE FRANCESCO MARIA I.

Se il chiaro Apelle con la man dell' arte
Esemplò d' Alessandro il volto, e 'l petto,
Non finse già di pellegrin subjetto
L' alto vigor, che l' anima comparte.
Mà Titian, che dal cielo hà maggior parte,
Fuor mostra ogni invisible concetto ;
Però il gran Duca, nel dipinto aspetto,
Scuopre le palme entro il suo cuor consparte.
Egli hà il terror frà l' uno e l' altro ciglio,
L' animo en gl' occhi, e l' alterezza in fronte,
Nel crin spatia l' honor, siede il consiglio.
Nel busto armato e nelle braccie pronte
Arde il valor, che guarda dal periglio
Italia sacra, e sua virtudi conte.

II.

ON DUCHESS LEONORA.

L' union de' colori chi lo stile
Di Titian distese, esprime fora
La concordia che regge in Leonora,
E le ministre del spirto gentile.
Seco siede modestia in atto humile,
Ed honestà che in vesta sua dimora,
Vergogna il petto, e 'l crin le vela e honora,
L' effigia Amor lo sguardo signorile.

Pudicitia, e beltà nemiche eterne
  Le spatian nel sembiante, e frà le ciglia
  Il trono delle Gratie si discerne.
Prudenza il suo valor guarda, e consiglia
  Nel bel tacer, l' alte virtudi interne
  Gli ornan la fronte d' ogni meraviglia.

III.

SONNET BY BERNARDO TASSO, PRAYING TITIAN TO PAINT HIS MISTRESS'S PORTRAIT.

Ben potete con l' ombre, e coi colori,
  Dotto Pittor rassimigliar al vero
  Quella beltà, ch' ognor col mio pensiero
  Via più bella, ping' io fra l' herbe e i fiori :
Ma quelle gratie, che i più freddi cori
  Riscaldano, onde Amor ricco et altero
  Stende le braccie del suo dolce impero,
  Opra non è da chiari alti pittori.
Se potete ritrar quel viso adorno,
  Quel girar de' begli occhi honesti e santi,
  Che ogni rara beltà fà parer vile,
Con pace sia d' ogni pittor gentile,
  E statue e tempii al vostro nome intorno
  Ergeran lieti i più cortesi amanti.

APPENDIX X

(Page 410)

PETITION TO GUIDOBALDO II. DUKE OF URBINO, BY CERTAIN MAJOLICA-MAKERS IN PESARO

Most illustrious and most excellent Lord Duke,

To your most illustrious Lordship have recourse these devoted petitioners, Mo. Bernardin Gagliardino and Co., Mo. Girolamo Lanfranchi, Mo. Rinaldo and Co., all makers of vases and bottles, citizens and inhabitants of Pesaro; Mo. Piermateo, and Mo. Bartolomeo Pignattari, citizens and indwellers of Pesaro; and all the others who inhabit the county of Pesaro;—setting forth how they find themselves continually, from year's end to year's end, subject to all sorts of burdens and imposts, exacted on real and personal property, and paying it with the sweat of their labour. They greatly complain how it seems to them wrong that strangers of their craft come into this city and district with similar productions, to take bread out of their hand, at all seasons of the year, a thing not allowed to themselves in other countries. For which causes they propose to your most illustrious Lordship the following articles for your signature.

First, that your Lordship would concede to them that no one, stranger or townsman, shall, on any pretext, sell, or export for sale from the city and district, earthen vases of whatever sort, excepting covered pans and oil-pitchers, or other vessels exceeding the size of a *medrio;* declaring always that, at the fair, all may sell any kind of vases, but at no intermediate time, on pain of forfeiture, and a penalty of ten lire of Bologna for each offence, one-half to your illustrious Lordship's chamberlain, one-fourth to the informer, and the rest to the party enforcing it;

always excepting figured vases of Urbino, and white ones from Urbino and Faenza.

It is further desired that no inhabitant, not engaged in this art in the city or district, be permitted to purchase foreign productions for resale, except those imported during the fair; always under the like penalties on contravention hereof.

And, in order to satisfy your Lordship that no inconvenience may arise to the city from this, they bind themselves henceforward to see that it be constantly supplied with such vases as are required, and usually made therein, and especially with figured vases of beautiful and stately character, and this for the customary prices, these being in nowise altered; and, in case of their departing from this, your Excellency shall be free to cancel these articles.

* * * * * *

Confirmed and enjoined as asked, but during our pleasure.

Pesaro, 27th April, 1552.

Passeri, p. 34.

APPENDIX XI

(Page 411)

LETTER FROM THE ARCHBISHOP OF URBINO TO CARDINAL GIULIO DELLA ROVERE, REGARDING A SERVICE OF MAJOLICA

To the most illustrious and most reverend Lord, my singular Lord and patron, the Lord Cardinal of Urbino in Ravenna.

Most illustrious and most reverend Lord, my singular Lord and patron,

On arriving at Urbino, I ordered of Mo. Horatio [Fontana], *vasaro*, the service [*credenza*] commissioned by your most affectionate and most reverend Lordship, for the most illustrious Monsignore Farnese. And, as there will be so many vases done with grotesques, in addition to the white ones (as per inclosed list), I could not manage it for less than thirty-six scudi, which, if I am not mistaken as to what he gets from others, is very good treatment. All the white pieces will have on the reverse the arms of Farnese in small, and I feel certain that the service will give satisfaction. He promises to deliver it finished in little more than a month, and, as an inducement to serve you well, as I trust he will do, I have, at his request, advanced him some money. If your illustrious Lordship please, let M. Ludovico Perucchi be written to, that he may pay the above-mentioned sum on account of this. As soon as finished, I shall get Horatio to pack it well, in order to go safely, and shall despatch it to Rome in such way as you shall direct. And, having no more to say, I remain humbly kissing your hands, and commending you to our Lord God, that, in his favour, he ever give you all your desires. From Urbino, the 2nd of March, 1567.

Your most illustrious and most reverend Lordship's
most humble servant,
Your Archbishop.

List of white pieces with arms on the reverse.

1 large cistern.
1 large bason, and 1 bottle.
1 barber's bason, and small brush.
6 great, and 12 middling dishes.
6 large and 6 middling comfit dishes.
2 vases for vinegar and oil, 4 salts.
36 dishes, 50 smaller ditto.
50 plates, 24 ditto [*piadene*].

With grotesques.

1 large cistern.
1 bason and bottle.
4 cups on raised stands.
1 barber's bason and brush.
2 salts.

APPENDIX XII

COLLECTIONS OF ART MADE BY THE DUKES OF URBINO

THE extent and value of the works of arts amassed by a series of sovereigns, who, during nearly two centuries, were continuously patrons of arts in its best days, cannot be uninteresting topics of inquiry, and fall within the scope of these volumes, as an important test of the knowledge and taste of the collectors. The beautiful objects which Castiglione and others include among the attractions of the palace at Urbino have thus acquired an almost classic importance, and to identify them with those now familiar to the travelled amateur were a pleasing result. Much more would it be so could we realise an ingenious theory put forward in the *Quarterly Review*,[1] that, by ascertaining what were the pictures first offered to the enthusiastic gaze of the youthful Raffaele, we might even now trace those early impressions of beauty which, reproduced by his fine genius and taste, have been unanimously adopted as standards of pictorial perfection. This gratifying hope is, however, delusive. To the ravages of two invasions, succeeded, in both instances, by military usurpation, may perhaps be imputed the disappearance of almost every picture which could have existed in the palace previously to 1521, for very few such were found there on the extinction of the ducal house in 1631. In order to throw every possible light upon this matter, I have spared no researches at Urbino, Pesaro, and Florence, and, from a variety of inventories, I have collected the facts which are now to be stated.

The principal sources of this information have been, *First*, a

[1] Vol. LXVI., pp. 3–10.

list of "good pictures," brought to Florence, in 1631, from the wardrobe of Urbino. It is in the archives of the Gallery degli Uffizii, at Florence, in the autograph of Pelli, and is obviously the document frequently referred to by him in his Galleria di Firenze. *Second*, a note of the objects of art in the Urbino inheritance, as inventoried by Bastiano Venturi in 1654. This is in a folio volume of inventories, preserved in the wardrobe archives of the Pitti Palace, and includes the succession of Duchess Livia, as well as that of her husband, the last Duke of Urbino. *Third*, selections from a full inventory of the wardrobe of Urbino, dated in 1623, and now No. 386 of the MSS. in the Oliveriana Library at Pesaro. Of these documents, the first is, unquestionably, of most importance as to the identity and value of the objects enumerated; and the last, having been compiled by a person unacquainted with art, cannot be much depended upon.

We may, however, estimate the extent of the collections in the different palaces of Francesco Maria II. from the Venturi inventory, and from another dated in 1623, which is No. 460 of the Oliveriana MSS. In the latter there are enumerated as at Pesaro (besides a series of sixty-two portraits in the gallery, sixty-nine maps, and a hundred and thirty-five plans of cities) eight hundred and forty-three pictures. This large amount includes apparently all the framed engravings, embroideries, and miniatures; and a great proportion were portraits of the ducal family and their connections. The small number which have the painters' names assigned to them renders this, the fullest list, of little interest. In the same palace are mentioned sixty-four pieces in marble, chiefly busts; and in various other palaces and chapels were some other pictures, seemingly of minor importance. The Venturi catalogue enumerates only ninety pictures, seventy miniatures in oil, eleven embroideries, twenty-nine tapestries, eighty bronzes, enamels, and carvings, and fifty-one works in marble and stone. These seem to have been the principal objects reserved out of the inheritance, the remainder having probably been given away or sold at Pesaro and Florence. This selection bears evidence of care and connoisseurship; but that of Pelli having the best pretensions to these qualities, the pictures it names are fully given in the first of the lists here subjoined, ending with No. 50. In the two subsequent ones, from Nos. 51 to 95, are included all other Urbino pictures of any moment which I have been able to glean from the inventories now described, and from other sources. To each picture is added such information regarding its identity as extended inquiry and observation have enabled me to hazard. Imperfect as it is, it will interest those who visit Florence, and may save them from very troublesome and often fruitless inquiries, which occupied me for many weeks.

I. PELLI'S LIST OF THE URBINO PICTURES.

Raffaele.

1. Madonna, Christ, and St. John Baptist, on panel. Pelli in a marginal note states this to be the *Madonna della Seggiola*, although he admits that a different extraction is by some assigned to that masterpiece. No picture thus described appears in the Pesaro inventories; that of Venturi mentions one such, but calls it a copy after Raffaele. The Madonna della Seggiola, now No. 151 of the Pitti Gallery, is said by Passavant to have been in an inventory of the Tribune, dated 1585, of course long antecedent to the Devolution of Urbino.

2. Madonna, Christ, St. John Baptist, and another Figure, on panel, large. In the Pesaro inventory, the Christ is said to be in arms; in the Venturi, two pictures are noted of the Madonna, Christ, St. John Baptist, and St. Elizabeth, but both are called copies of Raffaele. No work now in the Florence galleries answers this description.

3. His own Portrait on panel. It is described but not named by Venturi, and unquestionably is the small picture now among the portraits of painters in the Uffizi, No. 288. (See above, vol. II., p. 223.)

4, 5. Julius II., on panel, and the same on paper. Of this famous portrait several repetitions contest the palm of originality. The two best probably are those in the Pitti, No. 79, and in the Tribune, both on panel; the former, perhaps, has the advantage in breadth and mellow colouring, and I have heard the latter ascribed by Italian connoisseurs to a Venetian pencil.*[1] Con-

*[1] The Pitti portrait is an inferior replica of that in the Tribune of the Uffizi.

sidering the relationship and intimacy of the Pope with the Dukes of both dynasties, there can be little doubt that they possessed an original likeness, as well as the original cartoon mentioned above. The latter has passed into the Corsini Gallery, at Florence, and is admirable in bold character as well as in preservation. The pricked outlines attest its having been used more than once; and the first painting from it is understood to have been presented by his Holiness to the Church of the Madonna del Popolo, at Rome, a fane greatly favoured by the della Rovere. The Pesaro list includes the cartoon, and Venturi the panel portrait, which, according to the annotator of the last edition of Vasari (Florence, 1838), was that in the Tribune, the head alone of the Pitti one being, in his opinion, by Raffaele, the rest by Giulio Romano. Passavant, however, adjudges the palm of merit and originality to its rival in the Pitti collection, and considers it the Urbino picture.

TITIAN.

6, 7. DUKE FRANCESCO MARIA I., and his DUCHESS LEONORA, on canvas. These are justly considered among the choicest portraits of this master, but are painted in very different styles, the Duke being treated with extraordinary freedom, the Duchess in a severe and somewhat hard manner, suited to her stiff matronly air. They ornament the Venetian room at the Uffizi, Nos. 605 and 599, and the former supplies a frontispiece to this volume. Another portrait of him from the same hand is mentioned in Pelli's note. (See above, pp. 48, 58, 371–3.)

8. DUKE GUIDOBALDO [II.] Of this portrait I find no trace, though it is named in the Pesaro list, and may be that described by Venturi as in an antique dress.*[1]

9. HANNIBAL OF CARTHAGE, on canvas. Mentioned in the Pesaro inventory, but not now known.

10. MADONNA, CHILD, ST. JOHN BAPTIST, AND ST. ANNA, on panel, large. No trace of this picture appears in any inventory, or Florentine gallery.

11. THE NATIVITY, on panel. Not mentioned elsewhere; it

*[1] Gronau thinks this portrait may be the so-called "Young Englishman" of the Pitti Gallery (No. 92). Cf. GRONAU, *op cit.*

or the following may be the picture painted with a moonlight effect, now No. 443, of the Pitti Gallery; or that described by Venturi as "a woman swaddling an infant."*[1]

12. QUEM GENUIT ADORAVIT, on panel; or the Madonna adoring her Child. This I have nowhere been able to identify. (See the preceding No., and also below, No. 20.)

13. MADONNA DELLA MISERICORDIA, on canvas. The Pesaro list tells us it came from the Imperiale villa, and contained the painter's portrait, with many figures. It is No. 484 of the Pitti collection, where it is assigned to Marco di Tiziano, the cousin and favourite pupil of Titian. Following the usual type, this "Madonna of Mercy" is represented as a gigantic female, whose outstretched arms infold under her ample mantle of compassion, six men, five women, and two children; the eldest of the group is evidently Titian, and the rest are, no doubt, members of the Vecelli family. The picture was probably votive, in commemoration of some signal mercy vouchsafed to his house.

14. THE SAVIOUR, on panel. A half-length figure in profile, perhaps the finished study for some large composition. It is noted in all the inventories, and was carried by the French to Paris, but is now in the Pitti Palace, No. 228.

15. ECCE HOMO, on panel. Also included in all the inventories, and probably the picture No. 330 of the Pitti Gallery, where it is called in the manner of Sebastian del Piombo.*[2]

16. MAGDALEN, on panel. This is now No. 67 in the Pitti collection; a half-length, half-nude penitent, with variations from the frequent repetitions of the same subject by this master; her eye, no longer tearful, is upraised with an expression of joyful hope: the penitent is at peace. (See above, p. 375.)

17. JUDITH, on canvas. In the Pesaro inventory it is described as on panel, and both there and in Pelli's note it is ascribed to Titian *or* Palma Vecchio, whilst Venturi assigns it to Pordenone. It is now in the Venetian room of the Uffizi, with the name of Pordenone, and is on panel.*[3]

18. NAKED WOMAN LYING, large, life-size, on canvas. All

*[1] This picture is not by Titian, but by Marco Vecellio.
*[2] This picture no longer hangs in the Pitti Gallery.
*[3] No. 619, Uffizi, I suppose. It is by Palma Vecchio.

The Bassani.

27. A Supper. This was, doubtless, the Cenacolo, No. 446 in the Pitti Gallery, assigned to Leandro Bassano.

28, 29. The building and entering of the Ark. These are, probably, the companion pictures in the corridor of the Uffizi, which seem poor copies, though ascribed to Francesco. Of the latter, representing the Deluge, there is on the same wall a large and fine replica with his name, and a picture of animals entering the ark with the name of Jacopo.

30. Composition of Figures and Animals. It is stated by the Pesaro list to have come from the chapel in the lower gardens of that city, and may have been the large picture of the Rich Man and Lazarus, now in the corridor of the Uffizi, where it bears the name of Francesco.

31–34. Four Pictures. As there are fourteen pictures of the Bassani in the Uffizi, and five in the Pitti, besides those noticed above, and several portraits, it would be idle to attempt identifying these four. All these eight works of this family are noted in the Pesaro list, but omitted in Venturi's.

Baroccio.

35. Portrait of S. A. S. This is probably to be read Sua Altezza Serenissima Francesco Maria II., the last Duke of Urbino, now an ornament of the Tribune. It is a half-length on canvas, in armour richly inlaid in steel and gold, his helmet by his side and a scarf across his shoulder, being, as we learn from the Pesaro list, the uniform in which he returned from his naval expedition; a circumstance which fixes the date in 1572, when the Duke was in his twenty-third, and the painter in his forty-fourth, year. Nothing can surpass the fluid harmony and pellucid colouring of this picture, equally remarkable for breadth and high finish, but the feeble design apparent in the arms renders it impossible to give by the burin a favourable impression of its merit. I have therefore preferred engraving for this work a much less brilliant portrait obtained by me at Pesaro. A repetition of the Tribune picture, less clear but still more charming, graces the select gallery of Baron Camuccini at Rome.

36. VISITATION OF THE MADONNA, on canvas, painted, according to the Pesaro inventory, for the chapel there, on the visit of Pope Clement VIII. in 1598. It has disappeared.

37. MAGDALEN, on canvas. There are two pictures of this subject, and another in the Venturi list, one on panel, one on canvas, the latter of which is described as "the Magdalen in the Wilderness." I have not found either of them; but a Magdalen in devotion with Christ, upon canvas, is noted in the Pesaro inventory, and may probably be the large and fine picture now in the Sala di Baroccio at the Uffizi, known as *Noli me tangere*, in which the Saviour appears to the Magdalen after His resurrection.

38. MADONNA, ST. FRANCIS, AND ST. UBALDO, on canvas, unfinished. No doubt one of the votive pictures commissioned on the birth of Prince Federigo. (See above.) It has disappeared.

39. PORTRAIT OF MAESTRO PROSPERO, a Franciscan monk, half-length, on canvas; called by Venturi a Minim Observantine friar. Not identified.

THE ZUCCARI.

40. PORTRAIT OF DUKE GUIDOBALDI [II.] IN ARMOUR, HIS HAND UPON A DOG'S HEAD. In the Pesaro inventory it is said to be on panel; in that of Venturi it is ascribed to Baroccio. It has disappeared, but a bad copy is preserved in the Albani Palace at Urbino.

41. ST. PETER IN PRISON, large. This picture is engraved at No. 373 of the folio work on the Pitti Gallery, and is said by Vasari to have been painted for Duke Guidobaldo II., by Federigo Zuccaro when about twenty-three years of age. It ranks among his best works; for though the idea is borrowed from Raffaele's fresco, the treatment and the effect of chiaroscuro are original and good. The heavy grated window and the monotonous colouring are however injurious to the work.

42. HEAD OF ST. FRANCIS, on canvas. Lost, unless it be the Vision of the Saint in a wide landscape, on panel, No. 482 of the Pitti Gallery, where it is called anonymous. The Pesaro list describes him as in a landscape, by Federigo Zuccaro.

43. CALUMNY, large, by Federigo, unnoticed in the other inventories, and undiscovered.

Mascherino.

44. Christ with Nicodemus, Nicolas, and two Angels, on canvas. Of this I can ascertain nothing.

Anonymous.

45. Pope Sixtus IV., on panel. The Venturi inventory notes a similar anonymous portrait, by Baroccio, and one on panel of a Pope by Titian. This and the following number may be the portraits quoted as Titian's by Vasari.

46. Pope Paul III., on panel. Perhaps No. 297 in the Pitti Palace, where it is ascribed to Paris Bordone, and of which I have seen several good repetitions. The Venturi inventory contains another panel portrait of an anonymous pope by Titian.

47. Duke Francesco Maria I. in armour, on canvas. Perhaps a copy of No. 6, above.

48. Duke Guidobaldo, on panel; unknown. Possibly the original of the likeness engraved for this work of Guidobaldo II.

49. A Lady in a dark antique dress, with a shell in her hand, on canvas. Of this nothing is known.

50. Magdalen nearly naked, on canvas, described in the Pesaro list as reading a book. Not found.

Having now gone through Pelli's note of selected pictures, we shall complete our materials for estimating the Urbino collections, by adding such other works as are mentioned in the Venturi and Pesaro inventories.

II. VENTURI INVENTORY.

Raffaele.

51. The Duke of Urbino, a profile in half-armour, on canvas. This was probably the portrait mentioned by Bembo in a letter, wherein he speaks of it as a much less successful likeness than that of the poet Tibaldeo.

52. Marriage of the Madonna, a copy on canvas, no doubt

from the fine picture now in the Brera at Milan, which was painted for the church of S. Francesco, at Città di Castello.

53. Lucrezia, copy on panel. Of this neither the original nor the copy are known.

Titian.

54. Madonna, Christ, St. Joseph, and St. Elizabeth, on panel. Not identified.

55. Madonna, Christ, and St. John Baptist, on panel. Not identified.

56. Portrait of a foreign Lady, small, on panel. Not found.

57. Portrait of a Man in an antique dress, on panel. Not identified.

58. A Man armed with a morion and shield, on canvas, *after* Titian. Not identified.

Baroccio.

59. Madonna with Christ in her arms, St. Augustin, and St. Francis, on canvas. Not found.

60. Christ in a Cradle, Madonna, St. John, and St. Elizabeth, on canvas. Not found.

61. St. Francis, on panel. Not found.

62. A Man with a chemisette, on canvas; probably the half-length of Duke Francesco Maria II., with six gold buttons, mentioned in the Pesaro inventory, and of which No. 162 of the Pitti collection seems a finished head study on paper.

63. Marchese Ippolito della Rovere, on canvas. Not found.

64. Monsignore Giuliano della Rovere, on canvas. Not found.

65. The Saviour with the Globe in his Hand, *after* Baroccio. Now No. 101 in the Pitti Palace, where it is called *by* Baroccio. A poor picture.

Antonio.

66. A Woman in an antique dress, on panel. This may refer to Antonello di Messina. Not found.

67. PETRARCH AND LAURA painted bookwise. This is doubtless a blundering description of the heads of DUKE FEDERIGO and DUCHESS BATTISTA of Urbino, by PIETRO DELLA FRANCESCA, placed like a diptych or book in the same frame. They have been engraved at Volume I., p. 120, of this work, from the originals among the miscellaneous Italian pictures in the Uffizi.

68. A FRANCISCAN FRIAR TEACHING MATHEMATICS TO ANOTHER PERSON, on panel. This is ascribed to Ghirlandajo or Signorelli, but the subject makes it more probably a work of PIETRO DELLA FRANCESCA, court painter to Duke Federigo. I have found no such picture.

GIORGIONE.

69. A DUKE OF URBINO, on canvas. Probably Guidobaldo I., but unfortunately lost.

HOLBEIN.

70. TWO DUKES OF SAXONY, bookwise, small. They are Frederick III. and John I.; now in the German room of the Uffizi, where they are ascribed to Lucas Cranach.

SCARSELLINO.

71. CHRIST RECEIVING ST. PETER, on panel; a small picture. Not found.

72. CHRIST WITH HIS FOOT UPON A SERPENT'S SKIN [*scoglione*], on panel; a small picture. Not found.

THE ZUCCARI.

73. A WOMAN WITH A COCKLE-SHELL IN HER HAND, on canvas. Not found.

74. MADONNA, CHRIST, AND ST. JOHN BAPTIST, on panel, after Jacopo * * * *. Not found.

L'ALEMANO.

75. THE NATIVITY, on panel. Not identified.

V. DANDINI.

76. AURORA, on canvas. Not found.

Il Cerretani.

77. The Nativity, on canvas. Not found.

78. Portrait of Queen Mary of France. This may have been Mary de' Medici by Scipione Gaetani, No. 192 of the Pitti Gallery.

79. Virtue expelling the Vices. Not found.

80–88. Six Dukes of Urbino and three Popes; all small pictures on canvas.

III. PESARO INVENTORY

Raffaele.

89. Madonna, Christ, and St. Joseph, on panel. Not found in the other inventories, nor in the galleries at Florence.

90. Magdalen, on panel; behind it the arms of Duke Francesco Maria II. and his Duchess Lucrezia d'Este. Not elsewhere known.

Titian.

91. The Duchess of Camerino in an antique dress, on canvas. Not found.

92. A Soldier in dark armour, on canvas. Not found.

Baroccio.

93. The Crucifixion, with the palace of Urbino introduced in the background, on canvas. Not found.

The Zuccari.

94. The Crucifixion, with a city below, on canvas. Not found.

Giulio Clovio.

95. A miniature, was probably the Pietà on vellum, No. 241 of the Pitti collection. A group treated with great breadth, and coloured with much delicacy.

The following pictures, in the Pitti palace, though not in the Urbino inventories, are closely connected with the family della Rovere, and the first of them must have come from thence.

96. Prince Federigo, by Baroccio, on canvas, No. 55. The babe lies in his cradle swaddled, his dress and coverlet embroidered in flowers and gold; inscription above, Federigo Priñ d' Urb° quando nacque 1605.

97. Vittoria della Rovere Grand Duchess of Tuscany, by Sustermans, on canvas, No. 116. She is in the character of the Vestal Tuccia, with a sieve under her arm, full of water; a half-length figure, stout and comely, with a pleasant expression.

98. The Grand Duchess Vittoria, her Husband, and her Son Cosmo III., by Sustermans, on canvas, No. 231. This picture is called in the catalogue a Holy Family; but though the grouping of the figures appears borrowed from some such composition, there seems no real ground for this alleged impiety. They are half-lengths; the Grand Duchess has a darker complexion, and is somewhat older than in the preceding number.

DENNISTOUN'S LIST
OF
AUTHORITIES FOR THE WORK.

THE following List, though by no means containing all the books which have been looked into or consulted (especially numerous periodicals), will afford a general idea of the authorities upon which this work has been founded. The MSS. specially noted are, however, but a small portion of what has been examined, in a variety of Archives, and in the Vatican, Minerva, Angelica, Gerusalemme, S. Lorenzo in Lucina, and Albani libraries at Rome; in those of the Borbonica and S. Angelo in Nilo at Naples; in the Laurentiana, Magliabechiana, Riccardiana, Maruccelli, and Pitti at Florence; in those of the University and S. Salvadore at Bologna; and in the public libraries of Pesaro, Perugia, Rimini, Cesena, Siena, Volterra, and Monte Cassini. In the Oliveriana at Pesaro alone, upwards of one hundred MS. volumes yielded notices of interest. The MSS. in the British Museum have also been freely consulted, and not without fruit.

Affo, Vita di M. Bernardino Baldi . . . . 1 vol. 8vo.
Agincourt, Histoire de l'Art . . . . 6 vols. folio.
Alberi, Relazioni Veneti . . . . 7 vols. 8vo.
Alberti, MSS. di Torquato Tasso . . . . . . 1 vol. folio.
Andreozzi, Notizie di Città di Castello . . . . . 1 vol. 12mo.
Antiquitates Picene . . . . 10 vols. 4to.
Archivio Storico d' Italia . . . . 10 vols. 8vo.
Ariosto, Opere Complete . . . . 5 vols. 8vo.
——, Orlando Furioso, translated by Stewart Rose . . 3 vols. 8vo.
Armanni, Famiglia de' Bentivoglii . . . . . . 1 vol. 8vo.
Atanagi Rime Scelte . . . . 1 vol. 12mo.
Audin, Histoire de Leon X. . . . . 1 vol. 12mo.

Baldi, Vita e Fatti di Federigo Duca di Urbino	3 vols.	8vo.
———————— Guidobaldo I. Duca di Urbino	2 vols.	8vo.
Baldinucci, Notizie de' Professori di Disegno	14 vols.	8vo.
Baruffaldi, Vita di Ariosto	1 vol.	8vo.
———————— Bernardino Baldi	1 vol.	8vo.
Bellori, Vita de' Pittori, Scultori, de Architetti	1 vol.	4to.
Bembo, Opere Diverse	6 vols.	folio.
Berni, Chronicon Eugubinum		
Bettinelli, Resorgimento delle Arti in Italia	1 vol.	8vo.
Biographie Universelle	80 vols.	8vo.
Biondi, Italia Illustrata	1 vol.	8vo.
Black's Life of Tasso	2 vols.	4to.
Blount, Censura Celebriorum Authorum	1 vol.	folio.
Boccaccio e Betussi, delle Donne illustri	1 vol.	12mo.
Boccalini, Ragguaglio di Parnasso	1 vol.	12mo.
Bonaparte, Sac di Rome	1 vol.	8vo.
Bonfatti, Memorie Istoriche di Ottaviano Nelli	1 vol.	18mo.
Borghini, il Riposo	1 vol.	4to.
Bossi, Istoria d' Italia	19 vols.	12mo.
Bottari, Dialoghi sopra le Arti di Disegno	1 vol.	8vo.
———, Raccolta di Lettere Pittoriche	7 vols.	8vo.
Bradford's Correspondence of Charles V.	1 vol.	8vo.
Brantôme, Capitains illustres e Dames illustres	3 vols.	12mo.
Brown, Rawdon, Ragguaglii sulla Vita di Marino Sanuto	3 vols.	8vo.
Bruschelli, la Cita di Assisi	1 vol.	8vo.
Buonaccorsi Diario	1 vol.	4to.
Burriel, Vita di Caterina Riario Sforza	3 vols.	4to.
Burtin, Traité des Connoissances necessaires aux Amateurs des Tableaux	2 vols.	8vo.
Calogeriana, Opuscula e Nuova Raccolta	90 vols.	12mo.
Cambray, Histoire de la Ligue de	1 vol.	8vo.
Campanno, Vita di Braccio Fortebracci e di Nicolo Piccinino	1 vol.	4to.
Cancellieri, Opere Varie	1 vol.	8vo.
Casa, della, il Galateo	1 vol.	12mo.
Carli, Zecca d' Italia	1 vol.	8vo.
Carmina Illustrium Poetarum Italiæ	5 vols.	8vo.
Castiglione, il Corteggiano	1 vol.	4to.
—————, Lettere e Opere	2 vols.	4to.
Cebrario, Economia Politica del Medio Evo	4 vols.	8vo.
Cellini, Vita Scritta da lui Medesimo	1 vol.	8vo.
Cicognara, Storia della Scultura	3 vols.	folio.
Cimarelli, del Ducato di Urbino	1 vol.	folio.
Collucci, Uomini Illustri del Piceno	6 vols.	folio.
Colonna, Vittoria, Opere e Vita di	1 vol.	8vo.
Comines, Memoires de Philippe de	3 vols.	8vo.

Commentaria Pii II. et Epistolæ . . . . . 1 vol. folio.
Comolli, Vita inedita di Raffaello da Urbino . . . . 1 vol. 4to.
——, Bibliographia Architettonica . . . . . 1 vol. 8vo.
Conca, Viaggio Odeporico in Ispagna . . . . 2 vols. 8vo.
Condivi, Vita di Michelangelo Buonarroti . . . . 1 vol. 4to.
Corio, l'Istoria di Milano . . . . 1 vol. 4to.
Crescimbeni, Istorio della Volgar Poesia . . . . 6 vols. 4to.
Cunningham's Life of Wilkie . . . . . . 2 vols. 8vo.
Dante, La Divina Comedia . . . . . . 3 vols. 8vo.
———————— translated by Carey . . . . 1 vol. 8vo.
Daru, Histoire de Venise . . . . 8 vols. 8vo.
Denina, Revoluzioni d' Italia . . . . . . 3 vols. 8vo.
Descamps, Vie de Peintres Flamands et Hollandois . . 3 vols. 8vo.
Didier, Campagne de Rome . . . . . . 1 vol. 8vo.
Discorsi Militari di Francesco Maria I. Duca di Urbino . 1 vol. 12mo.
—— Sopra gli Spettacoli Italiani nel Secolo XIV. . . 1 vol. 8vo.
Dizionario Geografico Universale . . . . . 12 vols. 8vo.
Dolce, Dialogo della Pittura . . . . . . 1 vol. 8vo.
Domenichi, la Nobilita delle Donne . . . . . 1 vol. 12mo.
Donato, Vita di Francesco Maria II. Duca di Urbino .
Duppa, Life of Michelangelo Buonarroti . . . . 1 vol. 8vo.

Eccardius, Corpus Historicum Medii Ævi . . . . 2 vols. folio.

Fabroni, Laurentii Medicis Vita . . . . . . 1 vol. 4to.
Fea, Notizie intorno a Raffaele . . . . . . 1 vol. 8vo.
Feretrense, de Episcopatu . . . .
Filelfi, Epistolæ Familiares . . . . . . 1 vol. 4to.
Fleetwood's Chronicum Preciosum . . . . . 1 vol. 8vo.
Fortebracci, Lettera della Famiglia Fortebracci . . . 1 vol. 8vo.
Fuseli's Life and Writings . . . . . . 3 vols. 8vo.

Gaillard, Histoire de François I. . . . . . . 5 vols. 8vo.
Galleria degli Uffizii di Firenze . . . . . . 5 vols. 8vo.
Gulluzzi, Storia della Toscana . . . . . . 5 vols. 4to.
Gaye, Carteggio d' Artisti . . . . 3 vols. 8vo.
Genealogies Historiques des Maisons Souveraines . 5 vols. 4to.
Gibbon, Recherches sur le Titre de Charles VIII. à la Couronne de Naples . . . .
——, Antiquities of the House of Brunswick . . .
Ginguené, Histoire Littéraire d' Italie . . . . 9 vols. 8vo.
Giovio, Raggionamento sopra i motti ed impresi . . 1 vol. 12mo.
——, Vita de' Dodeci Visconti . . . . . 1 vol. 12mo.
———— di Francesco Sforza . . . . . 1 vol. 12mo.
———— Illustrium Virorum Vitæ . . . . . 1 vol. folio.
Gordon's Life of Alexander VI. and Cesare Borgia . . 1 vol. folio.

Gresswell's Memoirs of Italian Literature . . . . . 1 vol. 8vo.
Grossi, Uomini Illustri di Urbino . . . . . . 1 vol. 4to.
Gualandi, Memorie delle Belle Arti . . . . . . 1 vol. 8vo.
Guicciardini, Istoria d' Italia . . . . . . 8 vols. 8vo.
———, Sacco di Roma . . . . 1 vol. 8vo.

Hallam's View of Europe in the Middle Ages . . . 3 vols. 8vo.
Hystoire de la Conqueste de Naples par Charles VIII. . . 1 vol. 8vo.

Kugler's Handbook of the History of Painting . . . . 1 vol. 8vo.

Lanz, Correspondenz der Kaiser Carl V. . . . . . 2 vols. 8vo.
Lanzi, Storia Pittorica dell' Italia . . . . . . 4 vols. 8vo.
Lazzari, Opera Miscellanea . . . . 6 vols. folio.
——, Memorie di Pittori Celebri di Urbino . . . . 1 vol. 4to.
——, Chiese di Urbino . . . . 1 vol. 8vo.
——, Guida di Urbino . . . . 1 vol. 8vo.
Lazzarini, Dissertazioni in Materia di Belle Arti . . . 2 vols. 8vo.
Leandro Alberti, Descrizione d' Italia . . . . . 1 vol. 4to.
Lectures on Painting, by Barry, Opie, and Fusseli . . 1 vol. 8vo.
Leoni, Vita di Francesco Maria II. Duca d' Urbino . . 1 vol. 4to.
Lettere de' Principi . . . . vols. 8vo.
——— degli Uomini Illustri . . . . 1 vol. 8vo.
——— Pittoriche . . . . 7 vols. 8vo.
Life of Joanna II. Queen of Naples . . . . . . 2 vols. 8vo.
Lindsay's Sketches of the History of Christian Art . . 3 vols. 8vo.
Litta, Famiglie Celebri d' Italia . . . . . vols. folio.
Lomazzo, Idea del Tempio della Pittura . . . . . 1 vol. 4to.
———, L'Arte della Pittura . . . . 1 vol. 4to.

Machiavelli, Opere . . . . 8 vols. 8vo.
Malvasia, La Felsina Pittrice . . . . 2 vols. 4to.
Mambrino Roseo, Istoria di Napoli . . . . . . 1 vol. 4to.
Mancini, Istoria di Città di Castello . . . . . 2 vols. 8vo.
Marchese, Galleria d' Onore . . . . 1 vol. 8vo.
———, Memorie dei Pittori Domenicani . . . . 2 vols. 8vo.
Marini, Saggio della Citta di S. Leo . . . . . . 1 vol. 8vo.
Mariotti, Lettere Pittoriche Perugine . . . . . . 1 vol. 8vo.
———, Italy . . . . 2 vols. 8vo.
Masse, Histoire d'Alexandre VI. et de Cesar Borgia . . 1 vol. 8vo.
Mazzuchelli, Vita di Pietro Aretino . . . . . . 2 vols. 8vo.
————, Notizie intorno Isotta da Rimini . . . . 1 vol. 8vo.
M'Crie's History of the Reformation in Italy . . . . 1 vol. 8vo.
Memorie concernenti la Città da Urbino . . . . . 1 vol. folio.
———————— la Devoluzione di Urbino . . . 1 vol. 12mo.
Mezeray, Abregé de l'Histoire de France . . . . 3 vols. 4to.
Mezzanotte, Vita e Opere di Pietro Perugino . . . . 1 vol. 8vo.

Michiel, Origine delle Feste Veneziane . . . . . 4 vols. 8vo.
Michiels, La Peinture Flamande et Hollandais . . . 4 vols. 8vo.
Milizia, dell' Arte di Vedere nelle Belle Arti . . . . 1 vol. 8vo.
———, Dizionario delle Belle Arte . . . . . . 2 vols. 8vo.
———, dell' Architettura Civile . . . . . . 1 vol. 8vo.
Milman's Life of Tasso . . . . 2 vols. 8vo.
Misserini, Vito di Raffaele . . . . 1 vol. 18mo.
Molini, Documenti per la Storia d' Italia . . . . . 2 vols. 8vo.
Montalembert, du Vandalisme et du Catholicisme dans l'Art 1 vol. 8vo.
Montanari, L'Imperiale di Pesaro . . . . . . 1 vol. 8vo.
Morbio, Municipia d'Italia . . . . 4 vols. 8vo.
Morelli, Notizie delle Opere di Disegno . . . . . 1 vol. 4to.
Mortali Spoglie di Raffaele . . . . 1 vol. 8vo.
Muzio, Historia de' Fatti di Federigo Duca di Urbino . 1 vol. 4to.
Muratori, Annali d' Italia . . . . 40 vols. 8vo.
————, Rerum Italicarum Scriptores . . . . . 25 vols. folio.

Nardii, Le Historie di Firenze . . . . 1 vol. 4to.
Nicholas's Chronology of History . . . . . . 1 vol. 2mo.

Odasio, Elogio di Guidobaldo II. Duca di Urbino . . 1 vol. 12mo.
Olivieri, Opere Diverse . . . . 3 vols. 4to.
Olympia Morata . . . . 1 vol. 8vo.
Orsini, Guida di Perugia . . . . 1 vol. 8vo.
——, Lettere Pittoriche Perugine . . . . . . 1 vol. 8vo.
——, Vita di Pietro Perugino . . . . 1 vol. 8vo.

Paciolo, Summa di Arithmetica e Geometria . . . 1 vol. folio.
Passavant, Leben v. Raphael . . . . 2 vols. 8vo.
Passeri, Istoria delle Pitture in Majolica . . . . 1 vol. 8vo.
Pelli, la Galleria di Firenze . . . . 2 vols. 8vo.
Pignotti, Storia della Toscana . . . . 5 vols. 8vo.
Platina, delle Vite de' Pontefici . . . . . . 1 vol. 4to.
Poggio de Varietate Fortunæ . . . . 1 vol. folio.
——— Vita di Nicolò Piccinino . . . . 1 vol. 4to.
Pontano, de Bello Neapolitano . . . . 1 vol. 4to.
Promis, Trattato di Architettura di Francesco di Giorgio . 2 vols. 4to.
Pungileone, Elogio Storico di Giovanni Santi . . . 1 vol. 8vo.
———————————— Raffaele Sanzio . . . 1 vol. 8vo.
———————————— Bramante . . . . . 1 vol. 8vo.
———————————— Timoteo della Vite . . . 1 vol. 8vo.

Quadrio, della Storia d'ogni Poesia . . . . . . 7 vols. 4to.
Quatremere de Quincy, Vita e Opere di Raffaele Sanzio, voltato in Italiano da Longhena . . . . . 1 vol. 8vo.

Racheli, Discorso intorno a Vittorino da Feltro . . . 1 vol. 8vo.
Raimondo, de Fluxu Maris . . . . 1 vol. 8vo.
Ranghiasci, Bibliographia Storica dello Stato Papale . 1 vol. 8vo.
Ranke die Römischen Päpste ihre Kirche und ihr Staat . 3 vols. 8vo.
Raoul Rochette, Catacombe di Roma . . . . . 1 vol. 8vo.
Ratti, Vita dei Sforza . . . . 1 vol. 8vo.
Raynaldi, Annales Ecclesiastici . . . . 8 vols. folio.
Reynolds's Discourses . . . . 1 vol. 8vo.
Ricci, Memorie Istoriche delle Arti della Marca di Ancona. 2 vols. 8vo.
Richa, le Chiese di Firenze . . . . 2 vols. 8vo.
Ricotti, Storia delle Compagnie di Ventura in Italia . . 4 vols. 8vo.
Ridolfi, le Maraviglie dell' Arte . . . . . . 1 vol. 4to.
Rinuccini, Ricordi Storici . . . . 1 vol. 4to.
Rio, La Poesie Chretienne . . . . 1 vol. 8vo.
Riposati, Zecca di Gubbio . . . . 2 vols. 4to.
Robertson's Reign of Charles XII. . . . . . . 3 vols. 8vo.
Roscoe, Life of Lorenzo de' Medici . . . . . . 3 vols. 8vo.
———— and Pontificate of Leo X. . . . . . 4 vols. 8vo.
———————————— voltata in Italiano da Bossi . . . 11 vols. 8vo.
Rosini, Istoria della Pittura Italiana . . . . . . 8 vols. 8vo.
Ruskin's Modern Painters . . . . 2 vols. 4to.
Russell's History of Modern Europe . . . . . . 5 vols. 8vo.

Sansovino, Famiglie Illustri d' Italia . . . . . . 1 vol. 4to.
Sanuto, La Guerra di Ferrara . . . . 1 vol. 4to.
Simonetta, Historia de Rebus Gestis Francisci Sfortie . 1 vol. 12mo.
Sismondi, Histoire des Français . . . . 31 vols. 8vo.
——————— des Republiques d' Italie . . . . 14 vols. 8vo.
——————— de la Renaissance de la Liberté en Italie 2 vols. 8vo.
————, de la Literature du Midi de l'Europe . . . 4 vols. 8vo.
Spalding's Italy . . . . 3 vols. 12mo.
Specimen Translations of Sonnets from celebrated Italian Poets . . . . 1 vol. 12mo.

Tarcagnotta, Istorie del Mondo, con agguinte di Mambrino Roseo . . . . 4 vols. 4to.
Tasso, Bernardo, Lettere e Vita da Seghezzi . . . 1 vol. 8vo.
——————, Amadigi . . . . 1 vol. 4to.
——, Torquato, Opere di, Raccolte da Rosini . . . . 30 vols. 8vo.
Tesoro Politico . . . . 12mo.
Ticozzi, Dizionario dei Pittori, &c. . . . . . . 4 vols. 8vo.
Tiraboschi, Storia della Literatura Italiana . . . . 16 vols. 8vo.
Tommasi, Vita di Cesare Borgia . . . . . . 2 vols. 12mo.
Tondini, Vita di Franceschino Marchetti . . . . 1 vol. 8vo.
Tresor Numismatique e Glyptique . . . . . . 1 vol. folio.

Trestour, Quadro Generale dello Stato Ponteficio . .
Tullia di Arragona, Poesie di . . . . 1 vol. 12mo.

Valle, Lettere Sanesi . . . . 3 ols. 4to.
Valturio de Re Militari . . . . 3 vols. folio.
Vasari, Opere Diverse . . . . 11 vols. 8vo.
Vermiglioli, Vita di Pinturicchio . . . . 1 vol. 8vo.
Vergilio, Polydoro da, Historia Anglicana . . . . 1 vol. folio.
———————, De Rerum Inventoribus . . . . 1 vol. folio.
Viardot, les Musées d'Italie . . . .
———, Notice des Peintres de l'Espagne . . . . . 1 vol. 4to.
Vigne, Andry de la, Vergier d'Honneur . . . . . 1 vol. folio.
Villani, Chronice Fiorentine . . . . 8vo.
Vinci, Leonardo, Trattato della Pittura . . . . 1 vol. 4to.
Voltaire, Essai sur les Mœurs . . . . 3 vols. 8vo.

Waagen, Art and Artists in England . . . . . . 3 vols. 8vo.
Watt's Bibliotheca Britannica . . . . 4 vols. 4to.
Watson's Philip II. . . . . 3 vols. 8vo.
Wilde's Love and Madness of Tasso . . . . . . 2 vols. 12mo.

Zanetti, Medaglie d' Italia . . . . 1 vol. 4to.
———, Memorie Istoriche di Rimini . . . . . . 1 vol. 4to.
———, Zecca di Rimini . . . . 1 vol. 4to.
Zazzara, Nobilita d' Italia . . . . 1 vol. 4to.

AUTHORITIES IN MS.

FROM THE URBINO LIBRARY AT THE VATICAN.

No. 1023, f. 23. Federici Urbini Ducis Vita, auct. Johanne Galli; written about 1565, at Città di Castello.

No. 938. Sketch of him by Aloysio Guido da Cagli, in Latin.

No. 1011. His life by Muzio Giustinopoli, more full than the printed edition.

No. 941. Vespasiano, Commentario de' Gesti e Fatti e Detti de Federigo Duca di Urbino: printed in Spicelegium Romanum, i. 94.

No. 980. Epitome Vitæ Rerumque Gestarum Federici Urbini Ducis, auct. Julio Cesare Capaccio Neapolitano, 1636.

No. 303, 699, 1293. Various Latin poems by Federigo Veterani as to Urbino.

No. 928, f. 16. Antichita di S. Leo, da Giulio Volpelli, 1576.

No. 702. Mariæ Philelfi artium et utriusque juris doctoris, equitis aurati et poetæ laureati, ad ill. atque inclyt. Principem Federicum de Monte-feretro, Comitem Urbinatem, Martiados, 1464.

No. 804. His vulgar poetry, *passim*.

No. 373, 710, and 709. Porcellii Feltria, and other poems laudatory of Duke Federigo and his house.

No. 373, f. 145. Naldi de Naldi, Volterræ Expugnatio.

No. 743. Panegericon Comitis Federici, per Antonium Rusticum de Florentia, 1472.

No. 1198. Federici Urbini Ducis Epistolæ. There are ninety-three of these, all in Latin.

No. 1233. Odasii, Oratio habita in Funere Ducis Federici.

No. 1236. Oratio habita in Funere Battistæ Urbini Comitissæ ; also in No. 1272.

No. 829, f. 551. Ricordi del Duca Federigo.

No. 1323, art. 5. Ricordi di Paolo Maria, Vescovo di Urbino.

No. 904, f. 43. Memorie di quanto si fece nel tempo che il Duca di Valentino prese lo Stato.

No. 1023, fol. 1, 297, &c. Various lives and notices of the della Rovere family by Fra Gratia di Francia.

No. 1682. Sundries as to Julius II.

No. 906. Baldi, Vita di Francesco Maria I. Duca di Urbino, colla Diffesa contra Guicciardini.

No. 1023, f. 255. Baldi Diffesa di lui, and other sundries as to him.

No. 1023, f. 50. Muzio, Vita di lui.

No. 818, f. 444. Il Batessimo del Principe Federigo.

No. 733, fol. 8. 11. Epigrammata in ejus Natalibus.

No. 818, f. 5. Nobilta della Casa di Montefeltro.

No. 736, 351, 368, and 405. Urbani Urbinatis Familia Feltresca.

No. 992. Cronico di Sinigaglia.

No. 819, f. 335. Ritratto delle Actioni di Francesco Maria I.

No. 489. De Rebus Gestis quæ contigerunt circa ann. 1509.

No. 1037. Memorie Storiche di Francesco Maria I.

No. 921. La Ricuperazione del suo Stato, nel anno 1521.

No. 904. Various Diaries regarding Guidobaldo I.

No. 928, f. 16. Volpelli, Storsa di S. Leo.

No. 907, f. 10. Centelli, de Bello Urbinate.

No. 989. Leoni, Francisci Mariæ I. Vita.

No. 924. Philippi Beroaldi, Defensio Francisci Mariæ I.

No. 632. Petrus Burgensis Pictoris, de quinque Corporibus regularibus.

No. 818, f. 560. Vita di Baldassare Castiglione.

No. 1248. Ordine e Offizii della Corre di Urbino.

No. 1677. Il Sacco di Roma.

No. 935, 1232. Documents regarding the Statistics of Urbino.

No. 497–8. P. Virgilii Historia Angliæ.

No. 908. First Sketch of Tasso's Gerusalemme.

No. 816, f. 62. Federigo Zuccari, Ragguaglio del Escuriale.

FROM THE OTTOBONIANA MSS. IN THE VATICAN.

No. 3141, f. 144–193. La Famiglia del Duca Federigo.

No. 1305. Giovanni Sanzi's Rhyming Chronicle of Duke Federigo.

No. 2447, f. 135, 3137, f. 81. Discorsi del Duca di Urbino.
No. 3141. *passim*. La Famiglia del Duca Federigo.
No. 3144, f. 51. Vita del Duca Francesco Maria II.
No. 1941, f. 172. Luttere di lui.
No. 3135, f. 321, 3184, and 3142. Miscellanies regarding Urbino.
No. 2510, f. 201. The Urbino Rebellion in 1572.
No. 3153, f. 90. Filippo Giraldi, Fatti del Duca Francesco Maria I.
No. 3137. Sundries regarding the Camerino Dispute.
No. 2607. Il Sacco di Roma.
No. 2624, 3152. Burchardi Diarium.
No. 2528, 2726, 2206, f. 17, 2441, f. 39. Sundries as to the Borgian Policy.

GENEALOGICAL TABLE

DESCENT OF THE VARANA, as connected with URBINO.

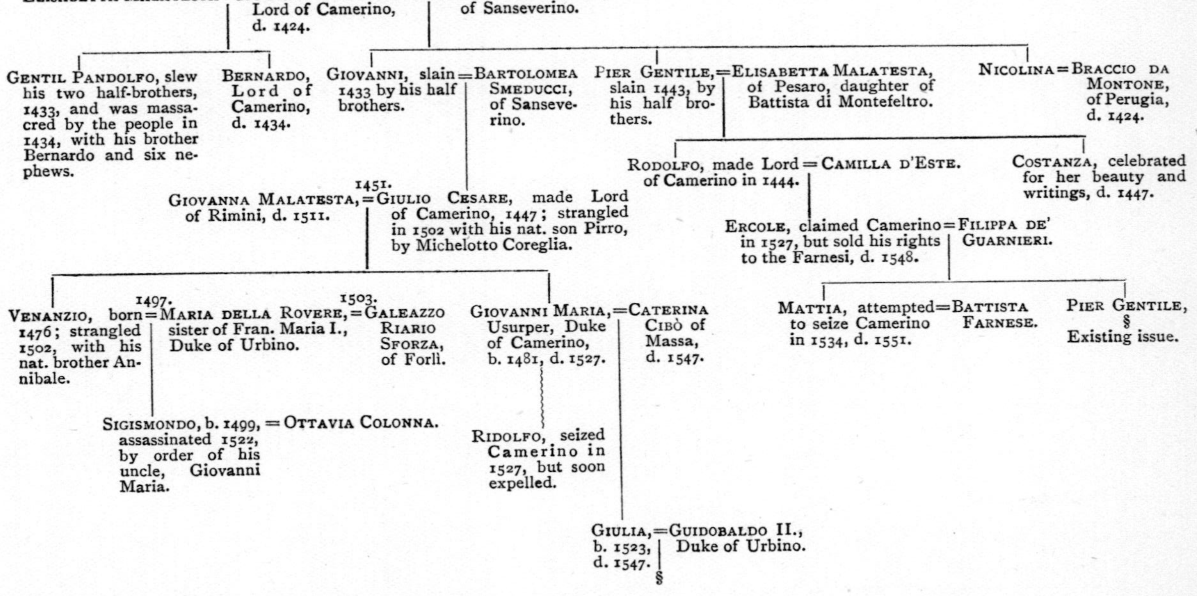

INDEX

INDEX

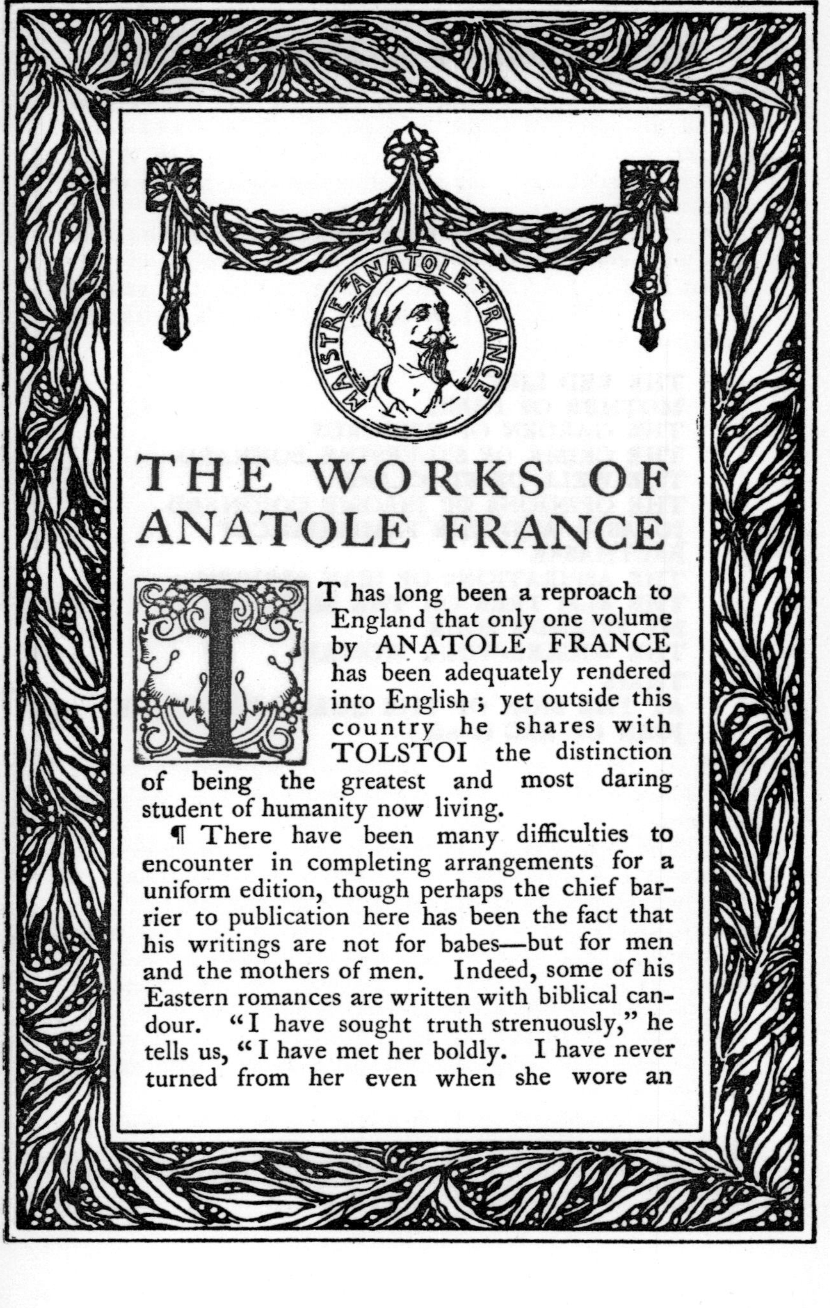

THE WORKS OF ANATOLE FRANCE

IT has long been a reproach to England that only one volume by ANATOLE FRANCE has been adequately rendered into English; yet outside this country he shares with TOLSTOI the distinction of being the greatest and most daring student of humanity now living.

¶ There have been many difficulties to encounter in completing arrangements for a uniform edition, though perhaps the chief barrier to publication here has been the fact that his writings are not for babes—but for men and the mothers of men. Indeed, some of his Eastern romances are written with biblical candour. "I have sought truth strenuously," he tells us, "I have met her boldly. I have never turned from her even when she wore an unexpected aspect." Still, it is believed that the day has come for giving English versions of all his imaginative works, and of his monumental study JOAN OF ARC, which is undoubtedly the most discussed book in the world of letters to-day.

¶ MR. JOHN LANE has pleasure in announcing that he will commence publication of the works of M. ANATOLE FRANCE in English, under the general editorship of MR. FREDERIC CHAPMAN, with the following volumes:

THE RED LILY
MOTHER OF PEARL
THE GARDEN OF EPICURUS
THE CRIME OF SYLVESTRE BONNARD
THE WELL OF ST. CLARE
THE OPINIONS OF JEROME COIGNARD
JOCASTA AND THE FAMISHED CAT
BALTHASAR
THE ASPIRATIONS OF JEAN SERVIEN
THE ELM TREE ON THE MALL
MY FRIEND'S BOOK
THE WICKER-WORK WOMAN
THAÏS
AT THE SIGN OF THE QUEEN PÉDAUQUE
JOAN OF ARC (2 vols.)

¶ All the books will be published at 6/- each with the exception of JOAN OF ARC, which will be 25/- net the two volumes, with eight Illustrations.

¶ The format of the volumes leaves little to be desired. The size is Demy 8vo ($9 \times 5\frac{3}{4}$ in.), that of this Prospectus, and they will be printed from Caslon type upon a paper light in weight and strong in texture, with a cover design in crimson and gold, a gilt top, end-papers from designs by Aubrey Beardsley and initials by Henry Ospovat. In short, these are volumes for the bibliophile as well as the lover of fiction, and form perhaps the cheapest library edition of copyright novels ever published, for the price is only that of an ordinary novel.

¶ The translation of these books has been entrusted to such competent French scholars as MR. ALFRED ALLINSON, HON. MAURICE BARING, MR. FREDERIC CHAPMAN, MR.

ROBERT B. DOUGLAS, MR. A. W. EVANS, MRS. FARLEY, MRS. JOHN LANE, MRS. NEWMARCH, MR. C. E. ROCHE, MISS WINIFRED STEPHENS, and MISS M. P. WILLCOCKS.

¶ As Anatole Thibault, *dit* Anatole France, is to most English readers merely a name, it will be well to state that he was born in 1844 in the picturesque and inspiring surroundings of an old bookshop on the Quai Voltaire, Paris, kept by his father, Monsieur Thibault, an authority on eighteenth-century history, from whom the boy caught the passion for the principles of the Revolution, while from his mother he was learning to love the ascetic ideals chronicled in the Lives of the Saints. He was schooled with the lovers of old books, missals and manuscripts; he matriculated on the Quais with the old Jewish dealers of curios and *objets d'art*; he graduated in the great university of life and experience. It will be recognised that all his work is permeated by his youthful impressions; he is, in fact, a virtuoso at large.

¶ He has written about thirty volumes of fiction. His first novel was JOCASTA & THE FAMISHED CAT (1879). THE CRIME OF SYLVESTRE BONNARD appeared in 1881, and had the distinction of being crowned by the French Academy, into which he was received in 1896.

¶ His work is illuminated with style, scholarship, and psychology; but its outstanding features are the lambent wit, the gay mockery, the genial irony with which he touches every subject he treats. But the wit is never malicious, the mockery never derisive, the irony never barbed. To quote from his own GARDEN OF EPICURUS: "Irony and Pity are both of good counsel; the first with her smiles makes life agreeable, the other sanctifies it to us with her tears. The Irony I invoke is no cruel deity. She mocks neither love nor beauty. She is gentle and kindly disposed. Her mirth disarms anger and it is she teaches us to laugh at rogues and fools whom but for her we might be so weak as to hate."

¶ Often he shows how divine humanity triumphs over mere ascetism, and with entire reverence; indeed, he might be described as an ascetic overflowing with humanity, just as he has been termed a "pagan, but a pagan constantly haunted by the pre-occupation of Christ." He is in turn—like his own Choulette in THE RED LILY—saintly and Rabelaisian, yet without incongruity.

A CATALOGUE OF MEMOIRS, BIOGRAPHIES, ETC.

WORKS UPON NAPOLEON

NAPOLEON & THE INVASION OF ENGLAND: The Story of the Great Terror, 1797–1805. By H. F. B. WHEELER and A. M. BROADLEY. With upwards of 100 Full-page Illustrations reproduced from Contemporary Portraits, Prints, etc.; eight in Colour. Two Volumes. 32*s*. net.

Outlook.—"The book is not merely one to be ordered from the library; it should be purchased, kept on an accessible shelf, and constantly studied by all Englishmen who love England."

Westminster Gazette.—"Messrs. Wheeler and Broadley have succeeded in producing a work on the threatened invasion of England by Napoleon, which treats of the subject with a fulness of detail and a completeness of documentary evidence that are unexampled."

DUMOURIEZ AND THE DEFENCE OF ENGLAND AGAINST NAPOLEON. By J. HOLLAND ROSE, Litt.D. (Cantab.), Author of "The Life of Napoleon," and A. M. BROADLEY, joint-author of "Napoleon and the Invasion of England." Illustrated with numerous Portraits, Maps, and Facsimiles. Demy 8vo. 21*s*. net.

THE FALL OF NAPOLEON. By OSCAR BROWNING, M.A., Author of "The Boyhood and Youth of Napoleon." With numerous Full-page Illustrations. Demy 8vo (9 × 5¾ inches). 12*s*. 6*d*. net.

Spectator.—"Without doubt Mr. Oscar Browning has produced a book which should have its place in any library of Napoleonic literature."

Truth.—"Mr. Oscar Browning has made not the least, but the most of the romantic material at his command for the story of the fall of the greatest figure in history."

THE BOYHOOD & YOUTH OF NAPOLEON, 1769–1793. Some Chapters on the early life of Bonaparte. By OSCAR BROWNING, M.A. With numerous Illustrations, Portraits, etc. Crown 8vo. 5*s*. net.

Daily News.—"Mr. Browning has with patience, labour, careful study, and excellent taste given us a very valuable work, which will add materially to the literature on this most fascinating of human personalities."

Literary World.—". . . Mr. Browning has examined all the available sources of information and carefully weighed his historical evidence. His discriminating treatment has resulted in a book that is . . . one that arrests attention by the conviction its reasoned conclusions carry."

THE DUKE OF REICHSTADT (NAPOLEON II.)

By Edward de Wertheimer. Translated from the German. With numerous Illustrations. Demy 8vo. 21*s.* net. (Second Edition.)

Times.—"A most careful and interesting work which presents the first complete and authoritative account of the life of this unfortunate Prince."

Westminster Gazette.—"This book, admirably produced, reinforced by many additional portraits, is a solid contribution to history and a monument of patient, well-applied research."

NAPOLEON'S CONQUEST OF PRUSSIA, 1806.

By F. Loraine Petre. With an Introduction by Field-Marshal Earl Roberts, V.C., K.G., etc. With Maps, Battle Plans, Portraits, and 16 Full-page Illustrations. Demy 8vo (9 × 5¾ inches). 12*s.* 6*d.* net.

Scotsman.—"Neither too concise, nor too diffuse, the book is eminently readable. It is the best work in English on a somewhat circumscribed subject."

Outlook.—"Mr. Petre has visited the battlefields and read everything, and his monograph is a model of what military history, handled with enthusiasm and literary ability, can be."

NAPOLEON'S CAMPAIGN IN POLAND, 1806–1807.

A Military History of Napoleon's First War with Russia, verified from unpublished official documents. By F. Loraine Petre. With 16 Full-page Illustrations, Maps, and Plans. New Edition. Demy 8vo (9 × 5¾ inches). 12*s.* 6*d.* net.

Army and Navy Chronicle.—"We welcome a second edition of this valuable work. . . . Mr. Loraine Petre is an authority on the wars of the great Napoleon, and has brought the greatest care and energy into his studies of the subject."

NAPOLEON AND THE ARCHDUKE CHARLES.

A History of the Franco-Austrian Campaign in the Valley of the Danube in 1809. By F. Loraine Petre. With 8 Illustrations and 6 sheets of Maps and Plans. Demy 8vo (9 × 5¾ inches). 12*s.* 6*d.* net.

RALPH HEATHCOTE. Letters of a Diplomatist

During the Time of Napoleon, Giving an Account of the Dispute between the Emperor and the Elector of Hesse. By Countess Günther Gröben. With Numerous Illustrations. Demy 8vo (9 × 5¾ inches). 12*s.* 6*d.* net.

*** *Ralph Heathcote, the son of an English father and an Alsatian mother, was for some time in the English diplomatic service as first secretary to Mr. Brook Taylor, minister at the Court of Hesse, and on one occasion found himself very near to making history. Napoleon became persuaded that Taylor was implicated in a plot to procure his assassination, and insisted on his dismissal from the Hessian Court. As Taylor refused to be dismissed, the incident at one time seemed likely to result to the Elector in the loss of his throne. Heathcote came into contact with a number of notable people, including the Miss Berrys, with whom he assures his mother he is not in love. On the whole, there is much interesting material for lovers of old letters and journals.*

MEMOIRS OF THE COUNT DE CARTRIE.

A record of the extraordinary events in the life of a French Royalist during the war in La Vendée, and of his flight to Southampton, where he followed the humble occupation of gardener. With an introduction by FRÉDÉRIC MASSON, Appendices and Notes by PIERRE AMÉDÉE PICHOT, and other hands, and numerous Illustrations, including a Photogravure Portrait of the Author. Demy 8vo. 12*s.* 6*d.* net.

Daily News.—"We have seldom met with a human document which has interested us so much."

Athenæum.—"As a record of personal suffering and indomitable perseverance against opposing circumstances the narrative of De Cartrie's escape to the Eastern frontier, in the disguise of a master-gunner, could not easily be surpassed."

WOMEN OF THE SECOND EMPIRE.

Chronicles of the Court of Napoleon III. By FRÉDÉRIC LOLIÉE. With an introduction by RICHARD WHITEING and 53 full-page Illustrations, 3 in Photogravure. Demy 8vo. 21*s.* net.

Standard.—"M. Frédéric Loliée has written a remarkable book, vivid and pitiless in its description of the intrigue and dare-devil spirit which flourished unchecked at the French Court. . . . Mr. Richard Whiteing's introduction is written with restraint and dignity."

Daily Telegraph.—"It is a really fascinating story, or series of stories, set forth in this volume. . . . Here are anecdotes innumerable of the brilliant women of the Second Empire, so that in reading the book we are not only dazzled by the beauty and gorgeousness of everything, but we are entertained by the record of things said and done, and through all we are conscious of the coming 'gloom and doom' so soon to overtake the Court. Few novels possess the fascination of this spirited work, and many readers will hope that the author will carry out his proposal of giving us a further series of memories of the 'Women of the Second Empire.'"

LOUIS NAPOLEON AND THE GENESIS OF THE SECOND EMPIRE.

By F. H. CHEETHAM. With Numerous Illustrations. Demy 8vo (9 × 5¾ inches). 16*s.* net.

MEMOIRS OF MADEMOISELLE DES ÉCHEROLLES.

Translated from the French by MARIE CLOTHILDE BALFOUR. With an Introduction by G. K. FORTESCUE, Portraits, etc. 5*s.* net.

Liverpool Mercury.—". . . this absorbing book. . . . The work has a very decided historical value. The translation is excellent, and quite notable in the preservation of idiom."

JANE AUSTEN'S SAILOR BROTHERS.

Being the life and Adventures of Sir Francis Austen, G.C.B., Admiral of the Fleet, and Rear-Admiral Charles Austen. By J. H. and E. C. HUBBACK. With numerous Illustrations. Demy 8vo. 12*s.* 6*d.* net.

Morning Post.—". . . May be welcomed as an important addition to Austeniana . . .; it is besides valuable for its glimpses of life in the Navy, its illustrations of the feelings and sentiments of naval officers during the period that preceded and that which followed the great battle of just one century ago, the battle which won so much but which cost us—Nelson."

SOME WOMEN LOVING AND LUCKLESS.

By Teodor de Wyzewa. Translated from the French by C. H. Jeffreson, M.A. With Numerous Illustrations. Demy 8vo (9 × $5\frac{3}{4}$ inches). *7s. 6d.* net.

POETRY AND PROGRESS IN RUSSIA. By

Rosa Newmarch. With 6 full-page Portraits. Demy 8vo. *7s. 6d.* net.

Standard.—"Distinctly a book that should be read . . . pleasantly written and well informed."

THE LIFE OF PETER ILICH TCHAIKOVSKY

(1840–1893). By his Brother, Modeste Tchaikovsky. Edited and abridged from the Russian and German Editions by Rosa Newmarch. With Numerous Illustrations and Facsimiles and an Introduction by the Editor. Demy 8vo. *7s. 6d.* net. Second edition.

The Times.—"A most illuminating commentary on Tchaikovsky's music."

World.—"One of the most fascinating self-revelations by an artist which has been given to the world. The translation is excellent, and worth reading for its own sake."

Contemporary Review.—"The book's appeal is, of course, primarily to the music-lover; but there is so much of human and literary interest in it, such intimate revelation of a singularly interesting personality, that many who have never come under the spell of the Pathetic Symphony will be strongly attracted by what is virtually the spiritual autobiography of its composer. High praise is due to the translator and editor for the literary skill with which she has prepared the English version of this fascinating work . . . There have been few collections of letters published within recent years that give so vivid a portrait of the writer as that presented to us in these pages."

COKE OF NORFOLK AND HIS FRIENDS:

The Life of Thomas William Coke, First Earl of Leicester of the second creation, containing an account of his Ancestry, Surroundings, Public Services, and Private Friendships, and including many Unpublished Letters from Noted Men of his day, English and American. By A. M. W. Stirling. With 20 Photogravure and upwards of 40 other Illustrations reproduced from Contemporary Portraits, Prints, etc. Demy 8vo. 2 vols. *32s.* net.

The Times.—"We thank Mr. Stirling for one of the most interesting memoirs of recent years."

Daily Telegraph.—"A very remarkable literary performance. Mrs. Stirling has achieved a resurrection. She has fashioned a picture of a dead and forgotten past and brought before our eyes with the vividness of breathing existence the life of our English ancestors of the eighteenth century."

Pall Mall Gazette.—"A work of no common interest; in fact, a work which may almost be called unique."

Evening Standard.—"One of the most interesting biographies we have read for years."

THE LIFE OF SIR HALLIDAY MACARTNEY, K.C.M.G., Commander of Li Hung Chang's trained force in the Taeping Rebellion, founder of the first Chinese Arsenal, Secretary to the first Chinese Embassy to Europe. Secretary and Councillor to the Chinese Legation in London for thirty years. By DEMETRIUS C. BOULGER, Author of the "History of China," the "Life of Gordon," etc. With Illustrations. Demy 8vo. Price 24*s.* net.

Daily Graphic.—"It is safe to say that few readers will be able to put down the book without feeling the better for having read it . . . not only full of personal interest, but tells us much that we never knew before on some not unimportant details."

DEVONSHIRE CHARACTERS AND STRANGE EVENTS. By S. BARING-GOULD, M.A., Author of "Yorkshire Oddities," etc. With 58 Illustrations. Demy 8vo. 21*s.* net.

Daily News.—"A fascinating series . . . the whole book is rich in human interest. It is by personal touches, drawn from traditions and memories, that the dead men surrounded by the curious panoply of their time, are made to live again in Mr. Baring-Gould's pages."

CORNISH CHARACTERS AND STRANGE EVENTS. By S. BARING-GOULD. Demy 8vo. 16*s.* net.

THE HEART OF GAMBETTA. Translated from the French of FRANCIS LAUR by VIOLETTE MONTAGU. With an Introduction by JOHN MACDONALD, Portraits and other Illustrations. Demy 8vo. 7*s.* 6*d.* net.

Daily Telegraph.—"It is Gambetta pouring out his soul to Léonie Leon, the strange, passionate, masterful demagogue, who wielded the most persuasive oratory of modern times, acknowledging his idol, his inspiration, his Egeria."

THE MEMOIRS OF ANN, LADY FANSHAWE. Written by Lady Fanshawe. With Extracts from the Correspondence of Sir Richard Fanshawe. Edited by H. C. FANSHAWE. With 38 Full-page Illustrations, including four in Photogravure and one in Colour. Demy 8vo. 16*s.* net.

⁂ *This Edition has been printed direct from the original manuscript in the possession of the Fanshawe Family, and Mr. H. C. Fanshawe contributes numerous notes which form a running commentary on the text. Many famous pictures are reproduced, including paintings by Velazquez and Van Dyck.*

THE DIARY OF A LADY-IN-WAITING. By Lady Charlotte Bury. Being the Diary Illustrative of the Times of George the Fourth. Interspersed with original Letters from the late Queen Caroline and from various other distinguished persons. New edition. Edited, with an Introduction, by A. Francis Steuart. With numerous portraits. Two Vols. Demy 8vo. 21*s*. net.

*** *This book, which appeared anonymously in 1838, created an enormous sensation, and was fiercely criticised by Thackeray and in the Reviews of the time. There is no doubt that it was founded on the diary of Lady Charlotte Bury, daughter of the 5th Duke of Argyll, and Lady-in-Waiting to the unfortunate Caroline of Brunswick, when Princess of Wales. It deals, therefore, with the curious Court of the latter and with the scandals that occurred there, as well as with the strange vagaries of the Princess abroad. In this edition names left blank in the original have been (where possible) filled up, and many notes are given by the Editor to render it useful to the ever-increasing number of readers interested in the later Georgian Period.*

THE DAUGHTER OF LOUIS XVI.: Marie-Thérèse-Charlotte of France, Duchesse D'Angoulême. By G. Lenotre. With 13 Full-page Illustrations. Demy 8vo. 10*s*. 6*d*. net.

*** *M. G. Lenotre is perhaps the most widely read of a group of modern French writers who have succeeded in treating history from a point of view at once scientific, dramatic and popular, He has made the Revolution his particular field of research, and deals not only with the most prominent figures of that period, but with many minor characters whose life-stories are quite as thrilling as anything in fiction. The localities in which these dramas were enacted are vividly brought before us in his works, for no one has reconstructed 18th century Paris with more picturesque and accurate detail. "The Daughter of Louis XVI." is quite equal in interest and literary merit to any of the volumes which have preceded it, not excepting the famous Drama of Varennes. As usual, M. Lenotre draws his material largely from contemporary documents, and among the most remarkable memoirs reproduced in this book are "The Story of my Visit to the Temple" by Harmand de la Meuse, and the artless, but profoundly touching narrative of the unhappy orphaned Princess: "A manuscript written by Marie Thérèse Charlotte of France upon the captivity of the Princes and Princesses, her relatives, imprisoned in the Temple." The illustrations are a feature of the volume and include the so-called "telescope" portrait of the Princess, sketched from life by an anonymous artist, stationed at a window opposite her prison in the tower of the Temple.*

THE TRUE STORY OF MY LIFE: an Autobiography by Alice M. Diehl, Novelist, Writer, and Musician. Demy 8vo. 10*s*. 6*d*. net.

Daily Chronicle.—"This work . . . has the introspective touch, intimate and revealing, which autobiography, if it is to be worth anything, should have. Mrs. Diehl's pages have reality, a living throb, and so are indeed autobiography."

HUBERT AND JOHN VAN EYCK: Their Life and Work.

By W. H. JAMES WEALE. With 41 Photogravure and 95 Black and White Reproductions. Royal 4to. £5 5*s.* net.

SIR MARTIN CONWAY'S NOTE.

Nearly half a century has passed since Mr. W. H. James Weale, then resident at Bruges, began that long series of patient investigations into the history of Netherlandish art which was destined to earn so rich a harvest. When he began work Memlinc was still called Hemling, and was fabled to have arrived at Bruges as a wounded soldier. The van Eycks were little more than legendary heroes. Roger Van der Weyden was little more than a name. Most of the other great Netherlandish artists were either wholly forgotten or named only in connection with paintings with which they had nothing to do. Mr. Weale discovered Gerard David, and disentangled his principal works from Memlinc's, with which they were then confused. During a series of years he published in the "Beffroi," a magazine issued by himself, the many important records from ancient archives which threw a flood of light upon the whole origin and development of the early Netherlandish school. By universal admission he is hailed all over Europe as the father of this study. It is due to him in great measure that the masterpieces of that school, which by neglect were in danger of perishing fifty years ago, are now recognised as among the most priceless treasures of the Museums of Europe and the United States. The publication by him, therefore, in the ripeness of his years and experience, of the result of his studies on the van Eycks is a matter of considerable importance to students of art history. Lately, since the revived interest in the works of the Early French painters has attracted the attention of untrained speculators to the superior schools of the Low Countries, a number of wild theories have been started which cannot stand upright in the face of recorded facts. A book is now needed which will set down all those facts in full and accurate form. Fullness and accuracy are the characteristics of all Mr. Weale's work.

VINCENZO FOPPA OF BRESCIA, FOUNDER OF THE LOMBARD SCHOOL, HIS LIFE AND WORK.

By CONSTANCE JOCELYN FFOULKES and MONSIGNOR RODOLFO MAJOCCHI, D.D., Rector of the Collegio Borromeo, Pavia. Based on research in the Archives of Milan, Pavia, Brescia, and Genoa, and on the study of all his known works. With over 100 Illustrations, many in Photogravure, and 100 Documents. Royal 4to. £3. 11*s.* 6*d.* net.

*** *No complete Life of Vincenco Foppa, one of the greatest of the North Italian Masters, has ever been written: an omission which seems almost inexplicable in these days of over-production in the matter of biographies of painters, and of subjects relating to the art of Italy. In Milanese territory—the sphere of Foppa's activity during many years—he was regarded by his contemporaries as unrivalled in his art, and his right to be considered the head and founder of the Lombard school is undoubted. His influence was powerful and far-reaching, extending eastwards beyond the limits of Brescian territory, and south and westwards to Liguria and Piedmont. In the Milanese district it was practically dominant for over a quarter of a century, until the coming of Leonardo da Vinci thrust Foppa and his followers into the shade, and induced him to abandon Pavia, which had been his home for more than thirty years, and to return to Brescia. The object of the authors of this book has been to present a true picture of the master's life based upon the testimony of records in Italian archives; all facts hitherto known relating to him have been brought together; all statements have been verified; and a great deal of new and unpublished material has been added. The authors have unearthed a large amount of new material relating to Foppa, one of the most interesting facts brought to light being that he lived for twenty-three years longer than was formerly supposed. The illustrations will include several pictures by Foppa hitherto unknown in the history of art, and others which have never before been published, as well as reproductions of every existing work by the master at present known.*

CÉSAR FRANCK: A Study. Translated from the French of Vincent d'Indy. And with an Introduction by Rosa Newmarch. Demy 8vo. 7*s.* 6*d.* net.

*** *There is no purer influence in modern music than that of César Franck, for many years ignored in every capacity save that of organist of Sainte-Clotilde, in Paris, but now recognised as the legitimate successor of Bach and Beethoven. His inspiration "rooted in love and faith" has contributed in a remarkable degree to the regeneration of the musical art in France and elsewhere. The now famous "Schola Cantorum," founded in Paris in* 1896, *by A. Guilmant, Charles Bordes and Vincent d'Indy, is the direct outcome of his influence. Among the artists who where in some sort his disciples were Paul Dukas, Chabrier, Gabriel Fauré and the great violinist Ysäye. His pupils include such gifted composers as Benoît, Augusta Holmès, Chausson, Ropartz, and d'Indy, This book, written with the devotion of a disciple and the authority of a master, leaves us with a vivid and touching impression of the saint-like composer of "The Beatitudes."*

JUNIPER HALL: Rendezvous of certain illustrious Personages during the French Revolution, including Alexander D'Arblay and Fanny Burney. Compiled by Constance Hill. With numerous Illustrations by Ellen G. Hill, and reproductions from various Contemporary Portraits. Crown 8vo. 5*s.* net.

Daily Telegraph.—"... one of the most charming volumes published within recent years. ... Miss Hill has drawn a really idyllic and graphic picture of the daily life and gossip of the stately but unfortunate dames and noblemen who found in Juniper Hall a thoroughly English home."

The Times.—"This book makes another on the long and seductive list of books that take up history just where history proper leaves off ... We have given but a faint idea of the freshness, the innocent gaiety of its pages; we can give none at all of the beauty and interest of the pictures that adorn it."

Westminster Gazette.—"Skilfully and charmingly told."

JANE AUSTEN: Her Homes and Her Friends. By Constance Hill. Numerous Illustrations by Ellen G. Hill, together with Reproductions from Old Portraits, etc. Cr. 8vo. 5*s.* net.

World.—"Miss Constance Hill has given us a thoroughly delightful book. ..."

Spectator.—"This book is a valuable contribution to Austen lore."

Daily Telegraph.—"Miss Constance Hill, the authoress of this charming book, has laid all devout admirers of Jane Austen and her inimitable novels under a debt of gratitude."

THE HOUSE IN ST. MARTIN'S STREET. Being Chronicles of the Burney Family. By Constance Hill, Author of "Jane Austen, Her Home, and Her Friends," "Juniper Hall," etc. With numerous Illustrations by Ellen G. Hill, and reproductions of Contemporary Portraits, etc. Demy 8vo. 21s. net.

World.—"This valuable and very fascinating work. ... Charmingly illustrated. ... Those interested in this stirring period of history and the famous folk who were Fanny Burney's friends should not fail to add 'The House in St. Martin's Street' to their collection of books."

Mr. C. K. Shorter in *Sphere.*—"Miss Hill has written a charming, an indispensable book."

STORY OF THE PRINCESS DES URSINS IN SPAIN (Camarera-Mayor). By Constance Hill. With 12 Illustrations and a Photogravure Frontispiece. New Edition. Crown 8vo. 5*s.* net.

Truth.—"It is a brilliant study of the brilliant Frenchwoman who in the early years of the eighteenth century played such a remarkable part in saving the Bourbon dynasty in Spain. Miss Hill's narrative is interesting from the first page to the last, and the value of the book is enhanced by the reproductions of contemporary portraits with which it is illustrated."

NEW LETTERS OF THOMAS CARLYLE.

Edited and Annotated by ALEXANDER CARLYLE, with Notes and an Introduction and numerous Illustrations. In Two Volumes. Demy 8vo. 25*s.* net.

Pall Mall Gazette.—"To the portrait of the man, Thomas, these letters do really add value; we can learn to respect and to like him the more for the genuine goodness of his personality."

Morning Leader.—"These volumes open the very heart of Carlyle."

Literary World.—"It is then Carlyle, the nobly filial son, we see in these letters; Carlyle, the generous and affectionate brother, the loyal and warm-hearted friend, . . . and above all, Carlyle as the tender and faithful lover of his wife."

Daily Telegraph.—"The letters are characteristic enough of the Carlyle we know: very picturesque and entertaining, full of extravagant emphasis, written, as a rule, at fever heat, eloquently rabid and emotional."

THE NEMESIS OF FROUDE: a Rejoinder to "My Relations with Carlyle."

By SIR JAMES CRICHTON BROWNE and ALEXANDER CARLYLE. Demy 8vo. 3*s.* 6*d.* net.

Glasgow Herald.—". . . The book practically accomplishes its task of reinstating Carlyle; as an attack on Froude it is overwhelming."

Public Opinion.—"The main object of the book is to prove that Froude believed a myth and betrayed his trust. That aim has been achieved."

NEW LETTERS AND MEMORIALS OF JANE WELSH CARLYLE.

A Collection of hitherto Unpublished Letters. Annotated by THOMAS CARLYLE, and Edited by ALEXANDER CARLYLE, with an Introduction by Sir JAMES CRICHTON BROWNE, M.D., LL.D., F.R.S., numerous Illustrations drawn in Lithography by T. R. WAY, and Photogravure Portraits from hitherto unreproduced Originals. In Two Volumes. Demy 8vo. 25*s.* net.

Westminster Gazette.—"Few letters in the language have in such perfection the qualities which good letters should possess. Frank, gay, brilliant, indiscreet, immensely clever, whimsical, and audacious, they reveal a character which, with whatever alloy of human infirmity, must endear itself to any reader of understanding."

World.—"Throws a deal of new light on the domestic relations of the Sage of Chelsea. They also contain the full text of Mrs. Carlyle's fascinating journal, and her own 'humorous and quaintly candid' narrative of her first love-affair."

Daily News.—"Every page . . . scintillates with keen thoughts, biting criticisms, flashing phrases, and touches of bright comedy."

ÉMILE ZOLA: NOVELIST AND REFORMER.

An Account of his Life, Work, and Influence. By E. A. VIZETELLY. With numerous Illustrations, Portraits, etc. Demy 8vo. 21*s.* net.

Morning Post.—"Mr. Ernest Vizetelly has given . . . a very true insight into the aims, character, and life of the novelist."

Athenæum.—". . . Exhaustive and interesting."

M.A.P.—". . . will stand as the classic biography of Zola."

Star.—"This 'Life' of Zola is a very fascinating book."

Academy.—"It was inevitable that the authoritative life of Emile Zola should be from the pen of E. A. Vizetelly. No one probably has the same qualifications, and this bulky volume of nearly six hundred pages is a worthy tribute to the genius of the master."

Mr. T. P. O'CONNOR in *T.P.'s Weekly.*—"It is a story of fascinating interest, and is told admirably by Mr. Vizetelly. I can promise any one who takes it up that he will find it very difficult to lay it down again."

MEMOIRS OF THE MARTYR KING: being a detailed record of the last two years of the Reign of His Most Sacred Majesty King Charles the First, 1646–1648–9. Compiled by ALLAN FEA. With upwards of 100 Photogravure Portraits and other Illustrations, including relics. Royal 4to. 105*s.* net.

Mr. M. H. SPIELMANN in *The Academy*.—"The volume is a triumph for the printer and publisher, and a solid contribution to Carolinian literature."

Pall Mall Gazette.—"The present sumptuous volume, a storehouse of eloquent associations . . comes as near to outward perfection as anything we could desire."

AFTER WORCESTER FIGHT: being the Contemporary Account of King Charles II.'s escape, not included in "The Flight of the King." By ALLAN FEA. With numerous Illustrations. Demy 8vo. 15*s.* net.

Morning Post.—"The work possesses all the interest of a thrilling historical romance, the scenes of which are described by the characters themselves, in the language of the time, and forms a valuable contribution to existing Stuart literature."

Western Morning News.—"Mr. Fea has shown great industry in investigating every possible fact that has any bearing on his subject, and has succeeded in thoroughly establishing the incidents of that romantic escape."

Standard.—" . . . throws fresh light on one of the most romantic episodes in the annals of English History."

KING MONMOUTH: being a History of the Career of James Scott, the Protestant Duke, 1649-1685. By ALLAN FEA. With 14 Photogravure Portraits, a Folding-plan of the Battle of Sedgemoor, and upwards of 100 black and white Illustrations. Demy 8vo. 21*s.* net.

Morning Post.—"The story of Monmouth's career is one of the most remarkable in the annals of English History, and Mr. Fea's volume is singularly fascinating. Not only does it supplement and correct the prejudiced though picturesque pages of Macaulay, but it seems to make the reader personally acquainted with a large number of the characters who prominently figured in the conspiracies and in the intrigues, amorous and political, when society and politics were seething in strange cauldrons."

FRENCH NOVELISTS OF TO-DAY: Maurice Barres, Réné Bazin, Paul Bourget, Pierre de Coulevain, Anatole France, Pierre Loti, Marcel Prévost, and Edouard Rod. Biographical, Descriptive, and Critical. By WINIFRED STEPHENS. With Portraits and Bibliographies. Crown 8vo. 5*s.* net.

*** *The writer, who has lived much in France, is thoroughly acquainted with French life and with the principal currents of French thought. The book is intended to be a guide to English readers desirous to keep in touch with the best present-day French fiction. Special attention is given to the ecclesiastical, social, and intellectual problems of contemporary France and their influence upon the works of French novelists of to-day.*

THE KING'S GENERAL IN THE WEST, being the Life of Sir Richard Granville, Baronet (1600–1659). By ROGER GRANVILLE, M.A., Sub-Dean of Exeter Cathedral. With Illustrations. Demy 8vo. 10*s.* 6*d.* net.

Westminster Gazette.—"A distinctly interesting work; it will be highly appreciated by historical students as well as by ordinary readers."

THE LIFE AND LETTERS OF ROBERT STEPHEN HAWKER, sometime Vicar of Morwenstow in Cornwall. By C. E. BYLES. With numerous Illustrations by J. LEY PETHYBRIDGE and others. Demy 8vo. 7*s.* 6*d.* net.

Daily Telegraph.—" . . . As soon as the volume is opened one finds oneself in the presence of a real original, a man of ability, genius and eccentricity, of whom one cannot know too much . . . No one will read this fascinating and charmingly produced book without thanks to Mr. Byles and a desire to visit—or revisit—Morwenstow."

THE LIFE OF WILLIAM BLAKE. By ALEXANDER GILCHRIST. Edited with an Introduction by W. GRAHAM ROBERTSON. Numerous Reproductions from Blake's most characteristic and remarkable designs. Demy 8vo. 10*s.* 6*d.* net. New Edition.

Birmingham Post.—"Nothing seems at all likely ever to supplant the Gilchrist biography. Mr. Swinburne praised it magnificently in his own eloquent essay on Blake, and there should be no need now to point out its entire sanity, understanding keenness of critical insight, and masterly literary style. Dealing with one of the most difficult of subjects, it ranks among the finest things of its kind that we possess."

MEMOIRS OF A ROYAL CHAPLAIN, 1729–63. The correspondence of Edmund Pyle, D.D., Domestic Chaplain to George II, with Samuel Kerrich, D.D., Vicar of Dersingham, and Rector of Wolferton and West Newton. Edited and Annotated by ALBERT HARTSHORNE. With Portrait. Demy 8vo. 16*s.* net.

Truth.—"It is undoubtedly the most important book of the kind that has been published in recent years, and is certain to disturb many readers whose minds have not travelled with the time."

GEORGE MEREDITH: Some Characteristics. By RICHARD LE GALLIENNE. With a Bibliography (much enlarged) by JOHN LANE. Portrait, etc. Crown 8vo. 5*s.* net. Fifth Edition. Revised.

Punch.—"All Meredithians must possess 'George Meredith; Some Characteristics,' by Richard Le Gallienne. This book is a complete and excellent guide to the novelist and the novels, a sort of Meredithian Bradshaw, with pictures of the traffic superintendent and the head office at Boxhill. Even Philistines may be won over by the blandishments of Mr. Le Gallienne."

LIFE OF LORD CHESTERFIELD. An account of the Ancestry, Personal Character, and Public Services of the Fourth Earl of Chesterfield. By W. H. CRAIG, M.A. Numerous Illustrations. Demy 8vo. 12*s.* 6*d.* net.

Daily Telegraph.—"Mr. Craig has set out to present him (Lord Chesterfield) as one of the striking figures of a formative period in our modern history . . . and has succeeded in giving us a very attractive biography of a remarkable man."

Times.—"It is the chief point of Mr. Craig's book to show the sterling qualities which Chesterfield was at too much pains in concealing, to reject the perishable trivialities of his character, and to exhibit him as a philosophic statesman, not inferior to any of his contemporaries, except Walpole at one end of his life, and Chatham at the other."

A QUEEN OF INDISCRETIONS. The Tragedy of Caroline of Brunswick, Queen of England. From the Italian of G. P. CLERICI. Translated by FREDERIC CHAPMAN. With numerous Illustrations reproduced from contemporary Portraits and Prints. Demy 8vo. 21*s*. net.

The Daily Telegraph.—"It could scarcely be done more thoroughly or, on the whole, in better taste than is here displayed by Professor Clerici. Mr. Frederic Chapman himself contributes an uncommonly interesting and well-informed introduction."

Westminster Gazette.—"The volume, scholarly and well-informed . . . forms one long and absorbingly interesting chapter of the *chronique scandaleuse* of Court life . . . reads like a romance, except that no romancer would care or dare to pack his pages so closely with startling effects and fantastic scenes."

LETTERS AND JOURNALS OF SAMUEL GRIDLEY HOWE. Edited by his Daughter LAURA E. RICHARDS. With Notes and a Preface by F. B. SANBORN, an Introduction by Mrs. JOHN LANE, and a Portrait. Demy 8vo (9 × 5¾ inches). 16*s*. net.

Outlook.—"This deeply interesting record of experience. The volume is worthily produced and contains a striking portrait of Howe."

Daily News.—"Dr. Howe's book is full of shrewd touches; it seems to be very much a part of the lively, handsome man of the portrait. His writing is striking and vivid; it is the writing of a shrewd, keen observer, intensely interested in the event before him."

THE LIFE OF ST. MARY MAGDALEN. Translated from the Italian of an Unknown Fourteenth-Century Writer by VALENTINA HAWTREY. With an Introductory Note by VERNON LEE, and 14 Full-page Reproductions from the Old Masters. Crown 8vo. 5*s*. net.

Daily News.—"Miss Valentina Hawtrey has given a most excellent English version of this pleasant work."

Academy.—"The fourteenth-century fancy plays delightfully around the meagre details of the Gospel narrative, and presents the heroine in quite an unconventional light. . . . In its directness and artistic simplicity and its wealth of homely detail the story reads like the work of some Boccaccio of the cloister; and fourteen illustrations taken from Italian painters happily illustrate the charming text."

MEN AND LETTERS. By HERBERT PAUL, M.P. Fourth Edition. Crown 8vo. 5*s*. net.

Daily News.—"Mr. Herbert Paul has done scholars and the reading world in general a high service in publishing this collection of his essays."

Punch.—"His fund of good stories is inexhaustible, and his urbanity never fails. On the whole, this book is one of the very best examples of literature on literature and life."

ROBERT BROWNING: Essays and Thoughts. By J. T. NETTLESHIP. With Portrait. Crown 8vo. 5*s*. 6*d*. net. (Third Edition.)

A LATER PEPYS. The Correspondence of Sir William Weller Pepys, Bart., Master in Chancery, 1758–1825, with Mrs. Chapone, Mrs. Hartley, Mrs. Montague, Hannah More, William Franks, Sir James Macdonald, Major Rennell, Sir Nathaniel Wraxall, and others. Edited, with an Introduction and Notes, by ALICE C. C. GAUSSEN. With numerous Illustrations. Demy 8vo. In Two Volumes. 32*s.* net.

DOUGLAS SLADEN in the *Queen.*—"This is indisputably a most valuable contribution to the literature of the eighteenth century. It is a veritable storehouse of society gossip, the art criticism, and the *mots* of famous people."

Academy and Literature.—"The effect consists in no particular passages, but in the total impression, the sense of atmosphere, and the general feeling that we are being introduced into the very society in which the writer moved."

Daily News.—"To Miss Alice Gaussen is due the credit of sorting out the vast collection of correspondence which is here presented to the public. . . . Her industry is indefatigable, and her task has been carried out with completeness. The notes are full of interesting items; the introduction is exhaustive; and the collection of illustrations enhances the value of the book."

World.—"Sir William Pepys's correspondence is admirable."

ROBERT LOUIS STEVENSON, AN ELEGY; AND OTHER POEMS, MAINLY PERSONAL. By RICHARD LE GALLIENNE. Crown 8vo. 4*s.* 6*d. net.*

Daily Chronicle.—"Few, indeed, could be more fit to sing the dirge of that 'Virgil of Prose' than the poet whose *curiosa felicitas* is so close akin to Stevenson's own charm."

Globe.—"The opening Elegy on R. L. Stevenson includes some tender and touching passages, and has throughout the merits of sincerity and clearness."

RUDYARD KIPLING: a Criticism. By RICHARD LE GALLIENNE. With a Bibliography by JOHN LANE. Crown 8vo. 3*s.* 6*d.* net.

Guardian.—"One of the cleverest pieces of criticism we have come across for a long time."

Scotsman—"It shows a keen insight into the essential qualities of literature, and analyses Mr. Kipling's product with the skill of a craftsman . . . the positive and outstanding merits of Mr. Kipling's contribution to the literature of his time are marshalled by his critic with quite uncommon skill."

POEMS. By EDWARD CRACROFT LEFROY. With a Memoir by W. A. GILL, and a Reprint of Mr. J. A. SYMONDS' Critical Essay on "Echoes from Theocritus." Photogravure Portrait. Crown 8vo. 5*s.* net.

The Times.—". . . the leading features of the sonnets are the writer's intense sympathy with human life in general and with young life in particular; his humour, his music, and, in a word, the quality which 'leaves a melody afloat upon the brain, a savour on the mental palate.'"

Bookman.—"The Memoir, by Mr. W. A. Gill, is a sympathetic sketch of an earnest and lovable character; and the critical estimate, by J. Addington Symonds, is a charmingly-written and suggestive essay."

APOLOGIA DIFFIDENTIS. By W. COMPTON LEITH. Demy 8vo. 7*s.* 6*d.* net.

*** *The book, which is largely autobiographical, describes the effect of diffidence upon an individual life, and contains, with a consideration of the nature of shyness, a plea for a kindlier judgment of the inveterate case.*

Daily Mail.—"Mr. Leith has written a very beautiful book, and perhaps the publisher's claim that this will be a new classic is not too bold."

BOOKS AND PERSONALITIES: Essays. By H. W. NEVINSON. Crown 8vo. 5*s.* net.

Daily Chronicle.—"It is a remarkable thing and probably unique, that a writer of such personality as the author of 'Between the Acts' should not only feel, but boldly put on paper, his homage and complete subjection to the genius of one after another of these men. He is entirely free from that one common virtue of critics, which is superiority to the author criticised."

OTIA: Essays. By ARMINE THOMAS KENT. Crown 8vo. 5*s.* net.

BOOKS AND PLAYS: A Volume of Essays on Meredith, Borrow, Ibsen, and others. By ALLAN MONKHOUSE. Crown 8vo. 5*s.* net.

LIBER AMORIS; OR, THE NEW PYGMALION. By WILLIAM HAZLITT. Edited, with an introduction, by RICHARD LE GALLIENNE. To which is added an exact transcript of the original MS., Mrs. Hazlitt's Diary in Scotland, and Letters never before published. Portrait after BEWICK, and facsimile Letters. 400 copies only. 4to. 364 pp. Buckram. 21*s.* net.

TERRORS OF THE LAW: being the Portraits of Three Lawyers—the original Weir of Hermiston, "Bloody Jeffreys," and "Bluidy Advocate Mackenzie." By FRANCIS WATT. With 3 Photogravure Portraits. Fcap. 8vo. 4*s.* 6*d.* net.

The Literary World.—"The book is altogether entertaining; it is brisk, lively, and effective. Mr. Watt has already, in his two series of 'The Law's Lumber Room,' established his place as an essayist in legal lore, and the present book will increase his reputation."

CHAMPIONS OF THE FLEET. Captains and Men-of-War in the Days that Helped to make the Empire. By EDWARD FRASER. With 16 Full-page Illustrations. Crown 8vo.

*** *Mr. Fraser takes in the whole range of our Navy's story. First there is the story of the "Dreadnought," told for the first time: how the name was originally selected by Elizabeth, why she chose it, the launch, how under Drake she fought against the Armada, how her captain was knighted on the quarter-deck in the presence of the enemy. From this point the name is traced down to the present leviathan which bears it. This is but one of the "champions" dealt with in Mr. Fraser's volume, which is illustrated by some very interesting reproductions.*

THE LONDONS OF THE BRITISH FLEET: The Story of Ships bearing the name of Old Renown in Naval Annals. By EDWARD FRASER. With 8 Illustrations in colours, and 20 in black and white.